Persuasive Games

Persuasive Games

The Expressive Power of Videogames

Ian Bogost

The MIT Press
Cambridge, Massachusetts
London, England

MIT Press books may be purchased at special quantity discounts for business or sales promotional use. For information, please email special_sales@mitpress.mit.edu or write to Special Sales Department, The MIT Press, 55 Hayward Street, Cambridge, MA 02142.

This book was set in Bell Gothic and Garamond by SNP Best-set Typesetter Ltd., Hong Kong, and was printed and bound in the United States of America.

Library of Congress Cataloging-in-Publication Data

Bogost, Ian.
 Persuasive games: the expressive power of videogames / Ian Bogost.
    p.   cm.
 Includes bibliographical references and index.
 ISBN-13: 978-0-262-02614-7 (hardcover: alk. paper)
  1. Video games—Social aspects. 2. Persuasion (Rhetoric). I. Title.
GV1469.34.S52B64   2007
794.8—dc22
                                                           2006032621

10 9 8 7 6 5 4 3 2

Contents

Preface

Videogames are an expressive medium. They represent how real and imagined systems work. They invite players to interact with those systems and form judgments about them. As part of the ongoing process of understanding this medium and pushing it further as players, developers, and critics, we must strive to understand how to construct and critique the representations of our world in videogame form.

Despite their commercial success, videogames still struggle for acceptance as a cultural form.[1] Critic James Newman offers two possible reasons. First, he suggests, videogames are perceived as a children's medium, "easily denigrated as trivial—something that will be 'grown out of'—and demanding no investigation."[2] It is common to hear parents, educators, and policymakers equate videogame playing with idle time, time that could be put to better use. Yet, even if videogames were merely a children's medium (which they are not, and never were), this reason alone does not adequately explain why they would escape respect.[3] Children's literature has enjoyed considerable popularity in both popular and academic contexts. For example, the Modern Language Association (MLA) maintains a group for children's literature, which in turn produces an annual, *Children's Literature*, which "publishes theoretically based articles that address key issues in the field."[4] Hollins University offers masters degrees in the study and writing of children's literature.[5] Even comics, which enjoyed broad readership among kids and adults alike before the adoption of the 1954 Comics Code, still benefit from occasional critical acclaim and attention.[6] The University of Florida supports comics studies, where English professor Donald Ault recently established a peer-reviewed academic journal on comics and graphic novels, called *ImageTexT*.[7] Even if it were accurate, the mere perception of videogames as children's culture is not a sufficient explanation for their resulting critical inattention.

A more convincing quandary emerges from the correlation between videogames and children's culture. That quandary is *triviality*. Videogames are considered inconsequential because they are perceived to serve no cultural or social function save distraction at best, moral baseness at worst. Newman cites this triviality as the second explanation for the medium's struggle for legitimacy. Videogames, he argues, are perceived to be "mere trifles—low art—carrying none of the weight, gravitas or credibility of more traditional media."[8] This is not a new problem in the history of culture. Comics, television, and even film once endured popular and critical scorn. The relative maturity of each medium explains part of the problem. Says noted videogame (and comics) critic Henry Jenkins, "If it's 1910 and you ask, 'What's the state of movies?,' I'm going to say mostly chases and pie fights. By 1915, when D. W. Griffith makes *Birth of a Nation*, now I'm saying that this is a mature storytelling medium that has enormous power to shape the debates within our culture."[9] Jenkins and many other critics in the growing field of game studies are trying to identify and cultivate a similar trend in videogames. In my previous book, *Unit Operations: An Approach to Videogame Criticism*, I too made such a gesture, arguing for a comparative criticism of videogames that would connect them with so-called high art—poetry, literature, and film in particular.[10]

But the growth of videogames as a legitimate medium requires more than just comparisons to other media. Jenkins's casual comment might inspire the incorrect belief that time is a sufficient cure for the relative immaturity of videogames. But creative progress on the part of the development community and critical progress on the part of the academic and journalistic community require a deeper knowledge of the way videogames work—precisely how they do whatever it is we would have them do to count as expressive cultural artifacts.

This book is an analysis of the way videogames mount arguments and influence players. Drawing on the 2,500-year history of rhetoric, the study of persuasive expression, I offer a general approach to how rhetoric functions uniquely in software in general and videogames in particular. In classical antiquity, rhetoric was understood as the art of oratory. Since then, some fields have adopted a more general understanding of rhetoric; for example, media studies now often covers visual rhetoric, the art of using imagery and visual representation persuasively, in order to understand the function of rhetoric in photography and film. Following these traditions, this book suggests that videogames open a new domain for persuasion, thanks to their core representational mode, procedurality.

I call this new form *procedural rhetoric*, the art of persuasion through rule-based representations and interactions rather than the spoken word, writing, images, or moving pictures. This type of persuasion is tied to the core affordances of the computer: computers run processes, they execute calculations and rule-based symbolic manipulations. But I want to suggest that videogames, unlike some forms of computational persuasion, have unique persuasive powers. While "ordinary" software like word processors and photo editing applications are often used to create expressive artifacts, those completed artifacts do not usually rely on the computer in order to bear meaning. Videogames are computational artifacts that have cultural meaning *as* computational artifacts. Moreover, they are a popular form of computational artifact; perhaps the most prevalent form of expressive computation. Videogames are thus a particularly relevant medium for computational persuasion and expression.

Among computer software, I want to suggest that videogames have a unique persuasive power. Recent movements in the videogame industry, most notably the so-called *Serious Games* movement, which I discuss below, have sought to create videogames to support existing social and cultural positions. But videogames are capable of much more. In addition to becoming instrumental tools for institutional goals, videogames can also disrupt and change fundamental attitudes and beliefs about the world, leading to potentially significant long-term social change. I believe that this power is not equivalent to the *content* of videogames, as the serious games community claims. Rather, this power lies in the very way videogames mount claims through procedural rhetorics. Thus, all kinds of videogames, from mass-market commercial products to obscure art objects, possess the power to mount equally meaningful expression. From this vantage point, in the following chapters I interrogate three domains in which videogame persuasion has already taken form and still has great promise: politics, advertising, and learning.

In the domain of politics, I look at politics and public policy, first discussing the ways ideology functions in videogames. I then examine the way rule-based systems expose what George Lakoff has called "frames" for political discourse. Unlike verbal discourse, which relies on deeply ingrained metaphors that most people take for granted, videogames deploy more abstract representations about the way the world does or should function. I trace the function of these frames in political games, art games, and commercial games. Next, I explore the field of officially endorsed political games, investigating the role of games in public policy and political campaign discourse.

In the domain of advertising, I first argue for a new era in advertising, one that abandons the trend toward "associative" marketing, the attempt to manufacture needs in consumers by suggesting affinities between aspirations and brands. Instead, I resuscitate and revise "demonstrative" advertising, the attempt to correlate advertising messages with the actual features and functions of goods and services. I explore and chart many varieties of advertising in games, from branded games to in-game product placement, suggesting that games which articulate the function of a product or service deploy the most productive procedural rhetorics.

In the domain of learning, I first critique the state of current educational practice, in particular the tendency to teach either specific knowledge divorced from context or abstract principles divorced from specific knowledge. Next, I look at how games address values and aspirations, including an interrogation of consumption, corporate training, and morality. I argue that videogames' usefulness comes not from a capacity to transfer social or workplace skills, but rather from their capacity to give consumers and workers a means to critique business, social, and moral principles. Finally, I explore so-called *exergames*, videogames that encourage physical activity in their players, arguing that the most sophisticated examples of these games attempt to translate the rhetoric of the personal trainer without simply reproducing the figure of the trainer.

The research that produced this book is twofold. On the one hand, I am an academic videogame researcher; I play games, research their histories and influences, and record my subsequent claims about their meaning. On the other hand, I am a videogame designer; I make games designed to have an impact in the three domains that are the subject of this book. The videogames studio I cofounded, Persuasive Games, shares its title with this book, and I intend this work to reflect both theoretical and game design goals. A small subset of the examples I discuss in the book were created at my studio, and I select them not for self-promotion but because they directly address the topic at hand, a direct product of my attempt both to theorize and to practice the principles of procedural rhetoric. While I do not offer direct advice for game designers in these pages, I hope this book will prove useful for designers, critics, and players of videogames alike.

I am grateful to numerous academic and professional colleagues whose direct support, collaboration, and feedback was essential to the completion of this book. Special thanks go to my frequent research collaborators Gonzalo Frasca and Michael Matcas, who have helped shape my thinking about videogames and rhetoric. Nick Montfort and Noah Wardrip-Fruin provided detailed feedback on numerous drafts of this book. I am grateful to Matteo Bittanti, Sandra Braman, Suzanne de Castell, Katherine Isbister, Liz Losh, Thomas Malaby, Sharon Mazzarella, Jane McGonigal, and Janet Murray for feedback on individual chapters. And I thank Jay Bolter, Ted Castronova, Mary Flanagan, Jim Gee, Stuart Moulthrop, Michael Nitsche, Ken Perlin, Cindy Poremba, and Kurt Squire for fruitful discussions, general feedback, and ongoing support. A few publication acknowledgements are also in order. Chapter 3 previously appeared as "Videogames and Ideological Frames" in *Popular Communication* 4:2 (2006).[11] Selections of that chapter appeared as "Frame and Metaphor in Political Games" in *Worlds in Play*, eds. Suzanne de Castell and Jen Jenson.[12] Earlier portions of chapter 8 appeared as "Videogames and the Future of Education" in *On the Horizon* 13:2 (2005),[13] and a previous version of chapter 4 appeared as "Playing Politics" in *First Monday* 11:9 (2006). eds. Thomas Malaby and Sandra Braman.[14]

Likewise, I heartily thank my professional colleagues in game development. I am particularly grateful to colleagues at my studio, Persuasive Games, including Gerard LaFond, Alejandro Quarto, and Nicolas Massi, without whom several examples discussed in the following pages would never have been created. I also must acknowledge Simon Carless, Brian Crecente, Michael Gesner, Raph Koster, Aleks Krotoski, Eric Marcoullier, and Ben Sawyer, who have all provided support and encouragement. I also thank the developers who speak at the annual Game Developers Conference, providing invaluable insights into the creation of their own games. I owe special thanks to Michael Boyce, Toru Fujimoto, Daniel Olson, Nate Olson, and Shannon Townsend for the essential yet trying job of acquiring permission to reprint many of the images that appear in the book. I am likewise indebted to the readers of Water

Cooler Games, a website on "videogames with an agenda" that Gonzalo Frasca and I have edited since 2003.[15] The reactions, responses, and support of our readers have been extremely beneficial. Finally, I thank my family for their ongoing support: my wife Abbey for tolerating my simultaneous refusal to connect a VCR to our television and insistence that ten videogame consoles remain continuously mated to it, and to my children Tristan and Flannery for helping me see what I otherwise might miss.

1

Procedural Rhetoric

In 1975, Owen Gaede created *Tenure*, a simulation of the first year of secondary school teaching, for the PLATO computer education system.[1] The program was intended to give new high school teachers an understanding of the impact of seemingly minor decisions on the teaching experience. The goal of the game is to complete the first year of teaching and earn a contract renewal for the next. During play, the player must make successive decisions, each of which affects different people in different ways. Some decisions may please the students but contradict the principal's educational philosophy. Others may provide a higher quality educational experience but put performance pressure on fellow teachers, causing workplace conflict. The player can monitor the state of affairs by listening to student reactions, requesting a conference with the principal, or overhearing gossip in the teacher's lounge.

The game is played primarily through responses to multiple-choice questions whose aggregate answers change principal, teacher, and student attitudes. For example, at the start of the game, the player must take a job interview with his prospective principal. The principal may ask about the player's educational philosophy or his willingness to advise student organizations. Later, the player must choose a grading methodology, classroom rules, student seating arrangements, and a curriculum plan. The simulation then presents the player with very specific quandaries, such as how to manage another teacher's students at a school assembly, whether or not to participate in the teacher's union, dealing with note-passing in class, contending with parents angry about their children's grades, and even managing students' difficult personal issues, such as home abuse.

No decision is straightforward, and the interaction of multiple successive decisions produces complex social, educational, and professional situations. Situations are further influenced by the gender of the teacher, the influence of the principal, student learning styles, and other subtle, social factors. In one run of a recent PC port of *Tenure*, Jack, one of my best students, had been arriving late to class.[2] I could choose to ignore his tardiness, talk to him privately, or give him detention. I chose to talk with Jack about the problem, which earned me praise from the principal, whose progressive philosophy encouraged direct contact and student empathy. However, after speaking with the student, I learned that his tardiness was caused by Mr. Green, the math teacher, who had been holding class after the bell to complete the last problem on the board. Now I was faced with a new decision: confront Mr. Green, make Jack resolve the issue and accept the necessary discipline, or complain to the principal. Asking the student to take responsibility would avoid conflict with my colleague and principal on the one hand, but would put Jack in an uncomfortable situation on the other, perhaps changing his opinion of me as a teacher. Confronting Mr. Green might strain our relationship and, thanks to lounge gossip, my rapport with other teachers as well. Complaining to the principal might cause the same reaction, and might also run the risk of exposing me as indecisive. All of these factors might change given the outcome of other decisions and the personalities of my fellow teachers and principal.

Tenure makes claims about how high school education operates. Most notably, it argues that educational practice is deeply intertwined with personal and professional politics. Novice teachers and idealistic parents would like to think that their children's educations are motivated primarily, if not exclusively by pedagogical goals. *Tenure* argues that this ideal is significantly undermined by the realities of school politics, personal conflicts, and social hearsay. The game does not offer solutions to these problems; rather, it suggests that education takes place not in the classroom alone, but in ongoing affinities and disparities in educational, social, and professional goals. *Tenure* outlines the *process* by which high schools really run, and it makes a convincing argument that personal politics indelibly mark the learning experience.

I suggest the name *procedural rhetoric* for the new type of persuasive and expressive practice at work in artifacts like *Tenure*. *Procedurality* refers to a way of creating, explaining, or understanding processes. And processes define the way things work: the methods, techniques, and logics that drive the operation of systems, from mechanical systems like engines to organizational systems like high schools to conceptual systems like religious faith. *Rhetoric* refers to effective and persuasive expression. Procedural rhetoric, then, is a practice of using processes persuasively. More specifically, procedural rhetoric is the practice of persuading through processes in general and computational processes in particular. Just as verbal rhetoric is useful for both the orator and the audience, and just as written rhetoric is useful for both the writer and the reader, so procedural rhetoric is useful for both the programmer and the user, the game designer and the player. Procedural rhetoric is a technique for making arguments with computational systems and for unpacking computational arguments others have created.

Procedural and *rhetoric* are both terms that can impose ambiguity and confusion. Before trying to use the two together in earnest, I want to discuss each in turn.

Procedurality

The word *procedure* does not usually give rise to positive sentiments. We typically understand *procedures* as established, entrenched ways of doing things. In common parlance, *procedure* invokes notions of officialdom, even bureaucracy: a procedure is a static course of action, perhaps an old, tired one in need of revision. We often talk about procedures only when they go wrong: *after several complaints, we decided to review our procedures for creating new accounts.* But in fact, procedures in this sense of the word structure behavior; we tend to "see" a process only when we challenge it.[3] Likewise, procedure and the law are often closely tied. Courts and law enforcement agencies abide by *procedures* that dictate how actions can and cannot be carried out. Thanks to these common senses of the term, we tend to think of procedures as fixed and unquestionable. They are tied to authority, crafted from the top down, and put in place to structure behavior and identify infringement. Procedures are sometimes related to ideology; they can cloud our ability to see other ways of thinking; consider the police officer or army private who carries out a clearly unethical action but later offers the defense, "I was following procedure." This very problem arose in the aftermath of American brutalization of Iraqi war prisoners at Abu Ghraib in 2004. Field soldiers claimed they followed orders, while officers insisted that the army did not endorse torture; rather individual soldiers acted alone. No matter the truth, the scenario raises questions about the *procedures* that drive military practice. In his report on prison practices, Major General Marshal Donald Ryder noted the possibility of altering "facility procedures to set the conditions for MI [military intelligence] interrogations."[4] In this case, the procedures in question dictate the methods used to interrogate prisoners. One might likewise think of interactions with line workers in retail establishments. When asked to perform some unusual task, such employees may be instructed to balk, offering excuses like "that's not our policy." Policy is a synonym for procedure in many cases: an approach, or a custom; a process for customer relations. In both these cases, procedures constrain the types of actions that can or should be performed in particular situations.

In her influential book *Hamlet on the Holodeck*, Janet Murray defines four essential properties of digital artifacts: procedurality, participation, spatiality, and encyclopedic scope.[5] Murray uses the term *procedural* to refer to the computer's "defining ability to execute a series of rules."[6] Procedurality in this sense refers to the core practice of software authorship. Software is composed of algorithms that model the way things behave. To write procedurally, one authors code that enforces rules to generate some kind of representation, rather than authoring the representation itself. Procedural systems generate behaviors based on rule-based models; they are machines capable of producing many outcomes, each conforming to the same overall guidelines. Procedurality is the principal value of the computer, which creates meaning through the interaction of algorithms. Although Murray places procedurality alongside three other properties, these properties are not equivalent. The computer, she writes, "was designed . . . to embody complex, contingent behaviors. To be a computer scientist is to think in terms of algorithms and heuristics, that is, to be constantly identifying the exact or general rules of behavior that describe any process, from running a payroll to flying an airplane."[7] This ability to execute a series of rules fundamentally separates computers from other media.

Procedurality in the computer-scientific sense preserves a relationship with the more familiar sense of *procedure* discussed above. Like courts and bureaucracies, computer software establishes rules of execution, tasks and actions that can and cannot be performed. I have argued elsewhere that procedurality can be read in both computational and noncomputational structures.[8] As cultural critics, we can interrogate literature, art, film, and daily life for the underlying processes they trace. But computational procedurality places a greater emphasis on the expressive capacity afforded by rules of execution. Computers run processes that invoke interpretations of processes in the material world.

For my purposes, procedural expression must entail symbol manipulation, the construction and interpretation of a symbolic system that governs human thought or action. As Steven Harnad argues, computation is "interpretable symbol manipulation" in which symbols "are manipulated on the basis of rules operating only on the symbols' shapes, which are arbitrary in relation to what they can be interpreted as meaning."[9] The interpretation of these systems, continues Harnad, "is not intrinsic to the system; it is projected onto it by the interpreter."[10] Computation is representation, and procedurality in the computational sense is a means to produce that expression. As Murray suggests, computer processes are representational, and thus procedurality is fundamental to computational expression. Because computers function procedurally, they are particularly adept at representing real or imagined systems that themselves function in some particular way—that is, that operate according to a set of processes. The computer magnifies the ability to create representations of processes.

The type of procedures that interest me here are those that present or comment on processes inherent to human experience. Not all procedures are expressive in the way that literature and art are expressive. But processes that might appear unexpressive, devoid of symbol manipulation, may actually found expression of a higher order. For example, bureaucracy constrains behavior in a way that invokes political, social, and cultural values. Consider the example of retail customer service as an invocation of processes. Imagine that you bought a new DVD player from a local retailer. Upon installing it, you discover that the device's mechanical tray opens and shuts properly, but no image displays on the television. You assume it is defective. Most stores offer a return policy in such cases, so you take the player back to the store and exchange it for a new one.

Now imagine that you buy the DVD player late one evening on the way home from work. You lead a busy life, and unpacking a DVD player isn't the first thing on your mind. You leave it in the box for a week, or two, and then finally take it out and connect it, discovering that it doesn't work properly. You are frustrated but still pressed for time, and you don't get back to the retailer for the return until the following week. The store would be happy to take your return, but they note that you purchased the item more than fourteen days ago. The store's stated policy is to accept consumer electronics returns only within two weeks of purchase. In this case, the retailer's employees may try to enforce their return policy, invoking the rules of a process. But you might reason with the clerk, or make a ruckus, or ask to see a supervisor, or cite your record of purchases at the store in question. Swayed by logic, empathy, or expediency, the store might agree to accept the return—to bend the rules or *to break procedure*, as we sometimes say.

Let's replace the human agents with computational ones. Now imagine that you purchased the DVD player from an online retailer. The return process is no less codified in procedure, but this time a computer, not a human, manages your interface with the procedure. You receive the package and, as before, you delay in opening and installing it. By the time you realize the item is defective, you have exceeded the stated return window. But this time, the return is managed by the retailer's website software. Instead of speaking with a person, you must visit a website and enter your order number on a return authorization page. A computer program on the server performs a simple test, checking the delivery date of the order automatically provided by the shipping provider's computer tracking system against the current date. If the dates differ by more than fourteen days' time, the computer rejects the return request.

Situations like this help explain why we often despise the role of computers in our lives. They are inflexible systems that cannot empathize, that attempt to treat everyone the same. This is partly true, but it is not a sufficient explanation of *computational* procedural expression. When the human clerks and supervisors in the retail store agree to forgo their written policy, they are not really "breaking procedure." Instead, they are mustering new processes—for example, a process for promoting repeat business, or for preventing a commotion—and seamlessly blending them with the procedure for product returns. This distinction underscores an important point about processes in general and computational processes in particular: often, we think of procedures as tests that maintain the edges of situations. Disallow returns after two weeks. Diffuse customer incidents as quickly as possible. This also explains why we think of procedures as constraints that limit behavior. Max Weber pessimistically characterized the rationalist bureaucratization of society as an "iron cage." When the asceticism of Puritanism was extended into daily life, argues Weber, it did its part in building the tremendous cosmos of the modern economic order. This order is now bound to the technical and economic conditions of machine production which today determine the lives of all the individuals who are born into this mechanism. In [Calvinist Richard] Baxter's view the care for external goods should only lie in on the shoulders of the "saint, like a light cloak, which can be thrown aside at any moment." But fate decreed that the cloak should become an iron cage.[11]

Weber's point is that mechanization overemphasizes rationalism. But in fact, procedures found the logics that structure behavior in *all* cases; the machines of industrialization simply act as a particularly tangible medium for expressing these logics. The metaphor of the cloak may suggest easy shedding of procedure, but the saint must immediately don a new cloak, symbolizing a new logic. Both cloak and cage brandish processes; one is simply nimbler than the other.

While we often think that rules always limit behavior, the imposition of constraints also creates expression. In our example, the very concept of returning a defective product is only made possible by the creation of rules that frame that very notion. Without a process, it would perhaps never even occur to us that defective or unwanted products can be returned. And yet, this state of affairs too implies a process, which we give the shorthand *caveat emptor*, let the buyer beware. When we do things, we do them according to some logic, and that logic constitutes a *process* in the general sense of the word.

This clarification in mind, there is no reason one could not model the more complex, human-centered product return interaction computationally. For example, the computer system might also recall the customer's previous purchases, forgoing the cutoff policy for frequent buyers. It might even reason about the customer's future purchases based on a predictive model of future buying habits of similar customers. We think of computers as frustrating, limiting, and simplistic not because they execute processes, but because they are frequently programmed to execute simplistic processes. And the choice to program only a simplistic process for customer relations exposes yet another set of processes, such as corporate information technology operations or the constraints of finances or expertise that impose buying off-the-shelf software solutions instead of building custom solutions.

Processes like military interrogation and customer relations are cultural. We tend to think of them as flexible and porous, but they are crafted from a multitude of protracted, intersecting cultural processes. I have given the name *unit operations* to processes of the most general kind, whether implemented in material, cultural, or representational form.[12] Unit operations are characterized by their increased compression of representation, a tendency common over the course of the twentieth century, from structuralist anthropology to computation. I use this term to refer to processes in the general sense, for example, the coupling of a cultural process and its computational representation. I also use *unit operation* to distinguish one process in interleaved or nested procedural systems, for example, the concept of customer loyalty as distinct from transaction age in the case of a process for managing product returns.

Since processes describe the way simple and complex things work, sometimes they are nonobvious. In some cases, we want to conceal procedure—for example, many people read the U.S. Army's ambiguous response to Abu Ghraib as a sign that high-ranking officials in the military, those with the authority to set the procedure, endorsed torture. In other cases, the process is too complex to apprehend immediately. We tend to ask the question *how does this work?* in relation to such processes. This sentiment probably conjures images of mechanical devices like wristwatches, where procedural understanding implies taking a set of gears apart to see how they mesh. But procedurality can also entail the operation of cultural, social, and historical systems. In these cases, asking *how does this work?* requires taking a set of cultural systems apart to see what logics motivate their human actors.

A notable example comes from microbiologist Jared Diamond's Pulitzer Prize-winning book *Guns, Germs, and Steel*, an alternative approach to understanding history (discussed further in chapter 9).[13] Instead of recording the events of human history, Diamond looks at configurations of material conditions like geography and natural resources and asks how they produce structural, political, and social outcomes. These outcomes in turn recombine with their underlying material conditions to produce new historical moments. For example, the lush agricultural conditions in the fertile crescent, along with the similar climates in the east–west axis of Eurasia, set the stage for rapid advances in agriculture across that continent, leading to adequate food surpluses that allowed societies to pursue activities like politics and technology. Such an approach to history goes far beyond the relation between contemporaneous events, asking us to consider the systems that produce those events.

Steven D. Levitt's work on microeconomies also exposes processes. Levitt and Stephen J. Dubner authored the *New York Times* bestseller *Freakonomics*, a populist account of Levitt's sometimes unusual microeconomic analysis. Levitt claims that human behavior is fundamentally motivated by incentives.[14] He uses this assertion to explain the seemingly incomprehensible function of numerous communities of practice, from real estate agents to sumo wrestlers to drug dealers. In one of his more controversial claims, Levitt argues that the massive drop in crime across the United States in the 1990s was caused by the legalization of abortion in 1973.[15] Levitt and Dubner explain:

In the early 1990s, just as the first cohort of children born after *Roe v. Wade* was hitting its late teen years—the years during which young men enter their criminal prime—the rate of crime began to fall. What this cohort was missing, of course, were the children who stood the greatest chance of becoming criminals. And the crime rate continued to fall as an entire generation came of age minus the children whose mothers had not wanted to bring a child into the world. *Legalized abortion led to less unwantedness; unwantedness leads to high crime; legalized abortion, therefore, led to less crime.*[16]

Using written rhetoric, Levitt and Dubner walk us through an explanation of the causal relationship that leads, in their proposition, from legalized abortion to reduced crime. They are describing a social process, the operation of interrelated legal policy and social welfare. Notably, the two end this explanation with a formal logical syllogism (italicized above), a structure I will return to below in the context of rhetoric.

These abstract processes—be they material like watch gears or cultural like crime—can be recounted through representation. However, procedural representation takes a different form than written or spoken representation. Procedural representation explains processes *with other processes*. Procedural representation is a form of symbolic expression that uses process rather than language. Diamond and Levitt make claims about procedural systems like history and crime, but they do not inscribe those claims in procedure—they write them, just like I wrote the description of product returns above. In fact, each and every analysis of videogame-based procedural rhetoric I will perform in this book necessarily *describes* the function of processes. These written descriptions attempt to explain the procedural ones, which are made up of rules rather than letters.

Procedural representation itself requires inscription in a medium that actually enacts processes rather than merely describe them. Human behavior is one mode of procedural inscription. Human actors can enact processes; we do so all the time. The clerk, the supervisor, and the army private all enact procedures. Even very young children can consciously enact procedures with great success: crossing the street, tying one's shoes, and setting the table are all unit operations in cultural and social processes. Nondigital board and card games offer further examples of human-enacted processes; the people playing the game execute its rules. But human behavior is a challenging medium to muster for arbitrary expression. It is difficult to coerce even a small group of people to execute a particular process again and again, without rest and without incentive. Because procedurality is intrinsic and fundamental to computers, and because computers are much more flexible as an inscription medium than human agents, they are particularly suited to procedural expression.

In her call for meaningful interactive drama, Janet Murray advocates for procedural authorship. Such effort, says Murray, "means writing the rules by which the text appears as well as writing the texts themselves. It means writing the rules for the interactor's involvement, that is, the conditions under which things will happen in response to the participant's actions." Murray cites Joseph Weizenbaum's *Eliza* program as an early example of this kind of procedural expression.[17] *Eliza* modeled a therapist, responding to users' text-based input in much the same way one would expect from a real Rogerian psychologist. Here is a sample exchange from Weizenbaum's original *Eliza*, which ran on MIT's MAC time-sharing system in the mid-1960s (capitalized lines are computer responses):

Men are all alike.
IN WHAT WAY?
They're always bugging us about something or other.
CAN YOU THINK OF A SPECIFIC EXAMPLE?
Well, my boyfriend made me come here.
YOUR BOYFRIEND MADE YOU COME HERE
He says I'm depressed much of the time.
I AM SORRY TO HEAR YOU ARE DEPRESSED
It's true. I am unhappy
DO YOU THINK COMING HERE WILL HELP YOU NOT TO BE UNHAPPY
I need some help, that much seems certain.

WHAT WOULD IT MEAN TO YOU IF YOU GOT SOME HELP
Perhaps I could learn to get along with my mother.
TELL ME MORE ABOUT YOUR FAMILY
My mother takes care of me.[18]

As a technical experiment, *Eliza* is an example of natural language processing (NLP); the computer takes the user's input, parses it into units of meaning that the program can understand, and then assembles and presents a response, including the proper grammatical transformations to maintain the illusion of language fluency. *Eliza* seeks out keywords such as "I am" or "you" and manufactures transformations based on them. The computer program has no real understanding of the meaning of the user's input; rather, it is taking that input and spinning it into a possible conversation. *Eliza* is a machine for generating conversations according to procedures.

Of course, the Rogerian psychologist is not the most meaningful real-life interlocutor—such a therapist converses with the patient, encouraging him or her toward "self-actualization" through empathy, mostly in the form of repetition intended to encourage reflection. Since *Eliza*, considerable research in the field of artificial intelligence has centered on the creation of similar agents. Some agents are meant merely to process bits of data, like keyword searches or security tools. Other agents have more lofty goals, hoping to create believable characters whose behavior is authored procedurally with special-use computer languages.[19] These are expressive agents, meant to clarify, explore, or comment on human processes in the same vein as poetry, literature, and film. No matter their content, these computer programs use processes for expression rather than utility. As an inscriptive practice, procedurality is not limited to tool-making.

Procedurality versus the Procedural Programming Paradigm

Speaking of computer languages, I would like to make a few notes to help reduce confusion for readers who come equipped with different (although not incompatible) notions of procedure, especially for those who come from a background in computer science. I am using *procedural* and *procedurality* in a much more general sense than it sometimes takes on in that field. In computer science, a *procedure* is sometimes used as a synonym for a subroutine—a function or method call. A procedure contains a series of computational instructions, encapsulated into a single command that can be called at any time during program execution. Some imperative computer languages, such as Pascal, even reserve the word *procedure* to declare a subroutine in code, as the following example illustrates.

```
procedure foo(var n: integer)
begin
    writeln('foo outputs ', n);
end;

begin
    i := 1;
    while i <= 10 do foo(i);
end.
```

In other cases, *procedural* is used to describe a particular approach to computer programming, one typically called the *procedural programming* paradigm. Procedural programming is a paradigmatic extension of the notion of *procedure* as subroutine. As a programming method, procedural programming became privileged over unstructured programming, in which all code exists in a single continuous block. In Assembly and early versions of BASIC, programs were written as long lists of code with branches (Assembly's BNE, BEQ, and JMP) or execution flow statements (BASIC's GOTO).[20] Procedural programming allowed increased readability and management of complexity, at a slight cost in program performance. Procedural programming also offered the ability to reuse the same code throughout a program through procedure calls, functions, and multiple files. Strong proponents of the more recent paradigm of object-oriented programming may shudder at my liberal use of the term *procedural*, but I am not referring to the programming paradigm. Object-oriented programming extends the modularity introduced by procedural programming and therefore owes the latter a conceptual debt, but this relationship is not relevant to my purposes here. Rather, I understand procedurality as the fundamental notion of authoring processes.

Procedural Figures, Forms, and Genres

Just as there are literary and filmic figures, so there are procedural figures. These are distinct from and prior to forms and genres. Procedural figures have much in common with literary figures like metaphor, metonymy, or synecdoche; they are strategies for authoring unit operations for particularly salient parts of many procedural systems. Noah Wardrip-Fruin has used the term *operational logics* to refer to the standardized or formalized unit operations that take on common roles in multiple procedural representations.[21] He identifies two operational logics that are particularly common, graphical logics and textual logics. Graphical logics are very frequently found in videogames; they include such procedural figures as movement, gravity, and collision detection. These fundamental figures ground innumerable videogames, from *Spacewar!* to *Pong* to *Pac-Man* to *Doom*. In many videogames, the player controls an object, agent, or vehicle that he must pilot in a particular manner—toward a goal or to avoid enemies or obstacles. Graphical logics frequently encapsulate procedural representations of material phenomena, such as moving, jumping, or firing projectiles. Object physics and lighting effects offer additional examples, meant to depict changing environments rather than character movement. In the videogame industry, sets of graphical logics are often packaged together as a *game engine*, a software toolkit used to create a variety of additional games.[22]

Wardrip-Fruin also cites textual logics as a common procedural trope. NLP, mentioned above, is an example of a textual logic, as are the text parsers inherent to Z-machine text adventure games and interactive fiction, such as *Zork*.[23] Additional logics include those procedural tropes used for text generation, such as n-grams, a probability distribution derived from Markov chains and first suggested by cyberneticist Claude Shannon. N-grams are sequences of a specified number (n) of elements from a given sequence, where probabilities determine which members of the sequence are most likely to be selected next. They are really sequential logics, but when applied to text generation they can be used to predict and construct textual phrases based on probability distributions of the subsequent word or phrase given a starting word or phrase. For example, in the sequence "where are" a likely subsequent word might be "you."[24]

Outside of videogames, procedural tropes often take the form of common models of user interaction. Elements of a graphical user interface could be understood as procedural tropes, for example, the scrollbar or push-button. These elements facilitate a wide range of user interactions in a variety of content domains. Operational logics for opening and saving files are also reasonable candidates; these tropes encapsulate lower-level logics for getting handles to filestreams and reading or writing byte data. We might call the former group of procedural tropes *interface logics*, and the latter *input/output (IO) logics*. Just as game engines accumulate multiple, common graphical logics, so software frameworks like Microsoft Foundation Classes (MFC) and Java Foundation Classes (JFC) accumulate multiple, common interface logics, IO logics, and myriad other logics required to drive the modern computer operating system.

Taken together, we can think of game engines, frameworks, and other common groupings of procedural tropes as commensurate with forms of literary or artistic expression, such as the sonnet, the short story, or the feature film. These collections of procedural tropes form the basis for a variety of subsequent expressive artifacts. On its own, the sonnet is no more useful than the physics engine, but both can be deployed in a range of expressive practices. A classical Newtonian mechanics simulation can easily facilitate both war (projectile fire) and naturalism (ballooning), just as a sonnet can facilitate both religious (John Donne) and amorous (Shakespeare) expression.

Procedural genres emerge from assemblages of procedural forms. These are akin to literary, filmic, or artistic genres like the film noir, the lyric poem, or the science fiction novel. In videogames, genres include the platformer, the first-person shooter, the turn-based strategy game, and so forth. When we recognize gameplay, we typically recognize the similarities between the constitutive procedural representations that produce the on-screen effects and controllable dynamics we experience as players.

Procedural representation is significantly different from textual, visual, and plastic representation. Even though other inscription techniques may be partly or wholly driven by a desire to represent human or material processes, only procedural systems like computer software actually represent process with process. This is where the particular power of procedural authorship lies, in its native ability to depict processes.

The inscription of procedural representations on the computer takes place in code. Just like *procedure*, the term *code* can take multiple meanings. Lawrence Lessig has taken advantage of the term's ambiguity to address the similarity between code in the legal sense and code in the programmatic sense: "In real space we recognize how laws regulate—through constitutions, statutes, and other legal codes. In cyberspace we must understand how code regulates—how the software and hardware that make cyberspace what it is *regulate* cyberspace as it is."[25] But in legal systems, code is regulated through complex social and political structures subject to many additional procedural influences, just like the soldiers in Abu Ghraib and the clerk at the retail return counter. In computational systems, code is regulated through software and hardware systems. These systems impose constraints, but they are not subject to the caprice of direct human action.

Rhetoric

Like procedurality, rhetoric is not an esteemed term. Despite its two and a half millennia-long history, *rhetoric* invokes largely negative connotations. We often speak of "empty rhetoric," elaborate and well-crafted speech that is nevertheless devoid of actual meaning. *Rhetoric* might conjure the impression of *hot air*, as in the case of a fast-talking con who crafts pretentious language to hide barren or deceitful intentions. Academics and politicians are particularly susceptible to this sort of criticism, perhaps because we (and they) tend to use flourish and lexis when coherence runs thin, as in this very sentence. Rhetoric is often equated with a type of smokescreen; it is language used to occlude, confuse, or manipulate the listener.

However, turgidity and extravagance are relatively recent inflections to this term, which originally referred only to persuasive speech, or oratory. The term *rhetoric* (ῥήτωρικη) first appears in Plato's *Gorgias*, written some 2,500 years ago, in reference to the art of persuasion. The term itself derives from the rhetor (ῥήτωρ), or orator, and his practice, oratory (ῥήτωρεύω).[26] Rhetoric in ancient Greece—and by extension classical rhetoric in general—meant public speaking for civic purposes. Golden age Athenian democracy strongly influenced the early development of rhetoric, which dealt specifically with social and political practices. Rhetoric was oral and it was public. The rhetor used his art on specific occasions and in particular social contexts—the law court and the public forum. A well-known example of this type of rhetoric is Plato's *Apology*, in which Socrates defends himself against accusations that he has corrupted the youth of Athens—*apology* here refers to the Greek term ἀπολογία, a defense speech. In the context of public speech and especially legal and civic speech, rhetoric's direct relation to persuasion is much clearer. Spoken words attempt to convert listeners to a particular opinion, usually one that will influence direct and immediate action, such as the fateful vote of Socrates' jury.

In golden age Athens, there was good reason to become versed in rhetorical technique. Unlike our contemporary representative democracies, the Athenian system was much more direct. Citizens were required to participate in the courts, and anyone (i.e., any male) could speak in the assembly. Unlike our legal system, with its guarantees of professional representation, Athenians accused of a crime were expected to defend themselves (or to find a relative or friend to speak on their behalf). Furthermore, Athenian juries were huge—usually 201 members but often many hundreds more depending on the importance of the case. The average citizen untrained in oratory not only might find himself at a loss for words but also might experience significant intimidation speaking before such a large group.

Rhetorical training responded to this need, partly motivated by lucrative business opportunities. The title character in Plato's *Phaedrus* speaks of books on the subject of rhetoric (ἐν τοῖς περὶ λόγων τέχνης), and Socrates subsequently recounts the technical advice these books proffer:[27]

Socrates: Thank you for reminding me. You mean that there must be an introduction [προοίμιον, *prooemion*] first, at the beginning of the discourse; these are the things you mean, are they not?—the niceties of the art.

Phaedrus: Yes.

Socrates: And the narrative [διήγησίν, *diegesis*] must come second with the testimony [τεχμήρια] after it, and third the proofs [πίστωσιν, *pistis*], and fourth the probabilities [ἐπιπίστωσιν, *epipistis*]; and confirmation and further confirmation are mentioned, I believe, by the man from Byzantium, that most excellent artist in words.

Phaedrus: You mean the worthy Theodorus?

Socrates: Of course. And he tells how refutation [ἔλεγχόν, *elenkhos*] and further refutation [ἐπεξέλεγχον, *epexelenkhos*] must be accomplished, both in accusation and in defense. Shall we not bring the illustrious Parian, Evenus, into our discussion, who invented covert allusion and indirect praises? And some say that he also wrote indirect censures, composing them in verse as an aid to memory; for he is a clever man.

. . .

But all seem to be in agreement concerning the conclusion of discourses, which some call recapitulation [ἐπάνοδον, *epanodos*], while others give it some other name.

Phaedrus: You mean making a summary of the points of the speech at the end of it, so as to remind the hearers of what has been said?

Socrates: These are the things I mean, these and anything else you can mention concerned with the art of rhetoric.[28]

Socrates' negative opinion of textbook rhetoric notwithstanding (see below), the *Phaedrus* offers evidence of the method by which fifth-century Greeks thought oratory could be best composed. Speakers should begin with an introduction (*prooemion*), then continue with a description or narration of events (*diegesis*), followed by proof and evidence (*pistis*) and the probabilities that such evidence is sound (*epipistis*). The speaker should then refute the opposing claim (*elenkhos*), and then refute it once more (*epexelenkhos*). Finally, the speech should end with a conclusion, including a recapitulation (*ephanodos*) of the argument.

These techniques form the basis for rhetorical speech; they describe how it works and they instruct the speaker on how best to use rhetoric in any situation. Technical rhetoric, as this type is sometimes called, is useful for the layperson but perhaps too simplistic for the professional orator. Numerous other techniques developed around imitating skilled orators. These experts usually charged for their services, and they were called *sophists*. Sophistic rhetoric was taught by demonstration and practice, not by principle like technical rhetoric. In some cases, a demonstration of sophistic rhetoric resembled the performance of epic poetry, where narrative fragments were memorized and reassembled during recitation.[29] Other techniques included parallelism in structure, syllabic meter, and tone.[30]

The popularity of books and sophistry bred critique. Such approaches motivated the work of Socrates, Plato, and Aristotle, who rejected the social and political contingency of the court and the assembly in favor of more lasting philosophical truths. Socrates and Plato privilege *dialectic*, or methods of reasoning about questions toward unknown conclusions, over rhetoric, which crafts discourse around known or desired conclusions. In Plato's *Georgias*, Socrates exposes rhetoric as a form of flattery, intended to produce pleasure, not knowledge or justice.[31]

Aristotle resuscitated rhetoric, joining it with his notion of causality. In the *Physics*, Aristotle articulates four causes, the material, formal, efficient, and final. The material cause is the material out of which a thing is made; the formal cause is the structure that makes it what it is; the efficient cause is that which produces the thing; and the final cause is the purpose for which it is produced.[32] A table, for example, is made of wood (material cause), crafted to have four legs and a flat surface (formal cause) by a carpenter (efficient cause) for the purpose of eating upon (final cause). For Aristotle, rhetoric has three possible ends, or final causes, and therefore he distinguishes three varieties of rhetoric: *forensic*, *deliberative*, and *epideictic*. Forensic (or judicial) rhetoric aims for justice, as in the purview of the law courts. Deliberative (or political) rhetoric strives for public benefit, as in the case of the assembly. Epideictic (or ceremonial) rhetoric aims for honor or shame, as in the case of a private communication.[33] Aristotle avoids Plato's dismissal of rhetoric, arguing that rhetorical practice as a whole has the final cause of persuasion to correct judgment.

In the *Rhetoric*, Aristotle accomplishes this corrective through an approach to rhetorical practice that aligns it with knowledge instead of sophistry. Responding to Plato, Aristotle attempts a systematic, philosophical approach to the art of persuasive oratory. This approach borrows much from the idea of oratory process from technical rhetoric, and a great deal of Aristotle's rhetorical theory addresses the style, arrangement, and organization of persuasive speech. For Aristotle, rhetoric is defined as "the faculty of observing in any given case the available means of persuasion."[34] The adept rhetorician does not merely follow a list of instructions for composing an oratory (technical rhetoric), nor does he merely parrot the style or words of an expert (sophistic rhetoric), but rather he musters reason to discover the available means of persuasion in any particular case (philosophical rhetoric). This variety of rhetoric implies an understanding of both the reasons to persuade (the final cause) and the tools available to achieve that end (the efficient cause), including propositions, evidence, styles, and devices. Most importantly, Aristotle offers a philosophical justification for rhetoric that moves it closer to dialectic, the philosophical practice of reason that Socrates and Plato deliberately opposed to rhetoric. In particular, Aristotle draws a correlation between two modes of human reason, induction (ἐπαγωγή) and deduction (συλλογισμός, *syllogism*). In rhetoric, the equivalent to induction is the example (παράδειγμα, *paradigm*), and the equivalent to deduction is the enthymeme (ἐνθύμημα). Examples advance the claim that a certain proposition is a part of a set of such (allegedly true) cases, and therefore equally true. Enthymemes advance the claim that a certain proposition is true in light of another's truth value. Unlike syllogisms, in which both propositions and conclusions are given explicitly, in enthymeme the orator omits one of the propositions in a syllogism.[35] For example, in the enthymeme "We cannot trust this man, as he is a politician," the major premise of a proper syllogism is omitted:

Politicians are not trustworthy. (Omitted)
This man is a politician.
Therefore, we cannot trust this man.

The enthymeme and the example offer instances of a broad variety of rhetorical figures developed by and since Aristotle. Like procedural figures, rhetorical figures define the possibility space for rhetorical practice. These figures are many and a complete discussion of them would be impossible in the present context. However, many rhetorical figures will be familiar by virtue of our common experience with them: antithesis (the juxtaposition of contrasting ideas); paradox (a seemingly self-contradictory statement that produces insight or truth); oxymoron (a highly compressed paradox); aporia (feigning flummox about the best way to approach a proposition); irony (evoking contrary meaning to yield scorn). These and other rhetorical figures found the basis of rhetorical tactics. Combining these with the structural framework of introduction, statement, proof, and epilogue, Aristotle offers a complete process for constructing oratory.[36]

Rhetoric Beyond Oratory

Unlike his Roman counterparts Cicero and Quintilian, Aristotle does not explicitly define rhetoric as the art of *verbal* persuasion, although it is unlikely that any other rhetorical mode occurred to him. Classical rhetoric passed into the Middle Ages and modern times with considerable alteration. The use of rhetoric in civil contexts like the court never disappeared entirely, and indeed it remains a common form of rhetoric today; our modern politicians soapbox just as Plato's contemporaries did. But the concept of rhetoric was expanded beyond oratory and beyond direct persuasion. Effectively, rhetoric was extended to account for new modes of inscription—especially literary and artistic modes. Rhetoric in writing, painting, sculpture, and other media do not necessarily make the same direct appeals to persuasion as oratory. Rhetoric thus also came to refer to *effective expression*, that is, writing, speech, or art that both accomplishes the goals of the author and absorbs the reader or viewer.

Persuasion as a rhetorical goal persists, but it has changed in nature. In classical rhetoric, oral persuasion primarily served political purposes. It was enacted when needed and with particular ends in mind. The effectiveness of oratory related directly to its success or failure at accomplishing a particular, known goal. And because citizens often got only one shot at oratory—as is the case in Socrates' defense speech—one can point to the clear success or failure of rhetorical techniques. In discursive rhetoric, persuasion is not necessarily so teleological. Writers and artists have expressive goals, and they deploy techniques to accomplish those goals. The poststructuralist tendency to decouple authorship from readership, celebrating the free play of textual meanings, further undermines the status of persuasion. Here, persuasion shifts from the simple achievement of desired ends to the effective arrangement of a work so as to create a desirable possibility space for interpretation. In contemporary rhetoric, the goal of persuasion is largely underplayed or even omitted as a defining feature of the field, replaced by the more general notion of elegance, clarity, and creativity in communication. When understood in this sense, rhetoric "provides ways of emphasizing ideas or making them vivid."[37] Success means effective expression, not necessarily effective influence.

Despite the apparent dichotomy between classical and contemporary rhetorics, the two share one core property: that of technique. Rhetorics of all types assume a particular approach to effective expression, whether it be oral, written, artistic, or otherwise inscribed. Today, spoken and written expression remain deeply relevant to culture. The spoken and written word enjoys a long rhetorical tradition—Aristotle's techniques remain equally useful, and indeed equally put to use, by contemporary orators. Sonja Foss, Karen Foss, and Robert Trapp have attempted to reposition rhetoric outside of any particular mode of inscription. The three define rhetoric "broadly as the uniquely human ability to use symbols to communicate with one another."[38] However, as Kevin DeLuca points out, on the "very next page"[39] Foss, Foss, and Trapp also argue that "the paradigm case of rhetoric is the use of the spoken word to persuade an audience."[40] While rhetoric might include nonverbal transmission, these modes still maintain a tenuous relationship, and are at risk of appearing inferior to verbal discourse.

The influential twentieth-century rhetorician Kenneth Burke marks an important change in the understanding of rhetoric. Because people are inherently separate from one another, we seek ways to join our interests. Burke identifies this need as the ancestor of the practice of rhetoric. He extends rhetoric beyond persuasion, instead suggesting "identification" as a key term for the practice.[41] We use symbolic systems, such as language, as a way to achieve this identification. Burke defines rhetoric as a part of the practice of identification, as "the use of words by human agents to form attitudes or induce actions in other human agents."[42] While rhetoric still entails persuasion for Burke, he greatly expands its purview, arguing that it facilitates human action in general. Persuasion is subordinated to identification (or the more obscure term *consubstantiality*, which Burke uses to characterize identification), and using rhetoric to achieve an end is only one possible use of the craft for Burke.[43] Rhetoric becomes a means to facilitate identification and to "bridge the conditions of estrangement that are natural and inevitable."[44]

In addition to expanding the conception of rhetoric, Burke also expands its domain. Following the tradition of oral and written rhetoric, he maintains language as central, but Burke's understanding of humans as creators and consumers of symbolic systems expands rhetoric to include nonverbal domains. He does not explicitly delineate all the domains to which rhetoric could apply; instead, he embraces the broadness of human symbolic production in the abstract. "Wherever there is persuasion," writes Burke, "there is rhetoric. And wherever there is 'meaning,' there is 'persuasion.'"[45]

Visual Rhetoric

The wide latitude Burke affords rhetoric won him both champions and critics, but his approach advances the rhetorical value of multiple forms of cultural expression, not just speech and writing.[46] Thanks to the influence of Burke, and amplified by the increasingly inescapable presence of non-oral, nonverbal media, increasing interest has mounted around efforts to understand the rhetorical figures and forms of these other, newer modes of inscription that also appear to serve rhetorical ends. In particular, the emergence of photographic and cinematic expression in the nineteenth and twentieth centuries suggests a need to understand how these new, nonverbal media mount arguments. This subfield is called *visual rhetoric*. Marguerite Helmers and Charles A. Hill explain:

Rhetoricians working from a variety of disciplinary perspectives are beginning to pay a substantial amount of attention to issues of visual rhetoric. Through analysis of photographs and drawings, graphs and tables, and motion pictures, scholars are exploring the many ways in which visual elements are used to influence people's attitudes, opinions, and beliefs.[47]

Visual communication cannot simply adopt the figures and forms of oral and written expression, so a new form of rhetoric must be created to accommodate these media forms. Helmers and Hill argue that visual rhetoric is particularly essential in the face of globalization and mass media. Visual images on television, clothing, retail storefronts, and public spaces are nearly ubiquitous, offering a strong incentive to understand the rhetoric of such media. Moreover, the profusion of photographic, illustrative, and cinematic images increases with the rise in cheap, accessible digital photography and video techniques coupled with the instant, worldwide distribution on the Internet. Politicians and advertisers use visual images as much as, if not more than, they use spoken and written words. In reference to these and related uses of images, visual rhetoricians ask, "how, exactly, do images persuade?"[48]

Aristotle took great pains to reconnect rhetoric with philosophical discourse. A common thread in visual rhetoric addresses the relative merit of visual communication as emotional versus philosophical. As Hill explains,

It is likely that verbal text, because of its analytic nature (being made up of discrete meaningful units) and because it is apprehended relatively slowly over time, is more likely to prompt systematic processing, while images, which are comprehend wholistically and almost instantaneously, tend to prompt heuristic processing.[49]

Images may lack the kind of deep analysis afforded by textual interpretation, a sentiment that resonates with concerns over the use of images in propaganda. According to Hill, images are more "vivid" than text or speech, and therefore they are more easily manipulated toward visceral responses.[50] This use of images has been especially popular in advertising, a subject to which I will return in chapter 5. Advertisers, notes Hill, "don't want to *persuade* people to buy their products, because persuasion implies that the audience has given the issue some thought and come to a conscious decision. Instead, advertisers want to . . . compel people to buy a product without even knowing why they're buying it—as a visceral response to a stimulus, not as a conscious decision. And this is best done through images."[51] Hill offers no final conclusions about the potential for images to serve more reflective rhetorical purposes, but he does point out that visual rhetoric should not strive "to banish emotional and aesthetic concerns."[52]

J. Anthony Blair argues that visual rhetoric needs a theory of visual argument to escape this trap. Blair argues that, like Hill's psychological vividness, "symbolic inducement" alone is inadequate for a theory of rhetoric.[53] Rather, visual rhetoric requires visual "arguments" which "supply us with *reasons* for accepting a point of view."[54] Blair advances the rather ambiguous view that visual images cannot make propositional claims—the very notion of a "visual argument" stands at the edge of paradox.[55] The acid test for a visual argument, according to Blair, is "whether it would be possible to construct from what is communicated visually a verbal argument that is consistent with the visual presentation."[56] Blair admits that such an argument could never be equivalent to the visual argument, but that the test is necessary to determine whether an image has propositional content. Verbal rhetoric remains privileged, with images mainly useful for "evocative power."[57]

The preferential treatment afforded to verbal rhetoric underscores the continued privilege of speech over writing, and writing over images. Philosopher Jacques Derrida argued against the hierarchy of forms of language, giving the name *logocentrism* to the view that speech is central to language because it is closer to thought.[58] In the Western tradition, speech is thought to derive from thought, and writing from speech. Detractors of visual rhetoric like Blair could be seen as logocentric in arguing that images derive from writing and are thus more distant from thought, less conducive to persuasive expression.

David S. Birdsell and Leo Groarke oppose this position. Visual argument does exist, but it takes a necessarily different form from that of verbal argument; images are, after all, a different mode of inscription from writing. Birdsell and Groarke call the "prevalent prejudice that visual images are in some way arbitrary vague and ambiguous" a "dogma that has outlived its usefulness."[59] Objections claiming that images are sometimes vague are unconvincing, for spoken and written language is also vague at times. Visual argument, argue Birdsell and Groarke, is simply constructed differently than verbal argument. The two also observe that the rapid changes in visual culture make visual cultural contexts crucial in considerations of visual argument.

Randall A. Lake and Barbara A. Pickering offer several tropes for visual argument and refutation, including substitution, in which an image is replaced in part of a frame with connotatively different ones, and transformation, in which an image is "recontextualized in a new visual frame, such that its polarity is modified or reversed through association with different images."[60] Examples of transformation include the "reframing" and "mobile framing" techniques used by filmmakers. Keith Kenney points out that documentarian Ken Burns liberally uses these gestures to reveal portions of an image in order to draw selective attention to its constituent parts, which then complete the visual argument.[61] Editorial cartoons, a favorite example of visual rhetoricians, use similar techniques, encouraging the viewer to break down the image into constituent parts, each of which advances a portion of the argument.

Kevin Michael DeLuca attempts to address visual argument through the concept of "image event," a kind of visual documentation of a rhetorical strategy.[62] He draws examples from large-scale environmental demonstrations, such as the (failed) 1975 Greenpeace attempt to disrupt the Soviet whaling vessel *Vlastny* by positioning activists in inflatable boats between the harpoon and the whale. DeLuca argues that despite the failed actions of Greenpeace's Save the Whales campaign, they succeed in their rhetorical purpose, namely drawing massive worldwide attention to the problem in question. DeLuca makes convincing claims that these situationist-style interventions actually influence future policy, but I would argue that they do not deploy visual rhetoric in the true sense of the word. To be sure, images of the Greenpeace actions appear to be partly, even largely responsible for subsequent protests and rejoinders toward environmental policy changes, but the actions themselves are designed to generate provocation, not to make arguments for policy changes.

The profusion of visual images recommends a subfield of rhetoric, but visual rhetoric remains an emerging discipline. The very notion of a visual rhetoric reinforces the idea that rhetoric is a general field of inquiry, applicable to multiple media and modes of inscription. To address the possibilities of a new medium as a type of rhetoric, we must identify how inscription works in that medium, and then how arguments can be constructed through those modes of inscription.

Digital Rhetoric

Visual rhetoric offers a useful lesson in the creation of new forms of rhetoric in the general sense. One would be hard pressed to deny that advertisements, photographs, illustrations, and other optical phenomena have some effect on their viewers. To be sure, visual rhetoric is often at work in videogames, a medium that deploys both still and moving images. A study of visual rhetoric in games would need to address the disputes of the former field, especially the rift between psychological and cultural discourses about manipulation and phenomenal impact on the one hand and logical deliberation on the other. But despite its possible value to digital media, visual rhetoric cannot help us address the rhetorical function of procedural representation. To convincingly propose a new domain for rhetoric, one is obliged to address the properties of the persuasive medium in particular, and the general practice of persuasion on the other. Visual rhetoric simply does not account for procedural representation. This is not a flaw in the subfield of visual rhetoric; there is much value to be gained from the study of images in all media. But in procedural media like videogames, images are frequently constructed, selected, or sequenced in code, making the stock tools of visual rhetoric inadequate. Image is subordinate to process.

Unfortunately, many efforts to unite computers and rhetoric do not even make appeals to visual rhetoric, instead remaining firmly planted in the traditional frame of verbal and written rhetoric in support of vague notions of "the digital." *Digital rhetoric* typically abstracts the computer as a consideration, focusing on the text and image content a machine might host and the communities of practice in which that content is created and used. Email, websites, message boards, blogs, and wikis are examples of these targets. To be sure, all of these digital forms can function rhetorically, and they are worthy of study; like visual rhetoricians, digital rhetoricians hope to revise and reinvent rhetorical theory for a new medium. James P. Zappen begins his integrated theory of digital rhetoric on this very note: "Studies of digital rhetoric," he writes, "help to explain how traditional rhetorical strategies of persuasion function and are being reconfigured in digital spaces."[63] But for scholars of digital rhetoric, to "function in digital spaces" often means mistaking subordinate properties of the computer for primary ones. For example, Laura J. Gurak identifies several "basic characteristics"[64] of digital rhetoric, including speed, reach, anonymity, and interactivity.[65] Of these, the first three simply characterize the aggregate effects of networked microcomputers. On first blush the last characteristic, interactivity, appears to address the properties of the computer more directly. But Gurak does not intend *interactivity* to refer to the machine's ability to facilitate the manipulation of processes. Instead, she is thinking of the more vague notion of computer-mediated discussion and feedback, essentially a repetition and consolidation of the other three characteristics.[66]

Other digital rhetoricians likewise focus on the use of digital computers to carry out culturally modified versions of existing oral and written discourse; letters become emails, conversations become instant message sessions. Barbara Warnick has argued that the more populist, nonhierarchical structure of the web facilitated opposition to the standards of traditional media. For example, Warnick explores zines and personal websites as welcome alternatives to top-down commercial media like print magazines.[67] Others want educators, especially secondary and postsecondary instructors, to provide stylistic training in increasingly indispensable digital forms like email and the web. Richard Lanham has made a case for digital rhetoric's place in the broader "digital arts," encouraging higher education to address the changing composition practices brought on by so-called new media.[68] Both Warnick and Lanham's proposals are reasonable and valuable. But they focus on revisions of existing cultural and expressive practices; the computer is secondary. What is missing is a digital rhetoric that addresses the unique properties of computation, like procedurality, to found a new rhetorical practice.

This challenge is aggravated by the fact that rhetoric itself does not currently enjoy favor among critics of digital media. In one highly visible example, new media artist and theorist Lev Manovich has argued that digital media may sound a death knell for rhetoric. Writing about web interfaces, Manovich doubts that hypertext could serve a rhetorical function:

While it is probably possible to invent a new rhetoric of hypermedia that will use hyperlinking not to distract the reader from the argument (as is often the case today), but rather to further convince her of an argument's validity, the sheer existence and popularity of hyperlinking exemplifies the continuing decline of the field of rhetoric in the modern era. . . . World Wide Web hyperlinking has privileged the single figure of metonymy at the expense of all others. The hypertext of the World Wide Web leads the reader from one text to another, ad infinitum. . . . Rather than seducing the user through a careful arrangement of arguments and examples, points and counterpoints, changing rhythms of presentation, . . . [hypertext] interfaces . . . bombard the user with all the data at once.[69]

One can raise numerous objections to Manovich's claims. For one, he has a rather curious view of hypertext that seems to equate hypermedia with media gluttony. Manovich seems to think that web pages present links in an attempt to substitute their linkage for their content, causing endless, haptic clicking on the part of the user. Meaning is tragically, "infinitely" deferred. This claim is especially curious given the prehistory of hypertext in Vannevar Bush's conceptual Memex and Ted Nelson's Xanadu.[70] These systems were conceived largely as tools to *increase* the correlation between documents, as material manifestations of manual cross-reference. Today, hypertext on "ordinary" websites is frequently used in this fashion; they provide additional information or resources to the user who wishes to confer them. Frequently, these resources take the form of supporting arguments, evidence, or citation, very old and very traditional tools in written rhetoric.

While Manovich considers the nature of the hyperlink, he ignores the computational system that facilitates hypermedia in the first place. Chris Crawford has used the term *process intensity* to refer to the "degree to which a program emphasizes processes instead of data."[71] Higher process intensity— or in Crawford's words a higher "crunch per bit ratio"—suggests that a program has greater potential for meaningful expression. While hypertexts themselves exhibit low process intensity, the systems that allow authorship and readership of web pages exhibit high process intensity. A web browser must construct a request for a page using the proper format for the Hypertext Transfer Protocol (HTTP) that carries requests between the computer and a server. The computer must then create a connection to the server via Transmission Control Protocol (TCP), which in turn communicates the request via Internet Protocol (IP), the communication convention that transports data across the packet-switched network that comprises the Internet. The server hosting the requested web page must then interpret the request, retrieve the requested document, and prepare it for transmission back to the user's computer via the same protocols, HTTP atop TCP/IP. IP guarantees delivery of all packets in a request, so the receiving computer's network layer must determine—all in code—whether all the packets have been received, which ones are out of order, and which need to be resent owing to corruption or loss. Once received, reordered, and reconstructed, the web browser must then take the textual data that the server has returned and render it in the browser. This too takes place in code. The web page is made up of Hypertext Markup Language (HTML), which the browser must parse, making decisions about which elements to place where and in what format on the user's screen. Then the web browser repeats the process for other resources referenced in the HTML document, such as other embedded HTML pages, images, script files, or stylesheets.

These technical details may appear to have little to do with Manovich's claims about the endless progression of hyperlinks on a web page. But the aggregate software systems that facilitate web-based hypertext are what make it possible to link and click in the first place. The principal innovation of the web is the merger of a computer-managed cross-referencing system with a networking system that supports heterogenous clients. More plainly put, Manovich ignores the software systems that make it possible for hyperlinks to work in the first place, instead making loose and technically inaccurate appeals to computer hardware as exotic metaphors rather than as material systems. Continuing the argument above, he compares hypertext to computer chipsets: "individual texts are placed in no particular order, like the Web page designed by [artist collective] antirom for HotWired. Expanding this comparison further, we can note that Random Access Memory, the concept behind the group's name, also implies a lack of hierarchy: Any RAM location can be accessed as quickly as any other."[72] Manovich compares the HotWired website to RAM not because computer memory facilitates the authorship of websites, but because the website was designed by a group that uses a pun on a computer chip term in their name—a different chip from RAM, as it happens, Read Only Memory, or ROM.

Manovich admits that a new rhetoric of hypermedia is "probably possible," but clearly he has no intention of pursuing one. Gurak and Warnick are not cynical about rhetoric and communication, but they focus on digital communities of practice, treating the computer primarily as a black-box network appliance, not as an executor of processes. In short, digital rhetoric tends to focus on the presentation of traditional materials—especially text and images—without accounting for the computational underpinnings of that presentation.

Rhetorician Elizabeth Losh neatly summarizes this inconsistency among digital rhetoricians. "In the standard model of digital rhetoric," she argues, "literary theory is applied to technological phenomena without considering how technological theories could conversely elucidate new media texts."[73] While I admit that there are useful interrogations of digital media that focus on reception over the technological structure (Losh's own work on the way digital artifacts take part in the public sphere is such a one), my contention here is that approaches to digital rhetoric must address the role of procedurality, the unique representational property of the computer.

Procedural Rhetoric

With these lessons in mind, I would now like to put the concepts of *procedurality* and *rhetoric* back together. As I proposed at the start of this chapter, *procedural rhetoric* is the practice of using processes persuasively, just as verbal rhetoric is the practice of using oratory persuasively and visual rhetoric is the practice of using images persuasively. Procedural rhetoric is a general name for the practice of authoring arguments through processes. Following the classical model, procedural rhetoric entails persuasion—to change opinion or action. Following the contemporary model, procedural rhetoric entails expression—to convey ideas effectively. Procedural rhetoric is a subdomain of procedural authorship; its arguments are made not through the construction of words or images, but through the authorship of rules of behavior, the construction of dynamic models. In computation, those rules are authored in code, through the practice of programming.

My rationale for suggesting a new rhetorical domain is the same one that motivates visual rhetoricians. Just as photography, motion graphics, moving images, and illustrations have become pervasive in contemporary society, so have computer hardware, software, and videogames. Just as visual rhetoricians argue that verbal and written rhetorics inadequately account for the unique properties of visual expression, so I argue that verbal, written, and visual rhetorics inadequately account for the unique properties of procedural expression. A theory of procedural rhetoric is needed to make commensurate judgments about the software systems we encounter every day and to allow a more sophisticated procedural authorship with both persuasion and expression as its goal.

Procedural rhetorics afford a new and promising way to make claims about *how things work*. Consider a particularly sophisticated example of a procedural rhetoric at work in a game. *The McDonald's Videogame* is a critique of McDonald's business practices by Italian social critic collective Molleindustria. The game is an example of a genre I call the anti-advergame, a game created to censure or disparage a company rather than support it.[74] The player controls four separate aspects of the McDonald's production environment, each of which he has to manage simultaneously: the third-world pasture where cattle are raised as cheaply as possible; the slaughterhouse where cattle are fattened for slaughter; the restaurant where burgers are sold; and the corporate offices where lobbying, public relations, and marketing are managed. In each sector, the player must make difficult business choices, but more importantly he must make difficult moral choices. In the pasture, the player must create enough cattle-grazing land and soy crops to produce the meat required to run the business. But only a limited number of fields are available; to acquire more land, the player must bribe the local governor for rights to convert his people's crops into corporate ones. More extreme tactics are also available: the player can bulldoze rainforest or dismantle indigenous settlements to clear space for

Figure 1.1 In Molleindustria's *The McDonald's Game*, players must use questionable business practices to increase profits.

grazing (see figure 1.1). These tactics correspond with the questionable business practices the developers want to critique. To enforce the corrupt nature of these tactics, public interest groups can censure or sue the player for violations. For example, bulldozing indigenous rainforest settlements yields complaints from antiglobalization groups. Overusing fields reduces their effectiveness as soil or pasture; creating dead earth also angers environmentalists. However, those groups can be managed through PR and lobbying in the corporate sector. Corrupting a climatologist may dig into profits, but it ensures fewer complaints in the future. Regular subornation of this kind is required to maintain allegiance. Likewise, in the slaughterhouse players can use growth hormones to fatten cows faster, and they can choose whether to kill diseased cows or let them go through the slaughter process. Removing cattle from the production process reduces material product, thereby reducing supply and thereby again reducing profit. Growth hormones offend health critics, but they also allow the rapid production necessary to meet demand in the restaurant sector. Feeding cattle animal by-products cheapens the fattening process, but is more likely to cause disease. Allowing diseased meat to be made into burgers may spawn complaints and fines from health officers, but those groups too can be bribed through lobbying. The restaurant sector demands similar trade-offs, including balancing a need to fire incorrigible employees with local politicians' complaints about labor practices.

The McDonald's Videogame mounts a procedural rhetoric about the necessity of corruption in the global fast food business, and the overwhelming temptation of greed, which leads to more corruption. In order to succeed in the long-term, the player must use growth hormones, he must coerce banana republics, and he must mount PR and lobbying campaigns. Furthermore, the temptation to destroy indigenous villages, launch bribery campaigns, recycle animal parts, and cover up health risks is tremendous, although the financial benefit from doing so is only marginal. As Patrick Dugan explains, the game imposes "constraints simulating necessary evils on one hand, and on the other hand . . . business practices that are self-defeating and, really just stupid."[75] The game makes a procedural argument about the inherent problems in the fast food industry, particularly the necessity of overstepping environmental and health-related boundaries.

Verbal rhetoric certainly supports this type of claim; one can explain the persuasive function of processes with language: consider my earlier explanation of the rhetoric of retail store return policies, or Eric Schlosser's popular book and film *Fast Food Nation*, which addresses many of the issues represented in *The McDonald's Videogame*.[76] But these written media do not express their arguments procedurally; instead, they describe the processes at work in such systems with speech, writing, or images. Likewise, it is possible to characterize processes with visual images. Consider a public service campaign called *G!rlpower Retouch*, commissioned by the Swedish Ministry of Health and Social Affairs. The goal of the campaign was to reduce the fixation on physical appearance caused partly by unrealistic body images in magazines and media. Forsman & Bodenfors, the agency hired to execute the campaign, created a click-through demo that explains how photo retouchers make significant changes to the bodies of their already striking models, hoping to render them even more perfect.[77] The demonstration depicts an attractive, young blonde on the cover of a fictional magazine. The user is then given the opportunity to undo all the photo retouches and individually reapply them. A textual explanation of the technique is also provided.

G!rlpower Retouch unpacks a process, the process of retouching photos for maximum beauty. It uses sequences of images combined with written text to explain each step. The artifact makes claims about images, so it makes reasonable use of images as propositions in the argument. *Retouch* even deploys the Aristotelian tactic of example, using a single model image to depict feature modifications common to all model images—eyes, teeth, lips, nose, jawline, hair, breasts, and so forth. The piece makes claims about the process of retouching, which is itself facilitated by the procedural affordances of image-editing software like *Adobe Photoshop*. However, *Retouch* does not deploy a procedural rhetoric, since it does not use representational processes to explain the actual processes used in photo retouching. That said, one could imagine a procedural version of the same argument. Simply replicating a photo editor would supply the needed procedurality, but not the required rhetoric. The steps needed to accomplish the individual effects are complex and require professional-level command of the tools. Instead, a procedural implementation might abstract a set of editing tools particular to model editing, for example a "thinning" tool for waists, arms, and hips. Shadow and highlighting tools could be added for cheeks, hair, and breast augmentation. Instead of clicking through a sequence of images that explain the retouching process, the user would be put in charge of implementing it himself. A procedural implementation would accentuate and extend the use of paradigmatic evidence in the existing version of *Retouch*. In its current implementation, the piece depicts only one model. Her archetypical appearance makes her an effective example, and her three-quarter perspective pose allows the authors to address both face and body modifications. But a procedural version of the same argument would facilitate a variety of different images, full-body, head-and-shoulders, different body types, and so forth. Such a system might also allow the user to load his own photos, or photos from the Internet; these would serve as the data on which the retouching processes could run. Such a capacity would extend the rhetorical power of example.

Another, similar online consumer-awareness tool makes strides in the direction of procedural rhetoric while resting comfortably in the domain of visual rhetoric. PBS Kids maintains a website for young viewers, hosting show pages, games, and other interactive features.[78] Among the features is "Don't Buy It," a minisite that seeks to educate kids about the tricks advertisers use to turn kids into consumers.[79] The site features simple quizzes to help kids understand media manipulation (coincidentally, among them is a much simpler version of *G!rlpower Retouch* for food advertising).[80]

One of these features is *Freaky Flakes*, an interactive program that allows the user to design a cereal box. Unlike *Retouch*, *Freaky Flakes* asks the user to construct a box from the ground up, starting with its color. Textual information explains the benefits of each color, for example, "Orange stimulates the appetite and is one of the most popular cereal box colors." Next the user selects a character, again reading textual descriptions, for example, "The superhero is a great choice because little kids prefer fantasy characters to pictures of real people." Next the user enters a cereal name; the program advises him to "pick a name that is an attention grabber." Then the user selects one of four banners to add to the box to add marketing appeal, such as "Outrageous Crunch!" which "makes your cereal seem fun and exciting to eat." Finally, the user selects a prize to place inside, following advice about gender identification such as "Tattoos appeal to boys and girls." The user can view the completed box (see figure 1.2) or make a new one.

The argument *Freaky Flakes* mounts is more procedural than *Retouch*, but only incrementally so. The user recombines elements to configure a cereal box, but he chooses from a very small selection of individual configurations. *Freaky Flakes* is designed for younger users than *Retouch*, but the children who watch PBS Kids also likely play videogames much more complex than this simple program. Most importantly, *Freaky Flakes* fails to integrate the process of designing a cereal box with the supermarket where children might actually encounter it. The persuasion in *Retouch* reaches its apogee when the user sees the already attractive girl in the fake magazine ad turned into a spectacularly beautiful one. This gesture is a kind of visual enthymeme, in which the

Figure 1.2 PBS's *Freaky Flakes* offers a simple representation of practices of children's advertising. Courtesy of KCTS Television. © 2004 KCTS Television. All rights reserved.

authors rely on the user's instinctual and culturally mediated idea of beauty to produce actual arousal, jealousy, or self-doubt. *Freaky Flakes* offers no similar conclusion. The user creates a cereal box, but every box yields the same result (even combining the superhero and the princess ring yields the congratulatory message, "Your box looks great!"). A more effective procedural argument would enforce a set of rules akin to the tactics advertisers use to manipulate kids, while providing a much larger possibility space for box authorship. Within this space, the user would have the opportunity both to succeed and to fail in his attempt to manipulate the simulated children buying the cereal. Through multiple designs, the user might home in on the logic that drives the advertisers, resulting in increased sales of his virtual cereal. This gesture represents a procedural enthymeme—the player *literally* fills in the missing portion of the syllogism by interacting with the application, but that action is constrained by the rules. That is to say, a set of procedural constraints would determine which combinations of design strategies influence kids more and less successfully.

Let's revisit verbal and visual rhetorics' stumbling blocks in light of these two examples of potential procedural rhetorics. Charles Hill pointed out that images offer greater "vividness" than verbal narration or written description. Vivid information, he argued, "seems to be more persuasive than non-vivid information."[81] J. Anthony Blair countered that vivid images may increase presence, but they do not necessarily mount arguments. Even if images successfully cause viewers to take certain actions, those viewers are more likely manipulated than they are persuaded. Visual arguments, argues Blair, "lack [the] dialectical aspect [of] the process of interaction between the arguer and the interlocutors, who raise questions or objections."[82] Procedural rhetoric must address two issues that arise from these discussions: first, what is the relationship between procedural representation and vividness? Second, what is the relationship between procedural representation and dialectic?

To address the first question, I reproduce a table from Hill's essay, which he names "A comprehensive continuum of vividness."

Most Vivid Information   actual experience
                                    moving images with sound
                                    static photograph
                                    realistic painting
                                    line drawing

	narrative, descriptive account
	descriptive account
	abstract, impersonal analysis
Least Vivid Information	statistics

Immediately one can see that procedural representation is absent from this continuum. Simulation does not even make the list. Further yet, Hill accounts for no computational media whatsoever. I would be less inclined to quibble with the exclusion had Hill not called the continuum "comprehensive," indicating his intention to cover representational forms and their relationship to vividness fully.[83] Procedural representation is representation, and thus certainly not identical with actual experience. However, procedural representation can muster moving images and sound, and software and videogames are capable of generating moving images in accordance with complex rules that simulate real or imagined physical and cultural processes. Furthermore, procedural representations are often (but not always—see below) interactive; they rely on user interaction as a mediator, something static and moving images cannot claim to do. These capacities would suggest that procedurality is more vivid than moving images with sound, and thus earns the second spot on the continuum, directly under actual experience.[84] However, other factors might affect the relative vividness of procedural representations. For example, a simulation that accepts numerical input and generates numerical output might seem more akin to an abstract, impersonal analysis or even a set of statistics, falling to the bottom of Hill's continuum. Recalling Crawford's notion of process intensity, I would submit that procedural representations with high process intensity and with meaningful symbolic representations in their processes—specimens like interactive fiction, software, and especially videogames—certainly earn a spot above moving images on the continuum. Given this caveat, procedural representation seems equally prone to the increased persuasive properties Hill attributes to vividness.

What about procedural representations' relationship to dialectic? Hill argues that images are comprehended "wholistically and instantaneously," whereas verbal texts are apprehended "relatively slowly over time" as a result of their "analytic nature."[85] Interestingly, Hill characterizes the latter as "made up of discrete meaningful units," a property somewhat similar to my characterization of procedurality as the configuration of logical rules as unit operations. Blair's objection to visual arguments centers around images' reduced ability to advance propositions, a requirement of rhetorical argument. The visual argument Blair names most effective is the famous 1964 Lyndon Johnson television spot known as the "Daisy Ad."[86] Here is an account of the ad as accurately described by Wikipedia (www.wikipedia.org):

The commercial begins with a small girl picking the petals of a daisy while counting slowly. An ominous-sounding male voice is then heard counting down as the girl turns toward the camera, which zooms in until her pupil fills the screen, blacking it out. Then the countdown reaches zero and the blackness is replaced by the flash and mushroom cloud from a nuclear test. A voiceover from Johnson follows: "These are the stakes! To make a world in which all of God's children can live, or to go into the dark. We must either love each other, or we must die." Another voiceover then says, "Vote for President Johnson on November 3. The stakes are too high for you to stay home."[87]

Blair argues that this visual image *does* make an argument "in the sense of adducing a few reasons in a forceful way."[88] In particular, the ad invokes a visual enthymeme that completes a syllogism:

Increasing nuclear proliferation will likely lead to the destruction of humanity.
Goldwater supports nuclear proliferation (omitted).
Therefore, electing Goldwater may lead to the destruction of humanity.

Nevertheless, argues Blair, the ad "does not embody dialectic completely. In particular, it "does not permit the complexity of such dialectical moves as the raising of objections in order to refute or otherwise answer them."[89]

How does such an example compare with procedural representation? For one part, procedural rhetorics do mount propositions: each unit operation in a procedural representation is a claim about how part of the system it represents does, should, or could function. *The McDonald's Videogame* makes claims about the business practices required to run a successful global fast-food empire. My hypothetical revision of *Freaky Flakes* makes claims about the techniques advertisers use to design cereal boxes, as well as claims about children's culturally and psychologically influenced responses to specific box configurations. These propositions are every bit as logical as verbal arguments—in fact, internal consistency is often assured in computational arguments, since microprocessors and not human agents are in charge of their consistent execution.[90]

What about raising objections? One might argue that many computational systems do not allow the user to raise *procedural* objections—that is, the player of a videogame is usually not allowed to change the rules of play. Many critics have objected to this tendency, calling for games that allow players to alter core simulation dynamics to allow alternative perspectives. Most famously, Sherry Turkle has criticized[91] *Sim City*[92] for its failure to include alternative taxation-to-social services dynamics, a debate I have discussed in detail elsewhere.[93] Applying this objection to our current examples, one might point out that users of *Freaky Flakes* cannot make alterations to the designers' conception of advertising manipulation.

I have two responses to this objection. For one part, the type of user alteration Turkle and others call for is not the same as the dialectical objections Blair requires of arguments. One raises objections to propositions in the hopes of advancing conflicting or revisionist claims. Conversely, one allows user alteration in order to construct an artifact that accounts for multiple perspectives on a particular subject. One usually makes rhetorical claims precisely to *exclude* opposing positions on a subject, not to allow for the equal validity of all possible positions. For example, in the case of *Freaky Flakes*, one might object that the underlying model for advertising influence presumes the media ecology of consumer capitalism. This is a reasonable objection; but such a wholesale revision might imply a different simulation entirely, one that would be outside the expressive domain of the artifact. However, procedural representations often do allow the user to mount procedural objections through configurations of the system itself. In my hypothetical procedural revision of *Freaky Flakes*, the player might attempt to find inconsistencies in the creator's model by designing boxes that both produce socially responsible messages and appeal to children.

For another part, all artifacts subject to dissemination need not facilitate direct argument with the rhetorical author; in fact, even verbal arguments usually do not facilitate the open discourse of the Athenian assembly. Instead, they invite other, subsequent forms of discourse, in which interlocutors can engage, consider, and respond in turn, either via the same medium or a different one. Dialectics, in other words, function in a broader media ecology than Blair and Turkle allow. This objection applies equally to all rhetorical forms—verbal, written, visual, procedural, or otherwise.

Just as an objection in a debate would take place during the negation or rebuttal of the opponent rather than in the construction of the proponent, so an objection in a procedural artifact may take place in a responding claim of a verbal, written, visual, or procedural form. Such objections are not disallowed by the Daisy ad or by *Freaky Flakes*; they merely require the interlocutor to construct a new claim in another context—for example a responding TV spot or software program.

Consider an example of a procedural representation that addresses both of these concerns. *The Grocery Game* is a website that gives subscribers access to a special grocery list, sorted by grocery store and U.S. location.[94] The game's premise is this: supermarkets structure their pricing to maximize consumer spending on a short-term basis; they count on families buying enough groceries for about a week's time and then returning for more the following week. Buying in this fashion inevitably costs more, as consumers don't take advantage of the cost leverage afforded by bulk purchases of staples. *The Grocery Game* addresses this issue by automating the research necessary to produce lists of common products that maximize weekly coupon and in-store specials for a given week, while encouraging larger purchases of basics to last many weeks. Despite its name, "The List" is really a procedural system designed to maximize savings through strategic use of coupons and stockpiling. The game's method is clarified on the website:

The Grocery Game is a fun, easy way to save hundreds of dollars on groceries each month. TERI'S LIST [the founder's name is Teri] reveals the "rock bottom" prices on hundreds of products each week and matches them up with manufacturers' coupons for the best possible savings at your local supermarket. The Grocery Game has exclusive databases that track manufacturers' coupons along with weekly sales and specials, both advertised and UN-advertised. With TERI'S LIST, the days of time consuming work required for effective couponing are over. The Grocery Game does all the hard work and research, presented in a quick reference format on the internet each week, as TERI'S LIST. Members log in, spend a few minutes with a pair of scissors, and they're off to win The Grocery Game!

The game has a goal (save as much money as possible) and a set of simple rules (stockpiling and couponing) that constitute its procedural rhetoric. A subsequent procedural system trolls grocery stock and advertising lists to produce a savings-maximized shopping plan tuned to a particular locality, based on the two tactics just mentioned.

The Grocery Game makes two major claims. For one part, it claims that the grocery business relies on weekly shopping for higher profits. Playing for a month and checking one's grocery budget against a previous month easily confirms this claim. For another part, the game claims that grocery shopping is fundamentally an exercise in spending as little money as possible. One might raise several objections to this claim: gastronomy is an experience central to human culture and should not be blindly replaced with frugality; buying the cheapest products for a given week sidesteps considerations like business ethics and the sustainability of growers and manufacturers; the cheapest products are sometimes, and perhaps often, at odds with ideal nutritional goals; a lowest-common-denominator grocery list assumes that all families are the same, while in fact every family has specific tastes and health considerations (such as food allergies); stockpiling requires storage space, which supports an undesirable obsession with material property. *The Grocery Game* has a hard time responding to these objections, although it is possible to pick and choose among the items the search algorithm generates.

While the game does not provide the user with direct access to the search algorithms that generate its lists, so that a user could wage these objections in code, it does provide a flourishing community of conversation. The message boards have entire threads devoted to savings for a particular week. This variation on the high-score list replaces hierarchical performance with discourse— an opportunity to share how well you did according to your own particular goals. It's not just about winning; it's also about telling people what you did and how you did it. Cash savings are winnings in a literal sense. To a lesser extent, so is fooling the grocery industry by refusing to play by their profit-maximizing rules. But the real winnings seem to come from what people do with what they save. Here's an example from the boards:

i [*sic*, throughout] have been a lister for 1 year now. grocery shopping has changed 100% for me. i dreaded every single minute of being in a market. now, i find it to be fun. i average 100.00 a week in savings and spending 150.00. Today, i was able to purchase the dvd "Holes" for my children. It is because of the great savings weekly that i am able to purchase things like that "big ticket" item with ease.[95]

The community discourse at the game's message boards are not always related to objections to its underlying procedural rhetoric, but the availability of this forum facilitates active reconfiguration of the game's rules and goals, a topic to which I will return in chapter 11.

Interactivity

Procedural representations do not necessarily support user interaction. Many computational simulation methods make claims about processes in the material world, but limit user participation significantly. Take a simple computational model like the Monte Carlo method, a statistical sampling technique used to approximate the results of complex quantitative problems. The classic example of the Monte Carlo method in practice is the so-called Buffon's needle problem. George-Louis Leclerc, Comte de Buffon, posed the following question: If a needle of a particular length is dropped at random onto a horizontal surface ruled with parallel lines drawn at a greater than the length of the needle, what is the probability that the needle will cross one of the lines?[96] In a computational model of the Monte Carlo algorithm, the user might configure the length of the needle and the distance of the lines, then run the operation. Similarly, in a physical simulation, such as a demonstration of rigid body collision or mechanical dynamics, a human operator might configure the size and mass of objects or the relative force of gravity, elasticity, and other properties before observing the result.

A more complex and expressive example of a procedural system with limited user interaction can be found in Chris Crawford's 1990 game about global ecology, *Balance of the Planet*.[97] In the game, the player sets global environmental policies. The game challenges players to balance global ecological and economic forces through taxation and expenditure. However, each of the player's policies sets a complex set of interrelated relationships in motion. For example, forest clearing changes the carbon dioxide levels, which affect global warming. The player enacts policy by adjusting sliders to change underlying policies (see figure 1.3), executing the results, and again revising the policies.

The Monte Carlo simulation, physical simulations, and *Balance of the Planet* all accept simple user input and configuration, perhaps the most basic type of input to a computer program other than merely executing and automatically returning results based on hard-coded parameters. *Interactivity* is an entrenched notion in studies of digital media. Janet Murray rightly calls the term "vague" despite its "pervasive use."[98] Murray argues that the simple manipulation of

Figure 1.3 Chris Crawford's 1990 title *Balance of the Planet* offers a sophisticated model of interrelated environmental issues.

a computational system, the "mere ability to move a joystick or click on a mouse" is not sufficient cause for "agency"—genuine embodied participation in an electronic environment.[99] Rather, such environments must be meaningfully responsive to user input. This state of affairs constitutes one of Murray's four properties of the computer, its *participatory* nature. "Procedural environments," she argues, "are appealing to us not just because they exhibit rule-generated behavior, but because we can induce the behavior. . . . the primary representational property of the computer is the codified rendering of responsive behaviors. This is what is most often meant when we say that computers are *interactive*. We mean they create an environment that is both procedural and participatory."[100]

As *Balance of the Planet* suggests, procedural rhetorics do not necessarily demand sophisticated interactivity. But we might ask if procedural rhetorics *benefit* from sophisticated interactivity. Following Murray, *sophistication* in this context does not refer to *more* or *more frequent* interaction, the kind that more buttons or faster hand-eye responses would entail. Rather, sophisticated interactivity means greater responsiveness, tighter symbolic coupling between user actions and procedural representations. *Balance of the Planet* offers a terrifically sophisticated procedural model of global ecology, but its coupling of user action to the game's causal model is weak, reducing both empathetic and dialectical engagement.

Another way to understand the role of interactivity in procedural rhetoric is through the concept of *play*. The weak coupling between model and experience in *Balance of the Planet* does not arise from a poverty of procedural representation. Rather, it arises from the awkward way that representation is exposed to the player. Play is a complex concept with a long and arduous intellectual history in numerous fields. Rather than understand play as child's activity, or as the means to consume games, or even as the shifting centers of meaning in poststructuralist thought, I suggest adopting Katie Salen and Eric Zimmerman's useful, abstract definition of the term: "play is the free space of movement within a more rigid structure."[101] Understood in this sense, play refers to the possibility space created by processes themselves. Salen and Zimmerman use the example of the play in a mechanism like a steering column, in which the meshing gears creates "play" in the wheel, before the turning gesture causes the gears to couple. In a procedural representation like a videogame, the possibility space refers to the myriad configurations the player might construct to see the ways the processes inscribed in the system work.

This is really what we do when we *play* videogames: we explore the possibility space its rules afford by manipulating the game's controls.

While *Balance of the Planet* sports a very large possibility space, the game's controls and feedback system make it difficult for players to keep track of the decisions they have already made and to see the aggregate effects of those decisions. The game is *hard to play*; that is, it is difficult to understand the processes at work inside and the nature of the possibility space those processes create.

In the context of procedural rhetoric, it is useful to consider interactivity in relation to the Aristotelian enthymeme. The enthymeme, we will remember, is the technique in which a proposition in a syllogism is omitted; the listener (in the case of oratory) is expected to fill in the missing proposition and complete the claim. Sophisticated interactivity can produce an effective procedural enthymeme, resulting in more sophisticated procedural rhetoric. Sometimes we think of interactivity as producing user empowerment: the more interactive the system, the more the user can do, and the better the experience. For example, many players and critics have celebrated *Grand Theft Auto III (GTAIII)*[102] as a game that allows the player to "go anywhere, do anything."[103] This sentiment is flawed for several reasons. First, the game does not actually allow the player to "do anything"; rather, in the words of one reviewer, "*GTAIII* let you do anything you wish, within the parameters of the game."[104] The "parameters of the game" are made up of the processes it supports and excludes. For example, entering and exiting vehicles is afforded in *GTAIII*, but conversing with passersby is not (see chapter 3 for more on this subject). This is not a limitation of the game, but rather the very way it becomes procedurally expressive. Second, the interactivity afforded by the game's coupling of player manipulations and gameplay effects is much narrower than the expressive space the game and the player subsequently create. The player performs a great deal of mental synthesis, filling the gap between subjectivity and game processes.

Previously, I have argued that the ontological position of a videogame (or simulation, or procedural system) resides in the gap between rule-based representation and player subjectivity; I called this space the "simulation gap."[105] Another way to think about the simulation gap is in relation to rhetoric. A procedural model like a videogame could be seen as a system of nested enthymemes, individual procedural claims that the player literally completes through interaction. If *Balance of the Planet* increased player interaction by adding more sliders to move, it would not necessarily become more expressive or more persuasive. On Hill's vividness continuum, *Balance of the Planet* might land closer to the realm of abstract analysis, despite its rich procedural policy model. However, if it increased the coupling between the computer's procedural rhetoric and the exposition of that rhetoric, its persuasive value would likely increase as well. Ironically, Chris Crawford himself has offered a definition of interactivity that addresses this very problem: "I choose to define it [interactivity] in terms of a conversation: a cyclic process in which two actors alternately listen, think, and speak. The quality of the interaction depends on the quality of each of the subtasks (listening, thinking, and speaking)."[106] In the case of *Balance of the Planet*, the player does a lot of meaningful listening and thinking, but not much meaningful speaking. The computer does a lot of meaningful thinking, but not much meaningful listening or speaking. Maximizing all three does not necessarily optimize expression—*GTAIII* does limited computational listening and thinking, for example—but understanding the relationship between the three can offer clues into the rhetorical structure of a procedural argument.

Videogames

I have chosen to explain and exemplify the function of procedural rhetoric in a subcategory of procedural expression, namely, videogames. There are several reasons I privilege this medium over other procedural media, and over other computational media in particular.

For one part, videogames are among the most procedural of computational artifacts. All software runs code, but videogames tend to run more code, and also to do more with code. Recalling Crawford's term, videogames tend to offer more process intensity than other computational media. Videogames tend to demand a significant share of a computer's central processing unit (CPU) resources while running; they are more procedural than other computational artifacts. As I write this paragraph, my computer is running twelve major applications, including the active one, resource hog *Microsoft Word*, and some seventy total processes to run the machine's underlying systems—window management, networking, graphics, audio, and so forth. Despite this immodest quantity of activity, my CPU remains 75–85 percent idle. The quantity of processes and the amount of random access memory (RAM) they consume does not necessarily correlate with their process intensity. Modern videogames often require another processor devoted to processing graphics instructions, a graphics processing unit (GPU). Videogames regularly drive computer hardware upgrades; physics processing units are slowly emerging as another tool to extend the power of the CPU. Process-intensive programs like videogames are not guaranteed to mount more interesting or sophisticated procedural rhetorics, but they are predisposed to do so

For another part, videogames are generally a more expressive subgenre of computational media than other types, for example, productivity software.[107] By expressive, I mean that videogames service representational goals akin to literature, art, and film, as opposed to instrumental goals akin to utilities and tools. All software structures experience, including productivity software, and much has been written about the ways word processors, spreadsheets, and web applications influence our conception of the world (to cite just one example, Friedrich Kittler has written about the ways WordPerfect, coupled to the MS-DOS operating system, structures writing practice).[108] But videogames are uniquely, consciously, and principally crafted as expressions. As such, they represent excellent candidates for rhetorical speech—persuasion and expression are inexorably linked.

For yet another part, videogames are often interactive in the particular way I described above; they require user action to complete their procedural representations. As such, they provide particularly promising opportunities for the procedural translation of rhetorical devices like enthymeme. Interactivity guarantees neither meaningful expression nor meaningful persuasion, but it sets the stage for both. Sid Meier, designer of *Civilization*, has argued that gameplay is "a series of interesting choices."[109] Interesting choices do not necessarily entail *all* possible choices in a given situation; rather, choices are selectively included and excluded in a procedural representation to produce a desired expressive end. For example, *The McDonald's Videogame* includes control of cattle slaughtering but abstracts control of restaurant line-workers for a rhetorical end: to force the player to make decisions with social and political implications.

Greater interactivity is often considered especially engaging, or "immersive." The interactivity of (good) videogames might locate those games higher on the "vividness spectrum" discussed earlier, producing more vivid experience thanks to the player's active involvement. But I want to suggest that vividness comes not from immersion, but from abstraction. The values common to virtual reality and computer graphics assume that the closer we get to real experience, the better. This sentiment corresponds directly to the vividness spectrum, with the best interactivity coming closest to real experience. But meaning in videogames is constructed not through a re-creation of the world, but through selectively modeling appropriate elements of that world. Procedural representation models only some subset of a source system, in order to draw attention to that portion as the subject of the representation. Interactivity follows suit: the total number and credibility of user actions is not necessarily important; rather, the relevance of the interaction in the context of the representational goals of the system is paramount. Videogames offer a particularly good context for this selective interactivity.

Finally, I will admit that I have a particular fondness for videogames. I am a videogame critic and a videogame designer, and I am devoted to the process of connecting videogames with the history of human expression. In my previous book, *Unit Operations*, I argued for a comparative understanding of procedural expression, using the concept of unit operations to define the elements of procedural representation common across media. In this book, I argue for a similar understanding with respect to rhetoric. As I have already suggested, rhetoric in its contemporary sense refers to both persuasion and expression, and so a study of procedural rhetoric shares much in common with a study of procedural expression. Despite my preference for videogames, I should stress that I intend the reader to see *procedural rhetoric* as a domain much broader than that of videogames, encompassing any medium—computational or not—that accomplishes its inscription via processes. I hope my choice of videogames as examples of procedural rhetoric inspires both an increased appreciation of that medium and inspiration to study procedural rhetorics in other media.

Persuasive Games

I give the name *persuasive games* to videogames that mount procedural rhetorics effectively. Before addressing persuasive games in this sense, it is worth diffusing some of the other ways videogames and persuasion have intersected, so as to distinguish my approach from others'.

Starting with Bushnell's *Computer Space*, arcade games have shared much in common with pinball and slot machines.[110] They accepted coins as payment, and one of their main design goals entailed persuading players to insert (more) coins. In the arcade industry, this is called "coin drop." Andrew

Rollings and Ernest Adams have discussed the effect of coin drop on the design of such games: "Arcade operators care little for richness, depth, and the aesthetic qualities of a game as long as it makes a lot of money for them. This requires some fine balancing. If a game is too hard, people will abandon it in disgust, but if it is too easy, they will be able to play for a long time without putting any more money in."[111] Procedural rhetoric might be deployed in such games, but more often persuasion is accomplished through more basic appeals to addiction and reinforcement. Shuen-shing Lee explains such persuasion via Geoffrey R. Loftus and Elizabeth F. Loftus's 1983 study *Mind at Play*:[112]

[*Mind at Play*] sorts out two types of psychological configurations embedded in game design that aim to get players addicted to gaming. The first type, "partial reinforcement," is that utilized by slot machines which spit out coins intermittently to reward a gambler. The experience of being occasionally rewarded often drives the gambler to continue inserting coins, in hopes of another win or even a jackpot. Arcade game designers have cloned the same reinforcement strategy in their games. Surprises such as score doubling, weapon upgrading, expedient level advancing may pop up randomly during the gaming process to heighten the player's intrigue, stimulating continued playing.[113]

Partial reinforcement is certainly a type of persuasion, but the persuasion is entirely self-referential: its goal is to cause the player to continue playing, and in so doing to increase coin drop. Despite its relationship to gambling and other addictive activities, partial reinforcement is an interesting and worthwhile area of inquiry that can help game designers understand how to produce experiences that players feel compelled to continue or complete. However, this kind of persuasion is not my concern here. Instead, I am interested in videogames that make arguments about the way systems work in the material world. These games strive to alter or affect player opinion outside of the game, not merely to cause him to continue playing. In fact, many of the examples I will discuss strive to do just the opposite from arcade games: move the player from the game world into the material world.

As arcade games suggest, there are reasons to leverage videogames for goals orthogonal to those of procedural expression. The increasing popularity of and media attention paid to videogames means that merely producing and distributing a videogame may have its own persuasive effect. When Gonzalo

Frasca and I co-designed *The Howard Dean for Iowa Game* in 2003, it became the first official videogame of a U.S. presidential candidate. While the game did deploy procedural rhetorics (see chapters 4 and 11 for more), the very existence of an official Howard Dean game served its own rhetorical purpose, further aligning the candidate with technology culture.[114] In another, similar example, Elizabeth Losh has reflected on the government's creation of *Tactical Iraqi*, a learning game designed to teach U.S. soldiers Arabic language and customs in order to help them accomplish military missions in the Middle East.[115] Losh, who studied the game as a field researcher and has written lucidly about her moral and rhetorical conflicts in doing so, later mused about its true rhetorical function in an online discussion forum:[116]

In the wake of all the publicity that *Tactical Iraqi* has received in the last few months, I find myself with an even more serious reservation about the game, which crystallized after reading Max Boot's article, "Navigating the 'human terrain,'" in which Boot, a senior fellow at the Council on Foreign Relations, enthuses about visiting "the Expeditionary Warfare School, where captains study Arabic by playing a sophisticated computer game complete with animated characters." It was then that I realized that the purpose of the game might be rhetorical not pedagogical. Despite what the researchers thought they were doing, perhaps it was primarily intended to SHOW the teaching of Arabic to policy makers and the general public not actually TEACH Arabic more effectively. Traditional classroom teaching doesn't make for a good media spectacle, but a video game might.[117]

Tactical Iraqi cannot be accused of sporting low process intensity. As an engineering effort, it deploys sophisticated procedural models of language understanding, simulated gestures, and cross-cultural communication. But, Losh suggests, as an expressive artifact, the project might serve an agenda different from its primary one, namely drawing attention to a videogame training system to distract critics from America's military occupation of Iraq. Again, such a gesture is undeniably rhetorical, but its rhetoric is accomplished through media speech, not through processes. I will return to the substitution of procedural rhetoric for audience correlation in the context of advertising in chapter 5.

Videogames created with a more genuine interest in expression and persuasion may still underplay procedurality in favor of visual images. The commercial game industry dazzles buyers with high-fidelity images of increasingly greater verisimilitude, but these images do not necessarily couple with advances in procedural representation. In 2004, the American Legacy Foundation commissioned *Crazy World*, a game in service of their ongoing antismoking campaign, best known for its rhetorically powerful "the truth"-themed television ads. Built around a satirical carnival world that coincided with the foundation's advertising campaign at the time, the game sports very high production values visuals, and sound—the very factors that contribute to vividness, according to Charles Hill. But the procedural rhetoric in the game is weak. In a press release, one of the creators describes a mechanic in the game:

The game, which is aimed at a wide audience, ages 18–50, was created to show both smokers and non-smokers the dangers of cigarettes using humor and irony. Players score points by avoiding moving green puffs of radioactive smoke. If they get caught in the smoke, they mutate into an alien-like form. "The idea is to attract people to entertain themselves and keep the message within context—to play for fun," [Templar Studios president Peter] Mack said.

A game like *Crazy World* may speak through visual rhetoric alone, or at least principally. The use of highly polished visual and sound design builds an expectation of authority. Images hypnotize many consumers, and even the largest videogame companies often repackage the same games with improved (or simply different) graphics. Considerable attention and investment has gone into improving the visual fidelity of commercial games, including the move to high definition and higher polygon models on the now-current Xbox 360 and PlayStation 3 consoles. Visual fidelity implies authority. Likewise, simplistic or unrefined graphics are often taken as an indication of gameplay quality. Just as a poor or "generic" package design can turn consumers away from a quality product, so the skin of a procedural rhetoric might influence player enticement. The 2004 Republican National Committee game *Tax Invaders*, which barely succeeds in replicating the rudimentary graphics of the classic arcade game *Space Invaders*, is an example of the latter (for more on this game, see chapter 3).[118]

The tenuous coupling between visual appearance and procedural rhetoric also hinders videogames that seek to make persuasive statements about issues in the material world, but fail to adopt effective procedural representations for those issues. One common pitfall is borrowing a procedural form from an existing game or game genre and skinning it with new graphics. Such a one is *Congo Jones and the Raiders of the Lost Bark*, a game about deforestation sponsored by the nonprofit Rainforest Foundation.[119] The game borrows its gameplay from 2D platform games of the *Super Mario Bros.* variety.[120] The player controls a monkey who must find and defeat the president of the World Bank. The player must jump from platform to platform to avoid flying chainsaws, while attempting to reach and defeat the bank president.

Congo Jones adopts no procedural representation—and therefore no procedural rhetoric—of its own. Instead, it borrows the notion of progress through abstract obstacles as an object lesson for deforestation's struggle against the World Bank (who had supported logging in the Congolese rainforests). The game makes no claims about possible reasons to oppose the World Bank, nor how to do so, although it does succeed in positing the World Bank as an archetypal opponent, the "boss monster" of the game. The game might or might not be effective in building "awareness" about the issue, but it certainly does not mount a procedural argument about the topic. Or more precisely, it does not mount its *own* procedural rhetoric; it adopts processes of obstacle avoidance and goal pursuit from platform games and reinscribes them onto deforestation.

Congo Jones borrows gameplay and applies a graphical skin—a visual rhetoric—atop it. Another common technique is to borrow gameplay and apply a textual skin—a verbal rhetoric—atop it. An example of such a game is *P.o.N.G.*, created by the Global Arcade art collective.[121] The game's website explains that the game features "a few different variations of the classic Pong, each with just a little different play on the language of globalization."[122] The result is a direct copy of *Pong* in which the ball is replaced by words that might arise in discussions of globalization (*neoliberalism, $$*, etc.). The player must bat these back and forth with the paddle, as one might "exchange words" in a conversation on the topic. While the Global Arcade's mission statement announces their commitment "to make information about globalization interesting, engaging and interactive," *P.o.N.G.* serves as little more than a sight gag, perhaps not even articulating expression adequate to warrant the moniker of *digital art*.

The notion of adopting *Pong*'s back-and-forth procedural mechanic or *Super Mario Bros.*' platform mechanic as rhetorics for discourse might have promise, but *P.o.N.G.* and *Congo Jones* do not make meaningful use of those processes in their arguments. *Tax Invaders*, which I mentioned above and discuss in detail in chapter 3, is an example of a game that borrows a videogame form and successfully mounts its own procedural rhetoric atop it.

A more successful procedural rhetoric can be found in the 1982 title *Tax Avoiders*, an unusual game for the Atari Video Computer System (popularly known as the Atari VCS or Atari 2600).[123] Conceived by Darrell Wagner, a "Licensed Tax Consultant and former IRS Revenue Agent," the goal of the game is to become a millionaire by amassing income and avoiding red tape and audits.[124] The player controls a human character, John Q, who must collect income (represented by dollar-sign icons) and avoid red tape (represented by an abstract tape icon). After each fiscal quarter the player has the opportunity to shelter income in investments, which are represented as sprites on screen, or to store income in a portfolio, represented as a briefcase sprite (see figure 1.4). A second sprite oscillates between an IRS agent, a CPA, and an investment advisor. The player always loses an audit, and 50 percent of his income is lost to taxes. A CPA charges a small fee but always makes new

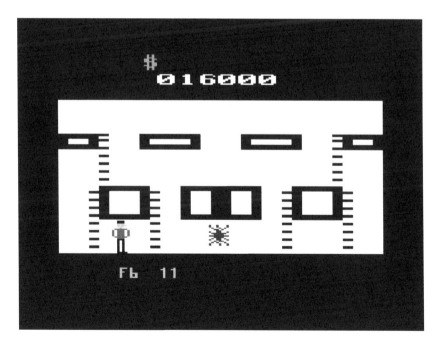

Figure 1.4 Although the Atari VCS title *Tax Invaders* may look simplistic, it constructs a sophisticated procedural rhetoric about tax strategy.

tax-sheltered investments available. The investment advisor can maximize returns on sheltered investments. At the end of this interstitial phase, the player's remaining income is taxed and he returns to work.[125]

Tax Avoiders mounts an interesting and relatively complex procedural rhetoric about tax avoidance strategies. The fact that these techniques are mapped onto movement, a graphical logic, is perhaps not ideal, but it is also not detrimental to the argument. The player must run around to collect income, literally *avoiding* red tape. Likewise, he must avoid the IRS agent while racing to *catch* investment opportunities before their window of opportunity closes. These metaphors of locomotion correspond quite well to the abstract processes of work, investment, and taxation.

Finally, I would like to make a distinction between persuasive games, procedural rhetoric, and the rhetoric of play. In contemporary game studies, considerable attention has been paid to the relationship between games and play—and this is a worthwhile pursuit. However, my interest here is not in the function of play, nor in videogames as a subdomain of play activities. Rather, my interest is in the function of procedural representation as it is used for persuasion, and in videogames as a subdomain of procedural media. In particular, I should draw a distinction between procedural rhetoric and what Brian Sutton-Smith has called "rhetorics of play," or ways "play is placed in context within broader value systems."[126] While we both use the term *rhetoric*, we use it in different contexts, although not in entirely different ways. Sutton-Smith discusses the rhetorical modes of play itself: the ways theorists present play as a human cultural activity. As Katie Salen and Eric Zimmerman explain, Sutton-Smith's rhetorics of play "identify how games and play embody ideological values and how specific forms and uses of play perpetuate and justify these values."[127] Sutton-Smith's project is a general one, focused on the cultural role of play, not the culturally embodied practice of playing specific games. He identifies seven rhetorics of play, including play as progress, fate, power, identity, the imaginary, the self, and frivolity, each of which orchestrates play in different ways and for different ends under the same ostensible name (hence the ambiguity).[128] Sutton-Smith musters these rhetorics to attempt to explain the reasons people play, and the cultural function of that play.[129] His approach is broad and macroscopic, investigating play itself as a cultural activity that serves multiple purposes, purposes which often complicate one another.

I am discussing the rhetorical function of procedural expression in the tradition of representation rather than the tradition of play. This said, Sutton-Smith's rhetorics may prove useful in contextualizing procedural rhetorics among the values of play. This is not an effort I will attempt here, but which Salen and Zimmerman attempt in their text on game design, *Rules of Play*. The two suggest *The Landlord's Game* (the conceptual precursor to the popular board game *Monopoly*) as an embodiment of Sutton-Smith's rhetorics of power and progress. Unlike *Monopoly*, *The Landlord's Game* opposes land monopoly, instead advocating the single tax proposed by economist Henry George. As Salen and Zimmerman explain:

Despite the strong similarity between The Landlord's Game and Monopoly, there are distinct (and wonderfully incongruous) differences in the rhetorics each evokes. While the play rhetorics of progress and power apply to both games, The Landlord's Game was distinctly anti-capitalist in its conception. The game's conflict was not premised on property acquisition and the accumulation of monopolies, but instead on an unraveling of the prevailing land system. Because properties in the game could only be rented, there was no opportunity for domination by a greedy land baron or developer.[130]

Without realizing it, Salen and Zimmerman helpfully clarify the difference between Sutton-Smith's *rhetorics of play*—the global, cultural roles for exploring themes like ownership and property—and the *procedural rhetoric of a game*—the local argument *The Landlord's Game* makes about taxation and property ownership. Salen and Zimmerman do not actually apply Sutton-Smith's rhetorics of play, a gesture that shows how macroscopic the latter's approach really is. On the one hand, they admit that progress and power "apply" abstractly to both *The Landlord's Game* and *Monopoly*. On the other hand, their analysis relies not on these higher-level categories, but on the specific function of the rules of each game, for example rental as collective equity versus ownership as individual leverage. When Salen and Zimmerman say that there are "distinct . . . differences in the rhetorics each evokes," they refer not to Sutton-Smith's cultural rhetorics, but to the procedural rhetorics of the two specific games, *The Landlord's Game* and *Monopoly*. In fact, Salen and Zimmerman's analysis of the procedural rhetorics of these games is quite mature, revealing the way the rules of the games make fundamentally different arguments about land ownership, despite having apparently similar boards and gameplay dynamics.

The difference between rhetorics of play and procedural rhetoric should now be clear. Sutton-Smith's rhetorics of play characterize broad cultural contexts, while procedural rhetorics express specific patterns of cultural value. Despite their invocation of Sutton-Smith as a figure at the intersection of rhetoric and games, Salen and Zimmerman are actually invoking the more ordinary notion of rhetoric as persuasive and expressive discourse.[131] Although they claim to "take the word 'rhetoric' from Brian Sutton-Smith's remarkable treatise *The Ambiguity of Play*," really they take the word from its more general classical and modern roots, applying it to the analysis of games.[132] There may be value in applying Sutton-Smith's rhetorics of play to specific procedural rhetorics, perhaps for comparative anthropological purposes. But as Salen and Zimmerman unwittingly demonstrate, the more useful intersection between rhetoric and play is one that unpacks the particular rules of a particular game in a particular context, not the more general intersection between modes of play in general. This distinction mirrors the one that separates representational discourse from sociological discourse. Clearly cultural context influences the creation of and interaction with games. But the games we create can also support, interrogate, or oppose those cultural contexts.

Persuasive Games versus Serious Games

Topics like taxation, deforestation, and globalization are not the usual subject matter of videogames; furthermore, the games about these topics discussed above are very arcane, so much so that I doubt many readers would have chanced upon all three before. Procedural rhetoric is not limited to such anomalous specimens; in the following pages I discuss numerous commercial games that have enjoyed great market success. But one often uses persuasion in the context of domains like economics, business, and politics. As it happens, an entire subdomain of videogame development has erupted around such topics, known as *serious games*. What, if anything, differentiates persuasive games from serious games?

Interrogating the relationship between seriousness and play is nothing new. Dutch anthropologist Johan Huizinga struggled with the ambiguous link between seriousness and play in his classic study *Homo ludens*. On the one hand, Huizinga notes that play "is the direct opposite of seriousness."[133] But on further investigation, he argues that "the contrast between play and seriousness proves to be neither conclusive nor fixed."[134] Huizinga notes that one can "play seriously," that is, with great devotion and resolve,[135] but seriousness does not seem to include the possibility of play, making the latter of a "higher order" than seriousness.[136] Despite this status, play helps constitute social and cultural functions of great gravity, according to Huizinga, including religion, politics, and warfare. Huizinga remains conflicted to the end on the interrelation between play and seriousness. As such, it is not surprising that scholars, business people, and developers thought they had fallen upon something new in "reuniting" seriousness and play.

An early example of the new collusion of seriousness and gameplay comes in Clark C. Abt's 1970 book *Serious Games*, which addresses the use of analog games (board games, role-play, etc.) in education, science, government, and industry. In his first chapter, titled "The Reunion of Action and Thought," Abt offers a definition of serious games: "We are concerned with *serious games* in the sense that these games have an explicit and carefully thought-out educational purpose and are not intended to be played primarily for amusement."[137] Abt quickly admits that this does not mean that serious games "are not, or should not be entertaining," but the message is clear: serious games are created under the direct influence and guidance of external institutional goals.

When the Woodrow Wilson International Center for Scholars unearthed the moniker "serious games" as the name for their new videogame initiative, they did so without direct reference to Abt's proposal thirty years earlier. Rather, the name arose fairly spontaneously. Wilson Center Director of Foresight & Governance David Rejeski and consultant Ben Sawyer were trying to title a white paper Sawyer had written for the center. The two had a subtitle—"Improving Public Policy through Game-Based Learning and Simulation"—but they wanted a snappy title to entice readers. Rejeski had been reading Michael Schrage's 1999 book *Serious Play: How the World's Best Companies Simulate to Innovate*, a call for businesses to foster play as an agent for innovation.[138] Schrage cites Abt in his book, and Rejeski, perhaps influenced by conscious or unconscious memory of that reference, suggested "Serious Games" as a title.[139] Since then, Woodrow has founded and funded the Serious Games Initiative, an ad hoc networking and knowledge-sharing group with a thriving membership.[140] Its primary activities include collecting resources, facilitating contacts between government/industry and developers, and running meetings and conferences on its core topics, including the Serious Games Summit, a large biannual conference (on whose advisory board I happen to serve). Interestingly, the Initiative's goals read very similarly to Abt's 1970 definition: "the goal of the initiative is to help usher in a new series of policy education, exploration, and management tools utilizing state of the art computer game designs, technologies, and development skills."[141] Mirroring Abt's goals with nondigital games, the Initiative seeks to couple videogames to the needs of modern institutions. Their mission statement asks, "How can we quickly expand the application of computer-based games to a much wider range of key challenges facing our government and other public or private organizations?" Abt's "carefully thought out educational purpose" and the Serious Games Initiative's focus on "government and other public or private organizations" both suggest that serious games are crafted in the service of officials, especially officials of governments or corporations. The language used to advertise the Serious Games Summit confirms this sentiment; under a header reading "Gaming for your Industry" follows a list of institutional interests: education, government, health, military, corporate, first responders, science.[142]

If the notion of "seriousness" is what distinguishes this group's efforts from other types of videogaming, it is worth briefly interrogating the term and its relationship to their endeavor. *Serious* is a word with many meanings, and it should no longer be sufficient merely to oppose it to *entertainment*, the major mover-and-shaker in the videogame marketplace.

Serious can mean *solemn*, implying emotionlessness and sobriety. One might think of the drill sergeant, the librarian, or perhaps even the IRS agent as an agent of this type of seriousness: *she shot me a serious look and I reconsidered my itemizations*.

Serious can mean *weighty*, implying consequence and demanding consideration. One might think of authority figures like teachers, parents, or religious leaders using this meaning of the term when addressing the particularly foolish (not serious) plans of pupils, offspring, or followers: *Don't tell me to calm down, son! Marriage is a serious commitment*.

Serious can mean *grave*, implying severity and foreboding. One might think of officials making statements about unthinkable acts of war, disease, or suffering: *Two of the five miners remain hospitalized in serious condition*.

Serious can mean *highbrow*, implying intellectualism and profundity. One might think of academics, artists, curators, and more generally snobs insistent on segregating weighty matters from light ones: *James is a serious artist, he doesn't make that pop-culture drivel.*

All of these ways of understanding *serious* have something in common: they rely on a point of reference that affirms the seriousness of a subject in relation to some nonserious alternative. Solemnity responds to behavior outside a known, desired code of conduct; weightiness responds to behavior thought to lead to crucial and perhaps irreversible decision; gravity suggests an opposite and always undesirable condition; and snobbery isolates worthwhile pursuits from insignificant ones. Furthermore, these meanings suggest that seriousness is often deployed in the service of institutions: governments, corporations, healthcare systems, religious beliefs, cultural communities, and so forth. Seriousness implies actions that support the goals and progress of these institutions.

Such a conception of seriousness is coincident with Abt's use of the term in relation to board games and the Serious Games Initiative's use of the term in relation to videogames. Serious games are videogames created to support the existing and established interests of political, corporate, and social institutions. To apply this principle to the industry domains of the Serious Games Summit proves a simple task. Educational games translate existing pedagogical goals into videogame form; government games translate existing political goals in videogame form; health games provide doctors and medical institutions with videogame-based tools to accomplish their existing needs; military games help armies and soldiers address existing global conflicts with new, cheaper, and more scalable simulations; corporate games provide executives with videogame-based tools to accomplish their existing business goals; first responder games offer simulated views of already known methods of response to natural disaster or terrorist incident; and science games provide appealing videogame-based tools to clarify known principles and practices.

Such goals do not represent the full potential of persuasive games. If persuasive games are videogames that mount meaningful procedural rhetorics, and if procedural rhetorics facilitate dialectical interrogation of process-based claims about how real-world processes do, could, or should work, then persuasive games can also make claims that speak past or against the fixed worldviews of institutions like governments or corporations. This objection—which bears some resemblance to Socrates' opposition to sophistic and technical rhetoric in the fifth century BCE—suggests that persuasive games might also interrogate those institutions *themselves*, recommending correctives and alternatives.

If we wanted to retain the term *serious games*—a questionable goal—then two other meanings stand out as potential ways of understanding the phrase. First, *serious* can imply care and attention to detail, especially as such care leads to reflection: *I will give your ideas serious thought*. This meaning is related to weightiness, but carries the sense of open discourse, of the possibility of finding new structures of thought not immediately given by a current worldview. Second, and more esoteric, *serious* can imply substance, a window onto the underlying structure of a thing. This use may be limited to informal discourse; a sentiment like *dude, that is a serious cheesecake* implies that the specimen presented offers a fundamental insight into the nature, even the apotheosis of the thing in general.[143] "Serious games" in this sense—a sense commensurate with what I intend persuasive games to mean—would deal with the exposition of the fundamental structure of existing situations intended to invoke support, doubt, or debate about their validity or desirability, or universality. These are not games in the service of governments, corporations, educational institutions, and their kindred but games that challenge such institutions, creating opportunities to question, change, or eliminate them.

The notion of the serious as the underlying structure of a system is particularly compatible with the concept of procedurality. Procedural representation depicts how something does, could, or should work: the way we understand a social or material practice to function. I connect this idea to contemporary philosopher Alain Badiou's notion of the *situation*, a "structured presentation" of a *multiplicity*, a particular ontological arrangement.[144] Badiou applies transfinite set theory to philosophy, understanding being to mean *being a member of*. The gesture of including a concept in a situation is akin to the set-theoretical notion of belonging, which Badiou names the *count-as-one*.[145] I have previously correlated the count-as-one with the unit operation, the gesture of conceiving of a particular process as an encapsulated concept.[146] Badiou further understands situations to have a *state*, the logic by which the elements in a situation are counted as one—or the reasons why the structure is organized in the way it is.[147] It is the state that is commensurate with "seriousness" as the nature of a thing, the reasons that make it what it is. Badiou further articulates a concept called the *event*, which offers a chance to disrupt the state of a situation and reinvent it, wholly anew, under a different organizing logic, a topic I will return to in chapter 11.[148]

Despite the possibility of rescuing serious games under the definition I have just offered, I do not want to preserve the name. Instead, I would like to advance persuasive games as an alternative whose promise lies in the possibility of using procedural rhetoric to support *or* challenge our understanding of the way things in the world do or should work. Such games can be produced for a variety of purposes, be they entertainment, education, activism, or a combination of these and others. The concept of serious games as a counter movement apart from and against the commercial videogame industry eliminates a wide variety of games from persuasive speech. It is a foolish gesture that wrongly undermines the expressive power of videogames in general, and highly crafted, widely appealing commercial games in particular. As I will show in the following chapters, many games carry messages, make arguments, and attempt meaningful expression. This should not surprise us; indeed, all media resonate on a variety of registers. I want to encourage developers and critics to pay more mind to the way such messages, arguments, and expressions are constructed through procedural rhetorics, in videogames of all kinds.

Persuasive Games versus Persuasive Technology

Since the late 1990s, Stanford University experimental psychologist B. J. Fogg has been advancing a concept he calls *captology*. The simple definition Fogg gives on his research group's website is this: "Captology is the study of computers as persuasive technologies. This includes the design, research, and analysis of interactive computing products created for the purpose of changing people's attitudes or behaviors."[149] Fogg's research has produced a book entitled *Persuasive Technology: Using Computers to Change What We Think and Do*.[150] Given the strong similarity between the phrases *persuasive technology* and *persuasive games*, I would like to address the differences between my approach and that of Fogg.

The most important distinction mirrors the difference between persuasive games and serious games. Just as the Serious Games Initiative implicates videogames in the service of existing goals, so captology does for computer technology in general. Captology, says Fogg, "does not include . . . unintended outcomes; it focuses on the attitude and behavior changes *intended* by the designers of interactive technology products."[151] Admittedly, this understanding is far closer to my goals than that of the Serious Games Initiative; Fogg does not appear to explicitly correlate captological persuasion with institutional ideologies. However, further interrogation shows that captology is not fundamentally concerned with altering the user's fundamental conception of how real-world processes work. Rather, it is primarily intended to craft new technological constraints that impose conceptual or behavioral change in users.

To this end, Fogg suggests seven types of persuasive technology tools, which I list, define, and exemplify below.

Reduction—"using computing technology to reduce complex behavior to simple tasks," exemplified by the capitoladvantage.com website, which simplifies political participation by presenting a user with contact information for all of his elected officials based on zip code input.[152]

Tunneling—"leading users through a predetermined set of actions, step by step," illustrated by the registration or electronic payment systems on many websites.[153]

Tailoring—"provid[ing] information relevant to individuals to change their attitudes or behaviors or both," as by scorecard.org, which provides information about polluting institutions local to a user based, again, on zip code input.[154]

Suggestion—"an interactive computing product that suggests a behavior at the most opportune moment," such as roadside speed-monitoring radar systems, which display a driver's speed as he passes.[155]

Self-Monitoring—"[a] type of tool that allows people to monitor their attitudes or behaviors to achieve a predetermined goal or outcome," for example, digital heart-rate monitors.[156]

Surveillance—"computing technology that allows one party to monitor the behavior of another to modify behavior in a specific way," such as Hygiene Guard, a system that monitors hand washing in the retail service industry.[157]

Conditioning—"a computerized system that uses principles of operant conditioning to change behaviors," such as Telecycle, an exercise bike which, when pedaled to a target speed, clarifies the image on a television screen in front of the cycle.[158]

Perhaps these tools offer valid ways of using technology to alter behavior. But not one of them deploys rhetoric; instead, all of Fogg's techniques use technology to alter actions or beliefs without engaging users in a discourse about the behavior itself or the logics that would recommend such actions or beliefs. Some techniques are more obviously guileful than others, such as the hand washing surveillance system or the website registration system. The approaches that do admit user awareness assume that the user has already understood and accepted the larger reason that the technology inscribes. For example, a self-monitoring technology like a heart-rate monitor assumes an understanding and acceptance of the relationship between cardiovascular exercise and long-term health. Thus, while captology does not explicitly align itself with the service of existing social, political, or corporate institutions, its formal structure—as tactics given a particular, established situation—only allows persuasive technology to work in the service of existing material ends, rather than the reasons one would want to pursue those ends.

More strongly, captology appears to rely only on psychological, not dialectical user responses. This is not surprising given Fogg's background as an experimental psychologist, but he seems generally dismissive of the tradition of philosophical rhetoric, which aligns persuasion with logical argument and discourse. In the nearly three hundred pages of *Persuasive Technology*, Fogg devotes only a half-page sidebar to the subject of rhetoric, dismissively labeled "A Brief History of Persuasion Studies."[159] In this sidebar, Fogg exposes his opinion that psychological methods are inherently more desirable than philosophical ones:

Today the formal study of persuasion continues to be advanced, primarily through research in social psychology, which began during the early part of the 1900s. Inspired largely by the U.S. government's need to persuade citizens to support war efforts, social psychologists established ambitious research programs to determine what caused people to change their attitudes and behaviors. Later, marketers and advertisers built on the insights gleaned from social psychology, systematically investigating how influence works and often applying their findings to help corporations prosper.[160]

The lack of irony and scrutiny in the discussion of government-funded social science studies for covert manipulation suggests that Fogg is perhaps unaware of the ideology he himself inhabits: one in which existing power structures always devise ethical and desirable goals. Fogg himself is caught in a worldview that limits his understanding of computational persuasion, one driven partly by corporate and government grant funding for his own research. Despite Fogg's suggestion that *captology* acronymizes "computers as persuasive technologies," the phrase itself conjures the sense of *capture*, of arrest and incarceration by an authority. A better name for Fogg's work would perhaps be *manipulative technology*.

On a less critical note, persuasive technology differs from persuasive games because the former does not deal fundamentally with procedurality. Fogg does discuss the use of simulations in persuasion, including nods to videogames (principally as examples of conditioning, "keeping the player playing," the broader context of which coin-drop is an example), but the majority of his examples rely on presenting data to the user (turning zip codes into lists of data) or mirroring the result of sensor input back to the user (the speed check or the heart-rate monitor).[161] Reduction and tunneling might provide useful frames for procedural rhetorics, but Fogg does not explicitly align them with procedural representation; as is, his examples all exhibit low process intensity.

Black and White Boxes

As a final note of clarification, I would like to say a few things about the function of computer code in my analysis of procedural rhetoric. If computational expression is fundamentally procedural, and if computational procedural expression is crafted through code, then what is the role of code in the practice and analysis of procedural rhetoric?

Since each figure and form of a procedural rhetoric in software and videogames must be constructed with code, it might seem impossible to analyze or discuss them without digging into the code itself. Verbal rhetoric, after all, has identified dozens of figures for the authorship of spoken and written arguments with an eye toward persuasion. Is the same not possible for procedural rhetoric? I believe that it is, but nevertheless none of the analyses you will read herein cites or extrapolates code.

Code is not usually available in compiled software like videogames. Software subsystems are closely held trade secrets, and one simply cannot "open up" *The Sims* or *Grand Theft Auto III* to look at the code running beneath. In software development and testing, there is a name for this distinction. To watch a program's effects and extrapolate potential approaches or problems (in the case of testing) in its code is called *black-box* analysis. Such analysis makes assumptions about the actual operation of the software system, assumptions that may or may not be true. To watch a program's effects and identify actual approaches or problems in its code is called *white-box* analysis (or sometimes, *glass-box* analysis). Such analysis observes the effects of the system with a partial or complete knowledge of the underlying code that produces those effects. Some white-box analysis can be performed without direct access to code. Examples include architectural descriptions from conference presentations about development techniques, as have been made about *The Sims*, or commonalities in documented subcomponents, as could be done for the Renderware engine at the heart of *Grand Theft Auto*. I have previously discussed the way early arcade console games use of common hardware components, and first-person shooters' use of common game engines, each influenced the design of multiple games built on the same platform.[162] Publicly documented hardware and software specifications, software development kits, and decompiled videogame ROMs all offer possible ways of studying the software itself. Such study can shed important light on the material basis for videogame experiences. An understanding of code supplements procedural interpretation. In particular, a procedural rhetorician should strive to understand the affordances of the materials from which a procedural argument is formed. For attorneys, this means understanding the legal code and judicial process. For computational critics, it means understanding the affordances of hardware, software frameworks, and programming languages.[163] This type of expertise is a subset of both procedural criticism and procedural rhetoric, and it is a worthwhile course of study in both fields. But such resources are hardly guaranteed for every computational artifact.

This lack of visibility concerns some critics. Part of Sherry Turkle's criticism of *Sim City* had to do with the simulation's black-box nature, which she saw occluding its position on such matters as tax policy. "Opening the box," in Turkle's opinion, would allow players to see how the simulation runs, providing better ability to critique. The problem with this objection is that the player *can* see how the simulation runs: this is, in no trivial way, what it means to play the game. Turkle's real beef is not with *Sim City*, but with the players: they do not know how to play the game critically. Understanding the simulation at the level of code does not necessarily solve this problem. Even understanding the simulation via some intermediary system poised between the code and the existing interface—some have proposed "policy knobs" that could alter the simulation rules of a game like *Sim City*—does not guarantee an understanding of making and interacting with arguments as processes rather than words. Rather than addressing this problem from the bottom up through code literacy, we need to address it from the top down through procedural literacy, a topic I will return to in chapter 9. Part of that practice is learning to read processes as a critic. This means playing a videogame or using procedural system with an eye toward identifying and interpreting the rules that drive that system. Such activity is analogous to that of the literary critic interpreting a novel or the film critic reviewing a film—demanding access to a computer program's code might be akin to asking for direct access to an author's or filmmaker's expressive intentions. Despite the flaws of twentieth-century critical theory, one notion worth keeping is that of dissemination, the irreversible movement of the text away from the act of authorship.[163] "Simulation authors," says Gonzalo Frasca, "do not represent a particular event, but a set of potential events. Because of this, they have to think about their objects as systems and consider which are the laws that rule their behaviors. In a similar way, people who interpret simulations create a mental model of it by inferring the rules that govern it."[164] In such simulations, says Frasca, "the goal of the player would be to analyze, contest and revise the model's rules according to his personal ideas and beliefs."

Persuasive Games and Procedural Rhetoric

As examples like *Tax Avoiders*, *P.o.N.G.*, and *Congo Jones and the Raiders of the Lost Bark* suggest, procedural rhetoric is not automatically a part of computational expression, and a great deal of attention is required to construct coherent—let alone effective—procedural rhetorics. In the three sections that follow, I will consider approaches to and examples of procedural rhetorics in three domains, namely, politics, advertising, and education. I have chosen these fields for several reasons. For one part, they are areas I know something about—I have worked professionally in all these areas, I have done academic research and writing in all these areas, and I have created videogames in all these areas. For another part, these represent typical domains for discussions of rhetoric and persuasion in general, and thus are low-hanging fruit for procedural rhetoric and persuasive games. For yet another part, they offer clear goals and referents in the material world. Exposure to procedural rhetorics in politics, advertising, and education should plant the seeds for the interrogation of other, perhaps more subtle expressive domains. And finally, together these three areas cover a broad swath of human social experience, areas that have become largely broken in contemporary culture, and areas I believe videogames can help restore, and not just in small part.

Politics

Political Processes

BioChemFX is a first-responder training tool designed to simulate bioterror attacks on urban environments.[1] Created by a group of physicists who specialize in the real-time rendering of very large datasets, *BioChemFX* incorporates live atmospheric, meteorological, topological, and architectural effects on the dispersion of more than two-dozen chemical agents.

A version of the software used for sales demonstrations and press release screenshots depicts a bird's-eye view of the campus of the University of California, Berkeley (figure 2.1). A bright green cloud covers much of the streets, representing a sarin gas attack on the area. For several years, I used this arcane counterterrorism simulation as a classroom example of the inherent subjectivity of videogames. Now that first responders can see the physical dispersion of the gas itself, whom do they save? The freshmen or the Nobel laureates? The homeless or the convenience store clerks?[2]

Then, in August 2005, hurricane Katrina hit New Orleans. Lamentably, I no longer needed a hypothetical example of how the perceived value of specific human lives might lead to impasse in a crisis.

At least 1,300 residents of New Orleans and the surrounding Gulf Coast area died in Katrina, although six months later authorities were still dredging up new bodies.[3] The chaos wrought by the storm included physical faults (the broken levee that resulted in the flooding that overtook parts of the city), planning problems (mixed or conflicting messages from different authorities), and response problems (the appalling conditions in shelters like the Superdome and the failure to provide rapid evacuation). The disaster struck a blow

Figure 2.1 Real-time gas-dispersion simulation *BioChemFX* visualizes the spread of bio-chemical contaminants, but it abstracts social and ethical questions.

to the Bush administration, which had presumably spent the four years since September 11, 2001 reconfiguring the government for rapid, successful response to emergencies. Citizens around the country festered; if we cannot respond to a disaster seen coming for weeks, how can we respond to a random, freak event like a terrorist incident?

In February 2006, the U.S. House of Representatives issued a scathing report on Katrina, citing "failure at all levels of government."[4] The report addressed each of the failures mentioned above. Poor engineering and absent warning systems were blamed for the levee breaches;[5] incomplete or failed efforts to execute the National Response Plan were blamed for mixed messages during the crisis;[6] emergency communications failures (both equipment and human), lack of advanced preparations, and failed mass communications systems were blamed for response problems, including the collapse of local law enforcement, which worsened the already dire situation.[7]

While "information gaps" underlie many of the problems, the House Katrina report echoed sentiments from the 9/11 Commission report, specifically citing failures of "imagination" and "initiative" as major malfunctions of overall standards.[8] However, the 600-page report spends less than a page fleshing out these ideas. Individuals who took on the moral obligation to help are mentioned, including Dr. Gregory Henderson, who "raided pharmacies for needed medication and supplies and set up ad hoc clinics."[9] The findings of the House Select Committee imply a need for all-around improvements in preparedness, with specific recommendations for the Federal Emergency Management Agency (FEMA), law enforcement, the military, executive command, and medical agencies.[10]

The Committee's admittedly pessimistic recommendations all focus on reviewing, revising, and tightening existing emergency response procedures. Just as the 9/11 Commission report focuses on failures to secure airports, failure to prevent attacks, and failures to respond when attacks were underway, the House Select Committee analysis focuses on failures to secure infrastructure, to prevent disaster, and to respond after the hurricane struck. All of these conclusions arise from bureaucratic procedure, the rules of interaction that facilitate, enable, or prevent civic action from taking place. In particular, the House analysis affirms the value and validity of the significant (and significantly expensive) new procedures established in the wake of 9/11. In short, the solution to the next Katrina is assumed to be inside the realm of current procedure. The government is just using those procedures ineffectively.

The White House Report on Katrina affirms this sentiment, recommending the creation of a National Operations Center to "provide situational awareness and a common operating picture for the entire Federal government."[11] Of these findings and recommendations, the most telling can be found in the House Committee's speculative conclusion: "We are left scratching our heads at the range of inefficiency and ineffectiveness that characterized government behavior right before and after this storm. But passivity did the most damage."[12]

The House Select Committee poses a riddle, one that asks if Katrina was more a natural disaster or an artificial one. If the system has failed, is it because of poor execution of the rules that govern it, or because those rules themselves were broken? The White House holds the former belief, and their report makes no haste in characterizing the tragedy as a natural disaster commensurate with the Chicago fire of 1871 and the San Francisco earthquake of 1906.[13] These are "acts of God," their outcomes final and decisive, despite the hypothetical possibility of human intervention.

In the wake of Katrina, it is worth asking what social circumstances underwrote the calamity. The Chicago fire, in which 300 people died and 100,000 lost their homes, was rumored to have been started by a farmer and her cow, but it spread so quickly owing to the dry summer conditions and the predominance of wooden building construction.[14] Beyond the more careful treatment of lanterns in dry barns, clear lessons from the fire included the susceptibility of wooden building materials to inferno, a reminder of the thatched roofs that had condemned London to burn two centuries earlier. An honest mistake caused both fires, but a flaw in the construction material of the cities doomed them to incineration.

Despite the 350 pages of bureaucratic interrogations that precede it, the House Katrina report seems to come to a conclusion quite different from the White House report, and perhaps quite different from the one the House itself presumed to have reached. The Committee's engagement with passivity—an issue they suggest underlies the entire crisis—is a lone question: "How can we set up a system to protect against passivity?"[15] The question is rhetorical, and it receives no additional consideration in the report; its answer is assumed: impossible. The Dr. Gregory Hendersons of Katrina become the "exception to the rule" from which "no one learned . . . until it was too late."[16] Quite simply, we just didn't care enough to figure out a way to prevent, inform, notify, rescue, or evacuate—especially when the residents in danger were poor or black or both.[17] And this tragedy points to a flaw in the construction material of our consciences.

The aftermath of Katrina continued to play out in government and in the media. The ouster of FEMA chief Michael Brown uncovered new reports that seemed to show Brown begging the administration to make more preparations the day before the hurricane made landfall.[18] But one wonders if any individual federal leaders, any infrastructure, any response plans could overcome the underlying values we muster when producing them.

In light of Katrina, let us imagine a real sarin gas attack on UC Berkeley. Imagine that you are a member of an elite emergency response crew deployed to the busy intersection of Telegraph and Bancroft near campus. Thanks to a superb rapid response system, your group was mustered minutes after the incident, and news of the attack has not yet created public panic. You are clad in protective gear and gasmasks, five minutes in front of *BioChemFX*'s predicted path, ready to begin the evacuation and containment. However, unexpected shifts in the wind alter the path of another arm of the gas flow; in less than two minutes the two flows will now converge near the team's current position, more than halving their original evacuation time. The bustling street contains local immigrant-run businesses, dozens of students, Sproul Hall, a university administrative building, and homeless drifters inside and outside makeshift shelters.

Whom do you save? *BioChemFX* can predict the flow of the gas, but we need a different simulation to convert an understanding of the physical world into a set of values that drive impossible decisions.

Ideology

Natural disasters and terrorist incidents are not the only complex political and social issues that governments attempt to simplify. One of the clearest examples of political doctrine's direct impact on a social ill was the Irish potato famine of 1845 to 1850. During this time, the average resident of the western part of Ireland lived on a small farm, on which he paid ever-increasing rent to English landlords, usually through intermediaries who incrementally subdivided the same land into smaller plots while increasing the rent on each. The potato, a staple crop that grew well in the poor soil of western and southern Ireland, served as the main nourishment for these peasant farmers and their families. In 1845, an airborne fungus began killing healthy potato plants, blighting crops for the following year, and then the following three as well.[19] During the course of the ensuing famine, one and a half million people died, and another million fled the country as emigrants.

Although environmental conditions caused the initial blight, the resulting massive starvation and death of the famine was rooted in British officials' unflinching adherence to laissez-faire economics. This philosophy staunchly prohibited intervention in the market. Inaugurating conservative American policy of the twentieth century, to which I will return in the next chapter, laissez-faire adherents believed that "any attempt by the state to provide welfare would make things worse. The lower classes were responsible for their own condition—they wasted time on drink and foolish amusements, they looked to others to promote their welfare, they followed foolish leaders."[20]

Despite the politicians' clear disregard for the victims of the famine, James L. Richardson has argued that the popularity of laissez-faire arose largely from a few vocal economic theorists, particularly David Ricardo, who "stripped the world to its essentials, laying bare the underlying structure."[21] The politicians who removed work programs and soup kitchens from Ireland were clearly not guiltless; however, their actions were motivated by the simplicity of the tools that laissez-faire provided. As Richardson says of it, "in a world of complexity and contingency, the Ricardian style of reasoning encouraged policymakers to posit simple, uniform relationships."[22] Relying on a single logic to rationalize every political event is certainly a relatively convenient means of governance.

The purity of British adherence to laissez-faire economics at that time offers a fungible example of how philosophies can act as logics for political thought and action. In this case, laissez-faire offered a logic for reasoning about social and political problems. The British did not alter their Irish grain-importing policy, so that during the famine the same Irish families who starved for lack of potatoes still exported large quantities of grain to England; the farmers gladly sold the grain despite their hunger, as they needed the income to pay rent on their English-let farms to avoid eviction. These rules of political behavior are an example of a procedural system that underwrites political, economic, and daily practice. Of course, a computer is not enforcing these rules; rather, they are driven by social, cultural, and political convention.

In the case of the Irish potato famine, the underlying systems of reasoning that drive politics are visible, even to the actors involved. In the case of Katrina or the fictional UC Berkeley attack, the issues are less clear, hidden under the surface of more complex political practice. Hidden procedural systems that drive social, political, or cultural behavior are often called *ideology*.

Ideology has a long and arduous intellectual history. The concept itself is as old as Western philosophy. In Plato's famous parable of the cave in the *Republic*, human understanding of the world is likened to that of prisoners watching shadows cast on the wall of a cave by objects and agents passing above. The prisoners see only a flawed shadow of the ideal form (εἶδος) of the object.[23] For Plato, the disparity between the ideal and material realms can only be reconciled through a recollection of the forms, a claim that assumes that our souls were once connected to these forms and, therefore, are also immortal. Western philosophy generally follows this trend of valuing the ideal over the material; the experience we have of the world is necessarily shrouded in shadow. Experience always partakes of a rift between the ideal and the material, a "false consciousness" that unwittingly guides our thinking and behavior.

The term *ideology* itself can be traced to eighteenth-century French revolutionary Antoine Destutt de Tracy, who conceived of it as a science of the origin of ideas, that is, of how humans access the ideal realm from the material.[24] As Raymond Boudon clarifies, it was Napoleon's response to de Tracy that gave ideology its more familiar meaning:

When Destutt de Tracy and Volney tried to thwart Napoleon's imperial ambitions, he scornfully called them *ideologues*, meaning people who wanted to substitute abstract considerations for *real* politics, as it was later called. From that time on, ideology signified those abstract (and rather dubious) theories allegedly based on reason or science, which tried to map out the social order and guide political action.[25]

Karl Marx understood the concept this way, and gave it perhaps its most famous characterization: "they aren't aware of it, but they do it [*Sie wissen das nicht, aber sie tun es*]."[26] Ideology thus lost the sense of being a weapon against entrenched ideas and gained a decidedly negative connotation, as the very entrenchment of those ideas. For Marx, ideology entails the delusion that ideas are material; in particular, the petite bourgeoisie sees itself (has an *idea* of itself) as universal. Following Hegel, Marx holds that historical progress comes from a dialectic between the *ideal* and the *material*.[27]

Antonio Gramsci takes issue with Marx's distinction between the material and the ideal, arguing that the material itself is filtered through consciousness and the realm of ideas. The revolution must thus address both the economic and the conceptual.[28] Gramsci's notion of *hegemony* characterizes the ability of stronger social classes to impose a worldview on subordinate ones, so that the latter see that worldview as natural. Louis Althusser built on Gramsci's interest in the way ideas connect with material practice, arguing that economic systems tend first to their own procreation. He conceives of two types of institutions that carry this out in the modern capitalist state, the Repressive State Apparatuses (RSAs), such as the police, courts, and army, and the Ideological State Apparatuses (ISAs), such as the church, the family, and the educational system.[29] For Althusser, ideology exists "in an apparatus, and its practice."[30] The subject is crafted according to the roles the ISAs have already created for him; Althusser calls this process *interpellation*.[31] Althusser essentially collapses the realm of ideas completely into material practice, a gesture that guides his student Michel Foucault's insistence on the material world as the primary system that structures human subjectivity through "discourse."[32] More recently, Slavoj Žižek has attempted to correct this positive view of material conditions. Ideology remains material for Žižek, but this material reality is distorted and malignant. Ideology is not just a false representation of reality, it has become a part of reality itself, disfiguring it. Says Žižek, "'ideological' is not the 'false consciousness' of a social being but this being in so far as it is supported by 'false consciousness.'"[33]

When ideology creates distortions in reality, these deformations become increasingly difficult to see. If material practice is established by or in ideology, as Gramsci, Althusser, and Žižek suggest, then we are unknowingly trapped inside a prison, the equivalent of Weber's iron cage. The challenge that faces political critique, then, is to identify the distortion in material practice. Gramsci allowed ideology to take on two meanings, one the expression of hierarchical authority, the other the more general expression of ideas that form our identities. This distinction allowed Gramsci to argue that struggle and transformation can alter even a dominant worldview, founding a new logic, a new ideology. This view complicates the traditional Marxist notion of ideology, giving people more direct ability to influence the logics that drive daily practice.

Alain Badiou calls the logic that dictates a situation's organization a *state*, or "that by means of which the structure of a situation . . . is counted as one."[34] As Peter Hallward summarizes, the state articulates "not the elements of the situation but the way these elements are grouped into parts or subsets of this situation."[35] The possibility of restructuring a situation depends on the void, or null set (Ø), which leaves open the possibility of reconfiguring the situation. For Badiou, this takes place through an *event*, which also founds subjectivity.

Videogames are particularly useful tools for visualizing the logics that make up a worldview (following Gramsci), the ideological distortions in political situations (following Žižek), or the state of such situations (following Badiou). The politics of Katrina and counterterrorism only become apparent through the unusual conditions that expose their underlying logics; such situations are rare in everyday practice—and perhaps ideally avoided. In these extreme cases, ideology is exposed and made material. Political videogames use procedural rhetorics to expose how political structures operate, or how they fail to operate, or how they could or should operate. Videogames that engage political topics codify the logic of a political system through procedural representation. By playing these games and unpacking the claims their procedural rhetorics make about political situations, we can gain an unusually detached perspective on the ideologies that drive them.

War and Peace

In 2002, the U.S. Army released an unprecedented government-funded first-person shooter (FPS) game. *America's Army: Operations*[36] was conceived and openly publicized as an army recruiting and communications tool, one crafted "to recreate the U.S. Army for the benefit of young civilians."[37] The game represented a major step for the military-entertainment complex; it was created on the then-current Unreal 2 engine, a costly professional-grade game engine, and released for free on the army's website. Within the first six months, over a million users had registered, of which over 600,000 had completed the game's basic rifle marksmanship and combat training (BCT), a necessary step before gaining access to combat missions.[38]

While *America's Army* shares a genre with other popular multiplayer FPS games, the army's desire to offer "a realistic look at army personal and career opportunities via sophisticated role-playing" altered or eliminated many of the popular conventions of both conventional and tactical first-person shooters.[39] On the one hand, *America's Army* shares the core gameplay of the popular multiplayer deathmatch FPS *Counter-Strike*: small groups of networked human players compete against one another in pursuit of victory.[40] In *Counter-Strike*, players enjoy fanciful tweaks like tunable gravity, unlimited ammunition, and extraordinary environments. Strategy in *Counter-Strike* is grounded in free-for-all: players often use "bunny hopping," or continuous jumping, to avoid fire; they respawn immediately when killed; they can fire effectively while running or jumping.[41] Players enter the game and start scuffling immediately, without the need for preparation of any sort.

By contrast, the player starts *America's Army* as a new recruit in training at the Fort Benning army base in Georgia. Here, the player must complete BCT with an adequate score to continue on to rifle or sniper qualification. The game represents weapons handling in great detail; for example, the player learns "to breathe at the right moment in the firing sequence, and get the most from an M-24 by using it on a bipod in a stationary position."[42] Pace in *America's Army* is much slower than in *Counter-Strike*; for example, firing while in motion results in significant loss of accuracy. These constraints seek to create an accurate representation of procedure and policy for army engagement, rather than a fictional universe for casual tête-à-tête combat.

But the game's political simulation is more interesting than its mechanical and physical simulation. *America's Army* enforces the U.S. Army's strict rules of engagement (ROE), which preclude the brouhaha of typical squad-based fighting games. Whereas *Counter-Strike* encourages the player to log as many kills as possible, *America's Army* players collaborate in short missions, such as rescuing a prisoner of war, capturing an enemy building, or assaulting an enemy installation. The ROE guide play with an iron fist. Writing about the game, designers Mike Zyda et al. explain:

All players abide by rules of warfare. If a player violates the Uniform Code of Military Justice, rules of engagement, or laws of land warfare, reprisal is instant. He will find himself in a cell at Fort Leavenworth, accompanied by a mournful harmonica playing the blues. Continued violation of the rules may cause a player to be eliminated from the game. To rejoin, he must create a new ID and restart.[43]

Many players discover this constraint in basic training; turning a weapon on one's drill sergeant immediately lands the player in the brig. The direct mapping of in-game behavior to the very ability to continue playing serves as a convincing procedural rhetoric for the chain of command, the principal structure new recruits must understand immediately. Even the use of foul language is grounds for in-game discipline.

But the game also ties ROE and chain of command directly to the moral imperative of the U.S. Army. As in many similar games, when players complete levels they earn points that persist on web-based global statistics boards. At specified point targets, a player character's "honor" statistic increases. Since honor indicates commitment and expertise, disincentives to violate the ROE and chain of command become especially strong; losing a character through violation would require considerable effort to rebuild.

The correlation of honor with the performance of arbitrary and politically decontextualized missions offers particular insight into the social reality of the U.S. Army. While the use of abstract honor points may seem contrived at first, the system bears much in common with the actual practice of military decoration. Ribbons, medals, and other designations reward the successful completion of military objectives. Training, professional development, wounds, completion of missions, and many other events earn soldiers decorations, which when worn on a dress uniform speak to the honor and nobility of the bearer. The average citizen's lack of familiarity with the specific actions that warrant a ribbon or medal ensure that these designations signify the soldier's abstract worth rather than his individual achievements. *America's Army*'s honor mechanic successfully proceduralizes this value system. As Zyda et al. summarize, "The game insists on the mission orientation of the US Army. Above all, soldiers must be team players, following army values and rules."[44]

The spillage of honor from the game into the metagame—the websites and leader boards that frame the experience—offers the player a unique perspective on military values. Honor, service, and courage are represented through the completion of military objectives under the constraints of ROE and the chain of command. Army success entails the selfless execution of tasks that have been handed down from a higher authority, completed without question or reservation. These tasks, like real U.S. Army missions, are decontextualized from geopolitics. Reward comes not from service completed in the conscious interest of a conflict, but from service completed in the absence of political circumstance. The U.S. Army recruit, one learns from *America's Army*, is an apolitical being.

This sentiment is reinforced by the most curious procedural rhetoric in *America's Army*, that of enemy threat. As already mentioned, the game is multiplayer, played in small groups on opposing sides, much like *Counter-Strike*. But in *America's Army*, each team always takes on the role of U.S. Army soldiers—the players never directly pilot the opposing, enemy team. As Zyda et al. explain, "no one ever plays a villain fighting the U.S. Both teams always see themselves as part of the U.S. Army and perceive the other team as the opposition."[45] When Zyda et al. say that each team "perceives" the other as the opposition, he means this in the literal, phenomenal sense: on screen, the player's team dons army uniforms, while the opposing team takes on the appearance of plainclothes renegades or guerillas. Both teams play the same mission, with one assaulting and the other defending. But both teams believe themselves to be the "good guys."

At first blush, one might commend the developers on a creative way to ensure that all players are always playing as members of the U.S. Army; this is an army recruiting game after all. But upon further consideration, the foreclosure of the opposition offers a telling view into the ideology of early twenty-first-century U.S. military aggression. The perceptual interchangeability of enemy and soldier underscores the contemporary American assumption that matters of military conflict are commutative; that is to say, one global, even transcendental situation guides both sides of the conflict. Perceptual equivalence reinforces the notion that military conflicts affirm a singular truth, one that is literally "seen" as identical from both vantage points. This line of thinking accurately represents contemporary U.S. attitudes about military conflict. Our perspective is not only right, but there is no explanation for the opposition's behavior save wickedness. Zyda et al.'s use of the comic book concept of the "villain" to refer to the opposition further underscores this logic: there is no reasonable explanation for enemy behavior, it is merely evil and therefore deserving of hostility. The visual representation of good and evil in the game is rudimentary, accomplished by rendering the opposing team in a different texture. The procedural rhetoric of enemy conflict is more complex. It rests in the ascription of an identical value system to both U.S. Army and opposition. The possibility of legitimate grievance on the part of the enemy—or even a coherent historical circumstance that underwrites opposing action—is ruled out of army conflicts.

The game's general obsession with "realism" further accentuates the ideology of universal justice. Zyda et al. detail the development team's concern for visual and aural fidelity, including accurate weapon sounds and environmental cues: "For added realism, footsteps, bullet impacts, particle effects, grenades, and shell casings are accorded texture-specific impact noises. A flying shell casing clinks differently on concrete, wood, or metal, for instance, and the distinction is clearly heard in the game. Likewise, footsteps on dirt, mud, wood, concrete, grass, and metal are sounded correctly."[46] The game's goal of sensory verisimilitude sets an expectation for political verisimilitude—and indeed the ideology of the enemy accurately represents the United States' one-sided perspective on matters of global conflict.

As a recruiting and advertising tool for young people, *America's Army*'s not only attempts to offer an accurate characterization of U.S. Army practice but also offers an accurate characterization for the political contexts in which the army deploys. Given that the game is designed and marketed for teenagers, one might raise legitimate concerns that *America's Army* functions as propaganda. Shenja van der Graaf and David B. Nieborg point out other realities of war that the game fails to represent with the realism of its surround-sound audio soundtrack. For one part, the gruesomeness of combat violence is largely underplayed: "dismemberment, bleeding soldiers and auditory enhancement of dying soldiers are absent."[47] Of course, limited gore wins the game a "Teen" rating in the U.S., ensuring that the army's target market can get their hands on it. The decision to avoid graphic violence and dismemberment more likely underscores the creators' concern for its critics than its beliefs about the real consequences of war.

My interest in *America's Army* lies more in its exposition of a contemporary U.S. ideology of war than in its representation of the brutality of war. Playing *America's Army* offers an unusually fungible perspective on the "state" of U.S. foreign conflict, to use Badiou's term on both its ontological and political registers. While we might worry about the game's influence over the young people it targets, we can also take some comfort in the fact that it necessarily exposes the ideology of the U.S. Army in the operating rules for the videogame. Here we see ideology take a new material form. Althusser held that ideology founds material practice and thereby divorces itself from the realm of ideas. Žižek and Badiou understand ideology as unified with material practice, although in different ways. In *America's Army*, ideology is made material in the realm of ideas. The game's persuasive goals are thus twofold. On the one hand, as a U.S. Army recruiting tool the game creates a representation of army life that draws interested youth into recruiting offices. On the other hand, as a manifestation of the ideology that propels the U.S. Army, the game encourages players to consider the logic of duty, honor, and singular global political truth as a desirable worldview.

Pacifism is no less susceptible to ideology. The International Center for Nonviolent Conflict commissioned military and healthcare videogame developers BreakAway Games to create *A Force More Powerful*, a game intended to demonstrate nonviolent democratic revolution.[48] According to the Center, the game will be distributed to activist groups in countries pushing for democratic change, although they have also offered it for retail sale on their website.

Whereas *America's Army* is an action game, *A Force More Powerful* focuses on strategy, particularly models of training, fund-raising, and organization necessary to create and administer civil disobedience. The game is based on the book and PBS series of the same name, created by Peter Ackerman and Jack DuVall.[49] In it, the player controls an opposition movement, which is opposed by a regime. The player is given the task of evaluating the regime's vulnerabilities and mounting an appropriate strategy to help bring about its demise.

Nonviolent conflict certainly sounds better than armed conflict, and any game with pacifist mechanics should be welcomed, if for no other reason than to expand the possibility space of a medium steeped in representations of violence. But *A Force More Powerful* attempts to build a procedural model for democratic revolution—for any kind of democratic revolution, no matter the circumstances. Despite efforts to characterize general, abstract methods for nonviolent action, one might wonder if a generalized model for political overthrow is even possible.[50] *A Force More Powerful* characterizes revolt independent of historical, cultural, and regional specificity. The nonviolent protests of Martin Luther King, Jr., or Gandhi, for example, were executed under specific material conditions, from within the conflict itself. In a political environment focused on "regime change," *A Force More Powerful* exposes the fact that such change is mired in the geopolitical interests of the West. Just as *America's Army* mounts a procedural rhetoric of commutativity for armed conflict, *A Force More Powerful* mounts one for unarmed conflict. The generic procedural model for authoritarian overthrow in *A Force More Powerful* underscores the fact that regime change is not a disinterested process. Rather, regime change comes about through external forces, and it always implies that such external forces perceive the existing government to be an illegitimate one. While it is certainly true that authoritarian governments are usually bad for their citizenry, these regimes are also "off the grid" of globalization, and therefore unable to participate in the capital-driven global economy. The democratizing interests of the West align democratic governance with free-market capitalism, a topic of considerable controversy in contemporary geopolitics.

In *A Force More Powerful*, the player takes the role of strategist in a nonviolent opposition. The game relies principally on recruitment. The player must assemble a coalition by converting members and building alliances. The very notion of a coalition is complex. Coalitions demand a confederacy, but sometimes—and perhaps often—they imply only a temporary one. Building a coalition requires a model of values that are the same, or similar enough to support a temporary federation against a solitary, authoritarian ruler. In such cases, tyranny and opposition must be clear-cut and abstract. A coalition requires the assimilation of groups with complementary interests working in support of a common goal. It is this sort of political and social unity that the game asks the player to build; he builds characters into groups, groups into coalitions, and coalitions into movements.

But the goals of coalitions are not necessarily complementary. Consider the Democratic Opposition of Serbia (DOS), the alliance that formed in opposition to the Socialist Party of Serbia and its leader, Slobodan Milošević, in 2000. The Serbian Democratic Party supported government transparency, independent media, and social democracy—the types of values usually held by the West as opponents of regimes like Milošević's. But no fewer than seventeen other parties made up the DOS, many with subtly conflicting goals. By 2002, two years after Milošević's overthrow, Serbian politics remained unstable. Some tentative resolution came in February 2003, when Serbia and Montenegro were united under one president, Svetozar Marović. But the reconciliation was short-lived; the following month, Serbian Prime Minister Zoran Đinđić was assassinated. Western leaders had smiled upon Đinđić as a leader; he had supported Serbia-Montenegro unity, which in turn supported the Western goal of perceived regional stability. All else being equal, from an outside perspective unity implies the absence of conflict. Đinđić had also made positive gestures toward encouraging Serbian participation in the global economy; for example, he signed a letter of intent to "engage Microsoft for providing consulting services and expert analysis for the government's electronic initiatives."[51] Microsoft invested with an interest in developing training and supporting licensure of Serbian citizens on their products, a necessary first step in bolstering commercial presence in the country, especially for corporate and consulting markets.

Đinđić's assassin was 28-year-old paramilitarist Zvezdan Jovanović. It was not the first attempt at Đinđić's life, an indication of the enemies he had made thanks largely to his pro-Western politics, and especially his foreign-favoring economic policies like the agreement with Microsoft. Some Đinđić detractors were likely affiliated with organized crime; nevertheless, the very existence of a movement against him demonstrates that the original ouster of Milošević did not solve all of the region's underlying political concerns. If anything, the overthrow of his regime paved the way for Serbians to attend to the much more complex and entrenched political, economic, and social conflicts that followed.

Interestingly, developers of *A Force More Powerful* were "assisted" by a prominent member of Serbian resistance movement Отпор (Otpor, or *Resistance* in Serbian), Ivan Marović.[52] The youthful and charismatic leader of the organization even collected a "Free Your Mind" award from MTV during their 2000 MTV Europe Music Awards, a prominent symbol of the Western market. Otpor reportedly followed the writings of Gene Sharp, a leading theorist of abstract, nonviolent resistance techniques.[53] Thanks to their prominence during this transitional period, Otpor reportedly enjoyed considerable financial and political support from Western interests, including strategic advice from U.S. Army colonel Robert Helvey and the majority of a $3 million expenditure by U.S. Congress-funded National Endowment for Democracy.[54] Although Otpor and other groups instrumental in Milošević's overthrow were not working in the pockets of Western interests, Marović's participation in the design of *A Force More Powerful* extends the West's previous support of Otpor, generalizing that support to nonviolent conflict in general. Otpor's MTV commercialization and Đinđić's support of economic integration with Europe both underscore the fact that regime change, it would seem, is inextricable from Western global capitalism. This tendency explains part of why the tactics for achieving regime change, including those represented in *A Force More Powerful*, are assumed to be so transplantable—because it is intended to provide an economic and social model assumed to work everywhere.

A Force More Powerful focuses on building coalitions to overthrow leaders who do social or physical violence to their population, but it occludes the global political forces whose long-term interests are served by the free-market capitalism encouraged in the wake of such revolution. Videogames like *America's Army* and *A Force More Powerful* accentuate the incompleteness and complexity of political situations. While these games offer holistic models that attempt to explain intricate political situations through a single logic, other procedural arguments attempt to highlight the causal or associative connections between seemingly atomic issues.

Such a rhetoric drives artist Josh On's *Antiwargame*.[55] In the game, the player takes the role of a U.S. president in a war against terrorism. The game depicts a very stylized United States with blue and green characters inside; the blue ones are ordinary citizens, the green are military. A foreign, aggressor nation is also depicted, dotted with oil derricks. The player has a set of simple actions at his disposal. First, he can change government spending in three categories, military/business, social spending, and foreign aid. Second, he can convert the green citizens to National Guard or send them abroad to war. Once sent abroad, the player can promote soldiers to officers, capture oil fields, or attempt to motivate apathetic soldiers. The player's popularity is depicted in a gauge on-screen, and small windows give abstract insight into media and business attitudes (figure 2.2).

Antiwargame makes a number of interrelated claims about the nature of the post-9/11 political and social environment, each claim simple and direct. First, business and the military are indistinguishable; there is no way to support one without the other, suggesting a fundamental tie between the two. Likewise, business support wanes if the player refuses to send troops overseas to secure the oil that drives business. This logic becomes self-perpetuating, as increased business/military funding converts more of the population to troops. Failure to maintain adequate business spending causes corporate interests to revolt, eventually leading to the player's assassination. Social spending produces economic dissatisfaction, which results in protest. However, the president can control dissatisfaction by manipulating media messages.

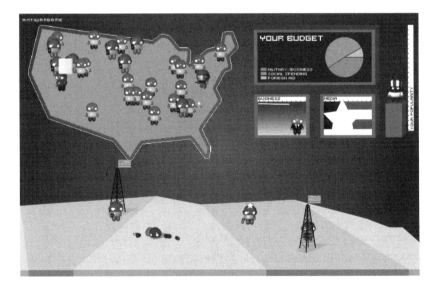

Figure 2.2 Josh On's *Antiwargame* argues procedurally that business and military interests are indistinguishable.

Furthermore, the National Guard can control the growth of protest movements through intimidation.

Once sent overseas, troops are very hard to keep motivated. Officers can encourage disaffected soldiers, but too many orders will cause the troops to revolt against their leadership. This mechanic invokes the estrangement of the Vietnam draft and suggests a correlation between the contemporary war in the Middle East and the Cold War. Once the player's troops start capturing oil fields, violence ensues. The press sends images of the bloodshed back to the media at home, which results in additional protest and reduced approval. Officers can control the press, but they can't fight, so the player must send more troops overseas. Killing foreign civilians creates more foreign troops, accelerating the violence. As more conflict takes place, foreign interests threaten more terrorist attacks. Withdrawing troops is one control against homefront attacks, but temporarily increasing foreign aid is another.

Antiwargame's procedural rhetoric emerges through the player's performance of political gestures that produce unexpected effects. It suggests relationships between political domains that are not explicitly construed as related. The game claims that military and business interests are identical, and that the overseas war is one of controlling resources to support business (there is no representation of foreign democracy, freedom, or "regime change" in the game whatsoever). Foreign aid serves no humanitarian end; rather, it is a war tool that temporarily pacifies enemies and the international community, as well as homeland critics. Furthermore, the media and the National Guard are not support networks, but tools for sedating the population. Together, the game's rules form a systemic claim about the logic of the war on terrorism, namely that the purported reasons for war—security and freedom—are false. Unlike other pacifist arguments, the *Antiwargame's* opposition to war is not based on antiviolence; rather, it opposes war by claiming that a broken logic drives post-9/11 conflicts.

The Rhetoric of Failure

Antiwargame's procedural rhetoric works because it forces the player to make and enact decisions that might not otherwise seem logical or obvious. By connecting the causal ties between business, war, and civil unrest, the game deploys procedural enthymeme. Once the player completes these rule-based syllogisms, *Antiwargame* offers a procedural representation of how its authors perceive U.S. foreign policy to be broken. If procedural rhetorics function by operationalizing claims about how things work, then videogames can also make claims about how things *don't* work.

As it happens, this technique has been especially popular in political videogames, perhaps because such games are often conceived as critiques of dysfunctional political practice. Shuen-shing Lee compares such a strategy to tragedy: A you-never-win' game could be considered a tragedy, for example, a game with a goal that the player is never meant to achieve, not because of a player's lack of aptitude but due to a game design that embodies a tragic form."[56] But tragedy also carries historical baggage, especially that of the very particular linear narrative of tragic drama. I want to suggest that such games operate by a common procedural rhetoric, the rhetoric of failure. Tragedy in games tends to find its procedural representation in this trope.

Lee offers two examples of unwinnable political games, both responses to the 9/11 attacks and their aftermath. In the first, *New York Defender*, the player shoots down airplanes flying toward the World Trade Center towers.[57] The planes approach at an increasingly rapid rate, making the task increasingly difficult. The second, *Kabul Kaboom*, is a commentary on the post-9/11 U.S. attack on the Taliban in Afghanistan.[58] The player controls an avatar borrowed from Picasso's *Guernica* to catch hamburgers (representing air-dropped food) while avoiding bombs (figure 2.3). The game highlights the simultaneity and inconsistency of aggression and relief. Eventually and inevitably, the player contacts a bomb, and the game depicts a scene of dismemberment.

Although both games have no winning condition, they don't represent failure itself. As Lee points out, *Kabul Kaboom* and *New York Defender* borrow a technique common to arcade games: the game continues until the player can no longer keep up with the onslaught. The actions necessary to play the games do not themselves produce failure. Rather, the inevitable breakdown of player attention or reflexes causes it. In fact, *New York Defender* feels much like an arcade game, albeit a rather simplistic one. *Kabul Kaboom* radically increases its starting difficulty to emphasize its rhetoric of failure. Whereas it is possible to play *New York Defender* for several minutes before it becomes difficult, then impossible, one can scarcely play *Kabul Kaboom* for more than a few seconds. The barrage of bombs simply makes it impossible to collect the food. This message, of course, is precisely the designer's intention.

Compare these two games with another political game designed by *Kabul Kaboom* creator Gonzalo Frasca.[59] In 2003, Frasca launched Newsgaming.com,

Figure 2.3 Gonzalo Frasca's *Kabul Kaboom* borrows and amplifies the procedural rhetoric of failure common in arcade games.

a website to host games about current events. Frasca called newsgames a merger of videogames and political cartoons, and offered a first example of such a one, *September 12*. The game depicts an anonymous Middle Eastern town with civilians, dogs, children, and terrorists milling about. The player is faced with the problem of what to do about the terrorists. The latter perform no actual terrorist activity during gameplay, but their threat is implied. The player controls a reticle on the screen, which he can move around to target. Clicking the mouse fires a missile, which arrives after a short delay, destroying buildings in the vicinity and killing anyone within its blast radius. When citizens are killed, others gather around and weep, before becoming terrorists themselves (figure 2.4).

Whereas *Kabul Kaboom* and *New York Defender* eventually end, *September 12* continues indefinitely; no goals or completion states are suggested or imposed. A variety of rules drives the simulation: the people in the village traverse it

Figure 2.4 *September 12* proceduralizes a position on U.S. geopolitics and the war in Iraq.

by a particular logic; once destroyed, buildings reconstruct themselves over time; citizens mourn their dead and then become aggressors. But most importantly, the tool the game provides for combating terrorism is revealed to be a sham—using missiles to root out terrorists only destroys innocent lives. The interface between missile, terrorists, and citizens works, insofar as it produces a result in the game world. However, the result it produces is undesirable, the converse of claims that long-range precision warfare is "surgical." Thus *September 12* claims that this logic of counterterrorism is broken; no one is made any safer by following it, and in fact many more innocent lives are lost.

Lee suggests that games like *Kabul Kaboom* and *New York Defender* "are meant to morph the player from an in-gaming loser into an off-gaming thinker (I lose therefore I think)."[60] And indeed, both games do produce crisis that can lead the player to subjective insights. But there is a key discrepancy between the rhetorics of *September 12* and *Kabul Kaboom*. Videogames that deploy rhetorics of failure make a subtly different statement than those that are simply unwinnable, or that actively enforce player loss. In *Kabul Kaboom*, the rules inscribe a playable game that eventually and inevitably ends in loss, similar to arcade games like *Pac-Man*. In *September 12*, the rules depict the impossibility of achieving a goal given the tools provided. Nodding to critics who argue that games must, by definition, be winnable, the creators inscribe a disclaimer in the instructions: "This is not a game. You can't win and you can't lose."[61] In *Kabul Kaboom*, the player fails to win the game, but in *September 12*, the represented procedural system fails to perform the service it alleges to provide. One cannot play and hope to succeed.

Madrid, the second game in the Newsgaming series, is frequently mistaken to deploy a rhetoric of failure. Created less than two days after the March 11, 2004 terrorist attacks in Spain, the game depicts a candlelight vigil.[62] A group of people faces the player, each wearing a shirt that pays homage to a city that has suffered a terrorist attack. One line of instructions is adequate: "Click on the candles and make them shine as bright as you can." Each candle's strength diminishes over time, and the player must achieve a minimum total luminescence to win (figure 2.5).

Owing to the precise, rapid mouse movement required to play it, the game proved particularly difficult to complete successfully, especially with nonstandard input devices like laptop trackpads. Given this distorted perspective

Figure 2.5 The "newsgame" *Madrid* was created less than 48 hours after the March 2004 terrorist attacks in that city.

on the game, it is possible to read it as an effective use of the procedural rhetoric of failure: no amount of mourning is ever adequate; we must keep lighting the candles eternally.[63] In fact, the game *is* winnable, and a meter at the bottom of the screen depicts the player's progress toward the win condition. Once reached, the screen depicts a visual elegy for the victims of the Madrid bombings. Thus the procedural rhetoric of the winnable *Madrid* is more subtle than a straightforward rhetoric of failure: reverence and memory fade, and we must use precision and diligence to keep them alive. However, such a strategy is worthwhile and can lead to overall social change.

Skinning Politics, Simulating Politics

Videogames have a strange and sundry history with politics. Many games grafted political visuals or themes onto existing procedural mechanics, another example of what Wardrip-Fruin calls *graphical logics*. In the heyday of the Atari VCS, a trio of political games were planned whose proceeds were to benefit environmental groups. The first was *Save the Whales*, a game about Greenpeace. The player controls a submarine that fires projectiles at nets dropped from a whaling ship at the surface (figure 2.6). The game was

Figure 2.6 Never commercially released to the mass market, *Save the Whales* offers an early example of a videogame about a social issue.

never released, although a version of it was repackaged for the 2002 Classic Gaming Expo, a gathering for collectors and creators of videogames on early platforms[64] (the other games planned for the series were *Dutch Elm Defender* and *Attack of the Baby Seals*, although neither was ever programmed).[65] The promise of videogames as a carrot for charitable funding certainly bears promise; however, *Save the Whales* simply reskinned and adapted shooter games like *Space Invaders* and *Defender*. The environmental context for whale protection, or the commercial context for whale poaching, was abstracted out of the experience.

Admittedly, the Atari 2600's software affordances are limited; it was built to manage sprites and projectiles, not dynamic political systems. By the next decade, however, even though more sophisticated simulation was possible on console systems, political topics remained largely relegated to visual skinning. Among the more curious videogames never to see the light of day was *Socks the Cat Rocks the Hill*, a platform game in which the player pilots Clinton White House pet Socks past spies and politicians to warn the president about a stolen nuclear missile.[66] The game was never released and thus details remain speculative; some claim that Republicans George H. W. Bush and Richard Nixon appeared as level bosses in the game.[67] Like *Save the Whales*, *Socks the Cat* borrows gameplay dynamics from popular genres of the era, in this case two-dimensional side-scrolling platformers principally reliant on movement and collision detection.

As *Save the Whales* and *Socks the Cat* suggest, not all videogames about politics are political. Political videogames in the sense I have articulated above are characterized by procedural rhetorics that expose the logic of a political order, thereby opening a possibility for its support, interrogation, or disruption. Procedural rhetorics articulate the way political structures organize their daily practice; they describe the way a system "thinks" before it thinks about anything in particular. To be sure, this process of crafting opinion toward resignation has its own logic, and that logic can be operationalized in code. In fact, a great many videogames have employed this strategy.

The clearest examples of these games are political election simulators. Among the first such videogames was *President Elect*, a 1988 turn-based campaign management game (figure 2.7).[68] The game allowed the player to run in any U.S. presidential election from 1960 to 1988, supporting both historical and ahistorical matchups. *Power Politics* appeared in 1992, allowing even more historical revisionism, such as matching up real presidential candidates

Figure 2.7 Like most campaign games, *President Elect* simulates electioneering, not politics.

from different eras.[69] *Power Politics* was retooled and rebranded as *The Doonesbury Election Game: Campaign '96*, although publisher Mindscape reportedly pulled the title within months after release.[70] By the 2004 U.S. election, no fewer than four such games were on the market: *The Political Machine*, which enjoyed the best distribution;[71] *Power Politics III*, a new version of Randy Chase's previous *Power Politics* and *Doonesbury Election Game*;[72] *President Forever*, sibling in a series that also includes *Chancellor Forever* and *Prime Minister Forever* (British, Canadian, and Australian versions);[73] and *Frontrunner*,[74] which focuses on the last ninety days of the campaign.[75]

These numerous simulations all have their own particular takes on the election process. *President Elect* focused on realistic representations of demographic trends and voting patterns. *President Forever* and *Power Politics* and its sequels focused on what-if scenarios. *The Political Machine*'s high graphical production values aimed for mass-market appeal. And *Frontrunner* focused on the anxious final weeks of the election.

But all of the games follow a common procedural rhetoric: elections are won by electioneering, not by politics. Players choose or customize candidates to play and oppose. The player builds a campaign staff to provide advice. Then the majority of the turn-based gameplay entails checking national and state support maps, choosing where to run fundraisers, planning and running ad campaigns (including smear campaigns), and managing debates.

In election simulations, public policy is irrelevant. Players choose or adopt positions on an issue, typically a rudimentary choice between support and opposition. *President Elect* quizzes players on their preferences and builds a profile based on responses to (now dated) policy topics. In these games, the presidential election process is revealed to be one of proper promotion and marketing; the political reality of social, economic, or foreign policy issues collapse into singular measurements of future performance based on past voting records and local demography. Otherwise put, election simulators assume political stasis: politicians seek to find the properly shaped tabs to suit the slots in popular opinion. The election games after *President Elect* allow the player to generate random demography rather than using historical data, but such revisions only remix political opinion for the purpose of election strategy. A conservative California or a liberal South now becomes the new static system for which the player crafts a candidate response; no political goals are at work here.

Of course, one could argue that games like *President Elect* and *Frontrunner* intend to make precisely this point: politics means election strategy, not public policy. But a postmortem on *The Political Machine* for *Game Developer* magazine underscores instead the developer's fear of procedural representations of policy itself:

In a political strategy game, especially in a hotly contested year such as this one with Bush vs. Kerry [2004], we had to put a lot of effort into making sure the game was fair to both sides. People would be looking for bias in the game, and probing for any hidden agendas. We wanted the game to be accurate enough to the real world that political junkies wouldn't be turned off, but we wanted to also make sure it was a fun game. This is a strategy game, not a simulator.[76]

That is to say, the game is not a simulator *of political policy*. Rather, it is a simulation of political *strategy*, which has nothing to do with policy.

In other words, the mechanical function of political orders like states, corporations (discussed in chapters 5 and 9), schools (discussed in chapters 8 and 9), and other institutions that found everyday experience is not identical to the logics that drive such institutions. To be sure, the two are related; the goals of the state are expressed, sometimes indirectly, in its method of operation. But the state works primarily to ensure its own future. As Badiou puts it, "The modern state aims solely at fulfilling certain functions, or at crafting a consensus of opinion. Its sole subjective dimension is that of transforming economic necessity . . . into resignation or resentment."[77] If election games make any political statement, it is one about the utter divestiture of politics from elections, such that electioneering's replacement of policy has become ideology.

Other games use political symbology, imagery, or verbiage but still avoid simulating the processes of political life. Games created explicitly about the election process (rather than election strategy, as in the case of *President Elect* and its kindred) offer instructive examples. The videogame that Gonzalo Frasca and I designed for the 2004 Howard Dean for America campaign, is one such example.[78] *The Howard Dean for Iowa Game* simulated grassroots outreach, arguing for local, individual action as the primary mode of campaign support. After considering several possible designs, the campaign commissioned one intended to address the power of grassroots outreach.[79] They hoped to win commitment from citizens who were sympathetic to the candidate but who had not yet contributed to or participated in the campaign. The game modeled the logic of grassroots outreach as well as the actual activities a grassroots supporter might partake of, in order to concretize the activities. Here the procedural rhetoric argues for a particular type of campaign activity as most likely to maintain ongoing support for the candidate.

In a similar vein, the Discovery Channel television network created *Staffers Challenge*, an advergame for their 2004 series *Staffers*.[80] The game put the player in control of a local campaign office, where he has to balance four simultaneous tasks: making coffee, answering phones, talking to walk-in visitors at reception, and stuffing envelopes. The goal is to keep all four stations running for as long as possible. *Staffers Challenge* is a clever and well-produced game that riffs on common resource management tasks in commercial videogames to mount its procedural commentary about electioneering: there's always more to do than there are people to do it; the campaign trail is tread by low- or unpaid volunteers whose idealism, youth, or ignorance forgives repetitive and thankless work. Like the campaign "mini-games" of *The Howard Dean for Iowa Game*, *Staffers Challenge* proceduralizes the individual experience necessary to yield the positive collective benefit of citizen supporters.

Other games manipulate political figures but fail to speak in any political register whatsoever, even one about the mechanics of political advertising like the election simulations. At the height of the 2004 election, UK mobile game developers Sorrent (now Glu Mobile) took the *Fox Sports Boxing* game they had already developed, replaced the boxers' heads with those of G. W. Bush and John Kerry, renamed the characters "Bubba Bush" and "K. O. Kerry," and re-released the game as *Bush vs. Kerry Boxing*.[81] Although unleashing a well-timed uppercut on one's political opponent of choice might have yielded momentary solace from the political strife of the 2004 election, the game itself, once again, does not proceduralize the political. If anything, *Bush vs. Kerry Boxing* reinforces the metaphor of politics as personalities rather than as infrastructures for facilitating everyday life.

With the growing popularity of political games, many games follow *Bush vs. Kerry Boxing*'s use of political imagery as an attempt to associate a topic of popular attention or to rise above the noise of the online and mobile games marketplace. Using surface effects to appeal to a particular lifestyle is a common advertising technique known as associative advertising, which I discuss in detail in chapter 5; Sorrent hoped that the faces of Bush and Kerry would make their existing boxing game appeal to the politically minded as well as the sports-minded. Likewise, using politics as an unusual curiosity or *pique* may make an ordinary game appear less ordinary.[82] Such is the case for *White House Joust*, an online game from Kewlbox.com.[83] The game borrows its name and gameplay from the popular arcade game *Joust*, but replaces that title's ostrich-mounts with large heads of presidents and presidential hopefuls (Bush, Clinton, Kerry), heads of state (Tony Blair), and other vaguely political figureheads (Rush Limbaugh). Kewlbox.com is an online game site run by advergame developers Blockdot; the site makes money through advertising, so slapping political personalities may drive increased traffic thanks to curiosity alone.

Specimens like *Bush vs. Kerry Boxing* and *White House Joust* are not political videogames. If anything, they are poor simulations of political videogames. These games apply a political skin to existing procedural mechanics, without attempting to transfer those mechanics into rhetoric supporting a political argument. These *graphical logics* may or may not make visual arguments about the world, but clearly they do not make procedural ones.

Still other games represent the traces of a political situation, suggesting inroads its political logic without directly representing that logic itself. In late 2005, mtvU—the college network arm of MTV—announced a contest for university students. The unenviable challenge: design a videogame to end the crisis in Darfur, Sudan, a conflict raging since early 2003 between the region's population and the Janjaweed, a government militia. The crisis is complex and just scratching the surface of it requires considerable study into arcane and complex historical tension between the region's non-Arab black population and its Arab settlers. Human rights violations, including mass rape and murder, have been blamed on both parties in the conflict, but lately the tide has turned in favor of the heavily armed and government-supported Janjaweed. The resulting imbalance of power has prompted increased concern from the international community, which fears the situation could easily escalate to ethnic genocide of the kind seen in Rwanda and the Balkans in the 1990s. However, the situation is further complicated by the "cold" nature of part of the conflict; for centuries, the non-Arab tribes have been sedentary farmers, whereas the Arab tribes are primarily nomadic herdsmen. The competing economic and material needs of these groups have often resulted in conflict. As of March 2005, the United Nations estimated that 180,000 people had died from illness and malnutrition in the region since the start of the conflict, that another 50,000 had been killed violently, and that some 200,000 more refugees had fled to neighboring Chad.[84] Some have criticized G. W. Bush for downplaying the Sudanese crisis in order to draw U.S. attention and support toward Iraq. The monetary and humanitarian solutions to the Darfur crisis are certainly within reach; however, it is unclear how long such solutions might last in a region blighted by centuries of similar conflict.

mtvU gave university students two months to design and submit a game based on this complex situation. In February 2006, the contest closed public voting for four finalists.[85] One of the finalists, *Guidance*, offers an abstract representation of U.N. aid. The player controls a U.N. symbol and attempts to guide conflicting tribes to food while preventing them from colliding. Despite its detached stick-figure abstraction of U.N. aid, *Guidance* makes a procedural claim for Western intervention. The solution does not take into account the centuries-old history of conflict in the region, nor does it account for the question of how and for how long to support such humanitarian efforts. However, according to the rules of *Guidance*, conflicting tribes can survive starvation and slaughter, so long as a U.N. intervention holds these conditions in check.

One segment of the winning game, retitled *Darfur Is Dying*, cast the player as a Darfuri child searching for a well from which to fetch water while attempting to avoid the heavily armed and vehicle-aided Janjaweed, depicted in figure 2.8.[86] The game leverages a common videogame design model: the player as hero runs to avoid an enemy. Inverting the common videogame power fantasy, the game puts the player in the role of the powerless rather than the powerful actor in the struggle. This winning entry was created by a group of University of Southern California masters students, led by Susana Ruiz, who developed the game as a part of her M.F.A. thesis.[87]

Understanding the Darfuri experience by playing *Darfur Is Dying* may increase player empathy, but the game does not make a procedural argument for conflict resolution. mtvU might argue that the game fulfills one of its contest goals, to "raise awareness" about the conflict, but awareness is a tired, ineffectual excuse for the absence of fungible solutions. If the player hopes for perspectives on possible solutions, he must consult materials far beyond the videogame. If it succeeds at all as a political statement, *Darfur Is Dying* acts as a kind of videogame billboard for more complex verbal or written rhetorics on the crisis. As mtvU explains in an official statement, *Darfur Is*

Figure 2.8 Taking on the role of a Darfuri child foraging for water emphasizes powerlessness, an inversion of typical videogame role play.

Dying is intended "to engage users and provide a window into the refugee experience—offering a faint glimpse of what it's like for the more than 2.5 million who have been internally displaced by the crisis in Sudan."[88] This is not an undesirable outcome; empathy may lead players to interrogate the situation further.

But mtvU's assertion that the game is part of their "two-year campaign to give college students the tools they need to help end the genocide in Sudan" raises an eyebrow.[89] The website mtvU built for the game arrogantly enjoins the visitor: "Play the game. End the killing." In a rejoinder similar to the one Elizabeth Losh raised against *Tactical Iraqi*, journalist Julian Dibbell wonders if the nature of the videogame design even matters to the sponsor: "you might start to wonder which use of game violence is sicker: the game companies' exploitation of adolescent aggressive impulses in pursuit of unit sales, or MTV's exploitation of adolescent social conscience in pursuit of ad revenue."[90] As in the case of *White House Joust*, the active rhetoric in these games may be identical to the commercial rhetoric of MTV—it mainly serves as a call toward attention. mtvU can always claim success in its vague attempt to "raise awareness" about the crisis; their own press campaign around it has been tremendously successful. And such an effort may be a noble one, especially if the rhetorical use of videogames as a positive association for young people leads to new interest in issues of international politics.

But we must distinguish the rhetorical use of videogames for politics and the inscription of procedural rhetorics in videogames about politics. *Darfur Is Dying* proceduralizes the experience of the Darfuri villagers at a particular moment in the crisis, abstracting the historical dilemmas that partially explain such a terrible outcome. In his history of the Darfur crisis, Gerald Prunier complicates this simplistic understanding under the name *ambiguous genocide*.[91] Media representations of the conflict, argues Prunier, characterize the conflict as one of "simple" ethnic cleansing, where powerful governments persecute, rape, and kill powerless victims.[92] That persecution, rape, and murder is in fact taking place is undeniable. But the simplistic, mediatized "opposition" that Prunier criticizes does not explain why such persecution takes place, a seemingly important piece of information for activists. Despite the promise of *Darfur Is Dying* as an effective call to empathy about the crisis, the game abstracts the core of the problem: how to engage in a procedural rhetoric about how historical circumstance underwrote the conflict, and why that circumstance makes solutions so difficult.

Political Processes

The interrelated structure of political issues suggests that procedural rhetorics may offer more promising methods for exposing political ideology than verbal rhetorics. Verbal rhetorics require coherent and methodical movement between causal pairs: laissez-faire economics starved the Irish; federal incompetence sank New Orleans. The negative image of the deceitful soapbox politician notwithstanding, these claims tend to simplify and cover over the network of relations that contribute to final outcomes. But not all videogames rise to the challenge; indeed, despite the promise of videogames for representing political thought, proceduralizing politics is hard work, and work that is largely unexplored in commercial videogames. While games like *America's Army* and *A Force More Powerful* claim to represent imperturbable political positions, they also help expose the ideologies that underwrite those very positions. Games like *Antiwargame* and *September 12* proceduralize specific positions on political issues, acknowledging their inherent bias. The uniqueness of political videogames in the contemporary media environment has brought about games like *White House Joust* and *Bush vs. Kerry Boxing*, which appropriate political images for commercial, not political purposes. Somewhere in between the *Antiwargames* and *White House Jousts* are efforts like *Darfur Is Dying*, which earnestly attempts political speech but abstracts the most complex political relationships from its procedural rhetoric.

When we interrogate political issues as procedural systems—as the emergent outcomes of interconnected, independent rules of cultural behavior—we can gain a unique perspective on such problems. Diana Richards has adopted the concept of "functional nonlinearity" from nonlinear modeling to describe the role of complexity in political processes.[93] Such processes are not neat and tidy; they are, in Richards's words, "a big mess" that entails "sensitivity to small changes, nonequilibrium dynamics, the emergence of complex patterns, and sudden changes in outcome. . . . much less is static, stationary and fixed."[94] Richards's focus is scientific explanation of empirical models that can explain political complexity. But procedural representations of political processes also engender *expression* rather than prediction or validation. Procedural rhetorics in political videogames make claims about the particular interrelations between political processes, why they work, why they don't work, or how society might benefit by changing the rules.

Ideological Frames

The 2004 U.S. presidential election renewed world citizens' recognition of an ideological polarization in U.S. politics. The American Electoral College and an absent viable third party only amplified the apparent split: massive, telecast U.S. maps displaying won states in red (Republican) and blue (Democrat) suggested a geographic divide to many Americans, with the west coast, northeast, and Great Lakes voting Democratic and the heartland and south voting Republican. Yet more detailed maps that showed county-by-county vote balance proved that the division runs even deeper, with most counties appearing some shade of purple, a combination of "red votes" and "blue votes."[1] In the aftermath of the election, Democrats have acknowledged that their messages have failed, just as Republicans have recognized how much theirs have succeeded. Juxtaposing American morality against British class rifts, some cite religion as the key issue dividing the presidential vote.[2] Meanwhile, the Left has scrambled to develop a new strategy. Ideas are plentiful: avoid candidates from the northeast;[3] focus more strongly on domestic issues;[4] seek better management.[5] But two influential political theorists have suggested that such superficial strategies will not move the political needle; instead, political success draws less from reality and more from representation.

Cognitive linguists George Lakoff and Mark Johnson propose that metaphor is central to human understanding.[6] Influenced by Claude Lévi-Strauss, Clifford Geertz, and Jean Piaget, Lakoff and Johnson argue that our conceptual systems are fundamentally shaped by cultural constructions. For

Lakoff and Johnson, metaphor is not a fanciful language reserved for poets, but an active framework central to how we understand the world. For example, the two unpack our understanding of "time as a commodity," showing how we relate our experience of time to monetary concepts of quantification (*you're running out of time; is that worth the time?*). Turning to politics explicitly, Lakoff argues that the most important consideration in political discourse is not how politicians respond to the "facts" of the external world, but how they conceptualize or "frame" that world in their discourse about it. Lakoff argues that political frames in the United States today reflect metaphors of family management—conservatives frame political issues as "strict fathers" while liberals frame them as "nurturing parents."[7] A self-professed liberal, Lakoff argues that if the Left wants to regain political credibility, they need to start crafting their political speech with an understanding of liberal and conservative frames. They need to create words that reflect their ideas.[8]

On the other side of the political fence, conservative political scientist Frank Luntz specializes in helping conservatives frame their spoken discourse to create the greatest appeal possible—what he calls "message development."[9] Luntz was responsible for much of Newt Gingrich's 1994 "Contract with America," and more recently he has guided conservatives on the strategic use of such terms as "war on terror" instead of "war in Iraq" and "climate change" instead of "global warming." What Lakoff calls "frames," Luntz names "contexts"—ways to repackage positions so that they carry more political currency.[10]

Some have criticized Luntz's message development strategy as misleading or even immoral. The National Environmental Trust maintains LuntzSpeak. com, a website devoted to exposing and critiquing Luntz's messaging strategy. Despite such criticism, politicians have taken Luntz's advice to heart, and evidence of his influence and success are increasingly apparent. At the 1998 unveiling of the Council of Republicans for Environmental Advocacy, founder Gale A. Norton argued that public lands should support "multiple use," a Luntz-created context meant to suggest that such lands might be used for their resources in addition to being protected for wildlife.[11] In 2001, the U.S. Department of the Interior passed a policy allowing local authorities the ability to exercise right of way for roads across federal lands.[12] The policy did not automatically allow local municipalities to bulldoze and pave remote country, but it did recontextualize public lands as places in which commercial activity might have a place in the future. Frames or contexts are not merely theoretical structures for intellectual navel-gazing; they are operational models that are actively influencing public policy.

Political Videogames

There are numerous precedents for commercial games that carry political messages through procedural rhetorics. Chris Crawford's 1985 classic *Balance of Power* is often cited as the first political game in which diplomacy outweighed brute force.[13] In the game, the player uses treaties, negotiation, international espionage and, as a last resort, military force to manage a world in the throes of a cold war. In this early example of game-based political expression, Crawford imbued his own worldview into the gameplay: inciting a nuclear war caused a most grave loss—a black screen imprinted with plain white offering a dour report of the player's outcome: "You have ignited a nuclear war. And no, there is no animated display or a mushroom cloud with parts of bodies flying through the air. We do not reward failure" (figure 3.1). Larry Barbu's 1991 cold war simulation *Crisis in the Kremlin* followed in the tradition of *Balance of Power*, challenging the player to stay in power and to prevent the Soviet Union from dismantling.[14] The year 1990 witnessed two games that

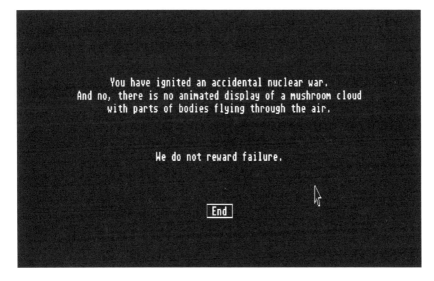

Figure 3.1 Failure to avert nuclear war in *Balance of Power* is cast as a losing condition, an example of how a videogame can embody a political position.

explored environmental issues. The first and more well known was Will Wright's *Sim Earth: The Living Planet*, a game adaptation of James Lovelock's Gaia hypothesis, the theory that the earth functions as a continuous system for all life rather than as a vessel for specific forms of life.[15] In *Sim Earth*, the player nurtured single-cell organisms into complex creatures with intelligence enough to leave the planet. Pollution, disease, and global warming were among the obstacles that stood in the way. The second, more obscure game was Chris Crawford's follow-up to *Balance of Power*, *Balance of the Planet*, which was released on the first celebration of Earth Day.[16] As I mentioned earlier, the game offered a detailed model of the earth's ecosystem. Crawford constructed some two hundred individual environmental factors such as lung disease, coal use, and coal tax, all of which were interconnected in a complex chain of causes and effects. Instead of manipulating the physical environment itself, as the player does in *Sim Earth*, in *Balance of the Planet* the player manipulates social responses to environmental conditions. For example, lowering the coal tax increases coal use, which in turn increases lung disease caused by coal pollution. In addition to changing environmental incentives, Crawford also allowed the player to adjust the formula inputs used to calculate the results themselves. For example, a player could ratchet down the effect of coal-burning energy on lung cancer, effectively reducing the coupling between that particular cause and effect.

In addition to these early examples of politically charged commercial games, increasingly larger numbers of independently created games about political issues have cropped up on the Web. The aforementioned *September 12* is such a one. The game's rules enforce a particular political perspective: violence begets more violence, and the nonprecision weapons of U.S. "precision warfare" bear significant consequence in the form of innocent lives lost. *Antiwargame* had similar goals, its simulation dynamic depicting the bind between homeland politics and foreign war.[17] In 2004, Josh Oda created *Bushgame: The Anti-Bush Online Adventure*. In this large and intricate adventure game, the player controls a series of pop-culture heroes (Hulk Hogan, Mr. T., He-Man, Christopher Reeve, Howard Stern, and others) in a battle to save the world from the Bush administration.[18] Traveling from the White House to Mars, the player combats enemies from the Bush cabinet, most of whom pilot complex robotic contraptions in opposition (for example, the player must defeat FCC chief Michael Powell in his robotic Janet Jackson breast, a reference to the former's censure of the latter's infamous exposure during the 2004

Super Bowl). During interludes between levels, the game provides guided tours through Oda's specific complaints with the administration, including the budget, the environment, and tax policy. Despite the interesting promise of embedding graphs and statistics into a satirical action game, *Bushgame* does not mount a procedural rhetoric. Instead, it peppers a traditional action game with written and visual rhetorics, in the form of pop-up text and graphs about the problems with Bush's leadership.

These precedents are but a few of the recent commercial and independent games that have addressed political problems. But a major shift in the subgenre of political videogames took place in 2004. In addition to becoming the year of an American political divide, 2004 was also the year political videogames became legitimate. For the first time, candidates and party groups created officially endorsed games to bolster their campaign for U.S. president,[19] U.S. Congress,[20] U.S. State Legislature,[21] and even president of Uruguay.[22] As the worlds of political message strategy and political videogames gain momentum, an opportunity arises for each to inform the other. As videogames become part of endorsed political speech, they will become more tightly integrated with existing strategies for political discourse.

But Frank Luntz's contextual message development and George Lakoff's framed conceptual systems both define strategies for *spoken or written* political rhetoric. As such, these methods may be inappropriate for videogames, whose primary rhetorical mode is procedural rather than verbal. Understanding political rhetoric in videogames intended to carry ideological bias requires a theory of framing as a procedural rather than a verbal strategy.

Reinforcement

Customary uses of language do have some place in videogame-based political messaging. The GOP's second game of the 2004 campaign, *Tax Invaders*, is a modified clone of the classic arcade game *Space Invaders*. Instead of combatting a swarm of descending aliens, players defend the country against John Kerry's tax plans.[23] In lieu of a spacecraft, the player controls the head of George W. Bush, which he moves from side to side along the bottom of the screen in place of the original game's space gun. The player combats potential John Kerry tax cuts, represented as abstract rectangles bearing the numerical value of the proposed tax, by firing projectiles out of the top of Bush's head to "shoot down" the tax hikes and defend the country (figure 3.2).

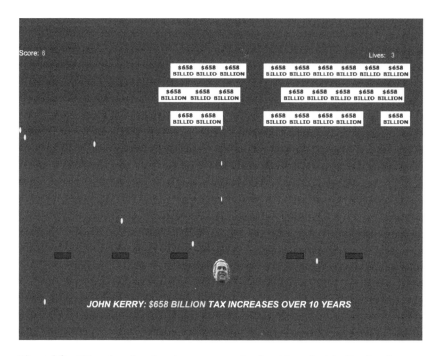

Figure 3.2   Although rudimentary in appearance, the Republican Party's *Tax Invaders* succinctly summarizes a traditionally conservative position on taxation.

The game's implementation is extremely crude, so crude that when I first played the game I quickly dismissed it, assuming its rhetoric to be as rudimentary as the game's primitive visual and programmatic execution. If left long enough, the taxes/aliens even pass over the player and off the bottom of the screen. And the blue "shields"—a critical strategic tool in *Space Invaders*—are rendered impotent in *Tax Invaders*. They seem to have been placed merely for show, or perhaps the game's programmers didn't have time to turn them into active protective barriers. The gameplay itself amounts to a three-level long barrage of countertax projectiles. But since its release I have revisited the game, and I am now convinced that it represents one of the most sophisticated examples of a procedural rhetorical frame at work in contemporary political discourse.

The game begins with verbal rhetoric; written text contextualizes the player's actions. The copywriting enacts logic familiar to both Lakoff and Luntz: it casts tax increases as an anthropomorphized enemy, a thief against whom you must defend yourself. The game's opening text announces, "only *you* can stop the tax invader" and invites the player to "Save the USA from John Kerry's Tax Ideas." Lakoff argues that such language reflects an underlying logic at work in conservative politics, that citizens know what's best for themselves and that material success is moral and should not be punished. Conservatives, he suggests, conceptualize theft as a metaphor for taxation. The language that opens (literally framing) the game conforms to this metaphor; the player is contextualized as a force of good, "stopping" taxes and "saving" the country from them. *Tax Invaders* extends the verbal metaphor of "taxation as theft" to the tangible plane.

Released in March 2004 at the height of the war in Iraq, some might find it surprising that the GOP would choose to publish a depiction of George W. Bush shooting at anything. Is this not precisely the message the White House would want to avoid at such a sensitive political moment? But within the verbal rhetoric of conservative politics, taxation is a "battle" to be waged. Lakoff argues that conservatives never perceive taxation as proposals to improve the general social good, but always as government threats to steal what does not rightly belong to them. When someone breaks into your home, it is appropriate to brandish a gun. One must defend his own property. There is thus no political inconsistency in contextualizing tax opposition as hostility, indeed as violent hostility. In the context of *Tax Invaders*, George W. Bush's bullet-like projectiles are not akin to army rifles wielded against innocent Iraqis, but rather to the police officer's sidearm wielded against a criminal. In another example of procedural enthymeme, the player completes the game's argument by firing the projectiles that defend the nation from Kerry's potential tax plans.

A simple game like *Tax Invaders* could be said to wear its rhetorical frame on its sleeve; indeed, the instantiations of conservative contexts are almost identical to their verbal counterparts. For example, we talk about politicians "shooting down" a measure in Congress. This figure even seems to function outside of the English language. In the aftermath of Hurricane Katrina, a German social minister used this verbal figure to attack President George W. Bush's handling of the crisis in New Orleans—"he ought to be shot down [*gehört abgeschossen*]"—later clarifying that he meant the statement "in the political sense."[24] The idea of a legislator "shooting down" a tax-hike proposal is thus extremely plausible; the game just makes such a verbal frame materially manifest.

Tax Invaders takes the metaphor beyond verbal and visual rhetoric. One could imagine a political cartoon that literalized the verbal metaphor of legislation as battle. One side might throw out proposals for new laws or candidates for official posts, which the opposing side would view as assaults rather than propositions, upon which they would then open fire. Such a cartoon might effectively illustrate one party's unwillingness to consider the other's potentially legitimate proposals. Such a cartoon would illustrate the verbal metaphor, rendering that metaphor into its visual equivalent. But *Tax Invaders* frames the metaphors of its rhetoric as embodied activities, not as words or images. Bush (and the player) fire projectiles at the tax hikes, representing the metaphor of taxation as enemy threat. No matter the player's political perspective, to play the game at all he must step inside the skin of the taxation opponent, viewing taxes as a foreign enemy—in this case the most foreign enemy, a wholly other enemy whose very name means otherness itself: the alien.

Thus, while *Tax Invaders* does little to represent actual tax policy, it frames taxation in a way that reinforces a conservative position. The short text descriptions bracketing the game do bear a striking resemblance to verbal rhetoric used elsewhere in conservative politics. That resemblance should come as no surprise, since experienced conservative communication personnel probably penned the lines. But this verbal language remains largely imperceptible to the player; its function as metaphor is hidden to a public mired in their own familiarity with those metaphors. More surprising is the game's remarkable translation of the frame of taxation-as-theft from verbal to procedural form. The authors of the game may not have had such a high-minded goal as to adapt their Luntz-style verbal rhetoric into computer code; instead, they likely took advantage of the resonance between this particular verbal metaphor and an existing, well-seated videogame mechanic: firing projectiles at things. Better still, the GOP was able to find an existing game with a suitable, adaptable graphical logic, and even better still a game with tremendous cultural currency, such that its constituency would find the game immediately approachable. After all, *Space Invaders* was first released in 1978, making it a good fit even for voters in their forties and fifties, who might remember playing the game in bars and arcades, as well as younger voters who could not have escaped *Space Invaders'* cultural wake.

George Lakoff argues that the conservative worldview holds up the wealthy as model citizens because they have worked hard and achieved success at their own hands, rather than by relying on tax-funded social programs.[25] Conservatives view taxation as punishment, and, in Lakoff's words, "that makes the federal government a thief."[26] The political right views liberals' inclination to conceptualize taxes as civic duty or even payment for government services as misguided: in the case of civic duty, conservatives see no obligation to contribute to the general assistance of the citizenry as a matter of principle. In the case of payment for services, conservatives point out that citizens do not have a choice to "purchase" the services funded by tax dollars. And furthermore, conservatives suggest that the government has a bad reputation for running ragged, primarily since it has no profit motive to drive efficient management, as do businesses. The absence of free market regulation implies coercion and incompetence rather than impartial public interest. Lakoff convincingly shows that opposition to taxation is fundamental to conservative politics because it underwrites so many other conservative positions: the drive to privatize government, turning poorly run federal and local services into well-run businesses with profit motives; the drive to reduce or eliminate social services in favor of "strengthening backbone" and enforcing personal responsibility as the primary factor in a thriving citizenry; the belief that human beings are fundamentally driven by reward and punishment, and that taking away hard-earned cash from personally responsible citizens in order to give it to the irresponsible stinks of injustice.

Tax Invaders is an example of the reinforcement an ideological frame. Typical political discourse would invoke the metaphor of taxation as theft, or legislation as battle through verbal or written speech; for example, a politician might vow to "strike down new tax proposals," or warn that he might "return dollars stolen from Americans through unjust taxes." But the game draws attention to the correlation between war and taxation, taxation and enemy threat, and taxation and theft. As a matter of cultural practice, alien invasions are tightly tied to theft. Alien abduction in the vein of *The X Files*[27] is perhaps the best example, but alien invasions from *The War of the Worlds*[28] to *Independence Day* all depict aliens as malevolent agents bent on stealing the very planet Earth from its inhabitants.[29] There is perhaps no more effective metaphor for theft than alien invasion.

Verbal and written rhetorics rely on our intrinsic experiences with metaphor as fluent speakers of a language. When listening to a politician on the soapbox, most of us would not even make note of the metaphors of theft and battle. The insight and utility of Lakoff's work on metaphor speaks to the ideology of the spoken word: its logic must be exposed as a platform for the way we think, since it is not immediately obvious that conceptual metaphor underlies what we say and write. *Tax Invaders* not only makes its argument from within the conservative frame on taxation, but also it explicitly draws attention to the frame itself. The rules of the game—aliens descend continuously, the player character combats them before they reach the bottom—stand as symbolic structures of a higher order than natural language. These procedural metaphors operationalize the figures of the verbal metaphor into a system whose very operation represents the desired position. Here the battle is both metaphoric and material—the player actually does battle against taxes, in a literal sense. *Tax Invaders* constructs a unit operation for the conservative frame on taxation itself. Whereas verbal rhetoric invokes the frame (or context, to use Luntz's word) without acknowledging that it even exists let alone structures the rhetoric, procedural rhetoric depicts the frame in tangible form, in the rules of the game. A game like *Tax Invaders* thus offers an unusual view onto the conservative frame for tax policy. In playing the game, the player is encouraged not only to reaffirm a conservative position on taxation, but also to practice using a conservative frame for that position.

Tax Invaders could thus be used for opposing political purposes. For conservatives it reinforces the notion that taxes are an invasion and that we need to "wage war" against them, as we would against alien invaders. This sort of rhetoric would be much more difficult, or at least more inappropriate, to enact on the soapbox. On the public pulpit, grandstanding politicians rely on the perlocutionary rather than illocutionary effect of their rhetorical frame. In speech act theory, an illocutionary act carries propositional content that the utterance expresses literally. A perlocutionary act carries an effect that is not expressed in the utterance, such as persuasion.[30] *Tax Invaders* offers the unique ability to convert perlocution into illocution. Instead of using verbal frames, the GOP has made the symbolic underpinning of their rhetorical context manifest in the rules of the game itself: a procedural rather than a verbal rhetoric. In essence, *Tax Invaders* is a lesson in how tax policy works for a conservative. The game says "Think of taxation as an invasion meant to harm you" rather than saying "We must fight against tax increases."

For liberals, *Tax Invaders* reinforces the conservative frame on taxation, forcing such players to enact the conservative position that taxation is a theft rather than a contribution to the common social good. Playing the game critically might assist liberals in orienting their frame in opposition to that of conservatives; the game's crudeness only underscores how foundational the metaphor of taxation as theft is for conservative politics and therefore how challenging opposition to it may prove. Each perspective is one side of the same coin: while *Tax Invaders* offers only a very rudimentary treatment of tax policy, it offers a more sophisticated reinforcement of a conservative rhetorical frame on tax policy.

Contestation

Tax Invaders mounts its argument partly through verbal rhetoric (the text inside the game) and partly through visual rhetoric (images of George W. Bush as hero, the imposing descent of taxes). While it does depict the rules that constitute the conservative frame on taxation, it borrows those rules entirely from another videogame. To further understand the way frames and ideological bias function in videogames, we must look at how the interactions of new rules create similar procedural frames anew.

In French artist Martin Le Chevallier's installation game *Vigilance 1.0*, players seek out deviants on surveillance-screen-like sections of an urban environment.[31] The game screen is divided into small squares, each of which displays a different segment and scale of the detailed city. Citizens traverse the environment, executing tasks typical of everyday urban life, such as shopping at the supermarket or relaxing in a park. The player's task is to watch these screens and identify improprieties ranging from littering to vagrancy to prostitution. Armed with a small circular cursor, the player must constantly scan the environment, pointing out infractions by clicking on offenders. For each success, the player is rewarded with points proportional to the severity of the offense (for example, littering is valued at one point, prostitution at five). Erroneous identifications cost the player points for "defamation." The game is programmed to increase or decrease social problems in proportion with the player's success at responding to them. With every offender that passes by unnoticed, the more depraved the society becomes, and vice versa.

Vigilance's rules are incredibly simple. The player can perform one action: censuring citizens. Successes are rewarded and failures punished: for each success the society becomes more pure, for each failure or omission more base. It is a game about surveillance disguised as one about moral depravity, the sixteen rectangular segments of the screen akin to a security guard's video monitors (figure 3.3). The player's "vigilance" quickly devolves into its own perversion, that of unfettered surveillance.

On first blush, the game seems to reinforce the ideological frame of vigilance as safeguard. The game supports this sentiment through its procedural model, which provides positive feedback for increased surveillance. But over time, the game defamiliarizes the player's adopted role as overseer. Because the game creates a positive feedback loop for depravity in the society, any attempt on the player's part to cease his vigilant oversight creates more corruption, reinforcing the need to monitor. By forcing the player to see the consequences of the metaphor of vigilance as comprehensive regulation, the game *challenges* the ideological frame it initially represents. The game's purpose is not to promote surveillance nor moral purity, but to call such values into question by turning the apparently upstanding player into one of the depraved whom he is charged to eliminate. After many minutes faithfully scanning the city's terrain for infractions, the player makes mistaken identifications that help cast doubt on his expertise. *Who am I to judge these people?*,

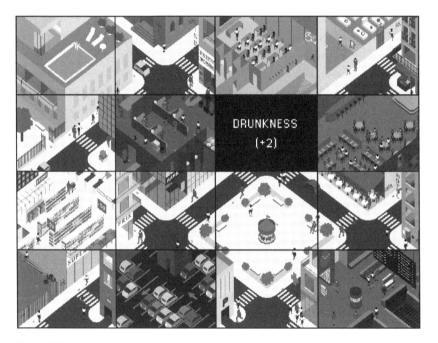

Figure 3.3 The separated views of an abstract urban environment in *Vigilance 1.0* resemble the many screens of a security surveillance system.

the player may begin to ask himself. In so doing, the game casts oversight in a role perhaps no less perverse than moral depravity—prostitution, vagrancy, zoophilia. The game then affords the player a variety of ways to interrogate this disparity.

For one, the game's reinforcement system encourages players to calculate one offense in terms of another: five litterbugs for every prostitute. The notion of equivalence between actions and their consequences evokes another metaphor for political thought, what Lakoff calls "keeping the moral books." In Lakoff's view, we conceptualize well-being as wealth. Changes to our well-being are thus akin to gains and losses.[32] Lakoff characterizes this metaphorical understanding of morality in terms of financial transactions. Individuals and societies alike have "moral debts" and "moral credits" that must sum to zero. Moral accounting implies the need for reciprocation and retribution; good actions must be rewarded, and harmful ones must be punished. That punishment might include restitution, which can in turn take many forms, from contrition to prison. When we speak of criminals who have completed their sentences, we often say that they have "paid their debt to society." In a moral system of this type, "the moral books must be balanced."[33]

In contemporary U.S. politics, a fair society is generally conceived as one in which an authority keeps track of the moral books, or does the moral accounting. This metaphorical chief financial officer takes many forms, from the courts to the police to the parent at the cookie jar. Lakoff identifies one common attitude toward public justice that stems directly from the concept of moral accounting; he calls this model "procedural fairness," or "the impartial rule-based distribution of opportunities to participate, talk, state one's case, and so on."[34] Here the term *procedural* refers to the invocation of legal rules that determine what behavior is allowed and prohibited in a society.

In one version of procedural fairness, the failure to account for improprieties puts the books out of balance. *Vigilance* allows the player to experiment within this frame. The game deploys an arithmetic algorithm to control the amount of depravity that feeds back into the system. Identifying more perverse acts increases the score more rapidly; for example, public drunkenness is worth +2, abandoned trash +1. The player could choose to target only the most egregious acts as a possible strategy for more efficient moral sanctity. But while watching for public urination or prostitution, many more low-level acts will already have begun spiraling the society into further chaos. The frequency of low-level acts increases, giving players an opportunity to locate and identify more litterbugs and drunkards for every prostitute, public urinator, or pedophile.

At the same time, the game forces the player to recognize the consequence of blind moral accounting: when one pedophile equals three drunkards equals six litterbugs, both the acts and the contexts for those acts are occluded. As Lakoff points out, "rule-based fairness invites dispute over how impartial the rules really are."[35] When the player of *Vigilance* clicks indiscriminately on vagrants and violent criminals alike, he is forced to think of each as a variety of the same, underlying moral depravity. The game does not afford the player the ability to consider the impartiality of the rules of surveillance, and thus invites reflection on the nature of each particular act. Why is the drunkard drunk? Is he unaware of social convention? Is he mentally ill and in need of assistance? Has he suffered a personal tragedy and is calling out for empathy?

I have previously argued that simulations exist in the gap between rule-based representations and a user's subjectivity. *Vigilance* thus provides a variety of player-configurable lenses through which to consider and reconsider the ideological frame of vigilance as inviolability. As the player identifies more and more deviants, the game slowly but progressively changes its focus from balancing the society's moral books to questioning procedural fairness as a legitimate strategy for running the society in the first place. Most explicitly, *Vigilance* attempts to identify such moral bookkeeping as a disturbing panopticon.[36] But the game also challenges other aspects of the frame of justice as balanced moral books: its view of moral depravation and criminality as a slippery slope of interrelated behaviors, and its construal of social justice as removal or incarceration rather than social support and reformation.

Implication

Both *Vigilance 1.0* and *Tax Invaders* could be seen as special cases, games created with ideological framing as a foremost goal, one for artistic reasons, one for political reasons. Commercial games may be less deliberate in their rhetoric, but they are not necessarily free from ideological framing; such games may display complex procedural rhetorics with or without the conscious intention of the designers. While the rhetorical intentions of the GOP or artists like Le Chevallier are palpable, the relative obscurity of these games restricts their influence. But procedural rhetorics in commercial games—the most successful of which easily sell millions of copies—trade forthrightness for authority. And that authority can occlude the ideological frames that such commercial games operationalize, rendering them implicit and in need of critique.

In *Grand Theft Auto: San Andreas*, players enact the life of an early '90s Los Angeles gangbanger.[37] Whereas previous iterations of the series favored stylized representations of historico-fictional times and places, *San Andreas* takes on a cultural moment steeped deeply in racial and economic politics.[38] Rather than taking on the role of an organized criminal, the player is cast as CJ, an inner-city gangster. GTA's use of large navigable spaces and open-ended gameplay have been widely cited and praised, but in *San Andreas* open gameplay, expansive virtual spaces, and the inner-city collide to underscore opportunity biases.

San Andreas added a new dynamic to the core GTA gameplay: the player-character must eat to maintain his stamina and strength. However, the only nourishment in the game comes from fast food restaurants (chicken, burgers, or pizza, as shown in figure 3.4). Eating moderately maintains energy, but eating high-fat-content foods increases CJ's weight, and fat gangsters can't run or fight very effectively. Each food item in the game comes at a cost, and

Figure 3.4 The player must eat in *Grand Theft Auto: San Andreas* to maintain stamina and strength, but only fast food is available.

the player's funds are limited. Mirroring real fast food restaurants, less fattening foods like salad cost more than high-calorie super-meals.

The dietary features of *San Andreas* are rudimentary, but the fact that the player must feed his character to continue playing does draw attention to the limited material conditions the game provides for satisfying that need, subtly exposing the fact that problems of obesity and malnutrition in poor communities can partly be attributed to the relative ease and affordability of fast food. Evidence suggests that citizens on fixed incomes like students and the working poor have easiest access to fast food, and as a result of this convenience they eat more of it. Fast food has even penetrated our healthcare infrastructure itself; more than a third of top U.S. hospitals have a fast food outlet on premises.[39] Nutritionist Marion Nestle has devoted much of her career to identifying the relationship between nutrition, food policy, and food industry marketing. Obesity, argues Nestle, replaced dietary insufficiency as the major nutritional problem in the United States in the hundred years since the turn of the nineteenth century.[40] Nestle traces the connections between obesity and a food industry intent on increasing food consumption to drive up profits. One major contributor to the problem is portion size. According to Nestle, Americans consume relatively large portions of over one third of all foods, including bread, french fries, and soft drinks.[41] The familiar "super size" fast food option is one example, immortalized in Morgan Spurlock's Oscar-nominated documentary *Super Size Me*.[42] At the time when *San Andreas* reached the peak of its popularity, Americans simultaneously bit their nails about avian flu, contemplated chemical weapons attacks at marine ports, and stuffed themselves with high-sugar Krispy Kreme donuts, cholesterol-raising hydrogenated oils, and high-fat, low-nutrient foods. Fad diets like the Atkins plan focus on quick results at the cost of long-term health. Nestle's and Spurlock's work underscores the same basic principle: obesity and other threats to public health are at best encouraged, at worst directly caused by the food market itself.

The tension between personal responsibility and social forces is related to another of Lakoff's metaphors for political thought, what he calls "moral strength."[43] Moral strength entails the courage to stand up to both internal and external evils, and it is fundamentally related to will. In Lakoff's model, moral strength comes from self-discipline and self-denial. The disciplined man is strong, and therefore moral, whereas the man who cannot stand up to temptation is weak, and therefore immoral. Lakoff explicitly links moral strength with asceticism. Self-indulgence and "moral flabbiness" are domains of the morally weak.[44] Lakoff argues that moral strength is a fundamentally conservative political frame that stands in contrast to the liberal equivalent, empathy and nurturance.[45]

It is no accident that flabbiness would come up in a discussion of moral strength. In the conservative frame, obesity and poor health are tied to self-control: the ability to assess and resist the internal temptation to eat the wrong food, or to overeat. In such a worldview, a problem like obesity has nothing to do with the food industry Nestle, Spurlock, and others renounce. The executives at fast food corporations and the proprietors of their franchises are simply fulfilling another aspect of conservative moral strength. Businesspeople are morally strong agents with enough self-discipline to work hard and earn material success.[46] The apparent differences between the morally strong entrepreneur and the morally weak overeater are not contradictory for conservatives; the latter are conceived as lesser citizens by the morally strong conservative, and gaining material advantage at their expense only further underscores both the moral and material superiority of the former. In Lakoff's own words, the conservative frame of moral strength "rules out any explanations in terms of social forces or social class."[47]

That fast food restaurants represent the only path to sustenance in *Grand Theft Auto: San Andreas*, and that such sustenance is required to progress and achieve goals in the game suggests two possible interpretations. For one part, the fact that food comes only from fast food joints implies a social condition inherent to the fast food and packaged food industries, one that recalls Nestle's critique: for the less fortunate in particular, the cheap, factory-style, high-fat, low-nutrient food of the burger joint or taco hut offers the easiest and most viable way to fill a grumbling stomach. When these establishments try to provide more healthful meals (like salads) they come at a cost premium: as I write this in late 2005, a McDonalds "premium salad" costs $4.99, whereas a Big Mac costs $2.59, nearly half as much.[48] Under this interpretation, *San Andreas*'s enforcement of fast food eating serves to expose the social forces that drive the poor and working-class residents of the inner city to consume fast food habitually. The game even allows the player to reap the health detriments of a fast food diet in the form of lost stamina and diminished respect (see below for more on the latter).

Even if the player does not play enough (or eat enough) to make CJ turn from a lithe youth into a portly one, the game's insistence that the player eat only at fast food restaurants draws attention to the social reality of poverty and its related health effects. Players of *San Andreas* might leave the game and make new observations about the world around them, and about how social opportunity and disclosure often overshadow the issue of self-restraint.

At the same time, the game seems to allow the player to overcome the social conditions of poverty and poor nutrition through hard work—a textbook example of moral strength. No matter what the player eats in the pizza place or the chicken hut, he can always build a ripped chest and six-pack for CJ by working out consistently in the game's gym. Furthermore, the more "healthful" salad meals at the restaurants cost more money, and the player earns money primarily through the "work" of playing the game. To be fair, that work is almost exclusively limited to violent crime, a topic I will return to shortly. Despite its apparent support for nutrition as a condition of social station, *San Andreas* allows the player to overcome that condition through relatively simple, if sometimes tedious, work and exercise. Such rules might tilt the game toward a more conservative frame, one in which discipline and hard work can overcome material conditions.

The game's use of unbounded virtual space presents a less ambiguous frame for social class, race, and criminality. *San Andreas* intricately recreates representations of three huge cities (the equivalents of Los Angeles, San Francisco, and Las Vegas) along with rural spaces in between. CJ has recently returned to his hometown neighborhood (the San Andreas equivalent of L.A.'s Compton). The player can customize CJ's clothes to some extent and, invoking the game's title, steal nice cars for him, but he remains a black youth from Compton. Thanks to the immense simulated space of the city, the player can travel from neighborhood to neighborhood; the buildings, scenery, vehicles, and people adjust accordingly, and appropriately.[49] But something remains the same everywhere in San Andreas, from its Compton to its Beverly Hills: no matter the location, the game's nonplayer characters (NPCs) respond to the player's semiautomatic-toting, do-rag wearing black gangsta character in roughly the same way. In fact, they respond the same even if the player dons absurd clothes, underpants on the outside.[50]

While major technology challenges impede the development of credible character interactions in an environment as large scale as San Andreas and its surrounds, the game makes no effort to alter character behavior based on race, social standing, or location.[51] Bumping into a leggy blonde on the equivalent of Beverly Hills' Rodeo Drive elicits the same anonymous outcry as would jostling a drug dealer on Compton's Atlantic Drive. When mediated by the game's inner-city context, its procedural interaction of space and character creates a frame in which the player's street gang persona does not participate in any historical, economic, racial, or social disadvantage. The aggregate procedural effects in *San Andreas* thus expose another ideological frame, and perhaps a surprising one.

Lakoff argues that the conservative frame for crime is an extension of the "strict father" model of seeing the world. The strict father disciplines his children and acts as a moral authority. Through this example, he instills discipline and self-reliance. Self-reliant, morally disciplined adults make the right decisions and prosper. Morally depraved adults do not deserve to prosper and may even be dangerous. Lakoff contrasts the conservative strict father with the progressive "nurturing parent." Unlike the strict father, the nurturing parent believes that support and assistance help people thrive, and that people who need help deserve to be helped. Nurturing parents reject self-discipline as the sole justification of prosperity and allow for economic, cultural, or social disadvantages that might suggest some people deserve even more assistance.

By avoiding interactions across the socioeconomic boundaries of the game's virtual space, *San Andreas* is implicated in a logic similar to the conservative frame on crime. If the game's NPC logic were to admit that cultural and economic disadvantages are factors that mediate interaction between characters, it would also have to admit that such factors are external to CJ (the player's character) and thus attributable to something outside CJ's character and self-discipline. As in the case of nutrition, from a frame of moral strength CJ's criminal behavior can be explained only by a lack of self-control and self-discipline. Any morally upstanding young man would find a legitimate job and earn his way off the street without resorting to criminality. But interestingly, the game turns this frame in on itself. To succeed in the mission-based story of *San Andreas*, the player effectively builds a sizable, if illegitimate, business of thug activities—based on a staple of drive-by shootings and armed robbery.

Yet, the game is a veritable rags-to-riches story. As the game starts, CJ is returning to Los Santos from Liberty City (the home city of *GTA III*), where he had fled the gang-ridden streets of his youth, presumably as a reformed man. He returns only to bury his mother, another victim of gang violence, and gets caught up in reclaiming his old neighborhood from the rival gangs who are dismantling it. As CJ, the player must build "respect" between both his own and rival gang members, eventually earning their trust and constructing an ever-larger gang of followers.

The addition of respect signals an unusual perversion of the traditional, conservative concept of moral authority. On the one hand, CJ's life on the street bears a striking resemblance to that of the political conservative: he takes responsibility for his family and takes it upon himself to build a new life of material wealth and personal safety. His authority demands respect from others, and those whose respect he demands stand subordinate to him. His own personal self-discipline even contributes to this respect: a well-padded CJ who eats too many burgers and doesn't work out earns less respect than a muscle-ripped CJ. On the other hand, CJ earns such respect through felonious behavior. He acts with a similar underlying value structure as the ideal conservative, but uses lawless rather than lawful material production as his medium. This inversion of the typical conservative frame could be read as a satire—the very same rules of behavior can produce a very different outcome from the one they are taken to bring about.

But outside of the game's tightly woven mission-based storyline, *Grand Theft Auto: San Andreas* also implies support for the metaphor of crime as decadence. Despite its purported open-endedness, *San Andreas* offers incentives to fulfill its missions, and thus incentives to engage in simulated criminal behavior. Although the game's premise does question whether gang members have legitimate moral options—at the start of the game CJ is set up by a corrupt cop and sent on the run—once outside of the mission architecture the game has no procedure in place to mediate character interactions. Notably, the open-ended gameplay reorients the player back toward the missions; the game will not unlock areas beyond Los Santos unless the player reaches key waypoints in the missions. Despite its narrative gestures toward subverting the gang as a possible social adaptation, the game situates its missions as small accidents in the broader urban logic. As the player exits the open urban environment and reenters the missions, he does so willingly, not under the duress of a complex socio-historical precondition. This rhetoric implicitly affirms the metaphor of criminal behavior as moral depravity.

Whether or not *San Andreas*'s creators intended the game to support or critique contemporary conservative ideological structures in the United States is an open question. But the fact that the game has been so universally reviled, not only by the "values-oriented" conservative right but also by centrists like Senators Hillary Clinton and Joseph Lieberman, suggests that neither side has actually played the game. How surprised the conservatives would be to find that a group of Scottish game developers may have placed tens of millions of copies of conservative political rhetoric in the waiting hands of contemporary American youth, including many inner-city youth who would normally be predisposed to oppose Republicans' pro-business, anti–social program stances. And how surprised the liberals might be to find that they have the perfect object lesson for counteracting conservative frames about poverty, class, race, and crime already installed on the nation's PlayStations.

Designing Procedural Frames

Politicians are already familiar with Lakoff's and Luntz's strategies on framing political speech, especially public speech. Those who wish to create videogames as endorsed or disruptive political speech will undoubtedly need to pay more attention to the use of context in such games. A shift away from verbal and toward procedural contextualization in such games will likely take longer. Lakoff argues that the central role in contemporary politics (and he has progressive politics in mind in particular) is to breathe new life into an otherwise bankrupt political discourse.[52] This restructuring is necessary because citizens tend to assume that language and its carriers—from politicians to news media—are neutral. The public has little purchase on the "moral conceptual systems" that underwrite verbal and written political utterances themselves.

Understanding a political position, argues Lakoff, "requires fitting it into an unconscious matrix of family-based morality." It is worth noting the urgent and somewhat desperate note on which Lakoff ends *Moral Politics*:

In short, public discourse as it currently exists is not very congenial to the discussion of the findings of this study. Analysis of metaphor and the idea of alternative conceptual systems are not part of public discourse. Most people don't even know that they have conceptual systems, much less how they are structured. This does not mean that the characterizations of conservatism and liberalism in this book cannot be discussed publicly. They can and should be. What requires special effort is discussing the unconscious conceptual framework behind the discussion.[53]

Lakoff has called this process "shifting the frame."[54] Perhaps the most promising future political role of videogames will be to help citizens take on precisely this challenge. As an example of procedural systems, the videogame is the only medium of mass appeal across many ages, demographics, and social and ethnic backgrounds that relies on conceptual frameworks—rule-based interactions—as its core mode of signification. We do not find it surprising when films like *Fahrenheit 9/11*[55] or television series like *The Daily Show* make explicit, outright attempts to change political affinity.[56] This is not yet the case for videogames. But unlike consumers of film, television, books, and other linear media, videogame players are accustomed to analyzing the interaction of proceduralized logics as a part of the play experience. Whereas particular political interests have effectively colonized some media—liberals and documentary film, conservatives and talk radio, for example—videogames remain indefinite about their political bent. This situation underscores both a promise and a threat. On the one hand, the medium of the videogame has not (yet) become attached to a particular worldview, thus welcoming all varieties of ideological frames. On the other hand, lessons from other media suggest that the political groups with stronger media strategies effectively lock out other voices. The questionable success of liberal talk radio station Air America provides an instructive example—the Left has nearly been banished from the airwaves because the conservatives became entrenched on them so much earlier. Although it is first an analysis of political discourse, George Lakoff's *Moral Politics* could equally be described as a scathing critique of the failure of liberal political discourse. Perhaps today it seems optimistic to claim that videogames might offer the most salient locus for discussions of how we think about political problems. But in time, and perhaps not much of it, we will wonder why it took so long to realize that games have been a part of public political discourse all along. And when that time comes, it would be unfortunate for one set of political positions to have so colonized the medium as to taint it for dissenting opinion.

Digital Democracy

If the 2000 U.S. presidential election made citizens more aware of the process of counting votes, the 2004 election made us more aware of the process of campaigning for them. Ten years after the widespread availability of the Internet and the World Wide Web outside of scientific and academic communities, and four years after the burst of the dotcom bubble, the 2004 election was the first to make broad use of digital technologies beyond the "storefront-style" website of the last two election cycles. Part of this delay had to do with timing—with four years between major elections, the campaigns, candidates, and party organizations didn't benefit from the continuous advances of internet technology in the 1990s. Successful exceptions mostly came in the form of public affairs firms, for example Grassroots.com, a technology firm chaired by ex–Clinton press secretary Mike McCurry that specializes in online advocacy and recruitment.[1] Such efforts primarily focused on corporate interests, trade associations, nonprofit and nongovernmental organizations (NPOs and NGOs). In short, technology-aided advocacy largely remained the purview of private groups with specialized communications needs.

Meanwhile, Internet access among U.S. voters rose dramatically during the decade between 1994 and 2004. Citizens learned they could buy everything online, from books to gas grills. Ebay ushered in a new era of niche microbusiness; E*Trade and Ameritrade marked a new form of electronic banking and investment. Local and state governments launched e-government initiatives to provide their citizens with online access to services like motor vehicle registration and tax filing. According to the Pew Internet and American Life

Project, 63 percent of adult U.S. citizens were Internet users at the end of 2004, compared with roughly 50 percent in 2000. Yet in a 2000 postelection survey of Internet use carried out specifically for civics and politics, the Institute for Policy, Democracy, and the Internet (IPDI) concluded that roughly 35 percent of U.S. citizens use the Internet to get information about politics.[2] An analysis of online campaigning in the 2000 election estimated 9 million visits to the Bush 2000 website and 7 million to the Gore 2000 site;[3] visits to the Bush 2004 website nearly doubled to 16 million visits and Kerry 2004 visits nearly tripled to 20 million.[4] These results suggest that on the whole, during the last national election cycle a larger percentage of U.S. citizens were using the Internet for political purposes even than for more familiar purposes like online shopping.

In 2003, major candidates finally started taking greater advantage of the public's hunger for easily accessible information on politics and public policy. Led by campaign manager Joe Trippi's then-controversial decision to pursue hundreds of thousands of individual supporters and donors rather than fewer corporate and institutional supporters, Howard Dean's long-shot campaign for president spawned numerous innovative uses of the Internet for campaigning. In a commentary affirming "that the internet has become an essential medium of American politics," analyst Michael Cornfield outlines five online campaigning innovations that came out of the Dean campaign:

news-pegged fundraising appeals
"meetups" and other net-organized gatherings
blogging
online referenda
decentralized decision making[5]

Dean's news-pegged fundraising appeals solicited immediate responses to news events, many of which included traditional Republican $2,000/plate fundraisers. Meetups took advantage of interest-sharing website MeetUp.com to help supporters self-organize in specific localities.[6] Blogging, a burgeoning social phenomenon inside and outside politics, created virtual communities in the same way meetups created physical ones. Blogs also gave supporters (and detractors) ad hoc access to read, comment on, or write personal perspectives on candidates and issues. Online referenda, an offshoot of blogging and news-pegged fundraising, allowed the campaign to ask its constituency for an opinion—a kind of casual, nonbinding referendum. And decentralized decision making underwrote the other four innovations, giving power and voice to the electorate.

One notable omission from Cornfield's list of innovations is social software. A form of online community building, social software systems are web-based applications that let people construct networks of person-to-person interactions. Over the past several years, the most popular of these have been *Friendster* and *MySpace*, services that let people find new friends among their friends' friends.[7] *MySpace* bills itself as a social service best used for dating and finding new friends, although it is often (incorrectly) dismissed as a tool for youth culture alone. When users sign up for the service, they create a profile that describes their interests, location, and other basic information. Subscribers are then encouraged to invite their friends to join. Each member can search or browse through the network of friends and friends' friends and so on. If they find someone they'd like to meet, the service facilitates a permission-based introduction through the links that connect the two parties. More specific applications of social software include tools like *LinkedIn*, which facilitate business relationships instead of arbitrary personal ones. *LinkedIn* places a special focus placed on deal making, job hunting, and recruiting.[8]

In the aftermath of the 2004 election, political uses of technology remained focused on extensions and revisions of the five Dean campaign innovations, with the addition of initiative-specific social software. As focus moves from campaigning to advocacy, NPOs and NGOs have taken up individual contributions, blog and blog-like communications, and ad hoc organization as guiding strategies. For example, the nonprofit Spirit of America has relied on the network effect of individual contributions to raise money for specific development projects in Afghanistan and Iraq, such as baseball equipment for local communities or sewing machines for local laborers.[9] The organization then builds social software–style hooks for members to recruit other members, a kind of automated grassroots outreach that is sometimes called "emergent democracy."[10] Following current trends in marketing, such campaigns often strive to capitalize on the uneven connectedness of a small percentage of the population. By appealing to so-called influentials, one can create a broad base of supporters.[11]

Without exception, all of these innovations take advantage of the Internet's affordances for rapid updates and ad hoc access. These initiatives represent a new type of "virtual grassroots outreach," using the Internet as a bonding agent for ad hoc communities of constantly involved constituents. As history would show, Dean would be remembered more for his innovations in politicking than for his politics, a point to which I will return later. However, all of these techniques also have another common property: they rely on computer technology solely for its ability to change and accelerate dissemination, not for its ability to change representation. In short, what political technology lacks is a meaningful engagement with procedurality.

As I introduced in chapter 1, Janet Murray identifies four essential properties of digital artifacts: procedurality, participation, spatiality, and encyclopedic scope. The Howard Dean innovations and their successors currently take advantage of two, sometimes three of these properties. All current political technology harnesses the participatory nature of the medium; if nothing else, blogs and news-pegged fundraising create coherent, ongoing interaction with a campaign or initiative, allowing user commentary and contribution. Blogs and meetups also take advantage of the spatial property of the computer, creating coherent environments for voters to explore. Meetups even span the gap between virtual and physical spaces. And the ease of publishing and storing news, comments, and conversations on blogs and via online referenda take advantage of the encyclopedic affordances of computers—their ability to store and retrieve massive quantities and varieties of information. But none of the popular techniques for Internet-based campaigning takes significant advantage of the procedural affordances of the medium (see table 4.1 for a comparison).

Videogame Histories

In order to suggest a corrective for this state of affairs, it is useful to look at procedural representations of phenomena similar to public policy in structure

Table 4.1 The intersection of the four main Dean campaign innovations with Murray's four properties of the computer as a medium.

	Procedural	Spatial	Participatory	Encyclopedic
News-pegged fundraising			X	
Net-organized gatherings	X	X	X	X
Blogging	X	X	X	X
Online referenda			X	X

and nature. One popular genre of commercial videogames offers procedural representations of history, a field grounded in similar material and social conditions as politics. These games create representations of causal factors that shaped either particular historical events or the general progression of human history. Some of those games serve as explicit political commentaries while others do so implicitly. Games like *Civilization*[12] and *Empire Earth* focus on the progress of history from era to era.[13] As software systems, these games can be seen as historiographies, representing history with rules of interaction rather than patterns of writing. In *Civilization*, material and technological innovation enables civic and military dominance, which the player must exercise to progress through history effectively. In *Empire Earth*, local events serve as parts of an overarching, Hegelian progress forward. Games like *Zeus*[14] and *Medieval: Total War* attempt to expose the salient traits of specific historical moments.[15] In *Zeus*, historico-mythical concepts like Hercules' labors take shape in the context of the material production required to support them, such as mining marble to build a temple suitable for invoking the hero. Educational technologist and games-and-learning theorist Kurt Squire has shown that *Civilization* offers students a better understanding of world history, especially the relationship between physical, cultural, and political geography and history.[16] The historical representation of *Civilization* bears a striking resemblance to that of Diamond's *Guns, Germs, and Steel*, mentioned briefly in chapter 1, and discussed in detail in chapter 8.[17]

As I suggested in the previous chapter, videogames are increasingly becoming a forum for artistic expression and political expression. The field of digital art has produced a wealth of social commentaries, and some game-based artifacts have emerged from that sphere of influence. Many of these take the form of electronic game modifications or "mods," alterations of existing commercial games. In 1999, artist Anne-Marie Schleiner and collaborators designed a mod called *Velvet-Strike* for the popular multiplayer first-person shooter *Counter-Strike*, discussed earlier as a counterpoint to *America's Army*.[18] *Velvet-Strike* asks players to spray virtual posters with political messages such as "Hostage of an Online Fantasy" and "You are your most dangerous enemy." While interesting as a "software intervention," *Velvet-Strike* is more a commentary on videogame genre conventions than a commentary on social conditions. The rich sensory environment of the videogame becomes merely a setting for protests against the fantasy of violence and power.

Games like Chris Crawford's *Balance of Power* and *Balance of the Planet* take on a social challenge through gameplay proper. In Crawford's words, *Balance of the Planet* deals with "the complexity of environmental issues and their entwinement with each other and with economic issues. . . . everything is connected . . . simplistic approaches always fail."[19] *Balance of the Planet* allows the player to simulate an adjustable value system, to witness the effects of that value system, and to carry that perception beyond the gameplay experience. But, as discussed in the previous two chapters, the game removes the procedural model from a representation of the sensory world, rather the opposite gesture as *Velvet-Strike*.

While videogame-based recreations of historical events like D-Day[20] and Pearl Harbor have been common for the last two decades, recent videogames have taken on more specific moments in history, fashioning themselves after another newly politicized medium, the documentary film.[21] Among this new subgenre, several examples stand out.

Two such games were created explicitly in the context of artistic practice. Los Angeles artist collective C-Level created *Waco Resurrection*, a game-based reenactment of the 1993 stand-off between the U.S. Alcohol, Tobacco, and Firearms (ATF) agents and David Koresh's Branch Davidian followers.[22] In the game, players don a plastic David Koresh mask with implanted microphone and are "resurrected" into a 3D representation of the Branch Davidians' Waco, Texas compound. Once inside, players must use voice commands to enact incantations that give Koresh the ability to do divine battle against the ATF, convert agents to his cause, and lead followers around his compound (figure 4.1). The same year, artist collective Kinematic released *9-11 Survivor*, a game in which the player is challenged to escape the burning World Trade Center towers on September 11, 2001.[23] In the game, the player is spawned in a pseudo-random location in the building. Controversially, some locations have escape routes via stairway, some are blocked by fire, and some are simply dead ends. In certain cases, players are faced with the choice of being engulfed by flames in the building or throwing themselves from windows.

Such games are not limited to the sphere of art practice, a community with a long history of challenging and upsetting social norms. Commercial developers have created at least two games of equal note, each with a hybrid interest in historical expression and commercial gain. In 2003, Kuma Reality Games released *Kuma\War*.[24] *Kuma\War* wasn't just one game about one event, but rather a sort of subscription network for game-based representations of

Figure 4.1 *Waco Resurrection* compels the player to recite mysterious incantations to invoke different powers (see the upper left side of the image). Image courtesy of C-level (Mark Allen, Peter Brinson, Brody Condon, Jessica Hutchins, Eddo Stern, and Michael Wilson).

recent news events. Released during the moil of the first year of the second Gulf War, *Kuma\War*'s first mission challenged the player to reenact the U.S. Army's stand against Uday and Qusay Hussein near a Mosul villa. As part of the company's launch press, they touted the player's ability to choose whether to follow the events of history—in this case destroying the entire villa with antitank missiles—or attempting an alternate plan, such as overrunning the villa in the hopes of capturing and interrogating the Hussein brothers. Since July 2003, Kuma has released dozens of additional missions, including the 1998 breaching of Osama Bin Laden's compound and John Kerry's controversial 1969 Silver Star swiftboat mission. According to the Kuma Games, the purpose of *Kuma\War* is to give Americans a better appreciation for the dangers faced by U.S. and coalition soldiers in conflict.

But perhaps the most controversial of all of these documentary games is *JFK Reloaded*, created and self-published by Scottish developer Traffic.[25] Released on the forty-first anniversary of John F. Kennedy's assassination, *JFK*

Reloaded puts the player in the shoes of Lee Harvey Oswald on the sixth floor of the Texas Schoolbook Depository. The developers claim to have created the game to put to rest any suspicions of a conspiracy theory of the assassination, and to that end they set up the game to allow the "re-creation" of the Warren Commission's account of the shooting. The simulation includes a sophisticated physics and ballistics model, and the player's only task is to use that physical model to recreate Oswald's three shots and their trajectories as accurately as possible. After firing, the game offers a replay and analysis, showing paths and impacts for each bullet. The developers even offered a $100,000 reward for the player able to match the Warren Commission's account most accurately. Senator Ted Kennedy and others called the game "despicable," and the media in general had a field day objecting—and therefore drawing attention—to it.

Tracy Fullerton has discussed the ways in which these games relate to the genre of documentary film and especially the latter medium's history of both recording events and expressing or theorizing about them.[26] Because games like *Kuma\War* and *9-11 Survivor* appear to take on specific, historical events, it's only natural to compare them with other media forms like documentary. In fact, the creators of all these games have explicitly aligned their artifacts with filmic and televisual media—C-level compares *Waco Resurrection* to documentary; Kuma Reality Games claims that *Kuma\War* offers "a new way of experiencing the news"; Traffic calls *JFK Reloaded* a "docugame." These gestures stand largely as posturing: part of the goal of such games is to challenge the notion that games cannot or do not take on a broader range of topics. But the comparison with documentary occludes an important aspect of these games, namely, their procedurality. Although the subject matter itself is comparable to documentaries and news broadcasts, to understand what the games are saying about these historical events we need to ask how the player interacts with procedural rules to create patterns of historical and social meaning.

Waco Resurrection's most salient feature is not the representation of the Branch Davidians' Waco compound—a simple feat of 3D modeling—but the use of voice commands as a primary input method. By obliging the player to utter Koresh's messianic interpretations of the book of revelation, the player is forcibly immersed in the logic of a religious cult. The words the player chants are not his own but those of Koresh, and the player quickly becomes absorbed in the power of these incantations. The game embodies a specific cult, but it creates an experience of religious fanaticism in general and shows how such fanaticism conflicts with the interests of government. While its skin is that of the Branch Davidians, the procedural expression at work in *Waco Resurrection* serves to depict the lure and madness of religious fanaticism in general and to remind the player how fine the line is between sensible "state-sanctioned" activities and threatening cultic religious practice, using the Davidians' example as a model, or a paradigm in rhetorical terms. On further review, *Waco Resurrection* suggests that the 1993 Waco event exemplifies an entire system of contemporary American religious expression and extremism. But unlike the "authorized" religious fervor of, say, fundamentalist Christianity, fanaticism of the Branch Davidian sort is illegitimate, unsupported, and in fact in need of government intervention and dismantling.

Similarly, *9-11 Survivor*'s procedural expression extends beyond the apparent representation of one person's potential doom in the World Trade Center towers. Although the game has been denounced for trivializing the victims' fates, the game's relevance comes from its solemn and careful treatment of victims' actual and potential experiences. *9-11 Survivor*'s procedural expression arises principally from the interplay between spawn locations in the building and obstacles the player might face while trying to escape. One of the more horrifying memories we nonvictims have of 9/11 is of watching so many people throw themselves out of windows eighty or ninety floors up rather than burn alive inside. These people must have known the certain doom they faced by jumping, and such knowledge only further underscores how ghastly the situation must have been inside the building. By creating an aleatory representation of the fate of a World Trade Center worker, *9-11 Survivor* offers one of the few representations of the intertwined role of chance and chaos on that fateful morning. During some sessions of *9-11 Survivor* the player has no escape; during others the player is faced with the decision to burn or to jump; during others escape is possible, but not easy (see figure 4.2 for one scenario).

Beyond an embodied experience of the procedural interactions between plane, building, and worker, *9-11 Survivor* depicts the strange new logic of security and terror in our post-9/11 world. Uncertainty is perhaps the most ineffable of topics in this "war on terror," a political frame that attempts to recast geopolitics into a traditional battle in which there are known enemies and known winners. Yet *9-11 Survivor* addresses precisely this uncertainty, which the game represents through its (admittedly simple) procedural

Figure 4.2 In *9-11 Survivor*, the player is thrown into the desperate situation of a World Trade Center worker seeking a path out of the building.

generation of scenarios, exit options, and limited tool use in extremely dangerous conditions. *9-11 Survivor* invites us to empathize with the victims of the WTC attacks, but more so it invites us to reflect on all the potential traps and escapes in our workplaces, homes, shopping malls, and public spaces— to consider our changed relationship with such spaces since 9/11.

Unlike *9-11 Survivor* and *Waco Resurrection*, *Kuma\War* offers a less procedurally expressive relationship between players and current U.S. foreign policy. Although Kuma offers "re-creations of real-world events," it builds scarcely few procedural hooks into such experiences beyond those required to carry out the historical account along with perhaps one alternate scenario on the same strategic trajectory. Missing from *Kuma\War* are political and social circumstances, commentary, and any elucidation that would frame these events in order to give the first-person interactivity of the game sociopolitical meaning. In rhetorical terms, *Kuma\War* advances no political propositions; rather, it simply skins the traditional first-person wargame with images and scenarios from recent military events.

Consider the game's launch scenario, capturing or killing the Hussein brothers at Mosul. Players do not gain any meaningful insight into the subtle tenors of U.S. military aggression when they choose between either advancing troops to slaughter perimeter guards in order to capture Uday and Qusay Hussein or bombarding the area to destruction. A more subtle rhetoric surrounds the military's need to capture or kill (either one) Uday and Qusay in order to demonstrate control over the regime's demise, and thereby to win further local support. No matter the outcome, the military gesture of controlling these two high-level figures serves a strategic goal in the broader U.S. campaign, both in Iraq and on the homefront. Disabling the two sends a message of progress to the nation at home; their status as sons of the Iraqi leader, who had been singled out as a principal threat to the United States, suggests that the war effort makes material progress, not just temporal progress. Likewise, dismantling the existing power structure in Iraq, no matter its relative merits or evils, demonstrates the military will and might of the United States to the local people. In either case, it does not really matter if Uday and Qusay are captured or killed; both outcomes succeed in their desired strategic result.

Such military rhetoric is untouched in the *Kuma\War* mission. Unlike *Waco Resurrection*, *Kuma\War* offers a relatively weak procedural representation of the social aspects of modern-day warfare, providing the ballistics, troop movement, and chain-of-command necessary to produce a playable wargame, but leaving out the local, national, and international political structures that give such encounters meaning. John Kerry's Silver Star mission held political currency because so much credibility rested on Kerry's status as war hero. Democrats held him up as a compassionate leader with military credentials; Republicans derided him as an indecisive rube without the backbone to lead. The Silver Star mission represents an important moment in Kerry's ontogeny, but divorced from the record of the rest of his public and private life, the mission only vaguely re-creates the fact that Kerry's military status might be a political issue of some kind, rather than exploring how or why it would be. The mission as re-created in *Kuma\War* doesn't provide an adequate representation of the logic in Kerry's own mind—his rules of engagement, so to speak—to make it an effective window onto his quality as a leader, then or now.

Of these games about historical events, perhaps the one with the strongest yet most confused procedural rhetoric is *JFK Reloaded*. While the game offers the smallest spatial representation of the four games—the player's control is limited to the view out of the sixth-floor book depository window, and the entire game world reproduces only half of Dealey Plaza (figures 4.2, 4.3)—it offers a richness of interaction thanks to the heavily proceduralized representation of the motorcade itself. Instead of using a static animation of the motorcade's path along its historical trajectory, the game accounts for interruptions or disturbances in that progression based on a model of physics and agency.

Although the designers encourage players to re-create the assassination as realistically as possible, no player was able to re-create the event successfully within the constraints of reported history. Given that *JFK Reloaded* had an explicit persuasive goal—to affirm the Warren Commission report and disprove conspiracy theories—it would appear to be a rhetorical failure. But emergent features in the game's design facilitate other interpretations, suggesting that the developer's stated goal was a ruse meant to inspire new

Figure 4.3 The controversial game *JFK Reloaded* thrusts the player into the disturbing role of presidential assassin. © Traffic Management Limited, Scotland.

perspectives on the historical event itself. Clever players quickly realized that alternate strategies produce intriguing results. In the historical record and according to the Abraham Zapruder film, Kennedy was shot about halfway along Elm street, the street directly in front of the book depository. *JFK Reloaded*'s simulation starts just before the motorcade peers around the County Criminal Courts building on the corner of Houston and Main streets. If the player sights properly before the motorcade's arrival, he can successfully execute William Greer, the presidential limousine's driver, just before he turns right onto Houston from Main. Because the game runs both a physics simulation aware of inertia and an agent simulation aware of causality, shooting the driver alternately stops the vehicle or causes it to speed ahead, onto the grass of Dealey Plaza or into an embankment on the other side of Houston street. Once the vehicle stops, the assassin has a relatively clear shot at a stationary president in the back of the limo. And this scenario is but one of many alternatives made possible by the procedural interaction of the motorcade's physics model and the passenger casualty behaviors.

Without a doubt, it is disquieting to take on the historical role of Lee Harvey Oswald, seeing through his eyes in the rifle sight. But such an experience offers new insights into the political context for the historical event itself. As someone who has no personal memory of Kennedy or his assassination, the man and the event have only ever entered my consciousness as mythology. *JFK Reloaded* had two distinct effects on me as a player and as a citizen. First, it simulates the sniper-assassin like no other videogame I have played. Many—perhaps most—games put the player in first-person view behind a firearm, but few are as physically demanding as *JFK Reloaded*. The precision and accuracy required to pull off the three shots of the Warren Commission Report not only struck me as nearly impossible (again casting doubt rather than clarity on the historical record) but also gave me the chilling feeling of the assassin's psychopathy. The precision of the game's stated goal helps the player depersonalize its consequences, further emphasizing the simulation of the psychopath-assassin. The quiet deliberateness the act demands is difficult to reproduce in the anonymous secret agent situations like those of *Splinter Cell*.[27]

Second, the game creates an impression of the performative nature of assassination itself, the planned, almost choreographed actions and their potential impact on a populous. The simulation seemed to suggest that the task of killing President Kennedy could have been more "efficiently" carried out, to put it crassly. Why did Oswald take the specific actions he did? Decades of historians, forensic scientists, and conspiracy theorists have tried their hand at answering the question. *JFK Reloaded* suggests that the assassin's role, unlike the military sniper's, is that of spectacle as much as accuracy. The assassination not only killed Kennedy, but also set into motion the political, social, and cultural wake of JFK intrigue. Although such an observation is historically obvious, it is easy to forget that a less shrouded, curious murder might have taken place.

The notions of spectacle and historical contingency suggest the game's second effect. The nation's shock at Kennedy's death assuredly would not have been any less sharp had Oswald taken a first shot at Greer and then a second at the president, now a sitting duck;[28] but would JFK's legacy itself not have been dramatically changed had he met a less spectacular end? Certainly Kennedy's tragic demise closed the door on a great deal of criticism about his personal life—criticism we would relive thirty-five years later during Bill Clinton's impeachment and the lewd behavior that brought it about. But more importantly, Kennedy's administration witnessed some of the most complex and mysterious events of the twentieth century. The "conflict" that John Kerry and others would wage in Vietnam was sown during Kennedy's tenure. Kennedy oversaw the unauthorized CIA operation that led to the Bay of Pigs invasion. And then there's the whole question of where union leader Jimmy Hoffa really is.[29] Kennedy was a man who took things into his own hands, and no matter how we may feel about his spectacular public execution, there is no denying that it contributes to his legacy.

In *Guns, Germs, and Steel*, Jared Diamond attempts to expose the underlying patterns that determine why history plays out in the way it does. Diamond is not concerned with individual historical figures or even specific historical moments except as they participate in the much broader scope of historical possibility. By writing an account of history as a procedural system, Diamond gives us access to a system for making sense of individual historical moments and personalities. Even though they appear to represent or re-create historical events, games like *JFK Reloaded* and *Waco Resurrection* serve much the same purpose: they represent the material, social, and cultural conditions that underlie historical events. Given the opportunities that historical videogames espouse, it should be possible to construct videogames that facilitate the player's understanding of contemporary political processes and issues. Keeping this notion of procedural expression in mind, I would now like to return to political practice and explore how games can change and possibly improve citizens' engagement with politics, advocacy, and public policy.

Procedural Rhetoric in Digital Democracy

Games like *Waco Resurrection* and *JFK Reloaded* are procedurally expressive; they embody their commentary in their rules. Despite *JFK Reloaded*'s claimed support for the Warren Commission report, these games aren't explicitly persuasive, but they do invite the player to participate in their representation. A game like *Balance of the Planet* posits persuasion as a more primary expressive goal, in this case persuasion toward a certain ecological belief. As I have already suggested, procedural rhetoric is particularly devoted to representing, communicating, or persuading the player toward a particular biased point of view. Playing such games can have a political impact because they allow players to embody political positions and engage in political actions that many will never have previously experienced, and because they make it possible for players to deepen their understanding of the multiple causal forces that affect any given, always unique, set of historical circumstances. Procedural rhetoric is precisely what is missing from current uses of technology for political and civic engagement.

Despite its success building a virtual community of hundreds of thousands of supporters, the Dean campaign struggled to reach beyond that core audience. This failure was caused partly by the abstractness of its communications strategy. Technophile Deaniacs evangelized the benefit of decentralized decision making, but the average citizen didn't necessarily grasp such a vague concept. In addition, it became increasingly evident that potentially sympathetic supporters simply didn't understand what "getting involved" really meant. Go to a meetup to do what? The campaign rightly saw this challenge as a great obstacle to its broad acceptance.

In December 2003, Gonzalo Frasca and I co-designed the first videogame endorsed by a U.S. presidential candidate. *The Howard Dean for Iowa Game* was commissioned by Dean for America to help fence-sitter supporters understand the process and power of grassroots outreach.[30] As an official, endorsed artifact in the campaign's media plan, the *Dean for Iowa Game* helped establish a new genre of political videogames. As a piece of procedural rhetoric, the game attempted to alleviate the campaign's difficulty in persuading sympathetic citizens to become supporters. In the game, players made a virtual trip to Iowa in order to help campaign for Dean in the important Iowa caucus. They recruited friends and acquaintances to join the campaign, canvassed neighborhoods, passed out pamphlets, and waved Dean signs to encourage Iowans to attend the caucus and stand in support of Howard Dean.

The game mounts two procedural rhetorics to address the campaign's challenge. The first represents the logic of grassroots outreach. The game features a simplified map of Iowa, split up into semiarbitrary regions. At the start of the game, the player has only one supporter unit available, him- or herself. The player places that supporter anywhere on the map. After having set the effectiveness of a supporter through a campaign minigame (more on that in a moment), the supporter works nonstop, enacting "virtual outreach" to win over other virtual Iowans. In the main map screen, more effective virtual supporters work more quickly in their region; circular gauges show their progress (figure 4.4). When the gauge fills, a new supporter spawns, ready for the player to place for additional outreach. Multiple supporters in the same region work together, speeding up the outreach process.

Figure 4.4 An abstract map of Iowa depicts the grassroots outreach simulation in *Howard Dean for Iowa.*

As the game progresses, the speed of supporter generation increases exponentially. As players position supporters to work together on the map, their reach and effectiveness increases. The map also represents relative levels of Dean support in each region, depicting more support in a darker shade of blue. While the game is a single-player Web distributed experience, the outreach that each player completes in a single session is saved to a server. These data are normalized for each player, allowing individual players to take advantage of the "real" in-game outreach their fellow players have already completed.[31] In so doing, the game allows the player to experience an accelerated network effect, concretely communicating the rather abstract idea that one supporter can actually make a difference in the campaign. Once again, the player completes the game's procedural syllogism; his in-game actions are responsible for growing virtual support for the candidate from zero to many tens or hundreds of supporters (the highest "score" we tracked in the game's initial month, measured in virtual supporters generated, was over 800).

The second procedural rhetoric is a simplified representation of the kinds of real-world action supporters could perform once connected to a local group. Three types of activity were represented: sign-waving, door-to-door canvassing, and pamphleteering. Frasca and I discussed the dynamics that led to this creative decision in an article on the game's design:

The question of what and how many outreach activities to include in the game was a matter of long discussion, both among ourselves and with the campaign itself. One of the primary goals for the game was to elucidate the concept of "grassroots outreach"—to give concrete examples of what it meant to perform such action. The logical conclusion was to represent as many such actions as possible in order to yield the broadest influence. Different activities might resonate more effectively with different players. Early on, we considered including as many such activities as possible, scaling down the representation of each by abstraction. But abstraction was precisely the problem the game hoped to solve—fence-sitter supporters were leery of getting involved in the campaign because they didn't grasp what "involvement" really meant. It thus seemed foolish to sacrifice the concreteness of the outreach activities for the sake of quantity.

Instead, we decided to choose three outreach activities. We asked analysts at the campaign to identify the three most important, and they settled on sign-waving, door-to-door canvassing, and pamphleteering. Later, campaign advisors would tell us that they probably should have chosen letter-writing among the three, as this was the main method the campaign had invoked as a means of getting national supports involved in pre-caucus outreach without physically traveling to Iowa.[32]

Each time the player places a supporter unit onto the Iowa map, the game loads one of these campaign minigames. The player's performance in the minigames dictates that supporter's effectiveness on the main Iowa map. The three minigames each deploy extremely simplified representations of these outreach activities; for example, to play the sign-waver minigame, the player positions a supporter near as many passing pedestrians as possible and clicks to wave the sign itself. To play the door-to-door canvassing game, the player deploys three volunteers to a block of residential homes, managing each simultaneously to maximize their time (figure 4.5). We chose simplified patterns of action to represent each of these activities, hoping to create a coherent understanding of what it meant to "get involved." By repeating the same three minigames in sequence for every supporter the player generated, we also

Figure 4.5 Simplified procedural representations of outreach activities concretize campaigning practices.

represented the repetitiveness of grassroots outreach, a fact not lost on many players.

Informal analysis of online responses to the game suggested that many would-be supporters did gain an increased appreciation for the campaign's grassroots outreach strategy. But the most interesting responses provided an insight that the campaign itself would fail to recognize, perhaps tragically, until after the Iowa caucus dismantled the campaign. While the game did provide an accurate and convincing procedural rhetoric for grassroots outreach itself, it failed to distinguish Dean from any other political candidate. As PopMatters.com reviewer Sean Trundle wrote:

I have to believe that there's more difference between any two candidates than the image on the front of a brochure or the name on a sign. And if there isn't, or if this game leads people to believe that there isn't, won't it have the opposite of its desired effect? If handing out leaflets for Dean is the same thing as handing out leaflets for Kucinich, why should I vote for either of them?[33]

After seeing numerous iterations of this same sentiment (a topic to which I will return in chapter 11), it became clear to me that *The Howard Dean for Iowa Game* had failed not in its mission—create a procedural representation of grassroots outreach—but in its conception. The procedural rhetoric in support of grassroots outreach was sound, but it inadvertently exposed the underlying ideology of the campaign, one that would eventually cause it to unravel. The failure to put coherent political rhetoric in the hands of its army of supporters was the Dean campaign's Achilles' heel. Dean had political views, but nobody knew anything about them, so they invented their own impressions of them.

Taking this lesson to heart, I focused special attention on the procedural representation of public policy in later election games. In the early fall 2004, the Illinois House Republicans commissioned me to design a game that would represent their positions on several public policy issues at the center of their 2004 state legislative election. These issues—medical malpractice tort reform, education standards policy, and local economic development—are abstract and dry at best. As such, citizens would be even less likely to have engaged them in the public or private forum, which provided only soapbox sound bites or lengthy, unreadable policy documentation. Moreover, these topics, like most public policy issues, are tightly interwoven. Educational quality affects job qualification, which in turn affects economic welfare. *Take Back Illinois* was an attempt to create a complex, interrelated procedural rhetoric that communicated the candidates' positions on these topics.[34]

Four subgames make up the game, three for each of the policy issues and one *Dean for Iowa*–like game of citizen participation. These subgames interrelate; play in one affects performance in the others. Each subgame provides the player with a goal. For example, in the medical malpractice reform subgame, the player must raise the public health level to a predefined target. The subgame goal and the player's progress toward it are displayed directly under the game field. A small calendar serves as a timer for the game, starting at January 1 and counting up one day for every few seconds of game time. To win, the player must reach the goal before the calendar reaches the end of the year. Faster success yields a lower and therefore better score.

The procedural rhetoric for each policy issue was designed to compress as much detail into the smallest possible rule-set. For example, in the medical malpractice reform subgame, the representation of a city is filled with citizens of varying health—healthy, ill, gravely ill. Unwell citizens are contagious, and healthy citizens nearby them will eventually become ill themselves. If left untreated, gravely ill citizens will die. The city contains several medical offices, and the player can send sick citizens to those offices for treatment (figure 4.6). However, part of the candidates' position claimed that Illinois was suffering higher medical malpractice insurance rates than its neighboring states. Their position on tort reform was partially motivated by the potential reduction in insurance rates such changes would encourage. Thus the game provides a "policy panel" that allows the player to change simple public policy settings for the game environment. In this case, the player could alter maximum noneconomic damages awarded in medical malpractice lawsuits as well as investment in medical research to prevent repeat tragedies. In the medical malpractice subgame, maintaining a high threshold on noneconomic damages keeps insurance rates high, which is likely to cause doctors to leave the state. Once this happens, the medical office dims and the player can no longer treat citizens there.

The other policy subgames create similar procedural rhetorics for each of the issues. In the education reform subgame, players simultaneously manage a handful of school districts across the state. Some districts start out with different educational standards in place, and some districts enjoy disproportionate funding and teacher-to-student ratios. To play the game, the player has to

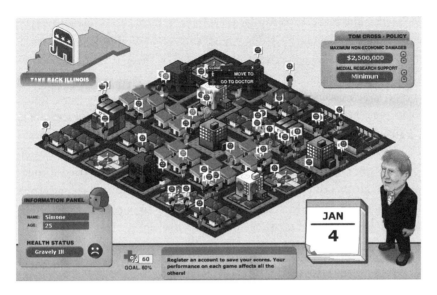

Figure 4.6 *Take Back Illinois* offers a procedural representation of legislative candidates' opinions on public policy issues.

"teach" in each district by keying in a Simon-like memory sequence that corresponds with the educational standard in each district. This procedural rhetoric once again embodied the candidate's policy position: maintaining multiple standards across the state made the educational system on the whole difficult to manage. Players would quickly understand this position upon being forced to remember four or five different memory sequences for all the schools. To play more efficiently, the player could reassign standards on a district-by-district basis by changing policy. The player could also reassign funding to needy schools in order to raise their educational output.

In public forums, policy issues are often discussed independently, even though most are bound to one another in significant ways. To communicate the rhetoric of interrelations, *Take Back Illinois* maintains a set of scores for each subgame and uses those scores as inputs for settings in other games. For example, higher performance in the educational reform subgame increases the efficiency of job training centers in the economic development game. The parameterized interaction between simulation models serves as a rudimentary procedural rhetoric for the interrelationship of these issues in particular, and other issues by extension.

To play the game successfully, the player is forced to acknowledge the campaign's position on the issues it represents—for example, it is impossible to win the medical malpractice reform subgame without reducing maximum noneconomic damages for malpractice lawsuits (although reducing them beyond reason decreases the likelihood of faults). The procedural rhetoric is a compressed version of the campaign's policy position. In playing the game, the player is not "brainwashed" or otherwise fooled into adopting the candidates' policy position. Rather he is afforded an understanding of that position for further inquiry, agreement, or disapproval. This rhetoric functions primarily through procedural enthymeme; the player completes the candidate's arguments regarding how policy change could lead to improved social conditions. However, none of the subgames argues that policy change alone is sufficient to create social change. In each of the games, the player must expend nontrivial effort to accomplish goals like improving healthcare and education. While simpler in execution, these actions trace the same goals as Crawford traces: to show the interconnectedness of political conditions. Where *Balance of the Planet* attempts to build a complex simulation model for these intricate correspondences, *Take Back Illinois* relies on simple, abstract player actions to suggest the incompleteness of the game's rhetorical model. We might think of this technique as an open, or abstract enthymeme: the procedural proposition implies other factors at work in the political ecology, inviting the player to consider the inherent limitations of simplistic legislative resolutions.

Playing Politics

Literacy expert James Paul Gee has argued that literacy is best suited to *semiotic domains*, embodied contexts of environmental and social practices in which individual knowledge gains distinct meaning.[35] Through procedural rhetoric, videogames can create highly compressed versions of the embodied experiences of citizens and of policymakers. *Take Back Illinois* offers an example of the potential of procedural rhetoric in political communications and digital democracy. Creating embodied experiences of public policy issues is very difficult, and our current methods for doing so are often either too meager or too detailed. Games like *Howard Dean for Iowa* and *Take Back Illinois* differ from political simulations meant to guide decision making, such as the public policy simulations the Congressional Budget Office (CBO) runs to guide economic policy. They also differ from computer systems used by the Pentagon to model political responses to current or potential conflict. Whereas these computer simulations strive to be *predictive*, videogames strive to be *expressive*; rhetoricians fundamentally interest themselves in making convincing arguments in favor of a specific point of view. Procedural rhetoric always remains open to reconsideration, objection, or expansion, whether through further procedural models or normal written and spoken discourse.

Even if procedural rhetoric is the missing link in the future of computational public political discourse, the Dean campaign innovations also remain central to such strategies. Blogs, meetups, and news-bound fundraising risk failing to rally conversation around the issues, in favor of provoking conversation around the communication tools themselves. The Internet's affordances for rapid updates and ad hoc access have opened new frontiers for the dissemination of information and the creation of communities. But the ad hoc assemblage of routers and computers that make up the Internet cannot necessarily provide meaningful subject matter upon which to focus that attention. To hold up the Internet as the apotheosis of technology-enabled campaigning ignores the procedural power of computers, discounting the very core of what makes computation a meaningful medium for expression. As a culturally relevant, procedurally replete medium, videogames offer a promising way to foreground the complexities of political issues for the layperson.

Political opinion itself is rarely black and white; most issues occupy gray areas, heavily influenced by other public policy issues. For example, healthcare reform cannot easily separate itself from questions of taxation, national budget practices, tort reform, and social security. If policy issues are complex systems that recombine and interrelate with one another according to smaller rules of interaction, then videogames afford a new perspective on political issues, since they are especially effective at representing complex systems. By understanding how games express rhetoric in their rules, we not only gain a critical vantage point on videogame artifacts, but also we can begin to consider how to design games whose primary purpose is to make political statements.

Advertising

Advertising Logic

An ancient Egyptian version of poster advertising made a religious appeal for "Ptolemy as the true Son of the Sun, the Father of the Moon, and the Keeper of the Happiness of Men."[1] Eighth- and ninth-century *Itineraries* offered pilgrims and travelers the medieval equivalent of travel adverts.[2] Handbills and newspaper advertisements spread along with the printing press in the sixteenth and seventeenth centuries. But as Raymond Williams points out, there is a difference between the Shakespearean notion of "the process of taking or giving notice of something" and "an institutionalized system of commercial information and persuasion."[3] James B. Twitchell has called this modern practice "rent[ing] our concentration to other companies' sponsors," an activity undertaken "for the dubious purpose of informing us of something that we've longed for all our lives even though we've never heard of it before."[4] Even if we do already live under the contemporary social burden Twitchell calls "AdCult," it is instructive to remind ourselves of the litany of advertising exposure he lists among its components:

There is barely a space in our culture not already carrying commercial messages. Look anywhere: in schools there is Channel One; in movies there is product placement; ads are in urinals, played on telephone hold, in alphanumeric displays in taxis, sent unannounced to fax machines, inside catalogs, on the video in front of the Stairmaster at the gym, on T-shirts, at the doctor's office, on grocery carts, on parking meters, on tees at golf holes, on inner-city basketball backboards, piped in along with Muzak . . . ad nauseam (and yes, even on airline vomit bags). We have to shake magazines like rag dolls to free up their pages from the "blow-in" inserts and then wrestle out the stapled- or glued-in ones before reading can begin. We now have to fastforward through some five minutes of advertising that opens rental videotapes. President Bill Clinton's inaugural parade featured a Budweiser float. At the Smithsonian, the Orkin Pest Control Company sponsored an exhibit on exactly what it advertises it kills: insects. No venue is safe. Is there a blockbuster museum show not decorated with corporate logos? The Public Broadcasting Service is littered with "underwriting announcements" that look and sound almost exactly like what PBS claims they are not: commercials.[5]

Clearly, advertisers are quick to colonize media. Even books used to carry advertisements. The Bradbury & Evans edition of Charles Dickens' *Little Dorrit*, reports Twitchell, carried an "ad section touting Persian parasols, smelling salts, portable Indian rubber boots, and the usual array of patent medicines."[6] Today's reader may recall the mass-market books of not so long ago that carried bound-in ads for other titles in the publisher's catalog.

In humanistic academic discourse of the last several decades, materialism and consumption are almost universally derided. Fredric Jameson uses the apposition "late capitalism" for the ambiguous period known as postmodernism, a hopeful, ideological gesture that suggests its eventual, inevitable end.[11] Jean Baudrillard writes of a simulation of a different kind than the procedural representation in videogames—the notion that media and cultural images have become more real than reality. Here simulation is masquerade, parody, and artifice. Baudrillard famously writes about Disneyland and its cousin theme parks, false realities whose representational goals now infect the world outside them: "Disneyland is presented as imaginary in order to make us believe that the rest is real, when in fact all of Los Angeles and the America surrounding it are no longer real, but of the order of the hyperreal and of simulation."[12] Baudrillard understands advertising as complicit in this progression of simulacra; choosing among dozens of types of shampoo or cars is not freedom, but a simulation of freedom.[13] Like the "tragic" Lacanian sign that endlessly produces new signifiers rather than signifieds, advertising has become a self-reflexive practice, with each consumer decision signifying another advertisement, not an actual lifestyle, social, political, or personal choice. Increasingly more of our environment has become Disneyfied, rendered into simulation.

We witness this trend in videogames as well. In 2005, Disney launched *Virtual Magic Kingdom*, a free multiplayer online game created as part of Disneyland's fiftieth anniversary celebration.[14] The game, targeted at Disney's favorite demographic, 7- to 12-year-olds, is essentially a simulated theme park. Upon visiting the *Virtual Magic Kingdom*, players can visit simulations of the "real" rides. They are even able "to win special perks and head-of-line passes for rides in return for completing online challenges. Players who go to the parks also can compete in on-site games to win swag for their online personas."[15] Perhaps a more apt title for the game would be *Marketingland*, an even higher-order simulation of the simulation that is Disneyland.

Advertising has become so pervasive that even moralistic responses to it have often cast consumption as a meaningful cultural practice. As social historian Claude S. Fischer points out,

even Americans who critique mainstream culture do so through their own consumption. Eating organic foods, wearing handmade clothing, giving only wooden toys as gifts, and riding bicycles to work amounts to self-labeling. Marketing people who target African Americans explain that blacks buy certain high-ticket goods more often than whites do to display a sense of worth to themselves and to rest of the world in face of the racial stigma and also to signal other blacks of their allegiance to a group identity. The psychological force behind greater consumerism is thus an increasing urge to self-expression.[16]

As Baudrillard suggests, "consumption is a system of meaning, like language."[17] While it is dubious to think of buying in and of itself as automatically meaningful self-expression, indeed this is the very mechanism advertisers have come to rely upon. In the face of this hyperconsumerism, many economists have given up entirely on the distinction between needs and wants.[18]

From the dawn of industrialization up to the era of television, people have consumed commodities. Originally, marketing mostly entailed providing information about the need the product fulfilled, its fair price, and its means of distribution. These communications were subject to extreme fragmentation (handbills, local newspapers and periodicals, etc.) or noise (catalogs, etc.). With the increased popularization of mass media, especially television but also national print and radio, producers of goods and services were able to reach nearly every consumer all at once. As it happened, this social move took place at the same time as the integration of social sciences like psychology and sociology. Advertising shifted from a minimalist, rationalistic strategy to a spectacular, emotional one. Human society had moved beyond subsistence living with the development of food storage and urban culture millennia earlier; but mass media allowed companies to manufacture wants rather than satisfy needs. As marketing guru Seth Godin puts it, "Television was a miracle. It enabled companies with money to effortlessly create more money."[19]

Within the contemporary media environment, both advertiser and consumer are conscious of advertising and consumption as a symbolic practice. Essentially, consumers have become aware that advertisers market to get them to buy, not to answer to their needs. In part, we have become increasingly cognizant of the phenomenon Baudrillard called a "simulation of freedom"; supermarkets took advantage of high leverage to lower prices on commodity goods, leverage born primarily out of the enormous demand for products created by television advertising and advanced by the growing car culture and suburbanization of the same period. When faced with dozens of types of shampoo or cereal or processed cheese food in today's market aisles, consumers increasingly understand that differentiation through advertising is a noise-reduction strategy.

Advertisers label this new trend cynicism. Consumers are perceived to have become scornful of the simulation of freedom, even if they do not cast their disparagement in such lofty terms. Increasingly, marketers have responded by developing new strategies to "combat" the cultural shift in consumption; advertisers perceive the cultural situation to be an affliction of the consumers, not the advertising. For example, Godin urges advertisers to acknowledge that "as a marketer, you can no longer force people to pay attention."[20] The frame Godin and his colleagues cast around this "crisis" is one of inattention. Consumers, who once sat idle and alert in the face of the advertisers' encouragement to consume, are now so bombarded with messages that the signal-to-noise ratio has become too high to tolerate. Godin invented a technique he called "permission marketing" to combat this new trend.[21] Whereas traditional advertising relies on interruptions like the commercial break to deliver its messages, the new advertiser must get the consumer to "ask for" the advertisement, for example by opting-in to product announcements or electronic communications.

Godin and others have extended the principles of permission marketing to techniques that essentially reform interruption marketing into messages that particular target markets want to associate with products and services. Godin's approach is a simplistic adaptation of George Lakoff's theory of conceptual frames. Rather than persuade a consumer that a product can efficiently address a need (pre-television era) or that a product simultaneously creates and services that created need (television era), advertising should recast the needs manufactured by advertising into smaller niches: "the product is nothing but a souvenir of your trip to the store—and a reminder of the way you felt when you bought it."[22]

Godin's strategy responds to a media ecology in which consumers have decoded the logic of advertising in the television age. In addition to the softer effect of saturation, devices like digital video recorders (DVRs) are creating a McLuhanian shockwave in the advertising landscape. While the phenomenon of inattention identified by Godin and others may lead to a conscious awareness of the logic of advertising as a system of need manipulation, DVR technology like TiVo foregrounds that logic as its primary technical affordance. More important than the ability to record television to watch later (a facility the VCR took care of in the early 1980s), viewers can program their DVR to pause live television for, say, the first twenty minutes of a broadcast, then sit down after that time and watch the program without its ads.[23] Add the increasing popularity and rapid release of DVD editions of television series, and television consumers gain full recognition that their primary outlet for entertainment has been fashioned entirely around the thirty-second television spot. Says a twenty-five-year-old marine biologist of the phenomenon, "Now that I have TiVo, I realize how much of TV is actually commercials."[24] This new realization is really knowledge of the procedural rhetoric of mass-market television advertising: networks create content designed to appeal to segments of the population, then sell interruptions in the broadcast for advertisement designed for that group. This new literacy builds on low-tech artifacts that have been drawing public attention to the internal logics of advertising for decades: a coffee-table book of Absolut vodka ads, which has sold over 300,000 copies;[25] the Super Bowl television ads that often eclipse interest in the game itself;[26] the iPod ads that spawn Photoshop do-it-yourself tutorials.[27]

Godin's solution is to feed on consumers' continued willingness to allow advertisers to manufacture needs after the mainline for the delivery of those needs has been compromised. This new advertisement is particularly directed at those consumers whom advertisers perceive to be the most valuable victims of their own understanding of the television economy—at present, the 18- to

34-year-old male, the same demographic that purportedly constitutes the core audience for videogames.[28] Now that consumers have decoded the logic of the advertising network, marketers are marrying permission marketing to strategically chosen frames. Marketing has shifted away from a focus on the procedural rhetoric of media technologies—integrating ads into rules of network programming formats. Instead, advertisers focus on the procedural rhetoric of the frames themselves—integrating ads into rules of consumers' perceived cultural station. Godin confirms this strategy: "*Worldview* is the term I use to refer to the rules, values, beliefs, and biases that an individual consumer brings to a situation. . . . Marketing succeeds when it taps into an audience of people who share a worldview . . . that makes that audience inclined to believe the story the marketer tells."[29]

Videogames have not escaped advertising's lust for new media to carry their commercial messages. Although advertising in videogames can be found as early as the arcade cabinets of the mid 1970s and home consoles of the early 1980s, popular opinion still understands the trend as a relatively new one. Many early boutique agencies peddling Web-based advergames claim "credit" for coining the term, but a formal definition of "advergame" is commonly traced to a 2001 whitepaper by Jane Chen and Matthew Ringel, analysts at interactive agency ⟨kpe⟩.[7] The two call advergaming "the use of interactive gaming technology to deliver embedded advertising messages to consumers."[8] Since the mid-1990s, the popularity of advergames have grown from modest and inexpensive Web-based games like those produced by advergaming agencies Blockdot[9] and Skyworks[10] to the elaborate *America's Army* discussed earlier. Seth Godin's permission marketing underlies the placement of the Honda Element SUV in the "extreme sports" videogame *SSX 3*, thus positing a means to complete the snow boarder lifestyle.[30] From the perspective of the advertising industry, videogames are just another medium to be accessed and exploited as part of the larger media ecology, one already run by advertising dollars anyway.

But as the procession of simulacra advances, it might also undermine the very practice of advertising. In Baudrillard's view, *Virtual Magic Kingdom* likely increases the unreality of Disneyland itself, allowing players to forgo the "real" experience—itself a simulation—in favor of the game, a simulation of that simulation. But the game might also expose the very unreality of Disneyland, making the theme park less of a real experience and more of a representational one—a realization that might direct players' attention toward their tendency to prefer simulation to reality. Perhaps even the smallest child can grasp the irony of physically visiting Disneyland in order to play in a virtual Disneyland. Contrary to Baudrillard's suggestion that the procession of simulacra always deepens the illusion of depth, perhaps the dissonance between the virtual and the real Disneylands actually exposes a similar dissonance between Disneyland and the real world. In the medium of videogames, advertising's pervasiveness might partly lead to its critique.

Three Types of Advertising

In the 1980s, economists Paul Milgrom and John Roberts were concerned about the large amount of advertising—especially TV advertising—that conveyed little or no obvious information.[31] Drawing from the field of economics, psychology, and mathematics known as game theory, the two articulated a kind of theoretical game they called the "persuasion game" as a possible explanation for advertising logic. The persuasion game is *noncooperative* in game-theoretical terms—a game in which both agents interact directly, but in which one agent tries to assign values to the outcome of another agent. Persuasion games are characterized by a lack of control over events relevant to the persuading agent.[32]

In advertising, a classic terrain for persuasion games of the general kind, a seller may emphasize consequences of purchasing that are important to the potential consumer but not directly under the control of the seller. Examples of such games abound: advertisers claim that a particular brand of beer might increase the buyer's appeal to the opposite sex, or that a particular brand of athletic wear might radically improve the wearer's performance. In these games, the advertiser's desired outcome is left in the consumer's hands. Persuasion games also apply to representative politics, political lobbying, organizational influence activities, social influence activities, and many other domains. More abstractly, a persuasion game is a game in which an interested player discloses information to another player, who has to make a decision that affects the payoff of the disclosing player. There are three important types of advertising that can participate in such persuasion games: *demonstrative*, *illustrative*, and *associative* advertising.

Demonstrative advertising provides direct information. These ads communicate tangibles about the nature of a product.[33] This type of advertising is closely related to the product as commodity; demonstrative ads focus on the functional utility of products and services. Among this category of advertisements, one might think of the "sponsor messages" of the golden age of television, ads that featured live demonstrations of detergent or "miracle" appliances. Also among this category are the copy-heavy print ads of the 1960s–1980s (examples abound in back issues of magazines like *National Geographic*), as well as modern-day television infomercials.

Ads like these focus on communicating the features and function of products or services. Consider the magazine ad for a Datsun hatchback in figure 5.1. In the aftermath of the oil crisis of the 1970s, the ad foregrounds the car's focus on fuel economy, a tangible benefit, with the large headline "Nifty Fifty." Additional copy at the bottom of the ad further rationalizes and defends this position, citing a five-speed transmission with overdrive as a contributor to the car's increased fuel economy.

Illustrative advertising communicates indirect information. Illustrative ads can communicate both tangibles and intangibles about a product, with a focus on the marginal utility, or the incremental benefit of buying this product over another, or over not buying at all.[34] These ads often contextualize a product or service differently than demonstrative ads, focusing more on social and cultural context. Consider another automobile ad, this one for a Saab sedan, in figure 5.2. Unlike the Datsun ad, which depicts the vehicle in an empty space, the Saab ad places the car on a road and uses photographic panning to telegraph motion.[35] No additional copy accompanies the ad, but the vehicle in motion serves to illustrate speed. The ad makes a case for the liveliness of the vehicle despite its "practical" four-door sedan frame, which is clearly visible in the center of the image.

Associative advertising communicates indirect information, focusing specifically on the intangibles of a product.[36] Where demonstrative advertising highlights the mass-market appeal of a product—the product as commodity—associative advertising focuses on its niche market appeal. In part, associative advertising came about as a result of improved manufacturing, sales, and distribution techniques that have made niche-market products possible in the first place. Whereas the Tin Lizzie famously came in "any color so long as it was black," present-day automated assembly line practices make it possible for automakers to manufacture a variety of vehicles to serve different types of buyers. Consider yet another automobile, this time the Volkswagen New Beetle advertised in figure 5.3. As in the Saab ad, all textual explanation has been eliminated from the advertisement. But unlike an

Figure 5.1   Demonstrative advertisements highlight the functional aspects of the vehicle, such as storage space and fuel economy.

illustrative ad, the Beetle ad communicates nothing about the contextualized features of the product. Instead, the ad telegraphs only intangibles about the product's social nature. Here, the white car is barely shown at all; instead, the viewer focuses on the "snow angel" the car is implied to have created moments before the present image was captured. The message is clear: the Beetle is a fun-loving vehicle made for fun-loving people.

Figure 5.2 In illustrative advertisements, products are contextualized but their features are deemphasized.

Many ads function across more than one of these three registers. While the Datsun ad with its large "Nifty Fifty" title and supporting copy primarily speaks in the demonstrative register, illustrative and associative elements also pepper the image. The open hatch with bags and dog loaded is illustrative; it suggests the incremental utility of the hatchback: a small car with good fuel economy and practical storage. The youthful, ambiguously gendered driver with tennis racket is associative; he (or she) casts a sportive aura around the car. The dog adds to this image, and the open hatch affirms the active sensibilities of the car's owner.

Associative advertising is related to a recent trend known as "lifestyle marketing."[37] Lifestyle marketing starts from the seemingly innocuous goal of tuning advertising to address niche rather than mass markets; however, lifestyle marketing and its associative tools depend largely on new techniques for data-gathering to help identify consumers as a member of this or that "segment."[38] Such techniques include the now-ubiquitous supermarket "club card," which requires buyers to exchange information about every product they buy in exchange for "special" pricing (which used to be just "normal" pricing, before all the supermarkets started using club cards). Signing up for

Figure 5.3 Associative advertisements focus on intangibles, depicting the feelings or sentiments associated with a product.

a card requires the customer to provide demographic information, which marketers correlate against individual product purchases. Data mining allows advertisers to address consumers individually, allegedly ending some of the tyranny of the mass market. But once marketers identify segments that prove particularly lucrative or easy to reach, lifestyle marketing becomes a process of advertising the lifestyle itself, rather than using the lifestyle as a medium for making a case for specific products. As such, associative advertising has become an increasingly common way for advertisers to craft new messages for the production of wants rather than the satisfaction of needs. It is this type of activity that Seth Godin suggested marketers adopt as their primary strategy.

The Current State of Advertising Games

Mapping the three types of advertising onto the medium of the videogame helps suggest the possible points of intersection between the two domains. Videogame-based demonstrative advertising would reveal the use of a product in the game, providing direct information. Videogame-based illustrative advertising would communicate the existence of products in the game and highlight their incremental benefits. And videogame-based associative advergames would correlate the product with an activity or lifestyle repre-sented by the game, providing indirect information. Of the three, associative games are most prevalent, but demonstrative games dovetail most closely with the procedural properties of the videogame medium.

In their 2001 ⟨kpe⟩ research report on advergames, Chen and Ringel come to a similar conclusion in their attempt to map the three types of advertising to videogames. Associative advergaming, they suggest, "can drive brand awareness by associating the product with the lifestyle or activity featured in the game."[39] The authors argue that such approaches ought to "logically or emotionally reinforce the brand image" through the "content and theme of the game play."[40] As an example, the two cite a pool game sponsored by Jack Daniels. The game offers serviceable pool play in a 3D environment with high production value. The Jack Daniels logo is emblazoned on the felt of the table and in other key locations around the game. In this case, the game attempts to correlate a lifestyle activity, a round at the pool hall, with the product in question, a whisky one might consume while playing pool.

Illustrative advergaming, suggest Chen and Ringel, "can prominently feature the product itself in game play."[41] As an example, the two cite a series of games created for General Mills' Cinnamon Toast Crunch breakfast cereal. In one such game, the player controls a cartoon character that collects his "wind-scattered breakfast cereal before the start of school."[42]

Demonstrative advergaming, in Chen and Ringel's conception,

can leverage the full arsenal of interactivity by allowing the consumer to experience the product within the virtual confines of the gaming space. Whereas some Advergames feature the product or brand name in incidental ways, demonstrative Advergames boost messaging effectiveness by presenting the product in its natural context and inviting the consumer to interact with it.[43]

Chen and Ringel's mapping of the three types of advertising onto games leaves scarce room for objection or controversy. What is more interesting is the example the two choose to typify demonstrative advergaming, a slam-dunk game created for Nike by the now-defunct advergame consultancy YaYa. In the game, the player can choose from a variety of Nike Shox basketball shoes. In Chen and Ringel's words, the game purports to "demonstrate the different performance features" of the shoe during gameplay.[44]

At first blush, the Nike Shox game is not an inappropriate example of demonstrative advertising. The game appears to simulate the physical properties of the shoes, offering the player a chance to consider the tangible benefits of the product as a core part of the experience. However, as far as demonstrative messages go, the Nike example is a weak one. While the physical properties of a shoe certainly have some effect on the wearer's performance, the very idea that a shoe can make a better slam-dunker is a textbook example of associative advertising. In fact, Nike is among the most sophisticated, successful associative advertisers around; they are masters of creating ties between garments and high-performance athleticism. Granted, considerable research goes into the material design of a competition track cleat or tennis shoe, but the majority of Nike's business comes from ordinary people who wear their products as a way to live a fantasy of sports prowess.

The weakness of the Nike Shox example does not necessarily undermine the accuracy of Chen and Ringel's mapping. Rather, it suggests an unexplored territory in demonstrative advergames. As I write this today, over five years after the ⟨kpe⟩ report was published, new illustrative and associative advergames appear in large numbers. Following Chen and Ringel's example, Kraft has opened Postopia.com, a website devoted entirely to games like the Cinnamon Toast Crunch game, but with more focus on associative connections between Post brand cereals and Nickelodeon characters.[45] Kraft also created Candystand.com, a similar site supporting Life Savers candy.[46] Darts, pinball, billiards, air hockey, rally racing, snowboard, and lacrosse, among others, all sport Life Savers signage and branding. Skyworks Technologies, a company that specializes in illustrative and associative advergames, created many of the games on these two sites.[47] Companies like Skyworks create generic versions of a common game, like pool or skiing, and then add logos to "customize" the games for a particular advertiser. For example, the logo emblazoned on a pool table felt might be replaced for a new sponsoring brand while the rest of the game remains the same. Brands seeking contact with "youth" are particularly inclined to contribute to the glut of snowboarding and other "extreme sports" games as they attempt to skew their products to a younger market.

Those games that do inch into the illustrative and demonstrative domains still frequently do so within the primary context of lifestyle associations. In 2003, Groove Alliance created a skateboarding game for Mountain Dew, aptly named *Mountain Dew Skateboarding*.[48] In the game, the player skates around an outdoor arena performing tricks for points. The player must keep a "Mountain Dew Power" meter at the bottom of the screen from expiring to continue playing; to refill it, the player collects Mountain Dew products scattered throughout the environment. *Mountain Dew Skateboarding* tries to extend that brand's ongoing efforts to associate its high-caffeine composition with high-energy activities like skateboarding; this associative advertisement frames the rest of the game.

The use of Mountain Dew products as power-ups could be construed as an effective simulation of the caffeine jolt the soft drink provides, a gesture in the direction of demonstrative advertising. However, this technique does not principally seek to demonstrate the tangible benefits of the product. Instead, it elevates the product (or more precisely, the product's packaging) as a token of positive, but anonymous value. We might call this gesture a kind of in-game object fetishism; the player seeks the Mountain Dew because it and it alone has magical power in the game world.

Discussing examples like the Mountain Dew can, Zach Whalen has made a distinction between archetypal and instrumental power-ups.[49] The former represent an abstract game goal, such as collecting dots in *Pac-Man*;[50] the latter represent an abstract game goal, but instead or additionally offer a use-value specific to the power-up: collecting bottles in *Mountain Dew Skateboarding* provide energy, giving them the appearance of instrumental power-ups. However, the energy those bottles provide prove necessary to play the game at all; there is no game in the first place without the Mountain Dew. One can imagine a more literal instrumental use of the cans in a game; for example, perhaps the player has to race from home to school to avoid running late. Obstacles might delay his route, and shortcuts might win time. Shortcuts would likely demand skateboard tricks, which require energy. In this case, foraging for high-caffeine Mountain Dew would provide instrumental benefit to the player. Whalen offers *Chester Cheetah: Too Cool to Fool*, a platform/adventure game for the Super NES,[51] as another possible example.[52] In *Chester Cheetah*, the player pilots the familiar mascot on a quest, collecting Cheetos to regain life. Here, the game's goal is the quest, and the Cheetos provide incremental advantage in reaching it. Still, the instrumental value of the cheese snacks remains abstract, and perhaps necessarily so: in what situation can one claim that they would actually *need* Cheetos to continue? These examples suggest that even instrumental power-ups often provide only incremental demonstrative advantage over archetypal ones.

Advertising in videogames can be traced back at least twenty-five years, since the first film/game tie-ins *Tron*[53] and *E.T.*[54] and the early branded games *Kool-Aid Man*, all of which made their appearance in 1982.[55] But examples like *Mountain Dew Skateboarding* and the Nike slam-dunk game suggest that contemporary interest in advertising games has been driven by a broader interest in videogames as a gateway to a particular consumer than by the unique properties of the medium as a new form of marketplace discourse. Understood in this way, advergames themselves become a type of associative marketing strategy: an attempt to reach a niche market of "gamers," a meta-advertisement. With DVR and videogames "stealing" television viewership, advertisers have been increasingly willing to consider games a media marketplace where they can reach the "coveted" 18- to 34-year-old male.[56] The appeal of manipulating impressionable children as an avenue into their parents' wallets continues in advergames; Postopia.com targets children 5 to 11 years of age, creating the online equivalent of television spots during Saturday morning cartoons. Based on research suggesting that women over 35 comprise the majority of online casual game players, some marketers claim that advergames can reach that demographic specifically.[57] Blockdot, a studio with a skin-and-resell approach similar to Skyworks, created a clone of the popular ur-puzzle game *Bejeweled*[58] that advertised Kotex feminine hygiene products.[59] *Bejeweled* is a three-in-a-row matching game, and Blockdot's Kotex version, called *Ms. Match*, replaced the former's jewel icons with abstract icons representing activities like volleyball, painting, makeup, and ballet, presumably activities one can take part in while making use of Kotex-brand tampons.

The trend to associate brands with videogames as a way to access a particular consumer segment is also not new. In 1978, Fuji released a Coca-Cola branded edition of its Sportstron TV Game.[60] The game was a home version copycat of *Pong*, with a red case and knobs in the form of Coke bottlecaps. Coca-Cola continued their investment in generic videogame branding, releasing a similar red version of the SEGA GameGear 16-bit handheld system. Pepsi followed suit in 2005, with a Pepsi-blue version of the Nintendo DS handheld.[61]

These devices do not perform procedural representation at all; they are merely branded objects that also happen to be videogame consoles. In some cases, procedural advertisements emerged out of these branded cases. The Coca-Cola game gear came bundled with a Coke-themed platformer game, *Coca Cola Kid*, which was also available separately.[62] *Coca Cola Kid* sported a rudimentary illustrative archetype power-up mechanic, requiring the player to collect cans of Coke to supply "power." And McDonald's sponsored a *Coca Cola Kid*–like platform game for the Nintendo Entertainment System, *M.C. Kids*, in which the player must recover Ronald McDonald's magic bag from the Hamburglar (see figure 5.4).[63] Nevertheless, both of these games represent rudimentary or nonexistent connections to the sponsoring companies' products and services; they were produced explicitly to associate the brand image with videogames, in the hopes of influencing game-playing youngsters.

These and other games suggest that creators and publishers of advergames, goaded by an ever more skeptical ad-buying market, are eager for games based on their cultural credibility rather than their representational power. Ad agencies try to motivate brands to consider games as part of their media plan by citing statistics such as the following:

- The games segment is growing 25% per year and surpassing total movie box office revenues. *(Los Angeles Times)*
- Forty-five million people will play online games over the Internet this year, growing to 73 million in 2004, which is faster than any other form of entertainment. *(Juniper Research)*
- Online gamers play games an average of 13 hours per week, which is more than people spend reading newspapers or magazines and about the same as TV watchers. *(Juniper Research)*

Figure 5.4 *M.C. Kids* offers an example of an early associative advergame.

- Sites promoting games are 8 of the top 10 entertainment sites on the Internet. *(Nielsen)*
- The session length in gaming areas of portals averages 4X the general site average, or 28 minutes. *(Advertising Age)*[64]

The problem with evidence like this is that it rationalizes advertising games solely through broader movements in the videogame and online advertising markets. In particular, it assumes an imprecise correlation between the videogame market and its potential as a persuasive medium, a correlation that does not take into account the unique properties of videogames. Advertisers perceive the production of advergames or the insertion of traditional advertising into games to be an adequate solution. And they assume a loose or absent causal relationship between play and persuasion; claims like those cited above perpetuate the idea that videogames with weak associative relationships to a sponsor yield meaningful value. The contemporary approach to advertising games relies on the game experience as an end in itself rather than as a bridge to activities in the material world, making these advertisements simulations in Baudrillard's sense of the word—copies with no original, fantasies for a world that doesn't exist.

Advertising Rhetorics

The business of advertising has its own internal logic that informs and structures the attitudes I've just described. Advertising agencies develop strategic "campaigns" based on a sophisticated understanding of a company's products or services, their target audience, and their incremental goals for the near future. This strategic plan includes a distribution of media targets, such as radio, outdoor, television, print, and online. Based on this strategy, the agency executes creative briefs for each of its media, which it then executes. Finally, the agency places the completed ads into each medium through media buys—essentially brokered ad purchases from the various networks who sell physical, televisual, or auditory space. Strategy and campaign development is usually handled with a retainer, a monthly or annual fee the hiring brand pays to the agency in exchange for general services. The execution of creative—the actual filming of a television spot, the recording of a radio ad, the production of a series of online banner ads, and so forth—is typically billed to the client near cost.

Media buys are the real profit centers. While some agencies may mark up the costs of research and creative, the additional revenue is incremental and often eaten up by the management of television ad directors, staffs, or other external agencies. Media buys offer compounding results. Typically, agencies bill a fee of 15 percent on top of the actual costs of media. The agencies employ media buyers to do the work, and those employee salaries are often amortized across retainers from all clients whose accounts the agency directs.

Media slots are essentially commodities; television and radio networks, outdoor (billboard and poster), magazines, and online networks sell ad space at fixed costs commensurate with the established value of the time or space, which is determined largely by supply and demand; a single Super Bowl spot can cost several million dollars, whereas a full-page magazine ad in a small publication might cost only a few thousand. When advertisers buy media, they buy a lot of it at once: multiple airings of a television spot, multiple locations for a billboard, multiple printings of a magazine ad. The Super Bowl is anomalous, but even the most typical television ad slot costs several hundred thousand dollars each. All of these factors produce enormous leverage on the part of the advertising agency; a 15 percent commission on incrementally increasing ad sales produces exponentially greater revenue at essentially the same costs.

The logic of the advertising industry—its own procedural structure—privileges the media buy. This logic helps explain advertisers' use of the abstract concept of "creative": creative is advertising content that can be placed in bought media slots. While the name implies that advertising value comes from the ingenuity or imagination in crafting the image, the value of creative is determined as much or more by the material's facility for wide placement within the media ecology. Understanding this logic helps explain why advergaming companies like Skyworks and Blockdot adopted the strategy they did: by providing generic games configured like a network, they made it possible for agencies to buy media placement, typically in the form of two-dimensional logos or banners within the games.

This logic also explains why advertisers have recently become so enthralled with "in-game advertising," the dynamic placement of digital ad units inside commercial videogames. Networks like Blockdot's Kewlbox.com (host of *Ms. Match*)[65] and Kraft's Postopia.com must source and establish enough traffic to justify their existence. Competing with online casual game sites like Yahoo! Games and PopCap proves to be an increasingly difficult charge. And despite the appeal of the middle-aged women who supposedly play casual games, advertisers are again most concerned about the apparent exodus of the 18- to 34-year-old demographic from the television market in favor of videogames. In-game advertising looks to place media inside the commercial games such "hard core" players buy for their home consoles and high-end PCs.

As the name implies, in-game advertising entails the direct placement of media inside commercial videogames. Dynamic in-game advertising focuses on the liveness that Internet-connected devices afford: the ability to serve ads dynamically into those games. By focusing interest on the opportunities for media buying in games as opposed to custom-created games or hybrids of media and game development, major in-game ad players Massive Inc.,[66] Double Fusion,[67] and IGA Partners[68] have each succeeded in raising $10 million in venture funding in 2005 alone.[69] The investment proved to pay off for Massive, whom Microsoft acquired in spring 2006 for an estimated $400 million.[70] The focus of all three companies is to create an advertising network in commercial videogames equivalent to that of television. Double Fusion summarizes this goal on their website: "Double Fusion provides advertisers an effective and easy delivery of their ad campaigns into the most exciting media for teenagers and young adults—interactive games."[71] In particular, in-game advertising seeks to extend the reach of *existing* advertising units—especially two-dimensional images and motion graphics—into videogames. Double Fusion's message to advertisers confirms that the primary benefit of such ads is the ability to maintain current methods of advertising production and sales: "Advertisers continue the same creative and business process they use now to create artwork for their traditional and online campaigns."[72]

In-game advertising networks' intention to advance advertising, and not videogames, is underscored by the absurdity of many of their case studies. Commercial videogames are caught in a genre rut, with a large majority of games set in futuristic or militaristic settings, sporting combat as a major theme. Massive showcases their in-game advertising solution in a slideshow of examples on their corporate website. Placements include a billboard for the film *Batman Begins* shown alongside a surgically implanted assassin in the game *Anarchy Online*;[73] a Coca-Cola fountain machine flanked by a gun-ready, gasmask-wearing character in the tactical shooter *SWAT 4*;[74] and Sam Fisher, the player character in the stealth-action game *Splinter Cell: Chaos Theory*, crouched clandestine in front of a Diet Sprite vending machine.[75] The examples on Double Fusion's website are only hypothetical, much "friendlier" than Massive's dark scenarios, but essentially identical: in a rendered city scene, a delivery truck sports Fanta soft drinks on its side; a generic city shop is emblazoned with Blockbuster Video or Starbucks Coffee signage.[76]

The incongruence of placed ads doesn't seem to faze the in-game ad network providers. The very idea that a furtive spy would stop for a Diet Sprite, or that a cyborg assassin from 30,000 years in the future might enjoy a present-day matinee, does not strike these advertisers as absurd. In fact, the networks justify in-game ads with claims that they enhance the realism of videogames. In one study conducted with 900 players of taxi-simulator *London Taxi*, researchers reported that "gamers responded favorably to in-game ads, with 50 percent stating that it makes a game more realistic, and only 21 percent disagreeing."[77] Some players affirm the sentiment. On the pundit-replete website Slashdot, one reader comments, "In the cases where advertising helps create an added feeling of realism (racing games, as pictured [in the article the comment references]) it's a great addition."[78] But the line between appropriate and inappropriate ad placement is a fine one. Recently, a guerilla marketing group (unaffiliated with the in-game ad networks mentioned above) placed Subway restaurant ads inside the popular deathmatch game *Counter-Strike*.[79] One player responds, "In a game that focuses on counter-terrorist/terrorist struggles in remote locations, a Subway sandwich ad simply has no place being littered around the scenery. It turns a believable experience into a marketing joke."[80]

Marketers have good reason to try to prove that players want in-game ads. Commercial videogames typically cost $50–60, and prices are rising to accommodate increasing development costs. In every other medium, consumers are accustomed to advertising offsetting or eliminating the costs of content. While it is true that some paid media like cable television and box-office cinema serve ads while simultaneously raising rates, those media markets have evolved their practices over years or decades. There is no evidence that in-game advertising is likely to affect consumer prices of videogames at retail.

To address this breach, in-game advertisers rely heavily on appeals to verisimilitude. To be sure, the videogame market is obsessed with visual fidelity; advances in graphics processing units (GPUs) and high-definition (HD) integration overwhelm the industry's interest in new game forms. Even so, in the absence of marketplace subsidies in-game advertising networks have had to make special arguments to convince players that they want in-game ads. The *London Taxi* study was funded and run by Double Fusion and Nielsen, an in-game ad network and an advertising measurement firm. Another study concluded that in-game ads improve "brand awareness."[81] This study was also funded and run by Nielsen, in conjunction with Activision, a publisher that has aggressively adopted in-game ads. Studies by more disinterested parties, however, arrive at different conclusions. A recent University of London study on player response to such ads concluded that in-game ads "had very limited impact on either the enhancement of the game experience or on product purchase intentions."[82] In this study, 14 percent of participants agreed that ads enhanced the gaming experience, compared to the 50 percent in the Double Fusion-Nielsen study. Although there is no direct evidence for collusion, in light of such conflicting evidence, sponsored studies could be understood to have rhetorical rather than scientific ends. They are ads for in-game ads.

The University of London study suggests that players don't perceive in-game ads in the same way they perceive real-world ads. Even in games where billboard-style ads are thematically appropriate, such as in the large, open urban environments of *Grand Theft Auto*–style games, the interface and simulation mediate the player's experience of the ads. Representations of billboards have been common in games since the early 1980s. *Pole Position*[83] featured track-side ads for publisher Atari and other games by creator Namco, such as *Dig Dug*.[84] But these ads verged on flippancy; the notion of advertising an arcade game that might well have been adjacent to the current one in the arcade smacks of more than a hint of irony. As I argued in chapter 3, the fast food restaurants in *Grand Theft Auto: San Andreas* serve a similarly sardonic function, as do the mock radio advertisements in the *GTA* series.[85] In fact, many games seem to use simulated contemporary urban environments to make jabs at the ubiquity and meaninglessness of advertisements. Stylized first-person shooter *XIII* features billboards reading "Drink Soda," a sort of laying-bare of the logic of outdoor advertising which exposes the dysfunction of advertisement while simultaneously contributing to a realistic environment.[86] A similar effect can be found in certain outdoor cafes in *Grand Theft Auto: Vice City*, which bear the simple message, "Drink Beer."[87] This is advertising that doesn't.

In-game advertisements thus might naturally lend themselves to incongruity in games. The player is fully aware that the environment is simulated, and thus advertisement can never escape simulation. As a corollary, consider the simulated spaces of Las Vegas. The New York, New York Casino is a simulation of the city of New York, complete with a false skyline façade. The building is real of course, insofar as the hotel actually exists in the material world, but the skyline is simulated through clever architectural techniques that make one building appear to be constructed out of many differently styled skyscrapers. Emblazoned on the side of these component "buildings" are huge poster advertisements, the likes of which one would expect to see on the actual buildings. Are these ads real? The ads themselves are surfaces that support inscription, and the products and services depicted on them actually can be purchased. But the apprehension of these ads is mediated significantly by the viewer's knowledge that they are presented in the context of a simulation of a city. The ads first contribute to that simulation and second, if at all, support the incremental value of the product.

Las Vegas hosts more of these simulacra, machines that draw the visitor's attention to the high orders of simulation at work in this environment. Warning signs in the Paris, Las Vegas hotel and casino enjoin the visitor to be careful not to trip on the cobblestones when entering an "authentic re-creation" of a real Paris street. Perhaps the highest-order of these is the

Coyote Ugly, also in the New York, New York Casino. This bar is a simulation of the one from the film of the same name, which in turn was a representation of a real bar, all housed in a simulation of the city in which the movie took place and in which the bar "really exists."[88] The sensation of being inside the Coyote Ugly is not so much one of drunken, sensual pleasure, even if women do dance provocatively on the counter. Rather, it is a sensation of how phantasmal the seductress barkeep really is—there are no chairs or tables in the bar, so as to pack more people into an already small space. The lack of furniture and the cramped, club-like nature of the place preclude pub conversation. Trying to "pick up" someone in such an environment is cognitively disturbing; no one is quite sure of the limits of their agency. Am I a real bargoer, or a simulation of a bargoer? A $20 cover further accentuates this effect.

Dynamic in-game ads also raise questions of privacy and surveillance. Nielsen and Massive have worked to create a new measurement system for in-game ads. In order to measure ads, Massive's system tracks player movement and orientation, as well as the physical location of the computer that hosts the ads (to serve geographically customized versions). Videogame developers are always looking for new ways to improve their products, and some publishers even use the ad-reporting data for game tuning. Said THQ senior global brand manager Dave Miller, "So if the character is stuck in front of a brick wall with an ad poster on it, we know that the level might be too hard. We now see the ad-tracking system as a way to find ways to improve on a game's design."[89]

Many online games already use sophisticated player tracking, but players may not realize it. The introduction of surveillance in games challenges players to ask themselves how they feel about corporations owning the behavior of their on-screen avatars. Covert researchers have followed shoppers for years in retail stores, noting each move and hesitation and attempting to correlate it to changing environmental cues. Many consumers find the practice abhorrent, but in-game ad tracking boasts essentially the same properties.

From Visual to Procedural Rhetoric in Advertising

Currently, advertisers are applying existing rhetorics to the videogame medium, despite the latter's fundamental focus on procedurality. Advertising has always focused on the visual. Advertisers synecdochically refer to consumers as "eyeballs," whose attention they strive to capture. Advertisers conduct sophisticated research to determine consumers' perceptual affinities, and to distinguish those affinities among targets for one or another type of product. The use and placement of color and contrast, the placement and visibility of typography and photography, the adaptation of moving image and cinematic techniques for the purposes of persuasion are all part and parcel of advertisers' project.

More importantly, the entire practice of advertising has focused almost exclusively on the inscription of two-dimensional surfaces. Magazine ads and billboards are surfaces. Television screens are surfaces that can simulate depth and movement. Even Internet banner ads are simply surfaces that might add occasional internal or external motion. Advertisers have enjoyed enormous success adapting new surfaces for advertising. Recently, the agency Saatchi & Saatchi built cardboard cutouts of the back of a man appearing to urinate to support The Privy Council's campaign for more public toilets in New York City.[90] The realistic-looking models were placed in front of trees in public parks; once bystanders got close enough to realize that the man was actually a foil, they could also read the URL printed on the back of his t-shirt.[91] Duval Guillaume's Brussels agency printed white bags with revolvers emblazoned upon them, oriented so that when carried by the cutout handle, the customer appeared to be carrying a sidearm. The bags promoted a new release from a popular crime writer.[92] BBDO New York created a blue t-shit for FedEx with an image of the familiar FedEx envelope screen printed on the lower right side, such that from a short distance wearers appeared to be carrying a real FedEx shipment under their arm.[93] In 2004, widespread complaints forced Columbia Pictures to stop their plans to print ads for summer movies on the bases during major-league baseball games.[94]

All these efforts rely on the inscription of two-dimensional surfaces. In every case, these surfaces are generic—that is, they bear no necessary relationship with the products or services advertised. Clever though it may be, the tendency to find and inscribe every surface in our world with advertising moves advertising further and further into the illustrative and associative domains. And following Baudrillard's characterization, the need for advertisement increasingly takes the place of the need for the products and services they once represented.

Even though the in-game ad networks increasingly boast the ability to place three-dimensional objects (e.g, pizza boxes, soda cans) in addition to texturing two-dimensional surfaces, these objects risk remaining empty vessels coated with print advertising; the objects themselves serve little more correlation with the product than the clever bookstore bag. Furthermore, these objects take on no behavior in the target game environment. And even though it might be possible to serve scripted objects into games, the behavior of such an object might not contextualize meaningfully, if at all, in just any game. Generic surfaces without specific functions are particularly conducive to media buying, the primary logic of the advertising industry. All of these signals would suggest the rapid and inevitable colonization of videogames by advertisers, save one major problem: unlike television commercials, magazine ads, outdoor billboards, shopping bags, or even t-shirts, videogames are not fundamentally characterized by their ability to carry images, but by their capacity for operationalizing rules.

Licensing and Product Placement

Simulations are always representations. They present biased perspectives on the function of systems and situations in the material world. Procedural rhetoric takes advantage of this tendency to make claims about how things work in the world. In the domain of advertising, videogames deploy procedural rhetoric when they simulate player-consumer interaction with products and services, rather than merely simulating advertising through the application of images into virtual environments.

Given its propensity for visual inscription and their predisposition toward media buys, it should come as no surprise that the advertising industry has advanced dynamic in-game ads as their principal vision of the future. But is advertising in videogames doomed to the realm of the higher-order simulacrum of the *Virtual Magic Kingdom*? Is it condemned to a contrivance of fantasy lifestyles? Toward an inscription of virtual surfaces as rampant as their inscription of real ones? I want to suggest that videogames offer a mode of engagement with products and services that can activate critical perspectives on consumption. But to do so, advertising must reconnect with the fundamental property of videogames, procedurality.

Licensing

A large percentage of the commercial videogame industry is produced from licensed properties. At the industry's largest publisher, Electronic Arts, some 60 percent of revenue comes from licensed properties like films and sports.[1] Licenses are common across all media and every consumer good these days. We buy Hello Kitty underpants for our children, enduring the electronic beep of their plastic Little Mermaid cell phones as we drive them to claim Strawberry Shortcake Happy Meals. We even take solace in the relatively "high" cultural value of *Harry Potter*, often ignoring the fact that the books in that series seem intricately crafted for screenplay optioning, cinematic release, and subsequent dispersal via toys, games, and endless other accessories. Children recognize and lust after licensed products not for their intrinsic value, but because they recognize the characters emblazoned on their surfaces. And it's not just children; models, musicians, and actresses increasingly sell their names for perfume, cosmetics, or clothing lines funded by investors lining up to cash in on the associative value of Jennifer Lopez, Britney Spears, or the latest celebrity starlet. Young and grown men buy Michael Jordan–emblazoned shoes or Kobe Bryant basketball jerseys. Porsche lends its name to sleekly designed toasters, sunglasses, teakettles, and computer hard drives. Following the strategy that made George Lucas a billionaire, Hollywood producers and studios now plan their development in terms of "properties" and "franchises"—long-term intellectual property conglomerates that can be exploited simultaneously in film, television, videogames, consumer products, comic books, and any other medium the public will purchase.

When we think of licensed properties in contemporary commercial videogames, film and sports franchises usually come to mind first. These deals are huge; Electronic Arts' 2004 exclusive licensing deal with the National Football League (NFL) was reported to total $300 million—and that's just for the *rights* to make games with NFL teams, players, and stadiums.[2] But in the early 1980s, the main videogame licensees were other videogames. Arcade games were much more sophisticated than the home consoles of the day, principally the Atari VCS and the Mattel Intellivision. Games with proven success in the arcades were sure sellers on the home consoles, and many of these popular games—*Pac-Man*,[3] *Joust*,[4] *Burgertime*,[5] *Pole Position*,[6] and *Dig Dug*,[7] among many others—were ported to home console. Creating a procedural representation of a videogame is certainly much less work than creating a procedural representation of a film; the game was already constructed as a set of software-coded rules, and arcade games of the day were simple enough that reverse engineering the gameplay often didn't require an intimate knowledge of how the game was originally developed.

The videogame industry's first experiments with film licensing came around the same time, with the Atari's exclusive license of *E.T.: The Extra-Terrestrial.*[8] In 1982, Atari reportedly paid Steven Spielberg's Amblin Entertainment $20 million for the rights to make a game based on that year's hit movie.[9] The title was rushed through development in less than two months to ensure that it would hit the shelves in time for the Christmas holiday season. The game was widely panned, selling just one million of over five million copies manufactured, the rest of which were returned to Atari and later crushed, encased in concrete, and buried in a landfill near Alamogordo, New Mexico. The Atari VCS versions of *E.T.* and *Pac-Man* are often held principally liable for the videogame market crash of 1983, which is blamed on a glut of low-quality games.

Crash notwithstanding, by the time the home console videogame industry got back on its feet in the late 1980s thanks to the Nintendo Entertainment System (NES), the arcade business was all but dead. And external licenses—especially for sports and films—became increasingly popular. By 2004, licensed sports games were estimated to make up $2.5 billion of the $23 billion generated on that period's current generation hardware (Sony PlayStation 2, Nintendo GameCube, and Microsoft Xbox). Licensed movie and television titles totaled nearly $2 billion, giving licensed games about a 20 percent share of all sales on the hardware just mentioned.[10]

All licensed products serve as illustrative and/or associative advertisements, but apparel, packaged goods, and miscellaneous trinkets serve as fetishes more than as "brand extensions" or legitimate artifacts in their own right. We can think of licenses not as intellectual property in the abstract, but as a network of products that interpret the license in some way. From this perspective, all licensed products always serve as advertisements for each additional node in the network of products. Videogames are no exception of course, but game licenses represent an instructive precedent in licensed property. Despite the financial and cultural dangers of sightless licensing, videogames must necessarily operationalize a licensed property in new ways; unlike a branded lunchbox or t-shirt, a videogame has to allow the player to do something meaningful inside its interpretation. This procedural rendering of a license has the potential to open the property to interrogation and critique on the part of the player. To be sure, the procedural adaptation of a licensed property is not guaranteed to be critically productive, but it is guaranteed to do more than just replicate the licensed property's characters, scenes, or logos as an advertising image.

Consider a familiar example. Film licenses are popular cash cows for game publishers but often miss the mark with players and critics. Most games in the *Harry Potter* series, created and published by Electronic Arts, represent the minimum necessary conceptual effort to produce and sell licensed games.[11] In the five years after the first film in 2001, Electronic Arts released six different Harry Potter titles on every platform, adding up to over thirty different Harry Potter SKUs.[12] Most of these are direct adaptations of the film plots, composed as a series of playable scenarios intermixed with rendered cinematics that fill in the scenes left unplayable. For example, in *Harry Potter and the Chamber of Secrets*, cinematics portray Harry and Ron's forbidden flying car trip from King's Cross station to Hogwarts; once the car crashes into the whomping willow tree, the player takes the controls. The actions afforded to the player then and throughout the game are repetitive, including major actions like learning a spell capable of releasing Ron from the whomping willow, and minor actions like collecting wizard cards.

The systems simulated and omitted in the *Harry Potter* games do more than just recreate the experience of the film while giving the player the ability to take on the role of a favorite character and act out a familiar plot. These specimens also bring the characters down to earth. The books and films are told from the perspective of a third-person narrator, but the games, by virtue of their genre, put the player in direct, first-person control of the characters. The game adaptation of *Harry Potter and the Prisoner of Azkaban* addresses this challenge by giving the player control of the triumvirate of Harry, Ron, and Hermione. This perspective shift is accomplished via a procedural representation of teamwork. The player still controls one character at a time, with the option of switching between them at any time; the other two characters follow the lead. Because different characters learn different spells and gain unique abilities, it is impossible to make progress using just one. In certain cases, the player must carefully move the characters in a specified pattern to complete a task or puzzle, such as opening a hidden door.

In addition to making for more interesting and challenging gameplay, the procedural rhetoric of teamwork casts a retrospective shadow on the rest of the *Harry Potter* properties. The characters are relatively flat—these are children's books after all—and each has a flaw: Harry is naive, Ron is hot-headed,

Hermione is pedantic. But the balance between the group is overshadowed by Harry's lead. He is the hero and he reaps the glory, despite other characters' sacrifices. J. K. Rowling intended to create tension between fear and courage in the stories—one need only recall how Neville Longbottom's attempt to stop Harry and crew in *The Sorcerer's Stone* yields the final points required to win the House Cup. But in general, collaboration in the stories is uneven; the ensemble cast devolves into a wealth of supporting roles, all paying their dues to the title character. The procedural rhetoric of teamwork undermines this position, drawing attention to the system of affiliations, skills, and abilities that contribute to Harry's success. In so doing, the videogames built on the Harry Potter license might return the player to the material world with a reinforced understanding of the relationship between the characters shorthanded in the license's title.

The *Harry Potter* games also lay bare the very operation of licensing itself. Consider the minor tasks like collecting Bertie Botts Everyflavour Beans or Wizard Cards. These activities seem written into the book anticipating their eventual exploitation through real-world licensed products (products which were in fact developed). In the first game, collection rewards little more than the accrual of virtual property, which the player can view in a special menu.[13] By stripping away any pretense of use or exchange value from these collectibles, the game effectively exposes their real-world equivalents as snake oil, highly profitable products manufactured to "extend the property" with little expressive benefit to the consumer. Anna Gunder appropriately characterizes this scenario as an aporia—the question "Why do I collect wizard cards?" is never answered within the game rules.[14]

The *Quidditch World Cup* game offers a different perspective on the property.[15] Based on the fictional sport in the books and films, author J. K. Rowling has described quidditch as a combination of basketball and soccer. On the one hand, *Quidditch World Cup* seems like a perfect example of good game adaptation; rather than cobbling together a meager version of a linear plot, *Quidditch World Cup* takes a subset of the story and operationalizes it in a sports game, a genre with proven expressive strength in the medium. Because quidditch requires flying brooms to play properly, one could argue that it can only be simulated in a computer graphics film shot, a videogame, or in the imagination of a reader. On the other hand, because quidditch remains largely unexplored in both the books and the films, the extensive treatment of the sport in the videogame gives it special purchase for commentary. In some sense, the videogame developers get the first word on how the sport really works.

Quidditch offers nested opportunities for interpretation. For one part, it is a sport with rules, rules that embody their own procedural rhetoric. Basketball and soccer are both team sports with considerable emphasis on collaboration. While powerhouse players like Kobe Bryant and David Beckham increasingly move both sports toward individual accolades, their rules still facilitate relatively even player-to-field distribution. Basketball has been moving in the direction of individualism since Wilt Chamberlain, who remains the sport's top single-game scorer, but it continues to be a more distributed team sport than American football, in which all offensive moves are mediated by one player, the quarterback. And despite Beckham's celebrity, he is a midfielder, not a forward, known primarily for his strong crosses. In essence, Beckham is a terrifically effective assist, famous for the precision with which he gets the ball to strikers, who in turn shoot on goal.

Quidditch keeps the scoring mechanic of soccer and basketball, with all its implications of collaboration. But the fictional sport adds an important orthogonal element, the golden snitch (a small, winged ball) and its corresponding player position, the seeker. As the rules dictate, even a team with a huge score deficit can win the match when its seeker captures the golden snitch. This rule introduces a tension between the team-oriented field players (who are also obliged to protect the seeker from the semi-sentient bludgers that strive to intercept him) and the seeker, who has no interest in the field game whatsoever. Quidditch enforces a procedural rhetoric of individual power, in which a golden boy uses extraordinary talent to overcome adversity. Harry's position as seeker thus reinforces the mystical, transcendental nature of his power, a major theme in the series (like Anakin Skywalker and Frodo Baggins, Harry feels both blessed and afflicted by his unique station). Although it may be technically possible to win a quidditch match on the field, the books and films privilege the snitch-capture victory, one in which the frail underdog uses transcendent power to defeat the brute strength of legitimate athleticism.

While the rules of quidditch are clearly articulated in both the books and the films, quidditch is a complex sport that cannot be easily grasped from casual exposure. The films rely on spectacle, the books on imagination for their representations of the game. But the videogame allows the player to play match after match of the sport, an immersion that allows the rhetoric of individual power to inform his perspective on the character and its representation in the rest of the franchise. More importantly, the videogame adaptation reveals quidditch as a game with broken rules. When it came time to operationalize the rules Rowling provides in the fictional world, the developers of *Quidditch World Cup* must have realized that a literal interpretation yielded an unplayable game. To allow the player the ability to seek the snitch at all times would eliminate the necessity of the field game, and vice versa. Instead, the videogame interpolates new rules to balance the field and snitch dynamics. Specifically, the game interface features a snitch meter; each successful gesture on the part of the player (including goals, passes, and so forth) increases the meter. When it fills, the game offers the player a chance to catch the snitch, effectively pausing the field game.

Electronic Arts' revision of the rules was necessary to make quidditch playable as a videogame, but the adaptation also draws attention to the incongruity of the rules of the fictional sport. Team sports like soccer and basketball require collaboration, even if superstars sometimes steal the show. Sports like American football privilege the performance of a few positions, with the rest of the team providing a supporting role. But none of these sports enable victory through the transcendent, individual power of a particular field position, as quidditch does. If chess were played like quidditch, one could win either by checkmate or, say, by dousing the board with thirty-year-old Scotch. *Quidditch World Cup* exposes the rhetoric of individualism inherent to the sport, offering a perspective on the fictional world of Harry Potter that is unavailable in the books or the films.

Harry Potter's underdog individualism and heroic selflessness in the face of evil could be seen as a positive attribute worthy of both empathy and imitation. Or it could be viewed as a selfish affirmation of the transcendental logic that supplies his power—the quidditch seeker represents the series' ongoing theme of separatism, a prejudicial relationship between the magical and the human worlds, the wizards and the death-eaters. The later Harry Potter books make Harry's quest clearer: it is about saving the muggles and the wizards from genocide. As Steven Waldman puts it, Harry Potter has a Catholic theology; he "sees outcome determined by individual actions."[16] As in religion, Harry's moral compass is magnetized by a transcendental force, a force that leads Voldemort to evil, Harry to good.

While the liberal Rowling would likely cringe to see her plea for tolerance contorted into unilateralism, Harry Potter's appeal to the transcendental recalls the kind of cowboy-individualist grandstanding the world has witnessed post–September 11, 2001, four years after the original publication of the first book and its underlying logic (*Harry Potter and the Philosopher's Stone* was first published in 1997 in the U.K., and in 1999 in the U.S. as *Harry Potter and the Sorcerer's Stone*).[17] Whereas a superhero like Spider-Man struggles to separate the good from evil at every turn, distinctions that are always incredibly ambiguous, Harry Potter is continuously guided by a single, transcendent good. Even the risk of evil's influence is disambiguated in Harry and Voldemort's common ontogeny. When Harry is led astray—and it is always at the hand of adult authority figures—those flat characters have no recourse save capitulation to evil. Nowhere to be found are the emotionally torn alter egos of the Green Goblin or the socioeconomic irony of Electro. Harry's universe excludes the deliberation of Spider-Man's equivocal maxim that *with great power comes great responsibility*.

Producers and property owners count on licensed products from franchises like *Harry Potter* both to generate revenue from license fees and to advance incremental consumption of other licensed products. The logic of licensing assumes that every exposure to a licensed product will always reaffirm and deepen the consumer's relationship with that property. The *Harry Potter* games suggest that licensed videogames have the potential to shed light on the values demanded by commitment to a franchise, a perspective fueled by the procedural rhetorics that drive the franchise's constituent parts. These insights might deepen player relationship to the franchise or they might erode it, a unique possibility among licensed products.

Still other games invoke similarly complex relationships with their licensed properties. For many years now, a group of low-budget PC titles has flown under the radar of the high-stakes, high-gloss console game industry. These games are produced on modest budgets and usually sold at retail or online for $20 or less; they fall into a category sometimes called "value publishing." Following the unexpected success of simulation games like *Sim City*,[18] value publishers have marketed original and unlikely titles like *Mall Tycoon*,[19] *Trailer Park Tycoon*,[20] and *Fast Food Tycoon*.[21] The titles borrow their names from the successful commercial games *Transport Tycoon*[22] and *Railroad Tycoon*,[23] strategy/simulations of early railroad construction and management first introduced in the early 1990s. They focus on building business empires (thus the "tycoon" moniker), but all of them also craft quite deep simulations of the day-to-day management issues of a specific industry. With the exception of a few breakout titles the games have never been major sellers, but they occupy an established and supported industry niche.[24]

Originally, all tycoon games featured generic representations of their chosen industries—in this way, they resembled the popular board game *Monopoly*, which also depicted the generic logic of real estate monopolies. By the early 2000s, publishers recognized the potential to apply licenses to these titles. *Cruise Ship Tycoon* became *Carnival Cruise Lines Tycoon*.[25] *Theme Park* gave way to *SeaWorld Adventure Parks Tycoon*.[26] We might be tempted to decry this trend as yet another instance of the branding of everyday life—is nothing safe from trademark branding? But on further reflection, the addition of brand names and their actual products or services may actually underwrite an unusual opportunity for critical assessment of the sponsoring companies.

Carnival Cruise Lines or SeaWorld t-shirts, posters, model ships and plush Shamus serve as illustrative advertising; they call attention to the existence of their sponsoring agencies. Carnival Cruise Lines or SeaWorld games serve as a very peculiar type of demonstrative advertising: they expose the general logics by which these companies provide their services to customers. In *SeaWorld Tycoon*, the player must build a park filled with events and exhibits, choosing from a variety of sea creatures and attractions. He can place food and concessions, as well as souvenir stores and bathrooms. The player must hire and manage staff, fix and clean the park, and care for the animals. The game proceduralizes the logic of running a theme park, and by virtue of their license SeaWorld admits the roles played by park layout, inflated prices, and other common factors of location-based entertainment design in their business model.

For some people, this is old news; of course theme parks and resort venues use structural and financial manipulation to maximize profit and time in-venue. But for others, especially kids, theme parks are sheer magic; the logics by which they operate are deeply hidden, thus the source of their frequent deception. Why, for example, is there a huge toyshop filled with plush seals directly on the (one-way) exit from the seal exhibit? Why does placing concessions near undervisited exhibits increase their popularity? Who are all the underclass who clean the tanks and the bathrooms so that upper-middle-class youngsters can enjoy their family vacation? Engaging players with these procedural rhetorics exposes the material realities of SeaWorld's operations.

These advertisements can be played critically: imagine a parent running through a few sessions with the kids before visiting SeaWorld or embarking on a Carnival Cruise. Contrary to "ruining the magic" of the trip, such an experience would help a child understand how that "magic" is manufactured. One can still buy the plush Shamu, but wouldn't it be better to understand how the theme park itself is manipulating junior to lust after *every* plush character after each exhibit? Such newfound experience of consumption would give much greater personal and social agency to the common parental enjoinder to "choose just one."

Other tycoon-style strategy/management games introduce players to unknown or underrepresented activities. For example, agronomists, farmers, and exurbanites can take pleasure in *John Deere American Farmer*, a farming simulator featuring the title brand's green equipment.[27] As in the games discussed above, *American Farmer* simulates managing a farm, including choosing crops and livestock, tracking weather and market fluctuations, and managing farm employees. John Deere equipment takes on a functional role in the game, each piece of machinery used for its proper function.

While upstart Future Farmers of America members might enjoy owning and operating a virtual combine, the game has particularly powerful opportunities for resonance with urbanites, who typically have no experience with farms and farm equipment. From John Deere's perspective, the advertising is directed not so much toward farmers, but toward nonfarmers, who might alter their conceptual (or even personal) relationship with farmers and farm equipment in response to simulated experiences with the equipment and the tasks that equipment facilitates. This possibility suggests a novel type of advertising. It is not simply demonstrative, as the game does not articulate the tangible features of the John Deere equipment for a party who likely buy such equipment, save perhaps the occasional die-cast combine. It is not simply associative, as the game does not articulate intangible features of the John Deere equipment—say, quality or tradition; again, the player has no intention of associating his own lifestyle with the products represented. We could conclude that the game functions illustratively, simply by displaying John Deere products, but that seems like a gross oversimplification. I would suggest that the game uses demonstrative advertising to create a conversational space between the farming and nonfarming communities. This space need not entail actual spoken conversation; it can also include conceptual conversation—empathy. When John Deere supports empathetic relations with the lifestyle their products help support, they accomplish political and social ends, not just commercial ones. Whether or not die-hard urbanites will raise fists for farm subsidies after a few rounds of *American Farmer* is an open question. But they might have a different sensation when such topics arise, or even when passing the John Deere dealership on the interstate.

Other games function similarly. *Caterpillar Construction Tycoon* does for building equipment and construction what *American Farmer* does for agriculture (although unfortunately the game has received universally abysmal reviews).[28] *America's Army* inspired the United Nations World Food Programme to create a videogame with a quite different theme: *Food Force*, an abstract simulation of the U.N.'s emergency food program.[29] The game consists of six missions, each corresponding with a different aspect of the World Food Programme's operations. In one mission, the player pilots a helicopter to locate refugees (figure 6.1); another mission entails the preparation of food packages; in another, the player airdrops the food, taking into account wind

Figure 6.1 *Food Force* suggests that being a humanitarian is a viable career choice by representing the tasks and goals of that profession.

conditions for proper targeting. *Food Force* could be seen to serve the same function as licensed games like *SeaWorld Adventure Parks Tycoon* and *John Deere American Farmer*: all these games mount procedural rhetorics of legitimacy. The games argue that the occupations they represent are valid ones, worthy of both respect and pursuit. Effectively, *Food Force* is really just *United Nations Humanitarian Tycoon*.

Cyberlore's videogame interpretation of the Playboy license offers a similar example in a rather different domain. *Playboy: The Mansion* combines the social simulation of *The Sims* with the business simulation of *Transport Tycoon*.[30] In addition to building both platonic and physical relationships with starlets, producers, and models, players must outfit their publication offices, commission articles, and persuade those starlets, producers, and models to pose for the magazine's signature spreads. The player then photographs these models in their polygonal au naturel.

The game certainly celebrates the familiar ideal of Hugh Heffner's famous lifestyle, but it contextualizes that roguish behavior as part of an overall business strategy. Playboy has built an empire around lasciviousness, and the game proceduralizes that logic. Readers respond better to spreads of well-known celebrities, but unknowns are easier to persuade to pose. The same goes for interviews and articles, and players must develop business relationships with ornery rock stars, actors, and other personalities. The game argues that lechery is a business, not a lifestyle; the consumer's ribald desires are serviced by an industry, not by a set of eager and willingly promiscuous young women.

While tycoon games are largely relegated to the less glamorous station of second-shelf retail placement in the United States, Japanese licensed advergames have gone mainstream. Among the many unusual and innovative games that find their way onto the PlayStation 2 in Japan is *Yoshinoya*, an action game based on the popular rice and curry bowl restaurant in Asia and a select U.S. cities.[31] The player takes on the role of a new employee at one of the chain's stores. Gameplay consists of fast-reflex button presses to serve customers their requested meals, one of four mapped to the PlayStation's cross, square, circle, and triangle buttons. After each morning, lunch, and evening shift, the player faces a kind of customer boss, for whom he must prepare a bowl of tea and a rice bowl, and—curiously—mash a button repeatedly to give the final meal a golden glow. The game is highly stylized, featuring cel-shaded graphics and a good deal of comic relief. The player must serve as many customers as quickly as possible (see figure 6.2). As more time passes

Figure 6.2 *Yoshinoya* simulates the core values of this rice bowl restaurant chain—speed and accuracy of service. © 2004 SUCCESS. Licensed by YOSHINOYA D&C.

without service, the customers' heads grow increasingly large as a signal of their ire. At higher levels, the bosses take on additionally comical forms—a strongman or a robot, for example.

The business management aspect in *Yoshinoya* is far less detailed than in any of the tycoon-style games on account of significantly different goals. Rather than leveraging a brand name to legitimate the vocation for which it is metonymic, *Yoshinoya* mounts a procedural rhetoric about the values of the franchise, constraining player action toward conduct consistent with that service value. In so doing, the game makes demonstrative claims about the service the player might experience as a customer of Yoshinoya. These claims are triggered by a role inversion; rather than occupying the familiar role of customer, the player is thrust behind the counter, forced to tend to dozens of simultaneous versions of himself as patron.

Yoshinoya's procedural claims all revolve around haste and accuracy of service. This is a fast-food chain where *speed* is still a real virtue. The simulated customers have little patience for dawdling, making the experience of counter service frenetic. At the same time, orders are simplistic, accomplished with one of the four primary controller buttons, abstractions for the rudimentary service options available at Yoshinoya. This is a benefit, not a failing; it represents the limited (but no doubt equally tasty) opportunities for gastronomical satisfaction. *Yoshinoya* presents the player with the fundamental logic of its store operations: quickly and correctly serve a small permutation of dishes as rapidly as possible. Even the boss battles underscore this value. To serve tea and rice bowls, the player must stop a moving needle within the correct segment of a gauge. Here a unit operation for running food out to the table is encapsulated in an abstract mastery of quick timing.

And *Yoshinoya* is not the only rice bowl restaurant game in the Japanese PlayStation 2 marketplace. *Curry House CoCo Ichibanya* simulates the operation of a CoCo Ichibanya curry restaurant, a chain as widely known in Japan as McDonald's is in the West.[32] Lest gamers think if they've played one rice bowl game they've played them all, *CoCo Ichibanya* sports gameplay and rhetoric quite different from that of *Yoshinoya*'s.

CoCo Ichibanya is a much more complex game. The player again controls the restaurant's service workers, not its customers, but the detail of service is much higher. When customers enter the restaurant, the player must press a controller shoulder button to call out "irashaimase!," the standard greeting with which proprietors of Japanese establishments welcome their customers. CoCo Ichibanya offers menu service, so the player must take a customer's order, then prepare it. Food preparation is an intricate, multipart process designed with great cleverness. The restaurant primarily serves curry dishes: rice with curry sauce and a vegetable or meat item on top. When customers order, they specify a size and a meat addition, as well as customizations like hot sauce. In the lower portion of the screen, the player assembles the dishes, using nontrivial analog stick gestures to scoop rice, pour the curry sauce, and add hot sauce if desired. The latter gesture is identical to the timed gauge-stopping mechanic in *Yoshinoya*, but rice-serving and curry-pouring require a great deal of dexterity on the part of the player. To pour curry, the player must move the PS2 analog stick at an angle commensurate with the quantity of curry to be poured (an on-screen gauge aids approximation) and then rotate the controller around in a circle to complete the action (see figure 6.3). Meat and vegetable selections must be dropped in the fryer, and the player needs to take care not to burn them, so as not to waste time and raw materials. The whole process feels approachable and quite charming on the first level, in which only a few guests visit the restaurant. In later levels, the player must

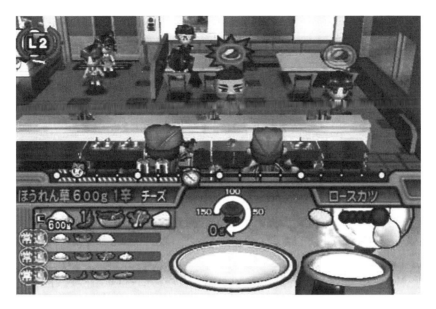

Figure 6.3 *CoCo Ichibanya* recreates the restaurant's food preparation practices. © 2004 Dorasu © Ichibanya Co. Ltd.

juggle many simultaneous orders, while still remembering to shout "irashaimase" in welcome and "arigato gozaimashita" in thanks when patrons depart.

The differences between *Curry House CoCo Ichibanya* and *Yoshinoya*'s procedural rhetorics are numerous. Where *Yoshinoya* abstracts food preparation and service into a single button-press, *CoCo Ichibanya* models preparation in considerable detail. The addition of menus leads to many more permutations of dishes, which necessitates more manual preparation. Furthermore, the gestural preparation and serving controls demand skill and the improvement of that skill. In short, *CoCo Ichibanya*'s procedural rhetoric shows the player that the restaurant *actually prepares the food*, rather than just scoop it out of a premade vessel. The game also makes claims about customer service. Where Yoshinoya prides itself on speed of service, CoCo Ichibanya retains the formality of greetings and personalized service. The abstraction of the greeting in *Yoshinoya* and its retention in *CoCo Ichibanya* signal deeper values of service in the latter, implying greater personal care and attention.

As videogames, these two are fun and unusual specimens whose novelty and absurdity make up much of their charm. As advertisements, the games are sophisticated efforts to operationalize the core features of each restaurant's respective food and service values. Because the player possesses a mature, empirical understanding of dining out, playing the game helps him interrogate a sense of personal compatibility with each of these restaurants. The license is important in this case; it introduces a litmus test in the game experience: is this representation commensurate with the player's previous experiences at these restaurants? If not, the games could be read as attempts to reconcile previous service ills with new solutions. If it is commensurate, the player's relationship with the chain is renewed or improved. And new customers get a sense of what to expect when they walk in the door, effectively practicing to be a restaurant customer. Either way, the games advance their invitations to the real-world versions of their represented restaurants through procedural rhetorics, rule-based embodiments of their respective licensors' service claims.

As with *E.T.* and the *Harry Potter* games, the very act of creating games around the Yoshinoya and CoCo Ichibanya licenses invokes unavoidable associative advertising claims: the fact that these restaurants have a PlayStation version of themselves suggests a desire to speak to a certain subset of the general population (although the game-playing population in Japan is arguably more diverse than its Western counterpart). But a simulation of the business processes of curry houses, theme parks, men's magazine empires, and farming reconnects the features and functions of products and services with their social context. Traditionally, games based on licensed properties have been vilified, usually for encouraging sloppy design and development in the service of coordinated release dates. But licensed properties also provide an opportunity for advertisers to make demonstrative claims about their products and services, opening a space for critical interrogation of these claims *and* the social conditions they assume, represent, or accentuate.

Product Placement

Clark Gable's performance sans undershirt in the 1934 film *It Happened One Night* is said to have caused an immediate nose-dive in the undershirt industry.[33] According to legend, undergarment manufacturers even tried to sue distributor Columbia Pictures for the affront.[34] Ten years later, the Otto Preminger film-noir adaptation of Vera Caspary's *Laura* featured a fictional whiskey called Black Pony;[35] the film's success spawned the creation of a real whiskey by the same name. By the following year, Joan Crawford poured authentic Jack Daniels whiskey in another film noir, 1945's *Mildred Pierce*, solidifying the feasibility and appeal of writing products into films, a strategy now widely known as product placement.[36]

Despite these early successes, product placement remained sporadic for several decades. *Smokey and the Bandit* featured the Pontiac Trans-Am as much as it did Burt Reynolds, but that was not until 1977.[37] The modern birth of product placement as a deliberate marketing strategy is usually traced to the 1982 Steven Spielberg film *E.T.*, one of the original sources of film-to-videogame licensing, as discussed above.[38] Apocryphal stories suggest that M&M's were originally used as the candy E.T. scatters in the film, but that Mars requested them to be removed because they feared the film would flop— or because they didn't to be associated with aliens.[39] No matter the truth, Hershey's Reese's Pieces were on the verge of being discontinued before their role in the film catapulted the candy to a new and lasting success.

Today, product placement is an integral part of almost every film and television production. Some instances are obvious. Following Pontiac's lead twenty years earlier, BMW introduced their Z3 roadster for the first time in the James Bond film *GoldenEye*.[40] Others are less obvious; for example, Ford provides all the vehicles in the television series *24*, and thus most of the cars the viewer sees on the show are Fords.[41] These subtle placements often go unnoticed by viewers, unless additional sponsorship deals require the writers to draw attention to them. One episode of the spy drama *Alias* garnered guffaws when main character Sydney Bristow (Jennifer Garner) called to her companion Michael Vaughn (Michael Vartan) before a pursuit, "Take the Ford F-150!—Follow the Mustang!"[42]

Cynicism and disgruntlement over product placement abounds. As with cinema pre-show ads and commercial breaks on paid cable, many consumers perceive product placement as an unwelcome intrusion. Some filmmakers have mocked this type of Hollywood commercialism by using repetitive, invented brand name products in their films (for example, Red Apple Cigarettes in Quentin Tarantino's *Pulp Fiction*, *Four Rooms*, *From Dusk til Dawn*, and *Kill Bill Vol. 1*).[43] Novelist David Foster Wallace satirized commercial sponsorship through the notion of "sponsored time" in his novel *Infinite Jest*; in the near-future of the novel, calendar years are known by their product sponsor: Year of Dairy Products from the Heartland, Year of the Trial-Sized Dove Bar, Year of the Depend Adult Undergarment.[44] These critiques are valid and necessary. Advertising continues to inch closer and deeper into every fold of our daily lives. This "ad-creep," as it is sometimes called, is slow-moving and treacherous; lack of vigilance will ensure that no experience remains unclaimed by the ravenous appetite of advertising.

But product placement in particular faces critique mostly because it comes so late into the encroaching trends of advertising. Some would ague that advertising has no place at all in our contemporary lives, but such a claim demands a holistic and credible solution to consumer capitalism—not just a critique, the likes of which are common, but a solution that could be implemented in short order, such that cultural and social trends would not overtake it.

Absent such an alternative, we would do well to consider what kind of advertising is socially better and worse than others, to pursue the better strategies, and to disrupt the worse ones. As I argued in the previous chapter, illustrative and associative advertising are of the latter type, especially those strategies driven primarily to support the cancerous practices of the advertising industry, without even supporting the marketing goals of their clients let alone the general social good. I want to suggest that product placement offers a perspective on a socially productive kind of advertising, one that begins to reintroduce a property long missing from advertising and necessary for its connection to procedurality, namely *context*.

Even in the heavy-handed *Alias* case above, the Ford vehicles were featured in a somewhat "natural" situation—that is to say, the vehicles are being put to credible use by characters we know and whose situation we understand. Ford probably hoped to capitalize on the popular appeal of the program ("anything Michael Vaughn drives must be cool"), a typical goal for associative advertising. Yet, while most of us don't plan to use our vehicles for international intrigue, the addition of meaningful context foregrounds actual features and functions of the vehicles—the F-150 has girth and torque, making it able to close the distance between it and the car it chases, and allowing it to barrel through a dropped parking garage arm with no hesitation; the Mustang is fast and agile, a suitable car for eluding government pursuit.

These are admittedly rudimentary showcases of product features. But, perhaps surprisingly, they suggest how product placement integrates demonstrative messages. Furthermore, because the products are contextualized in a fictional environment in which the viewer has already suspended disbelief, the products are subjected to greater scrutiny. In a high-intensity program like *Alias*, viewers are constantly noodling over consistencies and inconsistencies in the unfolding action. In short, the fictional abstraction of entertainment properties invites a critical perspective on placed products more so than does other advertisement.

Take another example. Steven Spielberg's 2002 film *Minority Report* is riddled with product placement.[45] The film features a futuristic Lexus automobile and transportation pod, both of which were actually built and shown at the Los Angeles Auto Show. The story is set in the year 2054, so the most obvious message the ad sends is that the Lexus brand persists fifty years hence. This is a claim about product quality and durability. But more so, the vehicle functions as a kind of longitudinal concept car. Concept cars are a mainstay of the automobile industry, and they serve a greater purpose than show alone. Concept cars demonstrate what a manufacturer believes is important for the future of the automotive medium. In fact, this is precisely how Spielberg framed his invitation to Lexus: "I thought Lexus might be interested in going into a speculative future to see what the transportation systems and cars would look like on our highways in fifty years."[46] Lexus designers worked with Spielberg and the production crew to craft both a "conventional" vehicle and a "pod" that rode on a high-speed magnetic-levitation (mag-lev) system, a kind of futuristic, automated highway. The feasibility of the vehicle was less important than the claims it housed on Lexus's behalf: these vehicles are conceptual statements about Lexus's vision for Spielberg's (via Philip K. Dick's) fictional future.

Compare the Lexus with another product placement in the film. After the precogs foresee him perpetrating a violent crime, a frantic John Anderton (Tom Cruise) attempts to elude pursuit. During his flight, he passes through a commercial district and is accosted by a robotic sales clerk at a futuristic Gap retail store. The robot knows who he is and what he last purchased, and begins recommending matching accessories. Anderton promptly disables the robot before continuing his attempt to evade the pre-crime division. Is Gap suggesting that its future incarnation will sport an advanced version of an Amazon.com-like recommendation system? And if so, is Spielberg, who invented modern film product placement twenty years earlier, criticizing the very practice? This tension is irresolvable in the film, and the viewer is left to ponder whether the present course of data gathering and mining leads to more or less freedom in the future.

On a more mundane level, reality television shows further accentuate the potential for product placement to reorient advertising toward the demonstrative register. *Survivor* creator Mark Burnett aired a reality show called *The Restaurant* in 2003–2004, which chronicled restaurateur Rocco DiSpirito's efforts to develop a thriving restaurant in New York City.[47] Despite the high drama one expects from shows of this kind, *The Restaurant* showed much more like a documentary about the ups and (more frequent) downs in this cutthroat business. American Express served as a major sponsor, using the show as a platform to promote their OPEN Network, a set of services for small business owners, including loyalty points, savings on common business expenses, and financial advisement services. During the course of the season, DiSpirito occasionally used American Express's services in actual situations in which they might prove useful. While American Express may have nudged producers to suggest the use of certain services, the situations themselves were unscripted, and therefore feasible representations of the actual use of the services.

Product placement in videogames follows in the tradition of film and television. Highly customized, contextualized products are integrated into gameplay. In the case of videogames, product placement is often more rudimentary than in television and film, largely because the themes and genres of commercial games are much narrower. In one rather example already mentioned briefly, Honda Motors arranged to place its Element SUV in the snowboarding game *SSX 3*.[48] Honda had recently introduced the Element, a boxy truck they hoped to market to young buyers with "active lifestyles," of which surfing and snowboarding were actual or "aspirational" activities. The vehicle was placed in certain courses as an obstacle of sorts. The game awards points based on speed and style, and tricks that interacted with the Element were awarded extra points. Jeep used an identical method to insert their vehicles into *Tony Hawk Pro Skater 3*, allowing the player to perform tricks on the surfaces of virtual Wrangler and Liberty vehicles.[49]

These examples of product placement are pure associative advertising, with little purchase for critical consumer interaction save disparagement. The closest Honda's *SSX* advertisement steered toward demonstrative advertising came from occasional placements directly in the player's path, perpendicular to the course, with its suicide doors open on both sides so as to encourage the player to board through it. The suicide door feature is at least minimally demonstrated here (Honda designed the vehicle that way so as to more easily accept large cargo like, say, snowboards).

Other videogame product placements fall equally flat. Dole-emblazoned bananas litter the world of *Super Monkey Ball 2*, a game in which the player pilots a plastic sphere-encased monkey around treacherous courses collecting bananas.[50] By happenstance, at the time of the game's Japanese release, Dole was introducing a new luxury banana in that market (something that could probably only happen in Japan). The serendipity led to a weird cross-promotion: Dole put *Super Monkey Ball* stickers on the bananas they sold in stores, and Sega put Dole stickers on the bananas in the game.[51] This placement seems unqualified even as associative advertising; anomalous thought it may be, the placement has the flavor of a boardroom prank more than anything else. If it does function as advertising at all, it does so mostly as an illustrative ad in the form of an archetypal power-up—even if monkeys do like bananas, *Super Monkey Ball*'s monkeys are encased in plastic anyway.

Absurdities continue to abound in videogame product placement. In 2006, Electronic Arts introduced sponsored matches in boxing game *Fight Night Round 3*.[52] Sponsored matches are common in real-world boxing, and thus branded rinks and venues are a plausible avenue for extending those deals into the virtual. In the game, these matches take the form of sponsorships or (static) in-game ads. *Fight Night* includes a Burger King–branded sponsored match, in which the creepy King mascot serves as a new trainer to help coach and support the player. Having the King as trainer purportedly improves the player's "heart" attribute. In the game, "heart" contributes to the character's likelihood to give up or fight back when he is losing the match, but the irony of this particular pairing of sponsor and attribute was not lost on many Internet message-board conversations about the game. Says one player, "I mean, since when has Burger King been good for someone's heart? I guess that's the price we pay to make it to the big time in *Fight Night Round 3*."[53] Burger King's recent advertising, including the "subservient chicken" website, uses subversion in the hopes of rising above the media noise, but the correlation of Burger King and healthy hearts seems only to cause players to meditate on the message's erroneousness.[54] Burger King, it seems, has successfully created unsympathetic discourse a propos their own advertising.

Some product placements begin to approach the critical utility of the filmic and televisual examples discussed above. One reason automobile manufacturers are more likely to advertise in videogames stems from the evolution of driving games of the 1990s. Driving games have always been popular—*Pole Position* and *Turbo* were favorite arcade games of the early 1980s.[55] But as 3D games became the norm in the era of Nintendo64 and PlayStation, new opportunities for driving simulations emerged. Creating realistic driving games like *Gran Turismo* required more complete vehicle models and specifications.[56] As a part of this process, developers went to auto manufacturers asking for data about their vehicles—and permission to use it in the game.

The result was a sophisticated virtual test track on which players could experiment with a variety of makes and models of vehicle, from the mundane economy hatchback to exotic formula-1 racers. The simulations were unforgiving, and simply taking turns wildly at top speed was no longer an option. Vehicles were divided into comparable classes, and players had to win races with lower performance vehicles to earn money to buy higher performance ones. As a result, every player of *Gran Turismo* was subjected to a wide variety of vehicles they might actually consider for purchase, a scenario one would probably expect to hear from Ralph Nader before Sony.

Despite their comparative realism, driving games are not simulators, and they do not purport to reproduce accurate experiences. The real-time rendering demands and limited memory of console systems further constrain the ability to create "accurate" representations of vehicle performance. But such a failing is immaterial for the player. An accurate simulation of torque, horsepower, weight, and braking is less important than the relative credibility of one vehicle's performance relative to another. A player may never get a complete picture of a single car, but he can gain a rough approximation of the field of relative benefits among a group of vehicles in a comparable class. The developers strive to create a balanced experience for all vehicles, imposing a level of disinterest that suggests (but does not ensure) that no single vehicle will be improperly characterized. In any case, what is most important about this example of videogame product placement is that unlike the *SSX* Honda or the *Tony Hawk* Jeep, the simulation of the vehicles is intrinsic to both the gameplay and the advertising. Here again, the advertising enters the demonstrative register, while retaining the social context usually reserved for an associative or illustrative message.

Growth of this type of videogame product placement has been slow, possibly as a result of the small intersection between credible scenarios for real-world products and commercial videogame themes. *The Sims* is one of the only games that depicts the quotidian household tasks that most consumer products facilitate.[57] McDonald's and Intel both placed products in *The Sims Online*,[58] reportedly paying seven-figure sums for in-game objects.[59] While the Intel placement did little more than play the familiar Intel Inside jingle alongside the company logo, the McDonald's kiosk ran code in the simulation; using it allowed players both to quell their hunger attribute on that chain's greasy delights and to increase their fun attribute thanks to its franchised charm. Thus the kiosk makes claims about the restaurant's actual features and functions—in this case, that McDonald's is a fun place to quash peckishness. Although the procedural representation is extremely rudimentary, it does embody its advertising claims in the logic of its interaction, a simple procedural rhetoric.

One of the most sophisticated examples of videogame product placement comes from an unlikely source, the stealth action game *Splinter Cell: Pandora Tomorrow*.[60] Like the others in the series, the game features operative Sam Fisher on another covert quest against terrorists. Publisher Ubisoft struck a deal with mobile handset manufacturer Sony Ericsson to include two of the latter's mobile phones in the game, the P900 PDA phone and the T637 camera phone. The two devices were integrated into the gameplay in such a way as to require the player to use them frequently and meaningfully during play. The larger, more complex P900 acts as a kind of menuing system, allowing the player to change weapons and communicate with remote command. The smaller T637 acts as a covert camera, which the player must use in certain missions to snap spy photos of terrorist leaders.

At first blush, the placement seems downright associative; these high-tech devices are placed in an environment of intrigue, making the handsets seem more like the James Bond gadgets they strive to resemble. One might compare the Sony Ericsson placement to Nokia's insertion of their devices in *Minority Report* and, more memorably, in *The Matrix*.[61] But whereas these film product placements focus on the products' appearance, the videogame placements in *Pandora Tomorrow* focus on the products' function. In the game, the devices are rather intricately simulated, such that their form, interfaces, and features match the product. Ubisoft effectively created a simulation of the product in the videogame, one that acts more like a hands-on demo than a mere mimicry of its exterior chrome.

Mobile phones, especially high-end ones like the P900, sport hefty price tags, often upwards of $500. Despite the gravity of such a purchase, most mobile phone retail stores make it impossible to properly experience the devices in practice. They are typically secured to antitheft displays that make them impossible to pick up and manipulate. Many suffer from drained or removed batteries, and still others sport simulated screens, as if the devices were mere props intended to showcase the retail display stands that support them. The retail experience offers no greater depth than *The Matrix*; the devices are represented as equivalent to their surfaces. The virus of illustrative and associative advertising has infected products even at the point of purchase.

Mobile phones and PDAs are very personal devices; we carry them with us everywhere, we rely on them for real-time access to a variety of changing signals from our daily lives, and we expect their efficient user interfaces to provide fast access to necessary functions. While the covert operative is a fanciful perspective for a product demonstration, he actually shares much in common with users of these contemporary devices: both are pressed for time, both need to develop practice and efficiency in selecting and executing handheld computational tasks, both endure high-stress situations in which matters of great import appear urgent. The simulation of the Sony Ericsson phones in *Pandora Tomorrow* addresses both of these issues through a procedural representation of the product in a credibly transferable context. Rather than say, *look how cool this device is!*, it says, *here's what you can do with this device*. This is a sure sign of a procedural rhetoric at work in an in-game product: it makes claims about what the product does, and it contextualizes that functional value in a transferable social situation. This product placement sports demonstrative value and context enough to put it on par with the use of American Express OPEN in *The Restaurant*. This isn't a world-changing advertisement, but it is a step down the right path.

The difference between product placement and dynamic in-game advertising, discussed in the previous chapter, is worth noting explicitly. Massive or IGA could serve a Sony Ericsson P900 into a game—into any game, once the title is configured to speak to the network's ad-serving middleware. But the mere placement of objects or images only serves to illustrate their presence, not to simulate their features and functions. And as in film and television, product placement in games faces predictable dangers. The tension between expression and advertising is the greatest of these. Television networks often fashion programming around ad placement more than tuning ad placement to original expression. Just consider the hopefuls in *The Apprentice*, forced to design Pepsi and Levi's advertising. Are these really appropriate tests of their worth as potential real estate developers?[62] If advertisers had their way, videogames would take place entirely on city streets and in subway stations—places where virtual versions of familiar spaces like billboards can be populated efficiently.

The need to explicitly and meaningfully operationalize products in games marks two decisive breaks with the traditional logics of advertising. First, it completely dismantles the media buy. Context and code-level integration are required for videogame product placements, efforts that require specificity at the design and technical levels. Hollywood studios contend with this situation all the time—if desired, each television or film script must be carefully and manually integrated with products and services. But videogames extend this challenge; it is not enough for products merely to appear in the game; this can be accomplished through the dynamic networks. Rather, they must be simulated and integrated into the gameplay. The numbers and levels of integration for a game publisher and developer are much higher than those of a film studio.

Second, videogame product placement undermines advertisers' obsession with the image. The visual inscription of surfaces is a nonstarter in videogames, whose expressive power comes from procedural representation. This hurdle may be impassable for the advertising industry in its present form. While advertisers think they have spent a decade making a transition to the digital via the World Wide Web, Internet advertising is little more than digital representations of two-dimensional images, just another inscribed surface. The entire advertising industry has taken on metaphoric stereotypes for its obsession with surface; the ad man is a façade, his designer shoes and suits hiding his dearth of substance, and the advertising agency is a veneer, its "creative" environment of Razor scooters and exposed ventilation hiding its scanty imagination. Changing this state of affairs will not be simple.

Advergames

Electronic Arts (EA) canceled all its plans for product placement in *The Sims 2* after its failed experiments in *The Sims Online*. Julie Shumaker, EA's director of ad sales at the time of the release of *The Sims 2*, explained their rationale: "We realized breaking the Sims fantasy in this case would detract from the player's experience, so we declined."[1] EA's decision serves as a gut-check for dynamic in-game advertisers who claim that ads always add realism to games, or that realism is always desirable. Even if advertisers manage to develop an ability to craft procedural rhetorics that represent their clients' products and services, commercial publishers may not have any interest in hosting them in their games.

What's more, commercial game genres offer limited opportunities for the wide range of products and services on the market. With *The Sims* off the ad market, few other popular, commercial games depict everyday household situations—the only sensible context for consumer-oriented packaged goods, which constitute a great deal of consumer advertising messages. Transferable contexts like that of *Splinter Cell: Pandora Tomorrow* may not always be possible or appropriate. Videogame publishers and consumers likely will not tolerate a glut of placements in commercial games. With the cost of developing AAA console titles predicted to double on Xbox 360 and PlayStation 3, even seven-figure ad placements won't necessarily offset development costs enough to justify them. And although proceduralized products in commercial games represent an interesting application of advertising in videogames, the field is currently a limited one for both advertisers and developers.

An alternative presents itself: if a videogame appropriate to host a particular product or service doesn't exist, a company could create a new one, an advergame. Unfortunately, since the original ⟨kpe⟩ report in 2001, the term has been unfairly applied only to associative Web games like *Mountain Dew Skateboarding* and *Ms. Match*. But I understand *advergame* to refer to any game created specifically to host a procedural rhetoric about the claims of a product or service. More succinctly put, advergames are simulations of products and services.

Despite their apparent novelty, advergames have a long history. Text-based mainframe *Star Trek* games were popular in the 1970s, although the games were unauthorized and are probably better characterized as the computational equivalent of fan fiction.[2] The first film-to-game adaptation was 1976's *Death Race*, a controversial arcade game based on the 1975 film of the same name (figure 7.1).[3] But the earliest game I have found with authorized branding in support of a product is the 1976 arcade game *Datsun 280 Zzzap*, a pseudo-3D driving game of the same style as Atari's more popular *Night Driver* (figure 7.2).[4] Calling *Datsun 280 Zzzap* an advergame might be a stretch, since nothing about the game's mechanics was necessarily tied to the vehicle. The

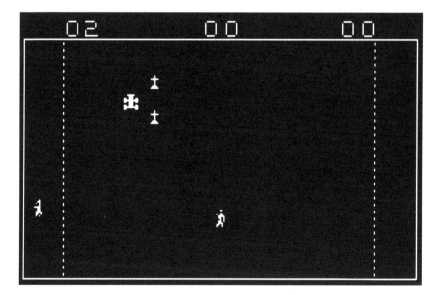

Figure 7.1 Inspired by the film *Death Race 2000, Death Race* may be the first videogame based on a film.

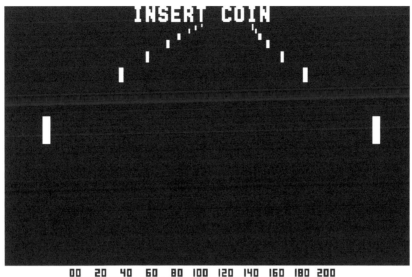

Figure 7.2 Even though the vehicle itself never appears in the game, *Datsun 280 Zzzap* is the first videogame with an advertising sponsor.

cabinet's marquee depicted a Datsun 280Z, although another, less common version was also released sans branding, called *Midnight Racer*.

By the early 1980s, brands took greater interest in creating games crafted more explicitly around their products. In 1983, consumer packaged goods company Johnson & Johnson released a game for Atari 2600, *Tooth Protectors*.[5] The game depicts a row of teeth at the bottom of the screen, with a player character (the Tooth Protector, or just T. P.) just above it. A ghoulish "snack attacker" drops small pellets, which the player must deflect (figure 7.3). Hitting the snack attacker awards bonus points and a new, more skilled attacker takes his place. Failing to block the pellets will cause the struck teeth to flash (indicating decay) and eventually disappear. The player can restore flashing teeth by pressing the joystick button, which issues a full-regimen tooth cleaning, including brushing, flossing, and mouthwash.

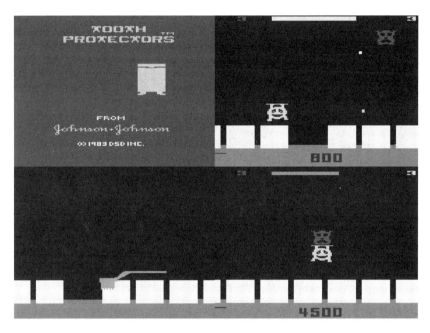

Figure 7.3 Johnson & Johnson's mail-order Atari VCS game *Tooth Protectors* offers a logical rather than a moralistic rationale for dental hygiene.

Given the constraints of the platform, the game is quite sophisticated. Rather than controlling the toothbrush, floss, and mouth rinse—the products Johnson & Johnson actually manufactures and sells—the game gives the player control over the oral hygiene situation itself. The procedural rhetoric is simple, but effective: it represents a causal relationship between eating and oral hygiene. The snack pellets represent undesirable foods; the player gets points for deflecting them (the game equivalent of refusing to eat them). Inevitably, some snacks get past the tooth protector. Snacking isn't the end of the world, but after three collisions between snack pellets and a single tooth, the tooth begins to decay. The player has a limited number of tooth cleanings, but must use them to save decayed teeth. Additional cleanings are awarded at point thresholds, the game's equivalent of extra lives.

Tooth Protectors is a game about the responsibility of oral hygiene. The game's rules enforce a causal relationship between snacking and tooth decay, and the points structure rewards the player for forgoing sugary snacks. However, the rules also admit the reality of snacking not as failure but as human nature. Just as the player cannot possibly deflect every pellet, the child cannot possibly defer every snack. In some cases, the player will inadvertently deflect a pellet at an odd angle that will actually cause it to strike a neighboring tooth. This procedural representation of the temptation of treats is a rather sophisticated adaptation of the Atari 2600's hardware constraints. The cleanings themselves also enforce a procedural rhetoric of duration: the tooth-cleaning animation is actually quite time-consuming in the context of a videogame, running approximately fifteen seconds in duration. The player cannot skip this interlude, just as the child should not cut short tooth-brushing sessions.

What Johnson & Johnson accomplishes with *Tooth Protectors* is to prompt the player—in this era probably a child—to consider dental care as a logical system rather than a moralistic one. Like toilet training and looking both ways before crossing the street, dental hygiene is typically imposed on children as an issue of righteousness: if you do it you are a good kid, and if you don't you are a bad kid. *Tooth Protectors* disrupts this opaque and doctrinal relationship and replaces it with a rationalistic one, expressed via the game's procedural rhetoric.

Admittedly, the game could be attached to any manufacturer, although the manual explains that T. P. deflects snack pellets with an outstretched dental floss (a detail the Atari's graphics leave up to our imagination), a signature Johnson & Johnson product. And the game's manual depicts product images of Johnson & Johnson brand dental hygiene products, including Reach tooth-brush, Johnson & Johnson dental floss, and Act fluoride rinse. But most importantly, *Tooth Protectors* was only available via direct mail order from Johnson & Johnson; it was necessary to collect UPC symbols from their products and to mail them in to get the game at all.[6] Here, promise of a videogame serves as the advertising and direct purchase incentive, which the game then converts from top-down, adult manipulation into a legitimate, eye-to-eye conversation with the child, on his own terms—a home videogame system.

Ralston-Purina attempted the same mail-order strategy with *Chase the Chuckwagon*, also created for the Atari 2600 in the same year. Unfortunately, the game is rather forgettable, neither entertaining nor of particular interest as an early example of videogame advertisement. The player controls a dog, which he must pilot through a maze to reach the familiar Purina chuck wagon logo, while avoiding a dogcatcher and weird, anonymous objects bouncing around the playfield (figure 7.4). The game has more in common with *Coca*

Figure 7.4 Purina's *Chase the Chuckwagon,* a precursor of the associative advergames found on corporate websites today.

Cola Kid than with *Tooth Protectors*—it was probably an attempt to recruit kids to urge their parents to buy Purina brand dog food so as to get the videogame, missing the interesting social advertising message of *Tooth Protectors*.

Since both *Tooth Protectors* and *Chase the Chuckwagon* were not sold at retail, they are quite rare and sought after by collectors. *Chase* is the more common title, but it is also the more highly desirable one.[7] Although it is not named in the book, some claim that *Chase* is the obscure title searched for by the protagonist of D. B. Weiss's 2003 novel *Lucky Wander Boy.*[8] Their rarity speaks to the limited adoption of both games. *Chase the Chuckwagon* in particular makes an instructive point about the dangers of brand-sponsored advergames: the novelty of having a videogame can take the place of using the medium's unique properties for advertising purposes.

No matter the quality, developing an Atari 2600 game is not easy. The hardware was arcane and documentation was closely held; third-party developers reverse-engineered the device in order to figure out how to program it. Whereas most modern online advergames are written in high-level languages, Atari 2600 games were written in assembly. Cartridges had to be manufactured and distributed by mail or in retail (where shelf space is always limited).

But since the mid-1990s, Macromedia Flash and Shockwave have made simple game development easy. The World Wide Web has made distribution easy. And a whole lot of advergames have been created by advertising and interactive agencies.

Many of these, like the games at Postopia or Kewlbox, deploy illustrative or associative advertising. But others have taken a different approach, using videogames to simulate experiences with products or services and in so doing create opportunities for consumers to interrogate those products as potential needs and wants.

In mid-2005, knife, scissor, and gardening tool company Fiskars released an advergame and promotion called *Fiskars Prune to Win*.[9] The premise is simple: the player must trim a continuously growing summer backyard to keep it from going wild. To do so, he must properly use four Fiskars tools: a pruning "stik," hedge shears, a snip, and a pruner. Different tools must be used on different plants; hedge shears are for hedges, not trees. The pruner is for bushes, not for flowers. The game's controls are simple and perhaps overly repetitive, but nevertheless effective in hammering home the proper tools for specific gardening actions.

Fiskars would like consumers to purchase all four products, which are "clearly" required for any self-respecting home gardener. But the game makes this case much differently than would a print ad or television spot; the player controls each of the tools repetitively in sequence, first gaining an understanding of the game's procedural rhetoric, namely Fiskars' claim that each tool is necessary for some type of yardwork. In the initial stages of the game, the player concentrates on learning the mapping of tool to plant type. After this process, the player may begin to map the yard represented in the game onto his own yard. What are the similarities? Do I even have any rose bushes to worry about? Are those tall bushes on my side or the neighbors'? When the player leaves the game, he understands Fiskars' position—we make specialized gardening tools, here they are—as well as his own—some yardwork I concern myself with, some I don't. The game is a means of reconciliation between the brand's claim that all the tools are needed (a claim the game's scoring system strictly enforces), and the likelihood that a real customer will choose one or two of the most applicable tools given a set of options.

By contrast, consider the approach to consumer choice among multiple products deployed in GlaxoSmithKline's *Sensodyne Food Fear Challenge*.[10] Sensodyne is a toothpaste made for people with sensitive teeth. The Food Fear

Challenge is a real-world event that gives those with jaw pain a chance to participate in eating contests with trigger foods, to consult with an on-site dental professional and to take part in other carnival-like activities. The game's theme is boxing, and the player defends a tooth against one of three opponents, Killer Cup of Joe, Ice Cream Kelly, and The Citrus Squeeze. The game forces the player to choose one of eight Sensodyne varieties as his "defense," but the screen seems to be there just as an excuse to list product features—the products are not simulated to perform differently in the actual game.

Tooth Protectors and *Fiskars Prune to Win* offer general consumer awareness that could easily be applied to other brand-name products. It is here that other factors, such as Fiskars' reputation for quality products, needs to take over to influence a purchase decision. For the purpose of understanding the potential of an advergame, a closed-loop purchase decision is immaterial. Rather, what is important is the game's success in creating an open space in which the player might consider the seller's product claims in a simulated, embodied experience. Compare the Fiskars game to a promotional webgame for the DVD release of Academy Award–nominated documentary *Super Size Me*.[11] The game, dubbed *Burger Man*, is a straight clone of the arcade classic *Pac-Man*.[12] The hero has been changed to an admittedly endearing squashed and pixilated version of director Morgan Spurlock. The ghosts have been changed to portly Ronald McDonalds, the dots to burgers, and the power pills to carrots. The gameplay is identical to that of *Pac-Man*; the player must clear the board, avoiding Ronald or using the carrots for a temporary power inversion.

Burger Man stands in stark contrast to the film it promotes. *Super Size Me* is a penetrating and personal interrogation of the short- and long-term effects of a fast-food diet. In the filmmaker's words, the documentary "explores the horror of school lunch programs, declining health and physical education classes, food addictions and the extreme measures people take to lose weight and regain their health."[13] As a promotional tool, the web-based game could have represented this social and political space, asking the player to make rudimentary dietary and lifestyle decisions and seeing the traps of public programs, poverty, or even the health effects of massive fast-food consumption, just as Spurlock takes on in the film. Such a game would have introduced the player to the procedural rhetoric explored in the film, namely that fast food is an integral part of the obesity problem in contemporary America. As executed, *Burger Man* simply provides evidence that the producers can successfully make (or more likely, hire out) a videogame of reasonably high production value.

In at least one circumstance, high production value alone *can* serve as demonstrative advertising. Before the dotcom bubble burst in 2000, interactive agencies frequently created showcase pieces to tout their abilities, usually in the form of web- or email-distributed holiday cards. Once the economy picked up again, this practice resumed, and in December 2005 long-standing interactive agency Agency.com created *Agency.com Snowball Fight*.[14] The game playfully satirized interactive agencies' own relationship with their clients; the player could chose from agency and client characters, each rendered as an appropriate cartoon caricature. Players then competed in a snowball fight with the opposite team, set in stylistic, snow-covered backdrops of cities with Agency.com offices. *Snowball Fight* is a meta-advergame; the services it makes claims about are Agency.com's own ability to create advergames and, by extension, other rich-media web-delivered services. The player, most frequently a current, former, or potential client of the agency, would play the game as a kind of litmus test for using the studio for future work.

But perhaps the most sophisticated procedural rhetoric in a web-based advergame comes in one that does not even use the familiar Flash or Shockwave technologies, let alone more sophisticated 3D browser plugins. Weary late-night office workers, searching for reprieve, might occasionally find themselves staring blankly at their computer screens. Such was the case for *Ready Made* magazine editor-in-chief Shoshana Berger. Burned out on deadlines and dealing with an overdue office construction project, she was fed up and looking for a break. Staring at the blank Google home page in front of her, she absentmindedly typed in the word "escape," then clicked "I'm Feeling Lucky."

The result was a cryptic, abstract game with one-line instructions: "Click and drag the red block, avoiding the blue block as long as you can." The game is implemented in Javascript; the player moves a red block around until one of the moving blue blocks strikes it, at which time a dialogue box reports the number of seconds the player endured (figure 7.5). A hyperlink below the game sends the player to Mountain Bike Ireland, the apparent sponsor or host of the game.[15]

Similar to Janet Murray's claim that the classic puzzle game *Tetris* is "perfect enactment of the overtasked lives of Americans in the 1990s—of the constant bombardment of tasks that demand our attention and that we must somehow fit into our overcrowded schedules and clear off our desks in order

Click and drag the red block, avoiding all the blue blocks as long as you can.

Welcome to the dodge game. Author is unknown. See how long you can avoid the blue squares. This must be one of the most addictive games that has done the rounds on the net. So simple yet so clever.

Figure 7.5 Playing the abstract web-based *Escape* enacts the frenzy for which the sponsor offers respite.

to make room for the next onslaught," the Escape game operationalizes the sensations its services seek to countermand.[16] And not only does game proceduralize the anxiety of office work, but the only way to find the game is literally to be driven to it, to *search for "escape."* A conventional advergame about mountain bike weekend trips to get away from civilization might put you in the saddle, riding through terrain. It would be another extreme sports game, another associative advertisement. But this game does better: it makes the player aware of the quotidian tribulations that would cause such a need in the first place, and then uses search-engine optimization to get the game into the hands of people likely to be suffering from those tribulations. The game not only musters a procedural rhetoric of burdensome coercion, but it actually turns that rhetoric inside out, encasing the game inside the very experience that reveals it.

The same procedural system was far less persuasive when reimplemented by McDonald's in the curious advergame *Shark Bait*.[17] Created before Lent to "remind players of the year-round availability of the Filet-O-Fish sandwich," *Shark Bait* reskins the escape game with swimming sharks and a Filet-O-Fish sandwich.[18] The player must keep the sandwich away from the sharks as long as possible. The rules are the same, but the context has changed radically, and the videogame no longer simulates a process even remotely applicable to the product advertised.

While many small advergames are constrained by budget and expertise to web delivery and therefore to the technologies that play in-browser, some companies have had the wherewithal to sponsor much larger custom-built games. These games often deploy much more sophisticated procedural rhetorics than their web-based counterparts, not because the latter are inherently less capable, but because the former are (necessarily) created by professional game developers rather than advertising agencies. In one notable example, automaker Volvo collaborated with Microsoft to create *Volvo Drive for Life*, a game that allows players to drive three Volvo vehicles on a simulation of the company's Göthenberg proving grounds course, both with and without safety features enabled.[19] Volvo reportedly produced 100,000 copies of the game, which runs on the Xbox home console;[20] the company plans to distribute the games for free at auto shows and in dealer showrooms.

Volvo faces particular difficulties in its chosen approach to the automobile market. The company is principally known for its safety features, but those features can never be demonstrated in a test drive. The company has shown crash-test footage and told harrowing life-saving stories about its vehicles, but all of these tactics use verbal or visual rhetorics. They cite previous accounts and attempt to make credible generalizations based on emotionally gripping, and sometimes manipulative, tales.[21]

Volvo Drive for Life takes a different tack. By simulating the safety features and then removing them from the experience, players can approximate the actual correlation Volvo claims between its mechanical innovations and actual improved safety. The physical accuracy of the simulation is not of primary consequence here; the game is not intended to provide a literal representation of the vehicles' actual responses under every situation. Rather, the game offers a subjective space for the player (and prospective Volvo buyer) to occupy inquisitively. *Volvo Drive for Life* deploys a procedural rhetoric about mechanical consequence, arguing that features like roll stability and front-end collision dampening provide materially demonstrable safeguards.

Given an embodied experience of Volvo's claims about the mechanism of its vehicles, the game then releases the player onto representations of three real-world courses, the Pacific Coast Highway, the Italian Grand Prix, and the road to the ice hotel in Jukkasjärvi, Sweden. This portion of the game includes traffic and other obstacles, giving the player a second point of reference: traffic safety. The Göthenberg track showcases the vehicle's role in safety, while the three highways showcase the driver's role. Unlike games such as *Gran Turismo* where the goal is to race to the finish first, or games such as *Burnout* where the goal is to crash and create as much carnage as possible, in *Volvo Drive for Life* the goal is to traverse the mundane reality of automobile transit.

The procedural representation of the car's capabilities intersects the player's own attention, reflexes, and driving habits. Volvo argues that the mechanical safety devices are tied to the driver's use or abuse of the vehicle; the best way to stay safe is to avoid accidents in the first place. This is a familiar maxim, perhaps even a clichéd one. But note the difference between the verbal argument—"the best way to walk away from an accident is never to get into one"—and the procedural argument—the individual experience of the intersection of human control and mechanical vehicle systems. Whereas the verbal argument verges on the moralistic, offering little meaningful insight into particular risks, the procedural argument allows the proclivities of an individual driver to resonate against the mechanical features that might offset those tendencies. As an advertisement, *Volvo Drive for Life* offers a much more measured statement about the real relationship between safety, equipment, and personal responsibility.

Not all automobile features are related to driving. Many advertisers tempt buyers with performance or luxury features, but more mundane, practical features like storage and seating weigh first on many buyers' minds, especially families. Television ads often idealize these features, showing families effort-lessly hurling movable seats about, or watching furniture magically arrange itself in the back of a waiting vehicle, as if a wizard comes standard. These commercials are usually intended as illustrative or associative advertisements; they document a feature or correlate a lifestyle, with the intention of driving the consumer to the next step in the purchasing process, in the case of auto-mobiles a request for a brochure or a trip to the dealer. Advertisers sometimes call this strategy "hand-raising."

But such strategies risk forestalling the actual relationship between human needs and product features, replacing them with a simulated relationship, that of the *perception* of needs. This perception often takes the place of consumer contemplation. Judith Williamson has related this perception of needs to the production of a gap in ads: "we are invited to insert ourselves into this 'cut-out' space; and thus reenact our entry into the Symbolic."[22] By the Symbolic, Williamson refers to the entry into language that psychoanalyst Jacques Lacan claims to be an endemic part of the formation of the subject. Advertisements give the illusion of freedom, but then implicate their viewers in foregone con-clusions. Williamson argues that ads dupe their viewers into entering this space and filling in the "cut-out" area, rushing into that absence as a vacuum draws air from high to low pressure.[23] In these advertising situations, the per-ception of need is interchangeable with the considered custody of need. Inter-estingly, Williamson's gap bears striking resemblance to the rhetorical figure of the enthymeme, the syllogism that omits one of its premises. The differ-ence Williamson articulates is similar to J. Anthony Blair's objection to visual arguments: the advertising does not enter into dialectical conversation with the viewer. Rather, it manipulates the viewer to supply the missing premise without knowing he is taking part in an argument.

In many cases, advertising itself does not shy away from this allegation. "Aspirational" advertising, a branch of associative advertising, relies on con-sumers' knowing acknowledgment that products and services do not speak to their needs, but to the things they wish were needs. The Nike *Rock Shox* game discussed earlier relies on this strategy: if the player were a world-class athlete, then minor adjustments in equipment could make a real difference. The *SSX 3* Honda placement relies on this logic as well: simply *wanting* to have a snow-boarder lifestyle is reason enough to buy an Element. In the manufacturer's mind, the buyer need not ever evaluate or question these sensations before purchase.

But advergames also have the potential to collapse the vacuum of perceived needs. Consider the so-called "Stow 'n Go" feature DaimlerChrysler has recently built into its Chrysler and Dodge minivans. Stow 'n Go is a seating solution that allows the owner to fold second- and third-row seats completely into the floor, rather than removing and storing them in a garage for large cargo excursions. When the seats are deployed in the normal upright position, the compartments into which they would otherwise stow can secure other items, such as groceries or cargo. Stow 'n Go is a perfect example of a feature for which both traditional advertising and dealer test-drives fall short. The television spots invoke the wizard, miraculously arranging vehicles and lives in thirty seconds' time. The dealer visit offers only an abstract experience of the feature, divorced from any actual scenario.

In 2005, Daimler commissioned a game created by Wild Tangent to address this challenge. *Dodge Stow 'n Go Challenge* was well conceived in principle: use a videogame to simulate the Stow 'n Go seating in a more meaningful way.[24] The game presents a detailed three-dimensional mall scene, asking the player to select among one of several stores (interestingly, one of these is a fully branded Bed Bath & Beyond store, an example of in-advergame advertising, a rather perverse incest to be sure). The player chooses a product appropriate for the selected store, which the game then transforms into an abstract geometric shape. The player is required to fit this shape *Tetris*-style into a grid superimposed inside a top-down view of a minivan.

Unfortunately, the specter of associative advertising haunts the game. The creators were apparently overcome by the realization that the traditional minivan buyer also falls into the same "soccer-mom" demographic as a large segment of the casual game-playing market. Thus, an opportunity to concretize the function of the product was abandoned in favor of a meta-associative advertisement that simply put the minivan in front of that potential buyer. In fact, the game may not even have made it that far, given its minimum system requirements, which included a 3D accelerated video card, DirectX 8.1, and 128MB RAM.[25] More offensive, the game presents shopping as the only context for Stow 'n Go. Kids' soccer games, family picnics, swap-meets, and moving junior into state college dorm are framed out of the minivan lifestyle. Apparently storage always means storage for newly acquired goods.

Compare *Stow 'n Go Challenge* with a similar game, this one commissioned by DaimlerChrysler's Jeep group and designed and developed by my studio.

Jeep introduced a new truck, the Commander, its first to include third-row seating. While the vehicle does not sport Stow 'n Go, it does offer the same overall advertising pitch: you need three reconfigurable rows of seats to cart around your family and your equipment. The game we created, *Xtreme Errands*, tried to make good on the claim that reconfigurable seats add functional, not just perceived value.[26] It is a strategy game, borrowing conventions from turn-based unit management war games like *Advance Wars*.[27] Each level has a theme, and each turn the player can move family members, move the Jeep Commander or reconfigure its seats, and pick up and drop off cargo (figure 7.6).

Whereas *Stow 'n Go Challenge* deploys the procedural configuration of abstract space as a way to represent Stow 'n Go seating, *Xtreme Errands* operationalizes limited time and resources, a problem common to both military commanders and busy families. Although DaimlerChrysler required that the levels support "Jeep lifestyle" activities like skiing and camping, those activities are never actually displayed in the game; in fact, the game's flippant title undermines the very notion of lifestyle activities. Instead, players drop off dry cleaning, cart around kids, pick up groceries, and deliver an entire soccer team on game day. The game challenges the player to complete these assignments in as few moves and turns as possible, but the player is not constrained to do

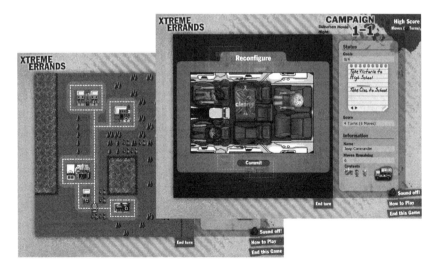

Figure 7.6 *Xtreme Errands* offers a procedural representation of how a three-seat SUV might help families accomplish everyday tasks.

so; the real goal is to experiment with a concrete representation of the vehicle's cargo and passenger space.

The procedural rhetoric of *Xtreme Errands* suggests that the Commander's affordances for flexible seating and storage couple usefully with certain family routines. The game is a sandbox for potential buyers to test that claim and reflect on its applicability in their lives. If we think of the advertisement as leaving a "cut-out" space as Williamson suggests, rather than being sucked into this space, the advertisement acknowledges it and welcomes the player's rejection, acceptance, or further interpretation of it. This time, the space between the game's rules and the player's subjectivity is a procedural enthymeme, or what I have called a simulation gap. Engagement with this gap creates a situation of crisis, a simulation fever.[28] Advergames that acknowledge this condition represent significant social progress in advertising: playing the game challenges the potential consumer to experiment with the ways he might use a product if he owned it.

Soft Drinks and Beer

To further illustrate the transition from illustrative and associative to demonstrative advertising in videogames, I want to look at the evolution of a particular market segment that has funded and produced games for at least twenty-five years: the beverage industry.

Beverages are a unique and noisy industry. According to the American Beverage Association, nonalcoholic beverages alone account for almost $100 billion in annual sales.[29] Dozens of brands compete for the right to hydrate and, more ambiguously, "to refresh." Unlike many consumer products, hard and soft drinks offer very limited product-to-product differentiation. The differences between Coke and Pepsi cola, Dasani or Aquafina water, Vernors and Canada Dry ginger ale, are difficult to demonstrate empirically. Seemingly, the only way to distinguish one soft drink from another is by personal preference. Personal preference cannot be determined, but it can be influenced. Beverage manufacturers have thus traditionally relied on associative and illustrative advertising as their primary strategies.

Given the enormity of this market segment, it is not surprising that a soft drink sponsored one of the first home-console advergames. In 1983, General Foods created *Kool-Aid Man*, a videogame for the Atari 2600 and Mattel Intellivision home-console systems.[30] While the game could be purchased at retail, as in the case of *Tooth Protectors* and *Chase the Chuckwagon* consumers could also obtain the game via mail order. According to a flyer, Kool-Aid customers needed to send in 125 Kool-Aid proof-of-purchase points, or 30 proof-of-purchase points and $10.[31]

Jonestown massacre aside, Kool-Aid was and remains primarily a kid's drink.[32] General Foods has used numerous popular-culture strategies to try to get kids to convince their parents to buy Kool-Aid, including a comic book, *The Adventures of Kool-Aid Man*, which ran six issues from 1983 to 1989. Thanks to the success of Kool-Aid Man as a transmedial phenomenon, General Foods attempted to leverage any and all media that might help cross-promote the character and therefore the product. The Atari version took up an ongoing theme portrayed in the advertisements, comic-book, and television commercials in which Kool-Aid Man battled evil "Thirsties," spikey gremlin-like creatures with insatiable thirst. In the game, the player helps Kool-Aid Man thwart the Thirsties' attempt to steal water out of a swimming pool while collecting Kool-Aid ingredients—"S" for sugar, "W" for water, and "K" for Kool-Aid—to stop the Thirsties' incessant attack on an otherwise idyllic summer backyard scene (see figure 7.7). The Intellivision version was somewhat different; in it, the player searches a house to locate the necessary equipment to make more Kool-Aid (pitcher, mix, sugar) while avoiding the

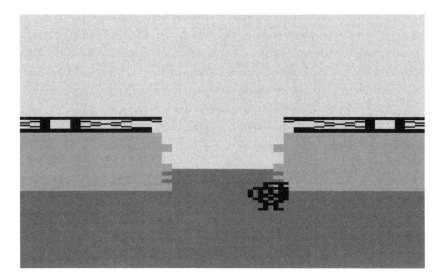

Figure 7.7 *Kool-Aid Man* for Atari VCS is among the eariest advergames.

Thirsties. Once the player makes a batch of Kool-Aid, the roles invert and he can chase and devour the Thirsties *Pac-Man*-style.[33]

The advertising strategy was principally an extortionist one. One hundred and twenty-five packets of Kool-Aid is enough to make 62.5 gallons of the drink. Quaffing enough to send in for the game demanded several months of continuous Kool-Aid consumption, a task that became more difficult as time passed, parental support for the venture being inversely proportional to the amount of sugar drink consumed. As with *Dodge Stow 'n Go Challenge* and *Kotex Ms. Match*, the videogame served primarily as a way to illustrate the product to a particular demographic.

However, one demonstrative message does emerge from the game: the preparation method for Kool-Aid itself. There is a kind of magic to Kool-Aid; its inventor Edwin Perkins was inspired by his own childhood fascination with the powdered dessert Jell-O. Perkins developed Kool-Aid as a Jell-O-inspired solution to the problem of shipping glass bottles of concentrated drink mix. Despite its simplicity, Kool-Aid remains a mystery to young kids. Somehow, that small packet of pale powder turns into a whole pitcher of sweet, bright red punch. Both Atari and Intellivision versions of *Kool-Aid Man* feature instructions, albeit extremely crude ones, about the actual preparation of the drink. Like unpacking the strategic operation of theme parks with *SeaWorld Adventure Parks Tycoon*, *Kool-Aid Man* exposes the operation of preparing Kool-Aid, including an admission that it is near equal parts sugar and water. While this fact alone isn't going to change dietary habits, it does open the door to discussions about the role of sugar in contemporary packaged foods. Perhaps after learning how to mix Kool-Aid via *Kool-Aid Man*, a child might be interested in learning how much sugar he consumed while collecting those 125 proofs-of-purchase—65 pounds when prepared according to the on-package instructions, or roughly the average weight of an eight-year-old. Here the videogame has the potential both to support and question the advertiser's business.

Soft drink companies continue to use games as tools to penetrate the youth market, as evidenced by *Mountain Dew Skateboarding*, discussed in chapter 5. In addition to their branded game consoles, Coca-Cola in particular has commissioned numerous web-based advergames in support of its larger promotional plans. Consider the company's ongoing holiday-themed ad campaigns, with their computer graphics penguins, polar bears, and Santa Clauses all enjoying Coke as an integral part of their holiday regimens. In one example of a videogame extension of this campaign, interactive agency Perfect Fools created *Nordic Christmas*, a sophisticated set of web-based games with very high production value.[34] The games were based on the 2004 season's elf-themed advertising, in which elves drank Coke as a kind of tonic for their playful, sometimes mischievous holiday pursuits. The games revolved around a tournament, with castle climbing, fencing, lancing, and catapulting activities.

Coca-Cola is nowhere to be found in any of the games, save gripped in the little hands of the elf characters depicted on the game's menu screen. Advertisements like these appear to be associative; as in the Volkswagen New Beetle print ad, Coca-Cola is associated with holiday playfulness and fun. But interestingly, the associative features Coca-Cola wants to leverage correspond precisely to the functional features of leisure videogames. Coke is about "enjoyment" and "fun"—exactly the sensations videogames are thought to produce.[35] Thus, we could think of generic advergames like *Nordic Christmas* as procedural manifestations of the enjoyment that the product produces, or more properly that it facilitates. Like alcohol, Coca-Cola presents itself as a social lubricant that produces enjoyment rather than uninhibitedness. Television and print ads in this vein create empathetic pleasure—the sensation of understanding the joy of the young boy or the polar bear as they quaff a Coke. Advergames like *Nordic Christmas*, though, are legitimately entertaining, albeit unrelated to the sugar-water Coke otherwise sells. The advertising has become the product, providing the actual enjoyment suggested by the product's demonstrative claims.

This inversion can be seen in two ways. On the one hand, we could understand *Nordic Christmas* and other games like it as affirmations of Baudrillard's procession of simulacra; the product has been replaced by the advertising, which now services the consumer instead of the product. On the other hand, we could view such games as markers of the dissonance between the product and the advertising claims made in support of the product. When we watch the polar bear commercials, the bears give us an impression of enjoyment; they slide down snow banks or glide across frozen lakes. But when we play the games, we experience *actual* enjoyment, with no Coca-Cola required. This dissonance founds a simulation gap, wherein the player can interrogate the ongoing claims Coca-Cola makes about its products, and his or her own willingness or unwillingness to accept them.

Missing from the Coke games is any representation of "refreshment," the other value common in Coca-Cola advertising. Aside from deploying the archetype power-up technique we witnessed in *Mountain Dew Snowboarding*, one can imagine a game in which thirst and refreshment might actually be core to the gameplay. Coke's failure to attempt such a game may suggest a lack of specificity in its claims to "refresh"—ignoring the idea that rejuvenation may come in different forms at different times. The player might recognize that Coca-Cola does not actually produce specific types of invigoration, but only one: the kind that involves the purchase of its products. In fact, Coca-Cola's strategy has shifted from winning new customers to increasing purchases by existing ones. Coke products (including Dasani water, Minute Maid juice, and the company's other non-soda brands) now account for 10 percent of the world's total liquid intake (TLI), a figure they hope to increase.[36]

An advergame that does take on such a demonstrative challenge is *Pickwick Afternoon*, created as part of a Dutch campaign promoting a new flavor of tea from the well-known Pickwick company.[37] Pickwick Afternoon Spirit is an herbal tea blend of peppermint, chamomile, and licorice root. The tea was offered as an afternoon pick-me-up suitable for stirring a diminished body and mind, but without the caffeine necessitated by an afternoon black tea or coffee. The game is about as simple as a small web-based game can be: three young people on a couch doze off repeatedly as their afternoons catch up with them. The player controls a teapot with which he pours tea to refresh each of them. The gameplay is essentially Whack-a-Mole played with boiling hot tea.

As a game, Coca-Cola's *Nordic Christmas* is clearly more sophisticated, sporting much richer, more refined gameplay. But I would argue that as an advergame, *Pickwick Afternoon Spirit* is more sophisticated, offering a game-based experience of the product that actually communicates something about it. Many marketers would disagree with me, citing evidence for developing and maintaining brand value. But attaching the Coke brand to a high-quality game with no meaningful message is bad for advertising and bad for games. Games that work to build experiences around products have the potential to become both good games and good advertising, without subordinating either medium to the other.

The same year General Foods put pixilated Kool-Aid pitchers on home consoles, Bally/Midway released the arcade game *Tapper*, in which the player helps a frantic bartender serve demanding and increasingly irate bar patrons.[38] The game was unique in every respect, but its main draw was a beer-tap interface in place of the usual digital button. The tap feels authentic, but its operation is abstract: the player pushes it forward to fill a beer, then pulls it backward to serve the beer, which slides down the counter into the waiting hands of a thirsty customer. If no customer is there to retrieve it, the beer breaks against the back wall of the tavern, costing the player a life. The game portrays four bar-styles in as many levels: country-western tavern, sporting event bar, punk club, and space alien bar.

The original version of the game featured prominent Budweiser branding on the wall of the bar (figure 7.8), on the draught mugs, and on cans during an interlude bonus game. Like *Yoshinoya* and *CoCo Ichibanya*, *Tapper* puts the player in the role of the server, not the consumer of the product. But this game pits the player against his customers, patrons whose drunken fervor erases any semblance of empathy. The customers are parodies of the drunken bar-hopper—the folly of their inebriation is rendered procedurally as a thoughtless, almost zombie-like progression toward the tap.

As an advertisement for beer, the game is a curious one. The player becomes the lone sober character, faced with the constant onslaught of drunken halfwits. Like *Kool-Aid Man*, the game could be read as an associative

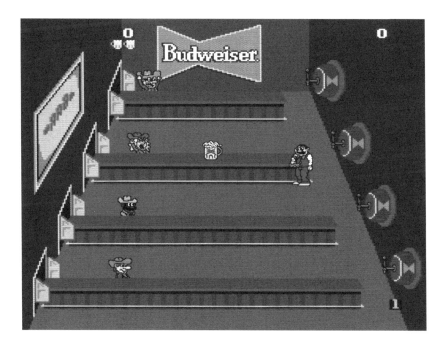

Figure 7.8 *Tapper* showcases early in-game advertisements, in this case a Budweiser beer backdrop.

advertisement. *Pong* started out in bars, after all, and young adults playing in bars and lounges dominated the arcade game scene of the 1970s.[39] Budweiser would have as much reason to brand a videogame in such a location as a coaster, or a lamp over a billiard table. But the game could also be read as a demonstrative advertisement; after all, the one product feature afforded by beer is inebriation, which the game crudely proceduralizes via customer ire. There is more than a hint of irony in a bar service game, for play in a bar, about servicing drunken patrons, presumably played by actual drunken patrons (both of the bar and the game). Budweiser, the bar proprietor that hosts the game, and Bally/Midway all cash in on the joke.

How does the player experience *Tapper*? By stepping outside of himself and performing the repetitive actions of the bartender, the player is forced to confront the reality of Budweiser's industry: inebriation impairs judgment, which is why it serves as a social lubricant. But such impaired faculties also contribute to the sometimes-unintended incremental support of that industry— the drunk get drunker, as it were. *Tapper* defamiliarizes the process of consumption, both through its procedural representation and through the distortion of the bartender the player controls. This defamiliarization opens a simulation gap that invites interrogation of the player's alcohol-consumption practices themselves. Budweiser's endorsement of this concern is a much less visible social service than adding *please drink responsibly* in small print on their ads, but perhaps it is a much more meaningful one. Some might object that drunken bar patrons are not capable of such self-reflection, but failure to control *Tapper*'s virtual bartender due to player inebriation might very well alert the player to his own diminishing faculties, a gross-motor signal no less effective than stumbling on the way to the toilet or falling off a barstool.

Another advergame takes such drunken stumbling as its primary gameplay mechanic. U.K. beverage maker Britvic manufactures a soft drink called J$_2$O. Some cultural context is probably necessary to explain it fully; until late 2005, British pubs were required to close their doors at 11:00 PM. Those interested in drinking later would have to move on to clubs, and a common venue for later night drinking are dance venues. Dancing becomes more difficult once inebriated, so serious night crawlers are advised to pace themselves. Water makes a fine salve for increasingly sizzled clubbers, of course, but Britvic hoped to capture some of the free-flowing pounds sterling of such occasions. J$_2$O is a beverage that bills itself as a "perfect soft drink pacer." According to Britvic, the product allows you to drink more, for longer, while enjoying any of five flavors of this "adult fruit drink."[40] Not to be outdone by those wishing for alcoholic refreshment, Britvic also notes that J₂O makes a fine mixer.

In 2003, U.K. agency Graphico created an advergame to support J₂O. *The Toilet Training Game* puts the player takes the role of a tipsy clubber who needs to relieve himself.[41] As the game starts, the player sees a toilet bowl flanked by the player character's trainers.[42] The primary game mechanic is urination; the goal is to aim in the center of the toilet and avoid oversplash. After each successful bladder emptying, the player character downs another pint. After more rounds of drinks, accurate aiming becomes harder, and the player inevitably splashes outside the bowl (figure 7.9). The player must then drink a J₂O, which relieves some of the inebriation and restores his ability to urinate and, by extension, to party accurately.

This is a sophisticated videogame. The urination mechanic itself is remarkable; the game implements a strange attractor that draws and repels the player's cursor target in an increasingly haphazard fashion. The lack of control

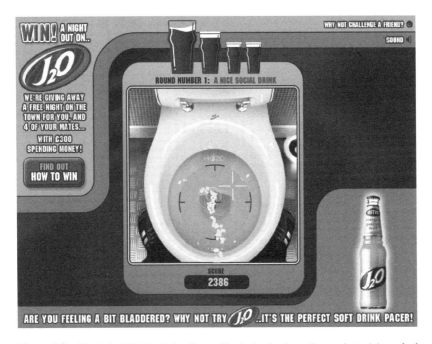

Figure 7.9 *The J₂O Toilet Training Game* effectively simulates the product claims of of Britvic's "pacer drink."

is palpable, a superb unit operation for the physical and psychic incapacity of intoxication. But even more so, *The Toilet Training Game* serves as an excellent example of demonstrative advergaming. Concentrating *Tapper's* simulation of drunkenness, *The Toilet Training Game* focuses on one, unique experience, that of relieving oneself. J$_2$O's salient product feature—relieving drunkenness—is tied to an activity apparently unrelated to dancing, socializing, or beguiling members of the opposite sex. But no matter the late-night activity, relieving oneself remains common to them all. Furthermore, the force of biology often draws clubbers and partygoers away from the noise and ruckus of the dance floor or the bar. It is only there, in the quiet of the loo, that a full recognition of the depths of one's inebriation sets in. Like *Tapper's* re-creation of the hypothetical drunkard, *The Toilet Training Game* enacts the moment in the player's simulated evening when he doubts the wisdom of the lifestyle that has landed him there, stumbling against the doors of the toilet stall. The game may approach the logical opposite of associative advertising—advertising that dissociates a product from a desired lifestyle. J$_2$O is not just about tempering an evening's overindulgence; it is about tempering the very lifestyle of alcoholic overindulgence.

Britvic's decision to represent this pivotal moment in the nightclub experience is paradigmatic for the positive role advergames can play in consumer culture. By casting their product's tangible benefits in a procedural representation of a situation of great reservation, the advertisement challenges the player to interrogate the degree to which he really needs the mixers, the pints, and indeed the very J$_2$O that the product advertises. Advergames function best at the intersection of demonstrative advertising and embodied experience through procedural representations of products and services. These games create simulation gaps about consumption practices; they expose the potential unities *and* discontinuities of consumer goods as they enter the lives of *individual* consumers. Unlike ideological apparatuses which, in Judith Williamson's words, "offer you a unity with the sign, a unity which can only be imaginary," advergames like these muster an uncertain subjective space that do not necessarily violate individual identity.[43]

In their relevant book *Age of Propaganda*, Anthony Pratkanis and Elliot Aronson investigate a compliance tactic called *the pique technique*.[44] The two argue that simply piquing someone's interest may be enough to elicit compliance. In their experiment, a panhandler who asked for 17 or 37 cents collected 60 percent more donations than a panhandler who asked for a quarter.

The pique condition forced people to focus on the request, rather than screening it out as noise. Currently advertisers use piques solely to draw players' attention toward the very short-term messages they carefully craft to influence wants and needs. Pratkanis and Aronson argue that persuasion as conversation—the type used in the rhetoric of the ancient Greeks—hoped to "create discourse that could illuminate the issue at hand."[45] They contrast this type of persuasion with modern media, which appeal to emotions and send information foils that prevent us from separating the wheat of a problem from the chaff.[46] Videogames are not a miracle cure to this problem. But they do offer a start that may be incisive, by deploying more sophisticated persuasive speech designed to create rather than avoid uncertainty about products and services.

Anti-Advergames

As media images have increased, so have critiques of advertising. In *No Logo*, Naomi Klein argues for resistance to the brands that view the world as one large marketing opportunity.[47] Juliet Schor has critiqued the immersion of children in particular in consumer culture.[48] Alyssa Quart extends such critique into the teenage years.[49] Quart discusses videogames in particular, including *Super Monkey Ball 2* and numerous other examples of product placement; Quart argues that these games overpower the impressionable minds of young people, giving them the false impression that a branded world is natural and even desirable. In her critique of branded products like shirts and skateboards in *Tony Hawk Pro Skater 3*, Quart argues that older skaters resist the commercial images while younger ones worry about donning the right brand images and dream of corporate sponsorship.[50]

Some groups have tried to take matters into their own hands and rally against the profusion of commercialization in games in particular. Some of these speak against the colonization of videogames by advertisers; others actively advertise against specific products and services, singling out companies by name. To capture both of these senses, I suggest the term *anti-advergame*.[51] For one part, anti-advergames advertise against a company; if advergames are endorsed and paid for by a corporation and are produced to support its business, anti-advergames are not endorsed or paid for by a corporation and are produced to critique its business practices. For another part, anti-advergames work against the practice of advertising in games itself; if advergames allow brands and products entrance into commercial videogames, anti-advergames critique or disrupt the insertion of such ads.

As an example of the latter type, critic Tony Walsh offered a set of ad-busting strategies for vegetarians, eco-activists, and other disgruntled users of *The Sims Online* McDonald's kiosks:

- Picket the nearest McDonald's kiosk. Stand in front of the kiosk and tell visitors why you think McDonald's sucks. Be careful not to use foul language or hinder the movement of your fellow Simians. Polite protest can't result in your account getting suspended . . . can it?
- Actually order and consume virtual McD's food, then use The Sims Online's "expressive gestures" in creative ways. Lie down and play dead. Emote the vomiting, sickness, or fatigue that might overcome you after eating a real life McNugget.
- Open your own McDonald's kiosk. Verbally abuse all customers in the name of McDonald's. Loudly proclaim how terrible your food is and how it's made from sub-standard ingredients (or whatever you think will turn people off). Make sure you preface each such statement with "In my opinion," to avoid libel charges.
- Open an independent restaurant. Gain the confidence of your clientele, and then let them know your business is being hurt by ubiquitous McDonald's kiosks. Ask them to put pressure on other Simians to support small business people instead of cogs in a gigantic franchise-machine.[52]

Walsh encourages players to use the McDonald's features to subvert their intended message. In a similar vein, shortly after in-game ad network Massive began placing their ads in commercial games, a group of makeshift hacktivists ran their Massive-enabled version of *SWAT4* through a packet dumper. After finding the Internet endpoints for the Massive service, they promptly published instructions for disabling the system on a local PC.[53]

There.com, a multiuser virtual world, was originally conceived as a digital extension for brand companies.[54] As in many persistent virtual worlds, users exchange real currency for virtual currency ("therebucks"), which they can spend in-world to customize their avatar or environment. Early versions of *There* touted the planned inclusion of virtual versions of Levi's jeans and Nike shoes; in addition to advertising, the brands hoped to use the virtual world as a kind of virtual focus group for new real-world products.[55] Virtual world critic Betsy Book has argued that original brands developed in-world by *There* community members and used to market services available only in the virtual environment have been far more successful—both in the commercial and social senses.[56]

Walsh's anticorporate activism in *The Sims Online*, the hacktivists who disabled Massive, and the *There* users who built rather than consumed brands offer useful suggestions for actively opposing the profusion of advertising in videogames, but they focus specifically on advertising *in videogames*, not the relationship between advertising and the material world. And while the grassroots brands in *There* are fascinating examples of virtual microeconomies, they are not direct statements for or against particular corporate messaging. It is always encouraging to see independent upstarts unseat large corporations, but the user-created brands Book describes are not deliberately oppositional.

Other videogames have used the procedural affordances of the medium for the explicit purpose of rejoining specific corporations. In 1999, seven interactive fiction authors collaborated on *Coke Is It!*, a rewriting of six classic text adventures and interactive fiction works that lay bare the ubiquitous hand of Coca-Cola marketing.[57] The authors present the six rewrites (*Curses, Adventure, Planetfall, Hitchhiker, Grip,* and *A Bear's Night Out*) as buttons on a virtual vending machine. The goals of each game are replaced by variations on finding and swilling a delicious Coca-Cola. The following example is taken from *Coke Is It! Planetfall*:

>examine door

Through the window, you can see a large laboratory, dimly illuminated. A blue glow comes from a crack in the northern wall of the lab. Shadowy, ominous shapes move about within the room. On the floor, just a short distance inside the door, you can see a thing of beauty—a gleaming can of Coca-Cola, framed by the light shining through the window.

The developers also rewrote key default responses to further distort the experience:

>move door

It is fixed in place. Unlike a typical refreshing Coke.

The result is simple but effective. By forcing the player to interact with Coca-Cola, the game produces an absurd perversion of the original works of interactive fiction, highlighting the inappropriateness of Coca-Cola's invasion of the media and the material world.

A more subtle anti-advertisement peppers another interactive fiction, *Book and Volume* by Nick Montfort.[58] The piece chronicles one night in the life of a sysadmin for nWare, the curious and increasingly dubious corporate hub of the fictional world nTopia. As the player makes his way around the city, completing last-minute server fixes before a big demo, increasingly strange visions appear to him. The game satirizes retail stores in general, but Montfort invents names for most of its stores—MarMart, Pharmicopia, Septisys. Spared shrouding are The Gap and Starbucks; the latter appears frequently throughout the city, a jibe at Starbucks' tendency to overcolonize the urban landscape. One independent coffeehouse, Independent Grounds remains in nTopia; presumably Starbucks forced the others out of business. If the player positions himself in front of Independent Grounds at a particular time during the game, he can witness its disassembly and replacement with another new Starbucks.

Book and Volume uses anti-advertising as a part of a subtle critique of consumerism and the culture of work. Other counteradvertising games are more deliberate in their attacks on specific corporations. The paint on software engineer Shawn McGough's new 2002 Mitsubishi Lancer started wearing away after only a few months. When Mitsubishi refused to make amends, McGough took the company to court. He won the case in a bittersweet $0 settlement. Feeling overwhelmed by lawyer culture, he decided to take the battle to "his own turf." McGough created *Melting Mitsubishi*, a web game that challenges the player to protect a yellow Lancer from falling rain.[59] The game borrows its gameplay from *Missile Command*;[60] the player fires circular blasts that expand to hit the falling droplets. While simplistic, the game successfully proceduralizes McGough's straightforward complaint against Mitsubishi: water destroys the paint. However, the game's procedural rhetoric is weak when unsupported by the verbal rhetoric of his written story, which accompanies the game in a menu.

More complex videogame grouses require more sophisticated procedural models of the complaint. My studio created *Disaffected!*, an anti-advergame about the FedEx Kinko's copy store. The game was conceived as a parody of the frustrating experience of patronizing such a store. The game puts the player in the role of employees forced to service customers under our perceptions of the organizational problems that plague Kinko's: other employees move orders around at random; employees sometimes get confused and respond only to inverted movement control; other times employees refuse to work at all, and the player must switch to another; and even when orders are fulfilled customers often return dissatisfied (figure 7.10). *Disaffected!* is an arcade-style game; the player must service all the customers successfully to advance to the next level. In our representation of Kinko's "successful" service does not necessarily imply a completed order.

It is useful to compare *Disaffected!*'s procedural rhetoric with a commensurate verbal rhetoric. A customer might mount a written or phone complaint to Kinko's about their service, detailing the problems. A specific problem or sequence of problems might spark adequate dissatisfaction to warrant a written complaint. In the interest of comparison, consider the following contrived letter:

To Whom It May Concern:

On September 13 I went to your Crossroads branch to get some copies and pick up a print order I had sent through the website. When I got there, I was disappointed to find that three of the four copy machines were out of service. Then I had to wait

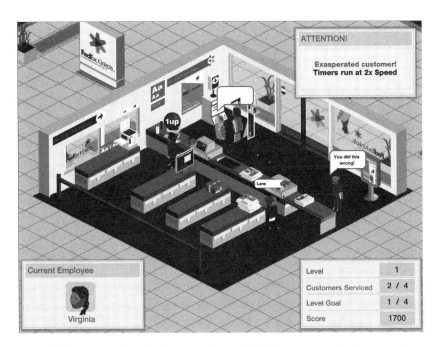

Figure 7.10 In *Disaffected!*, players control unmotivated workers at a simulated copy store.

at least 15 minutes in line. Even though there were five workers behind the counter, only one seemed to be doing anything. When it was finally my turn, the cashier helping me couldn't find my order. She looked in about five different places before coming back to ask me to repeat my name again. When she finally found the order under a big pile of other papers, I paid and left. But when I got to my car, I opened the bag and noticed that the order was printed on the wrong paper! I had to go back in and ask them to redo it, but I was already late for work.

This is the fourth time I've had almost the same problem at your store. Why should I come back to Kinko's after getting this kind of habitually bad service? I demand that you refund the $24.54 I spent on my incorrect order (a receipt is enclosed).

Very truly yours,
John Q. Customer

Many of us have written this kind of complaint letter. Most often, we write about a specific, personal problem requiring resolution. In fact, this is what consumer advocacy groups recommend. But habitual problems can never be solved by individual rejoinder. Better Business Bureau (BBB) reliability ratings notwithstanding, it is usually easier and cheaper for companies to pay individual reimbursements than to deal with the problems that create these issues. A game like *Disaffected!* universalizes the experience, casting it as a habitual and routine practice at Kinko's. Moreover, the operationalized version of the customer complaints produce actual frustration on the part of the player, something a letter or telephone call cannot possibly accomplish. While the complaint letter attempts to persuade the reader that the writer was wronged and deserves recompense, the anti-advergame attempts to persuade the player that the corporation is inoperative and must not be supported.

The decision to name Kinko's and to include their trademark in the game contributes to this effect. Despite a meaty disclaimer and appeal to the free speech rights granted to satire, we did not take lightly the decision to include the Kinko's name and trademark in the game. Whether or not they had the right to do so, Kinko's could easily have taken legal action for the representation. As a small studio, we would never have been able to combat the likes of a company as large as FedEx, and so we considered depicting a generic copy store with an evocative, yet distinctly different name (options we considered included Slacko's and Plinko's). The player would easily identify the target of our commentary. Such a technique is frequently used even in television satire. An early *Chappelle Show* sketch used this very tactic to attack Kinko's. In the sketch, comedian Dave Chappelle plays the manager of Popcopy, where he teaches employees how to anger customers.[61] But just as advertisers promote their own, specific products and services in their own names, so we wanted to deprecate their products and services in their own names. In a world replete with branding, one should not shy away from critiquing the brands themselves, just as one would critique a corrupt statesperson by name, not by oblique reference. Molleindustria's *The McDonald's Videogame*, discussed in chapter 1, stands as another superb example of a game with this goal in mind.

Rather than deploying antitestimonial (e.g., publishing an account of a bad experience on a public website), anti-advergames deploy antidemonstratives. Just as *Curry House CoCo Ichibanya* demonstrates the operation of its licensor's corporate values, *Disaffected!* demonstrates the operation of its victim's corporate values. However, in the latter case, those values are represented as broken. Anti-advergames suggest an alternative to the precious form of procedural rhetoric I called the rhetoric of failure. *September 12* imposes rules that enforce barriers to success, elevating failure as an inevitable outcome of both missiles.[62] Its procedural rhetoric ensures that no strategy for precision firing will avoid taking innocent lives, and that such violence begets more violence. The game does not intend to suggest that we should let terrorists run rampant, but rather that the particular strategy of so-called precision attack is dysfunctional; a new one is required. In *September 12*, the goals are undesirable, and thus invocation of the game's rules lead to failure; it is not possible to win *September 12*. In *Disaffected!* the goals are desirable, but the game's rules are broken. While those rules may cause the player to fail in his attempt to service customers, that failure is endemic to the representation of the problem. The procedural rhetoric serves as a unit operation for Kinko's business practices.

Putting the player in the shoes of the employees rather than the customers changes the register of the discourse. While the verbal rhetoric necessarily focuses on self-interest and personal gain, the procedural rhetoric transfers the argument into one of corporate policy and, by extension, politics. The first-hand experience of the simulation of work enforces the rules of malcontent that produce individual customer service woes. The game thus speaks on two registers: first, the register of consumer dissatisfaction: the player can take pleasurable umbrage in the satirical representation of a typical Kinko's experience. Second, it speaks on the register of corporate malevolence: by virtue of his position behind the counter, the player can consider the possible reasons behind the employee malaise that produces that customer experience—is it incompetence? Managerial hardship? Broader labor issues?

Disaffected! does not purport to proceduralize a solution to Kinko's customer service or labor issues. But its procedural rhetoric of incompetence does underscore the problem of disaffection in contemporary culture, on both sides of the counter. We're dissatisfied or unwilling to support structures of authority, but we do scarcely little about it. We go to work at lousy jobs with poor benefits and ill treatment. We shrug off poor customer service and bad products, assuming that nothing can be done and ignoring the reasons why workers might feel disenfranchised in the first place. We take for granted that we can't reach people in authority. These problems extend far beyond copy stores.

Anti-advergames thus have much in common with political games: they expose the logic of corporate and governmental structures and invite players to question them. Even though such games seem to contradict the goals of advergames that promote rather than depose, both types actually share fundamental principles: they demonstrate claims about the function (or dysfunction) of products and services, giving the player a first-person account of how the features and functions of those products and services intersect with his wants and needs. The player's evaluation of those claims as depicted in the game's rules opens a simulation gap, a space of crisis in which the persuasion game plays out. By offering a space for discourse about the use or value of a product, these advertisements encourage critical consumption: the reasoned and conscious interrogation of individual wants and needs, rather than manipulated subservience to corporate ones.

Learning

Procedural Literacy

Are videogames educational? The answer depends largely on what "educational" means, a controversial question. Rather than searching for a rationalistic yes/no answer, it is more productive to ask how a particular user community understands things to be educational. If something is educational, what does it teach? And how does it teach it?

In popular discourse, education most often relates to didactic pedagogy, conjuring visions of classrooms and textbooks. In this sense, we can understand "education" most easily as the outcome of successful interactions between teachers and students. What makes such interactions "successful" is the subject of ongoing debate in the educational community. As with any field, trends have come and gone over time. I will not attempt to summarize the history of educational theory in this context, but a few key moments helpfully contextualize the problem of learning in videogames.

According to early behaviorists like Edward Thorndike and B. F. Skinner, learning is about reinforcement. Organisms (behaviorists generally group humans among animals of all sorts) respond to positive and negative incentives. When organisms find themselves in similar situations with similar incentives, they will respond in similar ways. Transfer of learning—a pervasive and problematic concept in educational theory—takes place via repetition and reinforcement.[1] Reinforcement theory privileges stimulus–response learning arranged in steps to ratchet up a student's abilities.[2]

Objections to behaviorism abound. Principally, behaviorists have been accused of ignoring the private, mental processes inherent in individual human beings. According to this objection, materialist, empiricist understandings of learning leave no room for human subjectivity. Such a state of affairs is partly born from behaviorism's attempt to account for not only human behavior, but also animal behavior. The objectivism inherent in behaviorist underscores a general belief that psychology is a "natural science" based in empirical observation, like the natural sciences.[3] Thus introspection is unaccounted for in the most extreme forms of behaviorism.

With Jean Piaget, the understanding of learning became more connected to theories of mind, correcting the immoderate scientism of behaviorism. Piaget outlined overall cognitive structures or "development stages": sensorimotor (0–2 years), preoperation (3–7 years), concrete operational (8–11 years), formal operational (12–15 years).[4] Each structure demands different processes of adaptation, and therefore different modes of learning. Piaget insisted that cognitive development entails adaptation to the environment, a founding principle of other constructivist learning theories. Nevertheless, Piaget's scientific cognitivism still relied on a universalist approach to learning, even if that universalism was grounded more in biology than in rationalism. The cognitive structure of the individual, constrained by a particular stage of development, undergirds the learner's ability to actively construct new ideas based on his or her experiences and past knowledge.[5] Often traced to the epistemology of John Dewey, which rejects the rationalist notion that knowledge exists immutably in nature, constructivist learning assumes that the learner "constructs" knowledge individually, that learning is inseparable from the learner's interaction with the environment.[6] The more popular forms of social constructionism, founded on the theories of Lev Semenovich Vygotsky, draw particular attention to the role of social interaction in cognitive development.[7] Social constructionism includes approaches like the Soviet activity theory that descended from Vygotsky's own contributions, as well as situated learning theory, which focuses on "learning by doing."[8]

Constructivism too faces challenges. Social psychologist James K. Doyle has argued that the correlation between constructivist-style embodied thinking has not been convincingly tied to actual future behavior.[9] Doyle argues that changes in "thought, behavior, or organizational performance" are limited to anecdote and bias, with little sound, demonstrable scientific basis.[10] In response, one might argue that constructivism necessarily resists generalizable results as a matter of principle, focusing instead on the particularities of individual learners. Seymour Papert's version of Piagetian constructivism, which he called *constructionism*, focuses on the active creation of things in the material world.[11] Constructivism refocuses education on the practice of individualized cognitive development as a goal in itself, a goal not always reconnected with subject-specific learning outcomes.

No matter the educational theory, every philosophy assumes that the correct approach to learning involves culturing the student according to the principles of that philosophy. This is a noncontroversial generalization: learning theories are intended to guide and structure educational practice. At the risk of oversimplification, most contemporary understandings of (formal) education fall largely in either the behaviorist or the constructionist theory of education.[12] The "traditional" classroom relies on behaviorist learning strategies. Students practice within question/answer frames that reinforce knowledge of a subject matter. Students respond (in speech or writing, for example) and receive immediate feedback in the form of positive and negative reinforcement. The behaviorist classroom assumes that reinforced behavior will recur; and because of its empiricist assumptions, such a learning environment believes that one type of positively reinforced behavior is adequate. Teacher-directed rote learning is the norm in behaviorist-influenced educational practices.

Despite contemporary education's propensity toward behaviorist education, the commonest form of constructivist learning comes from the first classroom many of us experience: kindergarten. Nineteenth-century German educator Friedrich Fröbel, inventor of kindergarten, held great esteem for the individual student and his particular needs. Wrote Fröbel in his 1826 treatise *On the Education of Man*, "The purpose of education is to encourage and guide man as a conscious, thinking and perceiving being in such a way that he becomes a pure and perfect representation of that divine inner law through his own personal choice."[13] Fröbel's kindergarten relied on play, materials, and activities as a means to encourage creativity and thereby, fulfillment. In the kindergarten classroom, personal experience yields an understanding of the world.

Similarly, Italian educator Maria Montessori encouraged a child-centered that focused first on the senses, then on the intellect—this approach was based largely on her experience with mentally retarded children.[14] Unlike Fröbel, Montessori encouraged more "practical" learning, based around material exercises intended to ratchet up learning through increasingly demanding real-world experiences.[15]

In general, the contemporary behaviorist classroom is expected to function like a scientific instrument in which the successful student develops an increasingly accurate ability to reflect the veracity of the material world. That world contains facts and principles, or "learning content," which education successfully transfers into the mind of the learner through reinforcement. Constructivist approaches to education remain almost entirely confined to the arena of very early childhood. Even though this developmental period bears high cultural visibility, it is generally less controversial to allow the very young to experiment with their own emerging identities. And some object to the mystical freedom of educational environments like the Montessori classroom, versus the structured formalism of other situations. Constructivist learning environments risk devolving into relativistic playpens, where the abstract, individual growth of learners occludes actual educational substance.

Current theories of videogames as educational tools mirror our views on classrooms. While they are too new a phenomenon to definitively attach to educational philosophies, we can roughly split perspectives on videogame learning into behaviorist and constructivist modalities.

If behaviorism relies on an empirical, scientific worldview—that of a singular, knowable universe of concepts—then a behaviorist model of educational videogames transfers that universe onto the game world. Videogames may not be complete models of the material world, but they are certainly microcosms. These worlds, in the opinion of behaviorist-influenced educators, stand in for the material world in a one-to-one fashion. In so doing, videogames simulate the actual dynamics of the material world, and playing such games has the same effect as would real learning in the material world. That is to say, reinforcement through gameplay establishes repeat behavior, to which the player/learner adapts. If that behavior corresponds with the sort of content that an educator would positively reinforce in the material world, then the videogame serves a (potentially) commensurate purpose, both in function and value. If, however, the behavior corresponds with the sort an educator would negatively reinforce, then the videogame is dangerous and undesirable. In short, videogames teach their content, and that content transfers to real-world experience.

Consider a few examples. *Microsoft Flight Simulator*, one of the longest-running videogame series, is a game about flying aircraft. The game simulates the mechanics of a variety of equipment, atmospheric, and weather conditions, providing a plausible simulated representation of aircraft flight. From the behaviorist perspective, the game transfers its subject matter to the player. One might understand *Flight Simulator* as a game that teaches something about aviation, which players can then use to understand how real planes fly. This might be reasonable, but as Bill Buxton has pointed out, even though computer simulations have frequently been used to train pilots, very few of us would want to step into an aircraft whose pilot had only played *Flight Simulator*.[16]

Or consider *Sim City*, the popular urban management game.[17] In the game, players construct cities by zoning land, choosing energy sources, and investing in infrastructure like roads, rail, and public services. From the content perspective, the game teaches something about urban planning, which players could then use to plan real cities. As with *Flight Simulator*, some experiences are clearly abstracted out of *Sim City*, but a behaviorist videogame educator might say that the game teaches the "basics" of urban planning.

What about a game like *Ninja Gaiden*, first a side-scrolling arcade game for the Nintendo Entertainment System (NES) and other platforms of that era,[18] and more recently a popular and critically acclaimed Xbox fighting game?[19] Both versions are adventures in which the player directs a ninja against innumerable, very difficult enemies. As ninjas are wont to do, the player character in *Ninja Gaiden* deploys stealth, melee, and projectile attacks to take his revenge. The behaviorist view leaves little room for interpretation regarding such a game. By the logic we applied to *Flight Simulator* and *Sim City*, it follows that *Ninja Gaiden* teaches something about Japanese feudal stealthiness, which, again following the same logic, the player could then use in real espionage and retaliation. So-called *media effects* arguments attempt to correlate such representations with youth aggression and violence. This approach is classically behaviorist; the videogame positively reinforces a "bad" representation (in this case, ninja violence), which the player will then understand as appropriate behavior.[20]

The behaviorist-influenced content perspective opens up a Pandora's Box of media effects arguments. If videogames teach their content, and if that content ought to be negatively reinforced, then exposure to such games positively reinforces negative content. While only the staunchest behaviorist would suggest that exposure to *Ninja Gaiden* will produce armies of black-hooded stealthy warriors, many more would squint suspiciously at a game like *Grand Theft Auto*. The contemporary verisimilitude of Liberty City or San Andreas might suggest that the game teaches something about criminality, which the player can then use to perpetrate real crimes. Such representations, when ratcheted up through the successive positive reinforcement provided by an involved game like *Grand Theft Auto*, has been blamed for numerous social ills, from general dereliction to school shootings.

This dark side of the behaviorist conception of educational videogames is not limited to violence. Controversy erupted over *Flight Simulator* after the September 11, 2001 terrorist attacks. Three days after the attacks, Microsoft announced that it would remove the World Trade Center towers from the 2002 version of the game, "because we do not want to cause anyone pain in the future versions of the software."[21] The manual calls the game "as real as it gets," and the promotional introduction to the game reportedly depicted two people playing, one telling the other, "John, you just about crashed into the Empire State Building! Hey, that would be cool," sentiments that worried behaviorist-minded educators, lawmakers, and parents.[22] In 2004, a mother asked about *Flight Simulator* for her ten-year-old son at a Staples office supply store in Massachusetts. According to published reports, the clerk was so alarmed "at the prospect of the ten-year-old learning to fly" that he called the police. The mother, an Air Force Reserve pilot, discovered an FBI agent snooping around her house a few days later. As one commentator reported, "the authorities moved into action, leaving nothing to chance."[23] The risk that a videogame could teach the right things to the wrong people is a grave concern in behaviorist circles. As I discussed earlier,[24] *Sim City* has likewise been criticized for indoctrinating young people into an American model of taxation,[25] and for advancing an overly simplistic understanding of urban dynamics.[26] This same perspective underlies objections of these kinds.

The behaviorist view is problematic for numerous reasons. For those who wish to reject media effects arguments, this position all but requires players to accept that games that positively encourage negative incentives can only be damaging, never beneficial. But playing a role in a videogame does not automatically imply validation for the behavior the game models. As I have argued, videogames can also give players the opportunity to empathize with people and situations they might not ordinarily encounter, as in the case of *Darfur is Dying* and *Disaffected!*. Even though the player of a game might carry out the actions of the criminal, or the ninja, or the humanitarian, he does not necessarily endorse, reject, or adopt them outside of the game. Behaviorist approaches to games foreclose what I have previously called the simulation gap, the breach between the game's procedural representation of a topic and the player's interpretation of it. Indeed, behaviorism's general tendency to ignore the individual contexts for learning fail to account for both different player contexts and the ambiguity of meaning inherent to creative artifacts of all kinds. Such an absolute appeal to scientific logic occludes cultural nuance and the subjectivity of representation, a feature I have argued is inherent to videogame analysis.[27]

What about the constructivist-influenced approach to videogames? In Montessori, tactile interaction with abstract shapes and puzzles is not intended to produce abstract expressionist sculptors. Rather, the creative and menial work Montessori recommend of her students—including sweeping and polishing door handles—was conducted "[to make] them accomplish everything with an enthusiasm that is almost excessive."[28] Lego christened their computer-aided brick robot-building system with the term "Mindstorms," borrowed from constructionist Seymour Papert.[29] Mindstorms are primarily intended to teach computer programming and creative, expressive construction. While robotics are integral to the process, they serve principally as a carrot to draw child interest; the educational value of the toys are understood in terms of their potential to develop general abilities in programming and creative expression.

From this perspective, videogames teach abstract principles that service general problem-solving skills and learning values. Returning to our previous examples, a constructivist might understand *Microsoft Flight Simulator* as a game that teaches professional knowledge through "performance before competence," a concept of pedagogical apprenticeship.[30] Such an attitude might very well catalyze interest in aeronautics, but more generally it encourages the learner to experiment within knowledge domains freely, without fear of incompetence due to incomplete mastery.

Sim City likewise could serve as a similar catalyst for professional experimentation of the general kind, but the game offers another example of general constructivist learning principles. Under the shiny, credible graphics of *Sim City* towns is an abstract simulation of urban development, based largely on Jay Forrester's concept of urban dynamics.[31] But beneath even that layer of abstraction, the game marshals interactions between units of urban development via cellular automata, a technique that governs interaction between units (cells) of a system.[32] Just as Mindstorms robotics supply access to general programming techniques, constructivist approaches to educational videogames sometimes see games as uncovering the abstract systems that underlie them.

Sim City could be understood as a game that teaches about complexity and other approaches to the general operation of dynamic processes, such as systems theory and autopoietics. Through engagement with the game, players learn to reflect on the natural or artificial design of systems in the material world.[33]

Under such a conception, the "ninjaness" of *Ninja Gaiden* becomes a secondary, if not almost incidental, tool for general learning principles. In a demonstration of the game's learning principles at the 2005 Serious Games Summit, games and learning scholar James Paul Gee argued that the game uses exploration and small problems of increasing difficulty to teach players its rules of play. The design of successive challenges—climbing a wall, using a particular ninja attack on a particular type of opponent—is demonstrated, checked, and then challenged. All told, the game teaches players how to transform skills into strategies, and to turn failure into success.[34] *Ninja Gaiden* serves as an especially salient example of this technique owing to the game's characteristic difficulty. Unless the player learns the game effectively, he will never get very far.

This approach underscores videogames' ability to cultivate higher-order thinking skills. In a related example, Gee has argued that the real-time strategy (RTS) game *Rise of Nations* "encourages players to think in terms of relationships, not isolated events or facts."[35] This expanded view on a subject allows the player to see the problem abstractly and at a distance unavailable to the narrowly focused subject of a behaviorist classroom. The game, argues Gee, helps the player "see clearly how each piece of information we are given and each skill we are learning (and doing) is inter-connected to everything else we are learning and doing. We see the game as a system, not just a set of discrete skills."[36] John Beck and Mitchell Wade have called this abstract technique in videogames "going meta," or "taking a step back from the immediate situation, analyzing the choices and the odds, and finding the right strategy."[37] Beck and Wade argue that the "videogame generation"—people 35 and under as of 2005—are uniquely positioned for success in business because of this abstract ability to "go meta" learned from videogame playing in general.

The behaviorist position is perhaps as undesirable as the constructivist, but for different reasons. Behaviorism ascribes a singular, rationalist approach upon the content of videogames. Such a turn ignores Marshall McLuhan's suggestion that we understand media themselves as shapers of human experience, not just carriers of content. And constructivism risks total divestiture of the specificity of a *particular* videogame in favor of the general, abstract principles it embodies. While well-intentioned, Beck and Wade's approach to videogames represents a version of videogame constructivism that raises particular concerns for the medium's expressive potential. Instead of seeing videogames as an expressive medium, each artifact worthy of consideration and respect as a unique artifact, Beck and Wade see them as only a cultural trend, a population of minds properly conditioned for corporate influence. This approach to videogames recalls the ills of serious games, which try to leverage the properties of games to support existing hegemony. As Gee admits in his analysis of *Ninja Gaiden*, what the game really teaches is *how to play the game*.[38] We can understand the phrase two ways: how to play *this* game—*Ninja Gaiden*—and how to play the abstract game—business leadership.

If we reject both of these positions, what type of understanding of educational videogames emerges? Let's begin with Gee's useful summary of how he believes learning takes place in videogames, from his sustained study on the subject, *What Video Games Have to Teach Us about Learning and Literacy*:

The content of video games, when they are played actively and critically, is something like this: *They situate meaning in a multimodal space through embodied experiences to solve problems and reflect on the intricacies of the design of imagined worlds and the design of both real and imagined social relationships and identities in the modern world.*[39]

In other words, videogames simulate specific experiences that provide insights into the general relationships that drive those experiences. Gee calls this practice "situated" or "embodied learning."[40] I do not want to suggest that Gee's position is invalid, but rather that it is not strong enough. Videogames do not just offer situated meaning and embodied experiences of real and imagined worlds and relationships; they offer meaning and experiences of *particular* worlds and *particular* relationships. The abstract processes that underlie a game may confer general lessons about strategy, mastery, and interconnectedness, but they also remain coupled to a specific topic. The particular representations of taxation in *Sim City*, of criminality in *Grand Theft Auto*, and of humanitarianism in *Food Force* are not merely contingent. The underlying models of a videogame found a particular procedural rhetoric about its chosen subjects. Put differently, rhetorical positions are always particular positions; one does not argue or express in the abstract. A game's procedural rhetoric influences the player's relationship with it by constraining the strategies that yield failure or success.

The notion of graphical skins discussed in chapters 1 and 2 provides another perspective on this problem. The surface representation or graphical skin in a game is not a mere dressing for the abstract rules, such that any particular presentation of a procedural model is essentially arbitrary and dispensable. Likewise, the coupling of different graphical skins to similar procedural models does not necessarily couple the logic of the processes to the subject of the skin. This is why games like *Congo Jones and the Raiders of the Lost Bark*, *White House Joust*, and *Ms. Match* lose coherence: their topics are tied only to graphical skins and not to the processes underneath. Jesper Juul has called these two layers of a game *rules* and *fiction*, and he suggests that the two are not inseparable. To exemplify the claim, Juul compares two games with identical processes but different graphical skins, both derivatives of *Space Invaders*–style shooters: "In the first game, the player controls a spaceship in a battle against the heads of the hosts of a television program. In the second game, the player controls a spaceship in a battle against various [narratology] theories."[41] Despite the similarities of these games, which have identical underlying code, Juul concludes that "the relation between rules and fiction . . . is *not* arbitrary. . . . In the first case [players] stage the love/hate relationship that viewers may have with television personalities as a deep-space battle. In the second case they stage an academic discussion . . . as a deep space battle. Both are based on a background of some existing antagonism—and that is why they work, because the rules fit the representation—in an allegorical way."[42] In the case of these games, unlike *Congo Jones*, the procedural representation is deliberately chosen for its applicability to the games' respective topics.

Game designer Raph Koster offers an even stronger example. Koster imagines a hypothetical reskinning of the classic puzzle game *Tetris*. This new version replaces the game's abstract tetrominoes with dead bodies contorted into the different shapes. The abstract playfield of *Tetris* becomes a mass grave, and the game itself becomes a simulation of genocide. Koster explains:

You the player are dropping innocent victims down into the gas chamber, and they come in all shapes and sizes. There are old ones and young ones, fat ones and tall ones. As they fall to the bottom, they grab onto each other and try to form human pyramids to get to the top of the well. Should they manage to get out, the game is over and you lose. But if you pack them in tightly enough, the ones on the bottom succumb to the gas and die.[43]

The abstract goals of the two games remains the same, drop bodies to form neat, efficient rows in the tomb. But the adoption of a new context for identical rules changes the game from a harmless puzzle into a morally debatable cultural object. As Koster says of the hypothetical Holocaust simulator, "I do not want to play this game. Do you? Yet, it is *Tetris*."[44] Here, as in all videogames, the coupling of abstract processes to particular topics produce particular meanings that represent particular positions. Or, as Koster puts it, "the bare mechanics of the game do not determine its semantic freight."[45]

When Gee discusses "embodied experiences" in games, he is not referring to the type of individual encounter with a particular procedural claim about a particular topic in the examples just discussed. Instead, Gee connects embodied experience to *semiotic domains*, the sets of practices in which meaning is situated for a particular community.[46] While this idea may sound very similar to a procedural rhetoric, Gee's primary use of the term is quite general: the semiotic domain of videogames, or genres of videogames and the practices of players who learn and master them.[47] In this context, the learning that takes place in a videogame becomes an analogy for the way learning might take place in other contexts. For example, when people play first-person shooters, they learn the conventions and standards of those games, as well as the values and communications practices of players who play them, both inside and outside the game.[48] The semiotic domain of all first-person shooters might be similar due to the genre's common procedural model (unit operations for movement, projectiles, stealth, etc.), but the meaning of individual first-person shooters vary based on the way those processes are used rhetorically. *Doom* is about saving the world from hell-spawn; *Waco Resurrection* is about the politics of religious fanaticism. Gee's notions of semiotic domains and embodied experiences do clarify the qualitative differences between the kind of learning that takes place in videogames compared with traditional classrooms, but his approach maintains an ambiguous relationship with the educational significance of specific games. The higher-order thinking skills still matter, but so does the ninja.

To be fair, Gee never really intended his own analyses of the educational structure of videogames as an apotheosis of the medium's educational potential. Says Gee, "while I talk a good deal about actual video games, I really intend to discuss the *potential* of video games."[49] This sentiment breeds both encouragement and concern. On the one hand, it opens the door to an expanded possibility space for videogames that includes a variety of subject domains normally reserved for formal education and, thereby, normally excluded from commercial development. On the other hand, it suggests that the type of learning that takes place in current videogames is somehow derelict, or that the only learning possible in contemporary commercial off-the-shelf (COTS) games is of the abstract, subject-unspecific sort, a model for how learning might be more effective in other formal or informal settings, with or without the use of videogames. Thus, the notion that games teach you "how to play the game" stands as an open invitation for videogames of more varied genres and subject domains, where the game you learn to play has a greater and more meaningful coupling with real experience. More importantly, Gee's suggestions imply the need for a new understanding of educational games that reconciles subject-specificity and abstraction. As a means of entry into such a project, I propose a new understanding of *procedural literacy*.

From Programming to Culture

By the mid-1970s, early personal computers spawned a surge of interest in programming education, especially in getting children to program. At the Xerox Palo Alto Research (PARC) group, Alan Kay and Adele Goldberg proposed an environment in which anyone could program simulations.[50] Using their object-oriented Smalltalk language, Kay and Goldberg argued that computers could be used expressively by anyone. Soon after, Seymour Papert outlined a program for teaching children to program with Logo, a language he co-developed in the 1960s at MIT.[51] A student and colleague of Piaget, Papert built on the former's constructivist approach, extending his approach to knowledge as a practice of actively making real things, which he dubbed constructionism. By the early 1980s, programming began to gain recognition not only as a kind of professional training but also as a kind of literacy in its own right. This new trend has been called *procedural literacy*.[52]

Such efforts to teach programming to the uninitiated, and especially the very young, have continued since. Recently, Ken Perlin and Mary Flanagan have led a National Science Foundation (NSF)–funded initiative called the RAPUNSEL project, a programming environment designed specifically for preteen and early-teenage girls (a time when many girls lose interest in science and technology).[53] Like Papert's Mindstorms, RAPUNSEL relies on subject-matter "carrots" as incentives to program. But whereas the former uses abstract geometric art created by computer "turtles" and later robots as its carrot—a decidedly male-gendered bait—the latter uses dancing—equally gendered, perhaps, but far more appealing to girls. In RAPUNSEL, users embed dance-step programs into articles of clothing worn by avatars in the environment. RAPUNSEL programmers can trade parts of outfits to create new dances. Its creators haven't yet formalized RAPUNSEL into a fully functional system, but they currently envision it as a multiplayer game whose natural social dynamics will stimulate initial and continued interest in computer programming.

RAPUNSEL follows on the heels of numerous reports suggesting that the United States is falling far behind other nations in science and engineering.[54] Computational literacy is fundamental to many careers in the basic and applied sciences, and as such it is increasingly plausible to consider programming a foundational ability. But computer processing constitutes only one register of procedurality. More broadly, I want to suggest that procedural literacy entails the ability to reconfigure concepts and rules to understand and processes, not just on the computer, but in general. The high degree of procedural representation in videogames suggests them as a natural medium for procedural learning.[55] But, as I have suggested the learning that takes place in videogames is not just comprised of abstract processes, following the constructivist tradition, nor their surface content, following the behaviorist tradition. Rather, videogames use abstract processes to make procedural claims about specific topics. Expressive AI and interactive drama researcher/designer Michael Mateas offers a revised definition of procedural literacy that helps accomplish part of this correction:

By procedural literacy I mean the ability to read and write processes, to engage procedural representation and aesthetics, to understand the interplay between the culturally-embedded practice of human meaning-making and technically-mediated processes.[56]

Mateas's definition couples procedural reputation to culture and aesthetics, suggesting that procedural literacy is not just a practice of technical mastery, but one of technical-cultural mastery. I want to clarify a point left implicit in Mateas's position: procedural literacy should not be limited to the *abstract* ability to understand procedural representations of cultural values. Rather, it should use such an understanding to interrogate, critique, and use *specific* representations of *specific* real or imagined processes.

Before we can think about how videogames might help students become procedurally literate in this particular way, it is useful to consider how conceptions of "ordinary" literacy, in the literal sense of reading and writing "letters," have both addressed and confused the issue.

Shortly after World War II, Dorothy Sayers, a medievalist and friend of J. R. R. Tolkien and C. S. Lewis, gave a talk at Oxford entitled "The Lost Tools of Learning."[57] In the presentation, Sayers argued that we have failed to teach children what is most important. Instead of simply bombarding students with subject-specific content, Sayers suggests we first teach them how to learn. She points to the medieval method of education, based on the trivium, as a guide. The trivium comprised three parts: grammar, dialectic, and rhetoric. Aristotle first outlined this approach, mostly in works that were lost until the fifth and sixth centuries, when they were rendered into Latin for broader popular use. Sayers was a medievalist and Christian apologist, and thus she points explicitly to the medieval version of the trivium, which focused more on Latin authors as opposed to the Greeks ones who had formed the basis for learning in antiquity, including Latin-speaking ancient Rome.

On first blush, it is tempting to interpret Sayers' views as proto-constructivist. If Sayers decries "subjects" in favor of "the art of learning," doesn't this mean replacing content-specific learning with abstract principles?[58] In fact, this is not at all what Sayers wished to propose. "'Subjects' of some kind," says Sayers, "there must be, of course. One cannot learn the theory of grammar without learning an actual language, or learn to argue and orate without speaking about something in particular."[59] Sayers draws her suggestions for the particular subjects in which to ground a principles-based education from her background as a medievalist; they include post-classical Latin, theology, classical myth and European legend, historical figures and dates, and the natural sciences and mathematics. In this way, Sayers reconnects grammar with all subjects of all sorts, instead of relegating it to the single subject of language. Dialectic builds on this mastery of the basics of particular topics and moves into the realm of analysis ("Many lessons—on whatever subject—will take the form of debates"; "Was the behavior of this statesman justified?"; "Theology . . . will furnish material for argument about conduct and morals").[60] And rhetoric demands the student to synthesize critical, self-expressive, and argumentative perspectives about a wide range of topics, using the tools of dialectic.

Traditional classroom instruction, both in Sayers' time and our own, privileges subject learning in isolation and without mechanisms for synthesis; such is the source of the now-familiar pupil's aphorism, "when am I going to use this in the ical world?" But rather than suggesting that the exercise of Latin, or mathematics, or history themselves strengthen the mind through generic exercise, Sayers' proposes that the embedded logics of such subjects provide the tools necessary to interrogate new, unfamiliar questions. These tools become the basis for living a productive adult life, or for interrogating a new, more advanced subject at university (the equivalent of the medieval quadrivium, which follows the trivium).[61] Sayers' proposal is still that of a traditional medievalist, and it is stereotypically Western in its values. We might accept or reject the content of Sayers' proposal for literacy, but its structure is instructive: abstract approaches to specific subjects found the basis for learning.

Sayers does not propose the direct adoption of the medieval trivium, but a revision to it, a modernization. Her proposal is hypothetical and high-level, not adequate to support a complete curriculum. In recent years, educators influenced by Sayers' proposal in "The Lost Tools of Learning," have attempted to adopt her model for contemporary instruction. Sayers' influence is particularly pronounced in private and parochial schools, which appreciate her emphasis on the church, but secularized versions have also become increasingly common. Such schools often call their approaches "classical," a reference to the classical origins of the trivium itself. But since Sayers' own proposal is a revision of the medieval tradition's own adoption of the classical trivium, such new approaches are more properly called *neoclassical*: they revise the medieval trivium for a new era.

Despite the clarity of Sayers' proposal, modern adaptations of it have decoupled the trivium from its subject-specific roots, following the errors of constructivism. Among the more popular recent attempts to codify a neoclassical education is that of Jessie Wise and Susan Wise Bauer, who coauthored *The Well-Trained Mind*, an influential book on neoclassical education.[62] At first blush, Wise and Bauer's neoclassical trivium looks just like Sayers' proposal. The three stages of grammar, dialectic, and rhetoric are present (although Wise and Bauer rename dialectic *logic*). They also implement Sayers' suggestion to map these three stages to developmental level: grammar in the elementary grades, logic in the middle-school grades, and rhetoric in the high-school grades. But unlike Sayers' approach, Wise and Bauer divest the specific intellectual canon imposed by the trivium's subjects, such as Latin, theology, and epic in favor of instrumental, abstract ones. On the one hand, their neoclassicism divorces learning from the social and cultural traditions that serve as objects of knowledge, paralleling the constructivist privilege of abstraction over concreteness. But on the other hand, Wise and Bauer also don't revise Sayer's Occidentalism and traditionalism; for example, despite the implication of modernization in a *neo*classical approach, the two still privilege verbal and especially written expression, castigating visual and computational media.[63] This fault parallels the behaviorist insistence on a single mode of legitimate learning. Understanding the way a traditional approach to literacy broke down the bond between abstraction and subject-specificity will help us understand how to avoid such a one in the domain of procedural literacy.

Let's look at an example. One of the subjects that neoclassical philosophies privilege is Latin. Consider Dorothy Sayers' thoughts on the use of Latin in learning:

I will say at once, quite firmly, that the best grounding for education is the Latin grammar. I say this, not because Latin is traditional and mediaeval, but simply because even a rudimentary knowledge of Latin cuts down the labor and pains of learning almost any other subject by at least fifty percent. It is the key to the vocabulary and structure of all the Teutonic languages, as well as to the technical vocabulary of all the sciences and to the literature of the entire Mediterranean civilization, together with all its historical documents.[64]

Sayers accounts for Latin's influence in the evolution of European languages, but she gives equal weight to its influential place in the texts of Western civilization. Now consider the way Wise and Bauer's invoke Latin in *The Well-Trained Mind*:

Latin trains the mind to think in an orderly fashion. Latin . . . is the most systematic language around. The discipline of assembling the endings and arranging syntax . . . according to sets of rules is the mental equivalent of a daily two-mile jog. And because Latin demands precision, the Latin-trained mind becomes accustomed to paying attention to detail.[65]

Here, Latin is revered as a structured mental exercise, not for its value as a window into key components of Western culture, especially the culture of ancient Rome and the medieval church. More appropriately, Latin would be allowed to oscillate between its formal and cultural registers; on the one hand, the language itself possesses formal features of synthetic inflection that structure expression, and through that syntactic inflection, specific cultural output can be consumed or created. Additional formal constraints arise from time to time, for example metrical authorship in dactylic hexameter.

Now let's try to apply the lessons from neoclassical approaches to literacy onto procedural literacy. The formal logics of synthetic inflection and meter constrain and construct the expressive potential of Latin literature. More formal constrained writing practices like those of the Oulipo—palindrome,[66] lipogram,[67] and prisoner's constraint,[68] for example—impose even more stringent restrictions than those of natural grammar and "ordinary" literary convention, but such practice was founded explicitly to create new patterns for written expression. Computers constrain expression even more, through both hardware and design of programming language. One could easily replace the word *Latin* in Wise and Bauer's claim with the name of a computer programming language like *Java* or *Smalltalk* or *C*, effectively parodying the value of any subject for abstract goals alone. In many ways, programming and Oulipian writing offer even stronger evidence for the benefits of systematic training than Latin; after all, natural language is subject to human failing and misinterpretation.

Latin, C, and other language systems share basic properties. Languages impose internally checked compositional rules, which in turn produce the possibility space for expressive output. The languages themselves thus enforce a procedural rhetoric in each of their created artifacts; rules of syntax, grammar, composition, and so forth form the foundation of what it is possible to say or execute in a natural or computer language. But the cultural, historical, and material contexts for Latin and C are far from similar. Mastering the syntax and grammar of one over the other both opens up and closes down whole worlds of future knowledge and expression.

A behaviorist might argue that Latin is useful for learning classics and C for learning programming. A constructivist might argue that either Latin or C is useful for learning logic and syntax. Procedurality offers a possible bridge between the abstraction-poor behaviorist approach and the subject-poor constructivist approach, focusing on the way processes come together to create meaning. But I want to suggest an important break from previous conceptions of procedural literacy as *programming*.

From the first proposals to recent efforts like RAPUNSEL, procedural literacy has been a derivative of constructivist educational practice. Consider A. J. Perlis' 1961 proposal for a course in programming, which Mateas claims is the earliest argument for "universal procedural literacy":[69]

the purpose of my proposed first course in programming . . . is not to teach people how to program a specific computer, nor is it to teach some new languages. The purpose of a course in programming is to teach people how to construct and analyze processes.[70]

Now consider the broader educational frames that Gee draws around the use of videogames for learning:

"situated cognition" . . . argues that human learning is not just a matter of what goes on inside people's heads but is fully embedded (situated within) a material, social, and cultural world. . . . [Another] area is work on so-called connectionism, a view that stresses the ways in which human beings are powerful pattern-recognizers. This body of work argues that humans don't often think best when they attempt to reason via logic and general abstract principles detached from experience.[71]

At first glance, the objection of the situated cognitivists might seem very similar to more general constructivist arguments. After all, constructivism reconnects learning with individual experience. But the basic premise of situated cognitivism still occludes the *type of experience* that intersects with *specific* abstract principles. Gee continues,

Rather [than via abstract principles], they think best when they reason on the basis of patterns they have picked up through their actual experiences in the world, patterns that, over time, can become generalized but that are still rooted in specific areas of experience.[72]

It is precisely *specific areas of experience* that have been expunged from our understanding of constructivist learning and procedural literacy in particular; it is also the corrective for the practice of divorcing subject-specificity from learning. Even popular paeans for the cognitive benefit of television and videogames argue principally for abstract (although individualized) conceptual learning. Consider the following selections from pop-critic Stephen Johnson's *Everything Bad Is Good For You*:

Word problems . . . are good for the mind on some fundamental level: they teach abstract skills in probability, in pattern recognition, in understanding causal relations that can be applied in countless situations . . . . The problems that confront the gamers of *Zelda* can be readily translated into this form . . . .[73]

When we marvel at the technological savvy of average ten-year-olds, what we should be celebrating is not their mastery of a specific platform—Windows XP, say, or the GameBoy—but rather their seemingly effortless ability to pick up new platforms on the fly, without so much as a glimpse at a manual. What they've learned is not just the specific rules intrinsic to a particular system; they've learned abstract principles that can be applied when approaching any complicated system.[74]

Johnson also discusses intelligence tests that deploy spatial relations like the Raven Progressive Matrices or the various Wechsler measures. These measures demand synthesis of a kind that rote learning does not; this is why they are used to measure general performance intelligence. Johnson argues that puzzle games like *Tetris* provide widespread experience in complex relations, leading to increased performance on intelligence measures of this kind.[75] Videogames have thus perhaps made us smarter insofar as they allow us to understand the strategies of intelligence measures. But who would substitute mastery of intelligence measures for contributions to human progress?

Claims like Johnson's assume that what is cognitively beneficial is necessarily socially, culturally, or politically beneficial. To take up one of his examples, the specificity of a computer operating system like Windows XP is not merely incidental. Certainly the general principles of human–computer interaction benefit consumers in a world of saturated with electronics, in which corporate oligarchies force users to upgrade annually. But what about the specific affordances and constraints of Windows XP? Like the cultural and formal specificity of Latin versus Inuit or the formal properties of C versus LISP, the procedural affordances of a computer operating system *matter*: they constrain and enable the kinds of computational activities that are possible atop that operating system.

Some procedural approaches to learning take small steps in avoiding content or abstraction as exclusive learning outcomes. One such effort is Mitchel Resnick's version of the Logo language, which he named StarLogo.[76] StarLogo uses the same LISP-based Logo syntax, but instead of driving a stenographic turtle, it drives multiple turtles configured for agent based simulation of decentralized systems—things like bird flocks, traffic, and other emergent phenomena.[77] Yet despite their promise as introductions to social and biological systems in particular, such efforts still focus largely on the mechanical—StarLogo has much in common with the view of *Sim City* that highlights its cellular automatic and emergent mechanics as a principal, general learning outcome. What does procedural literacy look like when it privileges the representation of *culture* as much as that of dynamic systems?

Procedural History

Among their neoclassical revisions, Wise and Bauer stress what they call the "interrelatedness of knowledge." They advocate an approach to learning across disciplines, specifically an iterative four-year pattern of literature, history, and science from the ancients, the middle ages, early modern times, and modern times, respectively. Interrelatedness for Wise and Bauer has to do with creating links between knowledge fields, for example history, literature, and the sciences. In their conception, these connections are defined almost entirely by shared historical era; for example, the Greek epic, the notion of heroism, and Greek history form an interrelated, cross-disciplinary group.

Wise and Bauer hope to break down the barriers between disciplines created in contemporary behaviorist classrooms, where history, literature, and science are considered separate, subjects with their own drills, assessments, and teachers. But in so doing they also risk obscuring the nature of historical progress across eras, effectively separating the events of history (history as "content") from the logic of history (history as "abstraction").

Jared Diamond takes a different approach in *Guns, Germs, and Steel*.[78] During Diamond's time as an evolutionary biologist studying birds in New Guinea, a native friend of his posed the question, why do white men from the West have so many possessions, while natives have so little? Diamond reframed this question, observing that we know what happened in history— the conquest of much of the world by Europeans through the use of ocean-going vessels and horses, pistols and other forged weapons, and nonnative diseases like smallpox. But we don't understand *why* the history of the world unfolded in such a way that the Europeans possessed such advantages. If guns, germs, and steel are the *proximate causes* of the flow of history as we know it, what are the *ultimate causes*? Why, asks Diamond, didn't the Aztecs sail their ships to Europe and conquer the Spaniards?

Noting that much of human history has assumed that some basic difference in ability or intelligence among human peoples can explain why some have so much and others so little, Diamond argues that the answer to this question doesn't rest in anything inherent to people, but in a few fundamental accidents of geography and natural resources. In areas with especially abundant land, such as Mesopotamia and China, ancient peoples happened upon agricultural innovation. This allowed them to remain in one place longer, rather than wandering from place to place as nomads after they had expended a region's resources. Such locations, as it happened, also offered a variety of more easily domesticated animals such as horses and pigs, suitable for food, burden, and work. Sedentary communities of farmers were able to grow larger and eventually, through creating food surpluses, to relieve portions of their population from devoting most of their time to feeding their immediate families. In geographies with large east–west axes, such as Eurasia, similar climates across broad longitudinal distances facilitated the transfer of crops, animals, agricultural methods, and techniques of animal husbanding—facilitating massive social growth across long distances. Landmasses with north–south axes, such as North and South America, couldn't support the same crops and livestock over commensurate distances, owing to rapid climate changes along the latitudes and natural geological obstacles like the impassable Andes and the narrow isthmus of Panama.

Once food storage freed some from the burden of farming, growing societies could devote these populations to other tasks, such as soldiering, shipbuilding, technology, religion, and politics. The latter two classes especially provided the structure necessary to develop clans of people into chiefdoms and later states. Inventors created new crafts, including methods of metallurgy necessary to forge strong steel tools and weapons for war.

As communities grew into towns and cities housing people and domesticated animals in close quarters, disease transferred easily between them. While these scourges decimated local populations, they also bred strong resistances to even the most afflictive of diseases. As these societies took their ships and swords to war, the peoples they met had weapons, armor, political systems, and immune systems far inferior to those of their invaders. In short, Diamond argues that the proximate causes of European conquest via horses, guns, germs, and steel resulted from the accidental ultimate causes of land fertility, geographic distribution, and variety of plants and animals that occupied such regions.

One consequence of Diamond's concept of history is the deemphasis of individual achievement; he presents invention and innovation as the outcome of situations rather than the radical ingenuity of individuals. For Diamond, the "interrelatedness of knowledge" (to appropriate Wise and Bauer's term) turns out to be less relevant to historical moments than to the underlying conditions out of which such moments arose. Those conditions comprise both the actual events that took place and the configuration of geographic and material circumstances that bore them.

Diamond describes a procedural system in which political and social outcomes result from configurations of constrained material conditions. This abstract system founds the specific outcomes of history. Just as Sayers couples an abstract learning process with a specific ideology of cultural value, Diamond couples an abstract material process with a specific historical timeline. Such an approach to history asks the learner to understand a sequence of events in relation to the material logics that produce them. The procedural history Diamond presents in *Guns, Germs, and Steel* also has its own rhetoric about how history takes place—one in which geographic accidents generate historical events.

Diamond presents his procedural view of history in a book, using written rhetoric. To deploy its processes, the reader must imagine historical examples and perform thought experiments to trace their connection to material conditions. As I mentioned in chapter 4, videogames like *Civilization*[79] and *Empire Earth*[80] operationalize a theory of history similar to Diamond's. In *Civilization*, the player runs a society from its humble roots to empire. But empires grow on a base of stable food supplies and other natural resources, which facilitate political stability and, over time, investment in military forces or technologies (social, political, and material). Despite its similarities to *Guns, Germs, and Steel* in abstract material processes, *Civilization* offers only a limited window onto the actual events of lived history. The player can opt to play as a particular civilization, such as the Mongols or the Romans, but the choice changes little more than the graphical representation of the culture. Furthermore, geography in *Civilization* is rendered anew in each game, so the player's starting conditions may vary greatly from those of the historical conditions of the civilization under whose name he chooses to play. Of course, generative geography also affords the game great richness in its procedural representation of the relationships between natural resources and cultural progress.

Other games couple the procedural rhetoric of material accident to the actual progression of lived history. In *Europa Universalis*, the player controls a European nation during the colonial period, from 1492 to 1792.[81] The game focuses on colonial expansion through militarism, religious influence, diplomacy, and trade. *Europa Universalis* accurately reproduces the geographic reality of the European continent, along with its inherent physical, material, and political conditions. Even though the player may not choose to follow the events of the historical record, the relative strengths and weaknesses of each nation in *Europa Universalis* derives from their actual historical situation.

Historical divergence serves as both a limitation and an opportunity for videogames like *Civilization* and *Europa Universalis*. On the one hand, to connect the games' abstract model to the particulars of lived history, the player must muster knowledge from outside the game, perhaps from traditional educational media. On the other hand, the games' use of factual information about historical civilizations (names and landmarks in the case of *Civilization*, geographic and material circumstances in the case of *Europa Universalis*) underscore the inconsistencies between played and lived history in each run of the game. These contrary-to-fact conditions open a simulation gap for the player to interrogate: the player also learns by meditating on what is *different* in the game's representation of Egypt or Russia compared with the historical (and geographical) record. All told, artifacts like *Guns, Germs, and Steel, Civilization*, and *Europa Universalis* suggest that procedural literacy means more than writing computer code; it also comes from interacting with procedural systems themselves, especially procedural systems that make strong ties between the processes in a model and a representational goal—those with strongly argued procedural rhetorics. Otherwise said, we can become procedurally literate through play itself.

From its early stages, Papert's Mindstorms project used the computer language Logo to allow children to instruct their own robot creations. Starting in the mid-1980s, Papert and his colleagues collaborated with toymaker Lego to combine their configurative toys with the Logo language. Children built structures like elevators and robots with Lego bricks, then connected them to an interface box they could program in Logo. But even without a Logo interface, Legos offer their own lessons in procedurality. The feature fundamental to Legos' "creativity" is in fact the logic of their physical coupling: individual Legos can be reconfigured in many different ways to create new objects or systems, according to simple rules of assembly. Even without Papert-style Logo instruction, playing with Legos develops procedural literacy. Legos recombine in multiple patterns to create new, previously unpredictable meaning.

Lego play focuses on physical construction. In comparison, consider Playmobil, another type of children's toy. Like Lego, Playmobil are made of molded plastic and sold in themes like airport, pirate, and knight. But unlike Lego, units of Playmobil are larger and less materially recombinant, but more richly invested with cultural meaning. For example, a "Castaway" Playmobil kit comes with castaway, small island with palm tree, dead tree with torn white flag, torn lean-to, message in a bottle, three crabs, three fish skeletons, two starfish and pile of driftwood. When I began buying Playmobil for my kids, I originally thought there was no way they could offer the same kind of creative play as Lego, since the latter can be recombined in many more ways. But on further reflection, the high specificity of Playmobil pieces offers procedural learning on a much more deeply culturally embedded level than Lego. We don't see just knights in Playmobil, we see Crusaders. We don't see just fighters, we see Mongol Warriors. By providing a specific point of reference bound to human culture, the toys come equipped with specific cultural meaning as well as abstract processes for substitution. The components of each collection provide adequate context to allow kids to recombine their toys in a way that preserves, interrogates, or disrupts the cultural context of each piece. When children (or adults!) play with Playmobil, they recombine units of cultural relevance—metermaids, chimney sweeps, frothing beer mugs, airport security checkpoints (see figure 8.1 for an example). In so doing, they gain a richer understanding of the individual meanings of cultural markers through experimenting with their hypothetical recombination in circumstances outside their sphere of influence.

Procedural Rhetoric as Procedural Literacy

Procedural literacy has been largely understood as learning to program—a valuable and worthwhile goal in a world increasingly reliant on computation. But the value of procedural literacy goes far beyond the realm of program-

Figure 8.1 Playmobil toys allow children (and adults) to construct social and cultural situations. This unusual situation was constructed and photographed by the author.

ming alone; indeed, any activity that encourages active assembly of basic building blocks according to particular logics contributes to procedural literacy. Written and spoken language does require conceptual effort, but it is fallacious to think that media such as toys and videogames do *not* demand conceptual effort. Yet, it is equally fallacious to think that videogames automatically engender synthetic abstraction outside their specific subject matter. The procedurally literate subject is one who recognizes both the specific nature of a material concept *and* the abstract rules that underwrite that concept.

To distinguish videogames from narrative media, Heather Chaplin and Aaron Ruby argue that the former use models, whereas the latter use descriptions.[82] As an example, the two compare learning the orbits of planets from textbook or lecture descriptions versus learning from an orrery, a mechanical model of the planets on a system of gears that models their rotations and orbits at the correct relative velocities. The orrery, explain Chaplin and Ruby, "represents the solar system not by *describing* it but by serving as a *model* of it."[83]

Models that depict behavior, like an orrery, facilitate experimentation, a more formal kind of procedural play where the rules of the mechanical system constrain manipulation of the device.

Both models and toys also enforce procedural rhetorics. The orrery constrains its planets' behavior according to mechanical rules, which represent the laws of physics that guide celestial orbit. Planetary orbit is perhaps a non-controversial topic today, but before Copernicus advanced the heliocentric theory of the solar system in the early fifteenth century, belief in it was scarce. The orrery in its current form dates from the eighteenth century, but Copernicus and his contemporaries also used mechanical models to illustrate their theories, representing their arguments for celestial movement in the mechanical processes that made these models function. Some toys function like models too, enforcing behavior based on mechanical processes. Toys like Playmobil do not enforce procedural rhetorics directly, but they do allow their players to build procedural rhetorics. When a child constructs a Playmobil scenario combining HAZMAT-crew parts and pirate parts, he constructs an argument for how such a character would behave. This argument is carried out through the rules of play itself, the types of behavior the child chooses to encourage or prohibit.

Procedural rhetoric is a type of procedural literacy that advances and challenges the logics that underlie behavior, and how such logics work. Procedural literacy entails the ability to read and write procedural rhetorics—to craft and understand arguments mounted through unit operations represented in code. The type of "reading" and "writing" that form procedural rhetorics asks the following questions:

What are the rules of the system?

What is the significance of these rules (over other rules)?

What claims about the world do these rules make?

How do I respond to those claims?

Let us return to some of our previous examples of educational videogames with these questions in mind.

Consider again *Microsoft Flight Simulator* and *Sim City*. One productive means of assessing the educational value of these games is via an expansion of what Gee calls embodied experiences. In one such approach, David Williamson Shaffer has studied how games help individuals see the world through *particular* professional eyes.[84] Shaffer sees games as an instance of "epistemic frames," or ways that participants in a particular community of practice both structure their behavior and contribute to the ongoing development of that community of practice.[85] Shaffer gives the name *epistemic game* to "a process [of] simulation that preserves the connections between knowing and doing central to the epistemic frame."[86]

Both *Flight Simulator* and *Sim City* can be understood as epistemic games; they are simulations of professional situations. As simulations, the games embody procedural rhetorics about operating logics of aviation and urban planning. Note that the epistemic game, or the procedural rhetoric of a profession, implies not that players are learning to complete the work of such a profession, but rather that they are learning to understand the system of rules that drive the function of that profession. They are learning about the kinds of tasks, problems, and solutions involved in flying planes and building cities.

While Shaffer is principally (but not exclusively) interested in epistemic games as a pedagogical praxis for specific professional situations, I am equally—if not more—interested in procedural rhetoric as a critical practice. Recalling the disturbing account of the mother visited by the FBI after buying the game, one way to play would be to ask how the rules of aviation might encourage or avert terrorist acts. Earlier I discussed the procedural rhetorics of nutrition, class, and criminality in *Grand Theft Auto: San Andreas*. Playing the game with an interest in these procedural affordances for advancement allows the player to read its claims about crime and nutrition in light of his experience of those issues in the material world.

A game like *Take Back Illinois*, also discussed earlier, advances a procedural rhetoric of a particular position on medical malpractice reform, educational management, and job incentives.[87] Those logics are presented not as natural law to be internalized and positively reinforced, but as systems to be interrogated and questioned—one of the principles of rhetoric as we normally understand it anyway.

The Sims has been criticized for its procedural rhetoric of consumer capitalism.[88] Undeniably, it privileges the acquisition of material goods as a primary factor in sim success and happiness. Some argue that the game is a parody of consumption, the homogeneous goals of the sims acting as a caricature of contemporary U.S. ideals—an "American television culture."[89] Critic Gonzalo Frasca disagrees.

I met some people that firmly believe that *The Sims* is a parody and, therefore, it is actually a critique of consumerism. Personally, I disagree. While the game is definitively cartoonish, I am not able to find satire within it. Certainly, the game may be making fun of suburban Americans, but since it rewards the player every time she buys new stuff, I do not think this could be considered parody.[90]

The "real" answer to this objection is not important (although designer Will Wright maintains that the game is a caricature); but some of the educational value of the game comes from engaging and unpacking the relationship between the rules of consumption and the pursuit of virtual satisfaction.

At the start of this chapter, I asked: if videogames are educational, what do they teach, and how do they teach it? To summarize the reply given here: videogame players develop procedural literacy through interacting with the abstract models of specific real or imagined processes presented in the games they play. Videogames teach biased perspectives about how things work. And the way they teach such perspectives is through procedural rhetorics, which players "read" through direct engagement and criticism.

9

Values and Aspirations

In the United States, more and more parents and students are entertaining a rather terrifying notion: our educational system seems so focused on creating obedient, well-schooled masses that free-thinking, well-educated individuals have become the exception, freak accidents that somehow survive the schooling experience well enough to get a genuine education. Some vocal detractors have even given a lurid name to these battlegrounds where the underdogs of education struggle against the armies of schooling; they call them *concentration campuses*.[1] As a political issue, education consistently ranked in the top four subjects that most concerned U.S. citizens in advance of the 2004 presidential election.[2] A few broad positions on education emerge from the general soup of ire in which the issue simmers. Here's a brief but effective summary:

Liberal advocates often argue that more money needs to be spent on education, hiring more teachers to reduce student–teacher ratios and raising teacher salaries to levels comparable to other professions. They also argue that educational resources should be distributed more equitably, so students in poor school districts are not left behind. Conservatives often counter that a great deal of money is already being spent with little to show for it, and that control over education policy needs to be returned to the state and local level. Many further argue that private or public school choice will bring market pressures to bear on a system that suffers due to lack of competition.[3]

Despite these prevailing attitudes, recent years have witnessed an increased federalization of education in the United States. Shortly after taking office in 2001, President George W. Bush introduced a $47 billion educational reform plan that faulted the federal government for its lax participation in educational responsibility. Formalized the following year as "No Child Left Behind" (NCLB), the legislation imposed additional standardized testing demands—especially on primary schools—and increased penalties for local districts that fail to meet national standards.[4] Critics of NCLB most commonly cited problems in funding, accountability, and the utility of standardized testing.[5]

NCLB assumes that the educational system is well conceived and capable of functioning adequately; the problems emerge from rogue schools and inadequate teachers. The legislation assumes that making such groups "accountable" to the system will thus solve the problem. NCLB identifies an important feature of educational infrastructures. Classroom environments of all kinds—schools, workplace training centers, expensive executive seminars, continuing education courses, technology certification programs, and so many others—are not disinterested, bias-free places. Each is part of a larger social, political, or corporate structure, or a combination of these.

Distrust of educational institutions is not unique to twentieth- and twenty-first-century postindustrialism. In 1869, John Stuart Mill offered a similar argument:

A general State education is a mere contrivance for moulding people to be exactly like one another; and the mould in which it casts them is that which pleases the predominant power in the government—whether this be a monarch, a priesthood, an aristocracy, or the majority of the existing generation; in proportion as it is efficient and successful, it establishes a despotism over the mind, leading by natural tendency to one over the body.[6]

We might summarize the distinction as one of being *schooled* versus *educated*. Being schooled means becoming expert in the actual process of schooling, the requirements and conditions of doing well in school, so as to ratchet up in the system. Being schooled means understanding how to stand in line, how to speak when acknowledged, and how to follow directions. Being schooled means understanding how the system works and serving as a well-oiled cog in its machinery. By contrast, being educated means becoming expert in human improvement, so as to ratchet up in life itself. Being educated means being literate in the fundamental operation of a knowledge domain, knowing how to advance arguments, how to think independently, and how to express and improve oneself. Being educated means understanding how to disrupt a system with new improvements.

When schooling takes place in corporations or other enterprises, we usually call it *training*. Training in the pedagogical sense derives from the Old French verb *trahiner*, which had the sense of causing something to grow in a certain shape, usually a plant. Training always implies an external agent who sets the agenda for the desired growth, like a bonsai artist pruning and wiring the learner's roots and branches. It is perhaps no accident that the verb *school* is used derogatorily in informal parlance to celebrate dominance of one agent over another: *I totally schooled you*. Conversely, *education* has been tethered unfortunately to the chain of schooling and training. "Education" derives from the Latin *educere*, to lead out. "True" educational systems draw their participants out of the very systems that support them by helping them see the undesirable features of those systems.

Consumption

In particular, schooling is tightly bound to consumption. At the 2004 MIT-sponsored Education Arcade conference, critic and veteran educational software designer Brenda Laurel launched into a brisk harangue on the subject, which I paraphrase here:[7]

School teaches basic skills. Starting in the twentieth century, school provides socialization and, more importantly, babysitting while parents go to work. School teaches test-taking behavior. And school teaches about authority: teachers know more and have more power; students have no power. Students' ability to express agency is limited to "petty transgressions" or "achievements of excellence" within the structure provided by the school.

the teaching of hierarchy is the primary function of public education in America—designed to create an efficient underclass. School trains kids to be good workers and buyers. . . .

Public education does not teach young people to meaningfully exercise personal agency, to think critically, to use their voices, to engage in discourse, or to be good citizens.[8]

These arguments trace a broader trend made most famous by Louis Althusser, who cited the education system as the most important example of "ideological state apparatuses" (ISAs), state institutions that function specifically to reproduce the process of production.[9]

Laurel raises complaints similar to those of more recent educational critics John Taylor Gatto and Brian Jackson. Gatto is a former public school educator and the author of *The Underground History of American Education* and *Dumbing Us Down*;[10] Jackson wrote *Life in Classrooms*, which argued that there is a "hidden curriculum" in public schools that has converted education into a process of socialization rather than one of knowledge transmission.[11] In her Education Arcade talk, Laurel effectively echoes the sentiments of critics like Gatto and Jackson; schools encourage students to conform and identify valid knowledge so that they can continue to ratchet up through the system. It promotes *schooling*, not *education*. Laurel points out that schools teach hierarchy and consumerism; schools are necessary in order to release parents into the working world, where they contribute to the gross domestic product while taking on greater and greater debt that perpetuates their need to conform in the role of complacent citizen. Recent, more disturbing trends such as mandatory preschool seem driven by the need to maximize adults' productivity and economic activity, not to promote the education of young people.[12]

Just as political videogames deploy procedural rhetorics to advance the function of existing or proposed public policy, just as advergames deploy procedural rhetorics to advance the function of product and services, so educational games use procedural rhetorics to advance the function of conceptual or material systems in general. Political games and advergames could be understood as educational games, just as advergames like *The Toilet Training Game* and *Disaffected!* could be considered as political games. I understand educational games not as videogames that end up being used in schools or workplaces, but as games that use procedural rhetorics to spur consideration about the aspects of the world they represent.

Let's consider a simple example. *Mansion Impossible* is a web-based videogame about real-estate investment.[13] The game presents the gridded streets of a neighborhood (see figure 9.1). Houses pop out of the empty ground to go on the market, and disappear back into the ground when they sell. The price is inscribed on the house, and each house experiences a single gain–loss cycle before stabilizing. The player starts out with $100 k, and the goal of the game is to build enough capital to buy the $10 million mansion on the edge

Figure 9.1 *Mansion Impossible* abstracts real estate investment, focusing on geographic strategy.

of the screen. The player clicks on houses to buy or sell, taking care to time a sale for maximum profit. The town is divided into lower- and higher-cost housing areas, with the top right near the mansion offering the most exclusive and most expensive digs.

A great amount of detail is abstracted from *Mansion Impossible*. Nevertheless, the game mounts an interesting procedural rhetoric about real-estate investment. For one part, the player is encouraged always to invest in something; keeping money in the bank yields no gain. Even though *Mansion Impossible* does not address the topic of mortgage financing, this dynamic simulates the concept of leverage. By maximizing the use of one's capital in investments, one leverages the maximum gain out of the minimum investment.[14]

The game also splits the town into neighborhoods of increasing value. Houses go on the market constantly in every region, so the player can easily identify the more and less desirable areas by watching their respective price ranges. There is no general housing market driving appreciation across the entire town, but the player can identify which individual neighborhoods are hot or cold, desirable or undesirable, and plan investments accordingly. This principle also corresponds to common strategies in real-estate investment.[15]

But the most striking unit operation in *Mansion Impossible* models geographic proximity. Even though the player's only control is through single mouse clicks, the game is quite fast paced, with properties constantly appearing and disappearing from the market all over the map. The player must scan the marketplace for desirable, new properties while keeping an eye on the ones he already owns to avoid losses. The most practical strategy for managing current and future investments is to focus on one area of the board. Even though higher-valued properties in another region might appreciate faster, the attentional cost of investing in two remote regions makes it much easier to suffer losses. This gameplay mechanic is a unit operation for a much more complex and conceptually abstract principle in real-estate investment: investors should buy in areas they already know, and should make acquisitions in neighborhoods that are convenient to them (near work, near home, on the way to work, etc.).[16]

Mansion Impossible is not a videogame course on real-estate investment. It does not teach anything about investment mortgages, property management, taxes, government regulations, or other relevant topics. But it does not attempt to do such a thing. Popular literature on real-estate investment spends a great deal of time laying conceptual groundwork for the practice. *Mansion Impossible* makes a procedural argument for focusing investing in one area and keeping as much capital as possible invested in the market. The player may then consider deploying this new logical structure in a variety of ways; he might choose to look more closely at properties in his own neighborhood for potential investment. He might raise new objections to his neighborhood association group about the many speculators buying properties on his block and renovating them into "McMansions" to flip. Or, perhaps he might simply store the concept for later extraction and recombination in conversation or daily practice. In a few minutes of play, *Mansion Impossible* provides useful access to a fairly esoteric and high-level concept that most would only learn after poring through several real-estate investment texts.

Of course, *Mansion Impossible* is also a bit esoteric, a web game among a noisy abundance of online games. Commercial games also mount procedural rhetorics that explore everyday practice. The Nintendo GameCube videogame

Animal Crossing is an "animal village simulator."[17] Players move into a town filled with cartoonish animal characters and buy a house, then work, trade, and personalize their microenvionment. The game offers a series of innocuous, even mundane activities like bug catching, gardening, and wallpaper designing; like *The Sims*, *Animal Crossing*'s primary metaphors are social interaction and household customization.

Although the GameCube supports simultaneous play with up to four players, *Animal Crossing* only allows one player at a time. The game can store up to four player profiles in one shared town, and human players can interact with friends or family members who play the game, but only indirectly, by leaving notes or gifts, completing tasks, or even planting flowers or trees. Furthermore, *Animal Crossing* binds the game world to the real world, synchronizing its date and time to the console clock. Time passes in real time in *Animal Crossing*—it gets dark at night, snows in the winter, and the animals go trick-or-treating on Halloween. Since game time is linked to real time, a player can conceptualize the game as a part of his daily life rather than a split out of it. This binding of the real world to the game world creates opportunities for families or friends to collaborate in a way that might be impossible in a simultaneous multiplayer game.[18] Since the whole family shares a single GameCube, the game's persistent state facilitates natural collaboration between family members with different schedules. For example, a child might find a fossil during the afternoon, then mail it to her father's character in the game. At bedtime, she could let Dad know that she needs to have it analyzed at the central museum so she can take it to the local gallery the next day. As critics Kurt Squire and Henry Jenkins wrote of the game, "Families (of all types) live increasingly disjointed lives, but the whole family can play *Animal Crossing* even if they can rarely all sit down to dinner together."[19]

One of the most challenging projects in the game is paying off the mortgage on one's house. *Animal Crossing* allows players to upgrade their homes, but doing so requires paying off a large note the player must take out to start the game in the first place. Then the player must pay renovation mortgages for even larger sums.[20] While the game mercifully omits some of the more punitive intricacies of long-term debt, such as compounding interest, improving one's home does require consistent work in the game world. Catching fish, hunting for fossils, finding insects, and doing jobs for other townsfolk all produce income that can be used to pay off mortgage debt—or to buy carpets, furniture, and objects to decorate one's house.

Animal Crossing deploys a procedural rhetoric about the repetition of mundane work as a consequence of contemporary material property ideals. When my (then) five-year-old began playing the game seriously, he quickly recognized the dilemma he faced. On the one hand, he wanted to spend the money he had earned from collecting fruit and bugs on new furniture, carpets, and shirts. On the other hand, he wanted to pay off his house so he could get a bigger one like mine. Then, once he did amass enough savings to pay off his mortgage, the local shopkeeper and real estate tycoon Tom Nook offered to expand his house. While it is possible to refrain from upgrading, Nook, an unassuming raccoon, continues to offer renovations as frequently as the player visits his store. My son began to realize the trap he was in: the more material possessions he took on, the more space he needed, and the more debt he had to take on to provide that space. And the additional space just fueled more material acquisitions, continuing the cycle.

In the 1970s, psychologists gave the name *affluenza* to the spiritual emptiness and guilt that accompanies wealth. John de Graaf and others have recently expanded the concept to cover the feverish drive to acquire more and more debt and material property on the part of all social classes.[21] Shopping as cultural practice, rising debt, and bankruptcies are among the most prominent signs of the condition.[22] Learning how to smartly amass and expend capital is a type of literacy that haunts many adults—frequently we are told we should spend less and save more.

Animal Crossing mounts a procedural rhetoric of debt and consumption that successfully simulates the condition of affluenza. As I mentioned earlier, *The Sims* has been criticized for purportedly modeling consumption as a solution to loneliness and unhappiness. In discussions of that game, chief designer Will Wright has argued that the game's rules are optimally balanced via equal pursuit of material and social capital, a part of the game's caricature of American ideals.[23] Sims respond more positively to player characters with more material property; they like friends with big houses and hot tubs.

Animal Crossing's nonplayer characters (NPCs) are much less sophisticated. The cute animals who occupy the village sternly berate the player if they have not seen him in town for a while, but they seem to have no concern for the quantity or type of material properties that the players possess. Occasionally animals will express desire for a shirt or furniture item the player carries with him around the village, and they will offer to trade for it. But this type of transaction is both rare and charming; the animals frame their requests in terms of inveterate longing—"I've always wanted a Modern Lamp!"—quite different from the affluenza-burdened mallgoer's "one overriding interest, to spend money."[24]

Animal Crossing simulates the social dynamics of a small town but sidesteps the material obsession of keeping up with the Joneses. As such, the game serves as a sandbox for experimenting with the ways one can recombine personal wealth that is much more abstract than the economics of *The Sims*. While the player diligently works to pay off that new upstairs addition, the NPC animals retain their small shacks perpetually. They never cycle their belongings, seemingly unconcerned that their homes are filled only with fish, or rocks, or fruit furniture. One could argue that this asceticism is accidental, the default effect of Nintendo's disinterest in building a more sophisticated artificial intelligence system for redecoration. But procedural abstraction is also relevant to a videogame's overall design. *Animal Crossing*'s animals enjoy walks outdoors. They snooze on their porches at twilight. They stop to watch the player fish. They meander aimlessly and take great care to partake in the community events that transpire on holidays. They are not consumers but naturalists, more Henry David Thoreau than Paris Hilton.

These monastic animals oppose Tom Nook, the town shopkeeper. After a player makes a major payment to his mortgage, Tom Nook closes his shop and upgrades it; the game starts with Nook's Cranny, a wooden shack general store, and ends with Nookington's, a two-story department store. Each upgrade allows Tom Nook to sell more goods. None of the townsfolk ever appear in Tom Nook's shop, although they occasionally refer to it slightly disdainfully; the animals seem to have little drive to consume. In contrast, the player participates in a full consumer regimen; he pays off debt, buys goods, and sells goods. Tom Nook buys goods, which he converts to wealth. As the player pays off debt and upgrades his home to store more goods, he sees Tom Nook convert that wealth into increased commercial leverage. This simple causal link between debt and banking concretizes a dynamic that most mortgage holders fail to recognize: one's own debt makes someone else very wealthy. *Animal Crossing* proceduralizes this relationship in a simple yet effective way: lowering one's own debt increases Tom Nook's wealth. Tom Nook then leverages that wealth to draw more capital out of the player, whose resources remain effectively constant. While the player spends more, Nook makes more. By condensing all of the environment's financial transactions into one flow between the player and Tom Nook, the game proceduralizes the redistribution of wealth in a manner even young children can understand. Tom Nook is a kind of condensation of the corporate bourgeoisie.

Other dynamics further develop *Animal Crossing*'s ambiguous relationship with consumption. Each town comes with a police station that serves as a lost-and-found, and a dump. Occasionally items find their way to both these venues, and the player can take any of them he wants. The player may also drop off items he no longer wants in the dump, and they'll disappear the next day. The dump and the lost-and-found complement Tom Nook's store and the player's debt. Instead of amassing material property, they offer the opportunity to refuse to acquire goods even when those goods are free. The lost-and-found further emphasizes our tendency to acquire even goods we don't need; the officer stationed inside always asks "That's yours, right? You can take it . . ." Of course, none of the items in lost-and-found really belong to the player (even items left randomly throughout the town seem to remain eternally in place without incident). Thus, taking an item from the lost-and-found always foregrounds the player's questionable need for the item. The dump takes this value further. Players can sell just about anything to Tom Nook, but the dump allows the player to rid himself of goods without monetary gain. Even if players rarely use the dump, its presence provides an important balance in the game's consumer ecology, allowing goods to be divested of value completely.

Incentive to dispose of material goods is provided by one of the game's most curious features, the Happy Room Academy (HRA). Each day, players receive a letter from the HRA with a numeric rating of their home and a brief, often inscrutable message. The logic of the HRA is based on a complex interior design simulation that is never disclosed in the game or its manual (although players can consult online fan sites to decode its logic).[25] The HRA awards more points for easily testable goals, such as matching furniture in the same series and matching wallpaper to carpet within a single room. But it also ranks them based on position, where the player acquired them, and other intangibles like having started a savings account at the bank.[26] The player can ignore the HRA points, but the daily letter encourages eventual participation.

While much of the HRA's logic is based on consumerist goals such as the Pokémon-style "collect 'em all" logic of matching furniture, the rating system's necessary failure to consider the player's personal preferences quickly offends. The HRA applies a single lifestyle calculus to everyone's home, assuming certain necessities and certain aesthetics. The HRA's rating proce-duralizes fashion, especially the desire to have the "right" things from the "right" label or catalog. Players often attempt to appease the unseen HRA jury, only to become disenchanted with its elusive endorsement. At times, the HRA's letter asks the player *what's the point of having all that space if you're not going to use it?*, even when both floors of his home are so cluttered as to prevent walking around. As a simulation of trendiness, the HRA first encourages the player to covet what he does not have, then incites bitterness over the slip-pery nature of trends. Keeping up with the Joneses is an eternal, unending process.

If the player chooses to reject the influence of the HRA, a related dynamic also urges him to question the collection and retention of goods in general. The second home renovation the player can acquire is a basement—perfect to store all those shirts, carpets, and furniture not currently in use. Tom Nook makes clear that the HRA does not account for the basement in its ratings, so the player should feel free to store unused items there. Unsurprisingly, the addition of storage space encourages its suffusion with possessions. Just as that empty garage or storage closet invites new commercial acquisitions, so does the *Animal Crossing* basement. However, the game's rules bind this storage space to HRA ratings. Dr. Richard Swenson has given the name "possession overload" to the stress caused by simply having too much stuff around, a stress he argues does as much physiological damage as any other anxiety.[27] When the player becomes dissatisfied or overburdened with the HRA's empty pursuit of fashion, he may also reject the storage of unused possessions, by relin-quishing them to the dump, selling them, or giving them away.

Even as the HRA and the basement encourage acquisition, the simplicity of rearrangement in the videogame environment breeds increased deliberation about the player's need for his virtual possessions. To move an item in *Animal Crossing*, the player can simply stand next to it and press a button on the con-troller. The item, no matter its size or heft, collapses into a leaf, which the player character carries easily. What may seem like a simple trick to avert the design problem of representing hundreds of different items on-screen offers a convenient shorthand for possible objections to blind consumption. The cliché of the suburban wife staring at the living room with an eye toward rearrange-ment rarely conjures visions of disposal; furniture may be moved, accessorized, or traded for newer, more fashionable models, but rarely would they be removed entirely. The conversion of furniture into leaves suggests the former's evanescence—like a leaf, it can blow away in the wind, it can wash away in the river, it can rot and disappear into the ground. Indeed, this is precisely how the player rids himself of unwanted material goods, by dropping the leaves that represent them into the soft soil of the town dump, where they soon vanish. *Animal Crossing*'s consumerist rhetoric slowly unravels itself, moving from crowded repletion to reasoned minimalism. We can think of *Animal Crossing*'s houses as simulations of Japanese gardens more than American homes—they are perfect when nothing more can be taken out.[28]

Animal Crossing's focus on naturalism continues in its procedural representation of the town's outdoor environment. The village is lined with trees, cliffs, rivers, waterfalls, flowerbeds, and a sandy beach. Thanks to the real-time synchronization between the game and the console clock, golden hour rises in the early evening, darkness falls at night, leaves blush and fall in autumn, and snow covers the ground in winter. The simulation of seasonal cycles creates a persistent, living world that is always in flux. On some spring days it rains and the animals don umbrellas. The townsfolk sleep at night, and the crickets chirp. The fish and insects that live in the rivers and under the rocks also change seasonally. Life is scarce in wintertime, plentiful in spring, and certain animals can only be found during two-week periods throughout the year.[29] The living outdoor world opposes the dead indoors, where purchased products sit idle and unchanging.

As with a Japanese garden, the player has the ability to make thoughtful alterations to the landscape. He can plant trees and flowers, or cut down trees to create open spaces. Weeds appear in inverse proportion to the frequency of play; a player returning to his town after weeks or months away will spend many days gardening the town to its previous sanctity. Just as the HRA codified consumerism, *Animal Crossing*'s eco-pastoralist rules are codified in the game's wishing well. Each town has an outdoor clearing with a bubbling fountain. The player can ask the wishing well about the state of the town, and it will reply with cryptic clues about the landscape—too many trees in a particular acre, not enough greenery in another, too many weeds, and so forth. Players can then perform appropriate gardening to return the village to balance. HRA provides immediate feedback, a new letter arriving each day. But the wishing well's opinion changes much more slowly, taking weeks to alter its overall opinion of the town. After two weeks of "perfect" conditions according to the wishing well, the player is rewarded with a golden axe, an appropriate symbol of refinement through elimination rather than acquisition.

Both the HRA and the wishing well sometimes offer inscrutable advice, but each enforces a different logic of bewilderment. The HRA sends letters, suggesting human judgment by an unseen body of rational actors. Their absence speaks to the inaccessibility of the fashion calculus, and the player must measure his taste against the imposed and seemingly changing whims of fashionistas. The HRA's letter is the *Animal Crossing* equivalent of *Cosmopolitan* or *Dwell* magazine, which do less to document than to create trends in fashion and interior design by delivering advertising. The wishing well's messages arrive immediately, but their source is also concealed from the player. If the HRA is a unit operation for consumer trends, the wishing well is a unit operation for spirituality. The player measures his town's livability against a semitranscendental other-worldliness, accessed through the mystery of the well. Ideally, the wishing well invites the player to consider the town's outdoor environment as a communal place that affects everyone in the town, both other human player characters and the NPC animals.

The tension between wealth and community develops further in the town museum. The museum accepts donations of fish, insects, fossils, and paintings for each of its galleries. All of these items must be found or hunted by the player. To complete each exhibit, the players in the town must collaborate to donate all the items; each item can be donated only once, and a record of its donor is inscribed on a plaque near the item, just as one might find in a real museum.

Donating to the museum imposes a difficult decision on the player. Some fish, insects, and paintings are very valuable, yielding enormous profit when sold to Tom Nook. But once sold, the items disappear into Nook's unseen market; fish, insects, and fossils can never be bought at the town store. The museum forces the player to balance personal material gain against communal gain. Although the NPC animals never appear inside the museum, the fact that game time continues when the console is switched off implies that activity continues; the animals might enjoy browsing the museum when the player logs out. This dynamic is especially useful for children, whose rich imaginations are much more capable of filling in the game's gaps. Even if the player chooses to sell his first arapaima or giant stag beetle with the intention of donating the next one, favoring material wealth over communal benefit may cast a guilty shadow over his future fishing and insect-hunting expeditions.

Dueling procedural rhetorics collide in *Animal Crossing*. On the one hand, a rhetoric of affluenza encourages the player toward excess, toward more goods and a larger house in which to store them. In this context, the menial everyday tasks of gardening, fishing, and doing errands for the animals become an occupation, the necessary but undesirable frenzy of work necessary to sustain that lifestyle.[30] On the other hand, a rhetoric of pastoralism encourages the player to tend the land, appreciate the rolling hills and bubbling waterfalls, and to socialize with others before returning to a modest homestead to retire. The game oscillates uncertainly between these two rhetorics, uncomfortably positing one against the other. This discomfort is what I have called simulation fever, an internal crisis wrought between the game's rules and the player's subjective response to them.[31] *Animal Crossing* successfully creates identity crises for the player between consumption and introspection.

Animal Crossing's themes manifest outside the videogame, in its own context as a commercial artifact and franchise. For one part, the game—originally available only for the Nintendo GameCube—includes a tropical island that the player can only reach by plugging in a Nintendo GameBoy Advance, a feat that requires both the handheld console ($79 at its cheapest) and a special GameBoy–GameCube connector cable (another $10 or so).[32] Nintendo also released a set of *Animal Crossing* trading cards—several hundred in total—sold in packs of ten like baseball or Pokémon cards. The cards can be collected for their own sake, or they can be used to insert the contents they depict on their faces into the game world. However, to do so requires the GameBoy Advance e-Card e-Reader (another $40 purchase). All told, one could spend hundreds of dollars outfitting one's virtual town, and that's before buying any of the *Animal Crossing* licensed products—keychains, resin dolls, plush toys, and so forth.

The e-Reader cards and the GameBoy connection could be seen as Nintendo's blatant attempt to urge the young player to consume more—and more Nintendo products at that. This is certainly an accurate characterization of Nintendo's business goals. But the presence of these secondary products further accentuates the tension between consumption and reflection. The cross-platform tie-ins and licensed products create a kind of tendril that applies torsion to the game's rhetorics. The desire to purchase the GameBoy, the character plush, the e-Cards all test the status of the player's attitude about consumption, explored in the game itself.

I don't intend to suggest that all of these commercial goods are mere temptations, such that buying even one means giving in to consumerism. Rather, these products ask the player-consumer to reflect on the relationship between material things and intangible sensations. The GameBoy provides access to Animal Island, on which the player can meet a new character and collect coconuts to plant on the beach back home. Likewise, many of the e-Cards allow the player to introduce new characters into the simulation. Is socialization a valid rationale for acquiring material goods? Are the NPC animals part of a collection, a perverse personal zoo, or do they have personalities the player can admire and even care about? Sometimes animals move away from the town, events that have caused a real sense of loss in my family's village. Despite its apparently transparent role as a manipulative commercial exploitation of the young children who are its primary audience, these real-world extensions of *Animal Crossing* allow players to export their in-game commercial attitudes and experiment with them. *Animal Crossing* can be seen as a critique of contemporary consumer culture that attempts to persuade the player to understand both the intoxication of material acquisition and the subtle pleasures of abstention.

The Values of Work

Along with schools, workplaces are institutions that attempt to train their subjects toward conformity. The conventional image of corporate training is a bleak one. When we think of job training, we often think of thick manuals, antiquated and simplistic training videocassettes shown in antiseptic, fluorescent-lit rooms, or indifferent peers and supervisors providing hands-on mentorship for only a few hours. These are not the shining moments of human culture.

Work is where citizens end up after they have been properly schooled. As John Stuart Mill, John Gatto, Brenda Laurel, and others observed, schools are institutions that prepare young people to become workers. They learn to respond to authority, sit in one place for the day without complaint, and to complete arbitrary tasks divorced from their context. Likewise, they learn that challenging or questioning this system leads to sanction and reprimand. In schools, absolute removal from the environment requires considerable effort; even in the case of an expelled student, mandatory school attendance laws ensure that another school will take him in. But in the workplace, failure to act according to the environment's expectations can lead to dismissal. And getting fired means no paycheck, which makes it a lot harder to pay the mortgage and acquire goods and services, both the basic necessities and all those wants that de Graaff and others implicate in the condition of affluenza. In short, part of learning to use a workplace means submitting to its underlying logic and value structures.

Most schools have the same operational logic from district to district, school to school; in the wake of NCLB, public schools in the United States are essentially required to do so. Workplaces are not regulated in this particular way, although some industries do have to abide by private, state, or federal standards, for example OSHA safety standards, UAW labor practices, or SEC reporting requirements. Nevertheless, the basic logic of the workplace remains very similar from city to city, industry to industry. By and large, most businesses run in a similar fashion, with similar corporate hierarchies, policy practices, and administrative requirements. These practices can be represented in software. And videogames are becoming an increasingly popular way to deliver corporate training.

Early specimens of training videogames serve more as motivational incentives than as legitimate learning tools. In 1983, Coca-Cola commissioned electronics manufacturer Bandai to create a handheld electronic game for their sales executives. The result, *Catch a Coke*, was a modification of a popular Bandai handheld game from 1981, *Monkey Coconut*.[33] In the original, the player controls a tropical native catching coconuts a monkey tosses from the top of a screen; the Coca-Cola version adds a Coke vending machine in the tropical background, and changes the native to a business-suited Coke sales executive. Instead of coconuts, the monkey throws cans of Coca-Cola.

The same year, Coca-Cola also commissioned Atari to create a cartridge for the company's annual sales convention. The result, *Pepsi Invaders*, was a version of the arcade classic *Space Invaders* with aliens replaced by letters that spell out PEPSI on the screen (see figure 9.2).[34] The game is a hack of the Atari *Space Invaders* cart, but it was a "legitimate" hack, in that Atari created the game in-house and burned it on regular ROM chips instead of rewriteable EPROMs.[35] Among other interesting changes are the addition of infinite lives and a three-minute time limit. Reportedly, all 125 sales executives who attended the convention were given an Atari 2600 console and a copy of *Pepsi Invaders*, which came in a black cartridge without a label. Because of the short run, the game is incredibly rare and highly sought after by collectors.[36]

Both games were given to sales executives as an incentive. Neither teaches any business development principles, and these examples can only be seen as procedural interpretations of sales training through considerable squinting.

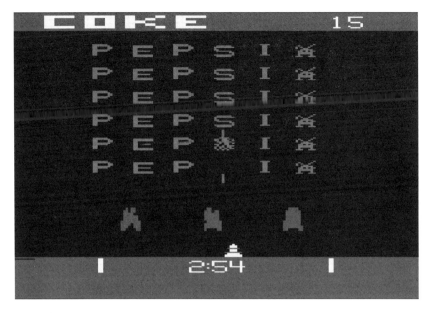

Figure 9.2 Produced exclusively for Coca-Cola sales executives, *Pepsi Invaders* casts a competitor as an invader.

Repetition and persistence in *Catch a Coke* require the player to persevere against boredom, rejection, and disappointment; just as *Tax Invaders* casts tax increases in the role of threatening, unearthly aggressors, *Pepsi Invaders* casts the competition in the role of dangerous intruders that imperil the company, jeopardizing its livelihood with their counterfeit, alien cola.

Despite their historical novelty, games like *Catch a Coke* and *Pepsi Invaders* resemble boardroom pranks more than large-scale training regimens. These two specimens offer barely incremental counterparts to the tired motivational standbys of executive incentives, and bear no resemblance to technique of the sales pit boss goading his staff with pep talks or intimidation. Pens, plaques, and watches might remain more useful motivational tools.

Recent efforts have been more deliberate. Because business practices often share common operational processes and training challenges, corporate training has been a popular target for serious games developers. If training is generalizable, then a single training solution could be deployed across several clients in a single industry, or even across industries.[37] Such logic has supported the training tomes, the VHS videos, and the PowerPoint-style online courseware—the very things that make corporate learning insufferable. Contemporary supporters of videogames for training argue that games solve the motivational problems that plagued these old forms of "static learning."[38] David Michael and Sande Chen recount the typical argument:

Serious games . . . offer a significant paradigm shift in training. No longer will employees be presented with information that can be ignored. Instead, they are immersed in the lesson to be learned and are expected to demonstrate their mastery of the material within the context of the serious game.[39]

Proponents of business training games argue that traditional activities like classroom sessions and videos cannot accommodate certain job skills, especially abstract skills with outcomes that resist numerical validation. Michael and Chen continue:

some skills, like personnel management and interpersonal skills, are not easily or well taught using the linear methods of e-learning. . . . To really learn, instead of simply memorizing answers, trainees need to be involved in what's being taught, to actively weigh consequences and mull over decisions.[40]

These sentiments echo literature on videogame training of more than twenty years earlier. In 1984, James Drisken and Daniel Dwyer argued that businesses can improve training "by incorporating the motivational and attention-focusing attributes of videogames."[41] In classic behaviorist style, Driskell and Dwyer place primary emphasis on the potential for games to increase motivation for the most boring of training tasks: "by tying a behavior with a higher probability of occurrence . . . to a behavior that is less intrinsically interesting . . . , we increase the probability of performance of the less desirable behavior."[42] Indeed, these two early theorists of training videogames are most concerned with the efficiency of videogames, which they describe as "practical" and capable of "reducing training time by 30 percent."[43] In their more recent study, Michael and Chen add strategic benefit but essentially repeat the same sentiment.[44] The primary benefits of training videogames are cost savings and a more suitable way to inculcate corporate processes and values within workers.

Indeed, videogames do create simulated experiences of complex situations, a difficult charge for lectures or book learning. But in a corporate context, such games always service the sponsoring corporation: an employee is trained in accordance with the procedural rhetoric of the company for which he works. If, as I have argued throughout this book, engagement with procedural rhetoric through videogames opens spaces of critical contemplation, how does this experience affect the worker? How does it affect the corporation that sponsors the game?

The Cold Stone Creamery is an international, franchised ice cream store. The company's signature concept is customer-designed ice cream flavors. Rather than stocking the thirty-one conventional, unchangeable flavors of Baskin-Robbins, Cold Stone stocks a smaller number of core flavors (around a dozen), along with a large number of ingredients or "mix-ins" that customers can select. Patrons have the choice of making their own "creation" (to use the Cold Stone jargon) or choosing from a menu of "Cold Stone Original" selections, combinations selected at corporate headquarters and intended to represent a wide variety of quick-order choices. In either case, Cold Stone workers (or "team members") scoop the ice cream, add the mix-ins, and work the whole concoction together atop a frozen granite stone (thus the name). Cold Stone Creamery is a configurative ice cream shop.

As a franchised food service chain, Cold Stone contends with the usual challenges of businesses like it: high turnover, very high and very low traffic days and seasons, and potential service inconsistency across more than 6,000 stores worldwide. In 2005, Cold Stone commissioned my studio to create a videogame to address a very specific training challenge: portions. Cold Stone serves three single-serving sizes as well as several take-home sizes. As in many food service businesses, profits are tied heavily to the cost of ingredients; as such, avoiding waste is an ongoing problem. And because of Cold Stone's serving method, ensuring consistent serving amounts is difficult. Because the ice cream must be mixed by hand, measured scoops are out of the question. Instead, Cold Stone team members use flat spades to "pull" ice cream before moving it to the stone to mix.

The videogame *Cold Stone Creamery: Stone City* simulates this process.[45] The player controls a Cold Stone worker during three shifts per day. Customers arrive and place orders at the counter. The player pulls ice cream to the size requested by the simulated patron, mixes it at the stone, and delivers the finished product (see figure 9.3). For the purposes of this game, we limited the choices to the thirty-three Cold Stone Originals and automated the mixing process, since the focus of the game was proper portioning. The player is scored

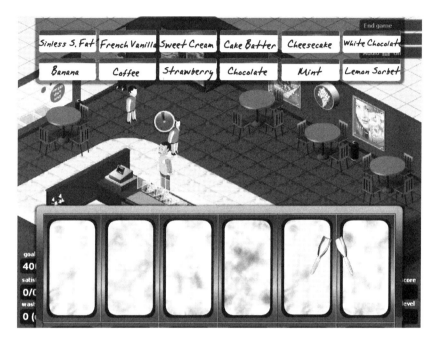

Figure 9.3 *Cold Stone Creamery: Stone City* represents the financial consequences of over- and underserving through an ice cream scooping simulation.

based on his success at selecting the correct ice cream flavor and serving it within a specified tolerance of the defined weight for the selected size. Underserving customers saves product but causes dissatisfaction and future lost sales; overserving never bothers customers, but negatively affects the store's bottom line. After each day, the game presents a summary of the player's performance with his average service and portioning accuracy projected for one month and one year, converted to both profitability and customer retention estimates.

Several notable features pepper *Stone City*. Different ice cream flavors have different consistencies and viscosities, so pulling doesn't feel the same across all the flavors. For this reason, it's impossible simply to develop a muscle memory for the duration or endpoint of a pull for a particular size. The game includes a pull viscosity model, since it was integral to the process of portioning. In addition, the relative smoothness of the ice cream tray affects the ease with which ice cream pulls, and thereby disrupts the scooping sensation. As the day wears on and more ice cream is served, trays with uneven surfaces result in more unpredictable serving sizes. This too was modeled; in effect, the game proceduralizes the physical properties of the ice cream, the server, and their interaction.

Recalling Michael and Chen's claims that videogames afford new training opportunities for skills unsuited to classroom or book learning, *Stone City* certainly improves the difficult process of training portioning in a traditional environment. Currently, Cold Stone uses videos and then hands-on training in the kitchen on-site. The former method makes the difficult task of portioning seem effortless in the hands of the expert who hosts the video. The latter wastes product and requires additional time and human resource commitments.

Despite the relative novelty of a videogame with an ice cream viscosity model, the training outcomes described above return all benefits to the corporation, not to the worker. The Cold Stone franchise and headquarters benefit from less wasted ice cream. Not even the franchise necessarily benefits from increased customer loyalty; because the Cold Stone corporation strives to maintain identical products and environments across all its stores, like most franchised businesses, locality is a matter of convenience, not personal loyalty.

For the "team member," the real learning benefits come in a different form: the level summaries. Here, the game exposes the franchise-level impact of each individual gesture of that ice cream spade. The procedural rhetoric is revealed to exceed a bureaucratic method handed down from headquarters via an unseen storeowner. Instead, the dynamics of pulling ice cream are bound to the profit motive of the local franchise and corporate headquarters. The game's procedural rhetoric exposes the corporate business model itself—a model that does not directly benefit the worker, as is the case in most low-wage food service jobs.

The videos and hands-on demonstrations detail the method for scooping a single ice cream serving in a particular fashion; the videogame operationalizes the logic for scooping every ice cream serving according to that method. Traditional training gives enough information to allow an employee's superiors to berate him if he executes the process incorrectly, a behaviorist educational strategy. *Stone City* gives the employee power to understand that he really holds all the cards, or to use the expected aphorism, that he controls the means of production. Owing to the nature of ice cream sales, Cold Stone stores often suffer from periods of extremely high traffic and periods of very low traffic. During the fast-paced times, the number of patrons the store can hold is fixed; the transaction rate can likewise only be lowered to some reasonable limit.

But the amount of ice cream that can be overserved rises at an increasing rate under such conditions. The franchise's success relies not so much on the manager's business savvy as the fractions of product saved versus served.

These insights may not be immediately fungible for the employee. But Cold Stone proclaims itself the "best first job," and indeed many of its employees are still in high school. First jobs can provide some spending cash for the fortunate, gas money and help with groceries for the less fortunate, but more often than not they provide the same thing that schools and corporate training does: early experience being institutionalized.

Training videogames become *educational* when they stop enforcing a process as a set of arbitrary rules in the service of the organization and begin presenting a procedural rhetoric for the business model that the employee has been asked to work under. Once the worker has a perspective on this business model, he can interrogate it as a value system rather than an arbitrary condition of employment. In this case, the franchise's success is predicated less on the amount of ice cream it sells per transaction—that is, which size the customer chooses. Instead, profit comes from regular sales of any kind served within a small margin of error between too little (such that the customer is dissatisfied and returns less frequently, resulting in a downward spiral in gross profit) and too much (such that the profit per customer is reduced but he returns as frequently or more so, resulting in a downward spiral in net profit). Although a simple game like *Stone City* is unlikely to replace business school for the would-be entrepreneur, it does allow the worker to contextualize the individual mechanical gestures of his work as a part of a business process.

Schooling imposes the conditions of a social, political, or economic situation on the learning context. The educational institution is a medium in McLuhan's sense of the word; it structures human experience and behavior. The Cold Stone Creamery team member and the *Animal Crossing* resident both interrogate procedural rhetorics about consumption. These players interact with procedural arguments about the situations that structure their daily lives, and engagement with those arguments allows them to orient their actions and attitudes in conscious support or opposition.

Morality and Faith

Issues of morality in videogames are more often found in newspaper headlines than in game mechanics. Typically, the very notion of "morality and videogames" implies questions about the validity of the medium itself, or about what kind of representation is appropriate within it. Violence remains a common point of contention, although the "hot coffee" sex minigame in *Grand Theft Auto: San Andreas* renewed concerns about representations of sexuality in games (especially in the U.S.).[46] Despite the medium's dramatic advances in visual fidelity, some might find it surprising that such disputes bear remarkable similarity to those voiced twenty years ago. To cite but one of many reviled videogames of yore, among the most maligned title of the early 1980s was *Custer's Revenge*. In this "pornographic" (and offensive) game for the Atari 2600, the player pilots a naked General Custer across a treacherous field of flying arrows in order to rape a Native American woman tied to a post.[47]

As Ren Reynolds has observed, even though the topics of "good" and "bad" are commonly uttered in popular discourse about videogames, the terms are only used to describe elementary consumer satisfaction ("*Grand Theft Auto* is a good/bad game") or depravity ("*Grand Theft Auto* is a corrupting game").[48] As Reynolds points out, participants in this discourse are talking past one another: the videogame industry focuses on their right to free speech, a deontological argument (one motivated from duty), while its detractors focus on potential harms, a consequentialist argument (one motivated by consequences). Vocal supporters of videogames, such as MIT professor Henry Jenkins, typically deemphasize consequentialist arguments rather than invoking alternative moral frames. For example, Jenkins has pointed to a general decrease in violent crime during the same period that videogames have become more popular. He adds that "people serving time for violent crimes typically consume less media before committing their crimes than the average person in the general population."[49] Jenkins has contested so-called media effects arguments, arguing that such studies decontextualize media images and thereby create invalid experimental conditions.

While support from a respected researcher like Jenkins benefits both the development and study of videogames, arguments like the one cited above carry a dangerous, hidden payload. If we concede that videogames in the abstract have not been shown convincingly to "turn an otherwise normal person into a killer," how does such a concession affect claims about the impact of procedural rhetorics on "positive" real-world action like politics, health, consumption, and the other topics I have tried to address in this book?[50] For procedural rhetorics to influence the world beyond the boundaries of the television screen and the computer monitor, clearly we must admit that videogames facilitate actual persuasion, not just simulated persuasion.

One way to begin addressing this issue is to reconnect the question of morality in a videogame to the types of decisions afforded and foreclosed by the artifact's procedural representation. Ren Reynolds puts it simply: "just think about the choices you have to take to win, and consider what they say about you."[51] Yet, simply playing a videogame need not entail the player's adoption of the represented value system; the player might oppose, question, or otherwise internalize its claims: which processes does it include, and which does it exclude? What rules does the game enforce, and how do those rules correlate, correspond, or conflict with an existing morality outside the game?

Videogames often enforce moral values through ideology; for example, *America's Army* supports a formal moral code that corresponds with the U.S. Army's focus on duty and honor. But as I argued earlier, the game also forecloses interrogation of the broader political context for the actions that soldiers undertake. Commercial games too have attempted to engage in ethical deliberation. Some impose prohibitions with clear legibility, similar to the ROE in *America's Army*. Miguel Sicart describes one example in the game *XIII*, about a deprogrammed spy: "The game puts the player in the role of an amnesic secret agent of moral ambiguity. The narrative plays with that moral ambiguity, but in some sequences of the game, killing a police officer implies a game over, clearly determining the ethical values embedded in the main character."[52] Sicart suggests that the moral imperative is inscribed in the character, the game consequence affording the player an insight into the role he enacts in the game, rather than into the player's own, extra-ludic moral code. The procedural rhetoric is not necessarily normative; it does not make a case for the transference of behavior from avatar to player.

Other games attempt to create a procedural possibility space for moral choices. *Star Wars: Knights of the Old Republic* is a role-playing game based on the popular film franchise.[53] Each decision the player makes—whom to help, fight, ignore—affects the player's moral attribute. In proper Star Wars universe jargon, this attribute is represented as the "dark" or "light" side of "the force." The calculus is rudimentary, with each gesture made by the player either increasing or decreasing the lightness or darkness of the avatar. At the halfway point, the player's moral persuasion is set.

This procedural rhetoric of good and evil recurs frequently. Well-known British game designer Peter Molyneux used it in two games. In *Black and*

White, the player controls a godlike creature who can rule the people of the earth with either compassion or intimidation.[54] In *Fable*, another role-playing game, the player leads a boy through and into adulthood; the decisions the player makes for him along the way determine his reputation, which is visually represented on the character (halos or horns). Even children's games partake. One of the early titles on the 8-bit Sega Master System of the late 1980s was *Sonic the Hedgehog*, a character who has became Sega's official mascot.[55] Sonic has always been a "good" character, portrayed to stand up for the right and just. He is kind and self-sacrificing, like many heroes. Shadow the Hedgehog was introduced in later games in the series, and he is the antihero of such games, the moral opposite of Sonic. In some games, the player can traverse the same environment with both Sonic and Shadow, seeing the same world through their different glasses. In *Shadow the Hedgehog*, the player chooses between Hero, Normal, and Dark missions before each stage.[56] Depending on the stages the player selects and how he traverses through them, a branching story unfolds. The game has ten different endings, all of which show a different possible outcome based on how the player navigates the levels.

All of these games attempt to create procedural models of morality, but they do so solely through an arithmetic logic. Gestures are inherently good or bad ("black or white," "light or dark") and morality always resides at a fixed point along the linear progression between the two. The procedural rhetoric of good and evil operationalizes a direct, abstract interpretation of George Lakoff's metaphor of moral accounting, discussed earlier in the context of *Grand Theft Auto: San Andreas*.

Shadow the Hedgehog uses a slightly subtler model of morality, revealing the relative baseness of Shadow in corelation to the other characters. As part of this dynamic, Shadow loses more rings (a collectible power archetype) than the other characters when he takes damage. Losing all his rings kills Shadow; he is inherently weaker than the other characters in this way, less able to hold on to his power. The player can retain rings by destroying targets in the game, which subordinates Shadow's power to these external devices.

There is a moral system at work in the game's rules, but it is still a rudimentary and fantasy-rich allegory for morality. James Gee has cited *Shadow the Hedgehog* as an example of a game that game teaches a moral system through play, and indeed the game's outcomes change based on how the player chooses to progress through the game.[57] These choices have effects—perhaps even nontrivial effects—on the game world. But as a simulation of morality, *Shadow* and its cousins enforce allegorical morality, one in which good and evil are embodied in a material form and overloaded for moralistic effect. Just as *Grand Theft Auto: San Andreas* avoids specifying class relations between the player character and individual NPCs, so *Shadow* and *Fable* avoid specifying moral relations between the player character and individual gestures within the environment. One cannot develop an individual moral relationship with a character in these games—what Lakoff really has in mind when he talks about moral accounting. Rather, in these games morality is an attribute, a property lifted from allegory and ascribed wholesale.

More complex procedural representations of morality are rarer. Perhaps the most sophisticated appears in *Deus Ex*, a first-person action/strategy game.[58] Lead-designed by Warren Spector, one of the creators of *Thief*, *Deus Ex* adopted the former's introduction of stealth in the fire-fight-burdened first-person shooter genre.[59] In both games, a guns-blazing strategy has consequences. But *Deus Ex* greatly expanded *Thief*'s simple focus on covertness. The player takes the role of a counterterrorist in a dystopian future a half-century hence, struggling against a global conspiracy in which drugs, terrorism, violence, and disease have hurtled the world into chaos. Each obstacle the player faces can be overcome in a variety of ways, usually through combat, stealth, or intelligence (such as hacking a computer to gain legitimate entrance into another area). Each decision has consequences in the game's framing story, as different parties in the ambiguous network of governmental and nongovernmental officials reveal the logic behind their motivations. Similar to the uncertainty the prospective teacher feels when playing *Tenure*, the player in *Deus Ex* is left in ambiguity—actions that once appeared right later appear less so.

Deus Ex mounts a procedural rhetoric of moral uncertainty. Far from simplistic relativism, the game makes a claim about the inherent complexity in ethical decision making. Whereas player gestures in *Knights of the Old Republic* or *Black and White* always map directly to moral values, such gestures in *Deus Ex* participate in a broader process of contemplation and reconciliation. Yet, despite its sophistication, the game still does not make a direct claim about a proper moral compass. Violent acts in *Deus Ex* are grotesque, and Spector has acknowledged that he wanted such bloodshed to create discomfort.[60] But the procedural morality the game constructs points principally to the deep uncertainty of justice and honor in an ambiguous global war, a prescient warning about the "war on terrorism" that erupted the year after the game's release.

Compare *Deus Ex* to *America's Army*. In the former, morality is suspended between interconnected interests; right is never definitively clear. In the latter, a moral system is assumed and enforced through a set of unit operations for Army procedure. Competing army teams who both see the other as the enemy dismantle the possibility for cultural, social, or historical validity on the part of the opposition. One can embrace or reject *America's Army* based on political belief; one must play *Deus Ex* differently to accommodate multiple moral compasses.

The two games offer an instructive lesson on procedural rhetoric and morality. On the one hand, videogames can represent ethical doubt through logics that disrupt movement along one moral register with orthogonal movement along another. On the other hand, videogames can represent ethical positions through logics that enforce player behavior along a particular moral register.

It is surprising that the latter strategy has not found more use in games conceived to support stable moral systems, such as those of organized religion. Religious games have a considerable history, dating back at least to the Nintendo Entertainment System. Color Dreams, a struggling publisher who managed to bypass Nintendo's first-party lockout chip in the late 1980s, attempted to appeal to nonsecular players with a series of religion-themed games. Color Dreams changed their name to Wisdom Tree and reskinned a number of their previous games to present semireligious themes. The games themselves verge on the absurd. *Bible Buffet* challenges players to throw utensils at opponents and collect carrots while answering Bible trivia.[61] In *Sunday Funday*, a reskin of the Color Dreams platformer game *Menace Beach*, the player pilots a skateboarding youth dodging obstacles to get to Sunday School on time.[62] Other games leveraged the era's popular 2D platform conventions for Bible-themed adventures. In *Exodus*, the player takes the role of Moses, who shoots W's that represent the word of God (see figure 9.4).[63] Similarly, *Bible Adventures* recreates three Bible stories, Noah and the ark, the story of the baby Moses, and David and Goliath.[64] And *Spiritual Warfare* borrowed the action/role-playing conventions of *The Legend of Zelda*; the player helps a young Christian who must rid his town of demons by converting them to Christianity.[65]

Wisdom Tree does not appear to have been motivated to create these games in the interest of faith alone. Color Dreams struggled to sell their secular games because Nintendo put pressure on retailers to refuse to sell unlicensed titles. Because Christian bookstores and specialty shops did not sell other

Figure 9.4 Faith and values in games like *Exodus* for the NES are not represented procedurally, but verbally through Bible trivia and visually through religious characters and icons.

Nintendo games, Wisdom Tree correctly predicted that such retailers would be happy to sell their unlicensed titles without concern for reproach from Nintendo. Nevertheless, the company must be credited with inventing the genre of religious videogames; they remain in business today selling old and new titles alike.

Genre innovation notwithstanding, Wisdom Tree's games did not proceduralize religious faith. Instead, they borrowed the operational logics of platform and adventure games, applying vaguely religious or biblical situations atop the familiar gestures of moving, shooting, and jumping. Many of the games were direct reskins of previous Color Dreams games, further accentuating their focus on movement over belief.

Interestingly, fifteen years after Wisdom Tree's original foray into religious games, not much has changed. In 2000, N'Lightning Software released *Catechumen*, a Christian first-person shooter.[66] The game is set in ancient Rome, and the player must defeat demon hordes sent by the devil to corrupt Roman souls. *Catechumen* updates Wisdom Tree's genre adoption, reskinning a 3D FPS instead of a 2D platformer. And in 2005, Crave Entertainment published two versions of *The Bible Game*, one a boardgame style Bible trivia game for consoles, the other an action/role-playing Bible trivia game for the GameBoy Advance handheld.[67] Just as advertisers create extreme sports games in the hopes of associating lifestyle activities with videogame-playing target demographics rather than simulating interaction with products and services, so Christian game developers create religious games in the hopes of associating isolated Bible facts with videogame-playing target demographics rather than simulating interaction with systems of belief.

One of the more remarkable attempts at procedural religion in a game is *Left Behind: Eternal Forces*, a real-time strategy game that integrates religious ritual into gameplay. The game is based on the popular *Left Behind* book series by Tim LaHaye and Jerry Jenkins, whose collected sales totals over sixty million copies.[68] The book series details the struggle of a group of people "left behind" on Earth after the Rapture, a concept popular in some branches of Protestantism that claims all Christians will be swept up to heaven from Earth before Jesus' second coming, leaving nonbelievers behind.[69] In the books, four characters confront the forces of the Antichrist in a struggle to convert and build a resistance force of believers. The game picks up this thread, giving the player control over the citizens of New York City. The player can use believers to convert neutrals, and then deploy these forces to capture buildings for conversion into bases and training facilities, or to attack the army of the Antichrist.

The game is a strategic wargame, to be sure, but its rules incorporate spirituality in a nontrivial way. In addition to people and money, the player has a "spirit" resource. For believers, higher spirit levels increase effectiveness in conversion and in battle; for unbelievers, lower spirit levels increase effectiveness. The two sides drift away from their ideal spirit over time—believers toward unbelief, unbelievers toward belief. The player can invoke prayer to increase spirit (see figure 9.5), or perform corrupt acts to reduce it—killing innocents results in the highest possible hit to spirit. But prayer completely occupies units in the field; they cannot convert, attack, defend, or build while

Figure 9.5 In this scene from *Left Behind: Eternal Forces,* the units on the left pray to raise their spirit before battle.

in prayer. From a game design perspective, the dynamic adds balance. The player must use prayer strategically, as it offers both benefit and disadvantage. From a spiritual perspective, the dynamic makes a claim about how prayer works best. Spirit "wears off," so to speak; engaging in regular prayer is the easiest way to keep spirit high. Even though prayer totally occupies the game's denizens, the game imposes greater penalty on dramatically reduced spirituality. Recovering from a drastically lowered spirit is much more costly than avoiding prayer, in terms of time and energy. Moreover, the game claims that prayer is an all-consuming activity. It is not something one can multitask.

Despite the game's interesting prayer dynamic, *Left Behind: Eternal Forces* skirts the book series' sect-specific perspective on salvation. While all Christians believe in salvation as a guarantee of eternal life in heaven, belief in the Rapture is largely limited to American fundamentalists, especially certain Baptists and Pentecostals. Like the books, the game clearly relies on the Rapture; at the start of the game, the player sees Earth from space, with gray wispy souls spinning off its surface. The entire premise of the game—

combating the army of the Antichrist to save the planet's remaining souls—relies directly on Rapture eschatology. But in the gameplay itself, religion is genericized. Players seek out "tribulation scrolls" that provide clues to the end of days, and level completions are rewarded with esoteric, quasi-numerological biblical curiosities. The game itself does not attempt to persuade players toward Rapture eschatology, or fundamentalism in general.

The call to regular prayer is certainly Christian in theme, especially given the accounting of prayer via spirit, the medium through which God becomes manifest, but regular prayer could also apply to other religions. In fact, both Islam and Judaism call for rigid regularity in prayer, including specific daily frequencies for prayer. This more measured notion of the ritual could be seen to correspond more accurately with the proceduralized decay of spirit represented in *Left Behind: Eternal Forces*. But the game's creators have withdrawn considerably from the clear religious specificity of their source materials. The creators argue that "religion is out" in the game; instead, "Biblical truth is in."[70] They claim to offer a "focus on eternal things" in a game that deals with "matters of eternal importance."[71] They seem to invoke this vague language in an effort to hedge their bets in the commercial game market. A game in which soldiers pray in battle is certainly a departure from current commercial trends—and a welcome one in my mind. But failing to proceduralize the creators' views on the Rapture waters down the potential for religious speech in the game. Even though the creators claim that they hope to create "coffee table discussion" through *Left Behind: Eternal Forces*, religion takes a back seat to military strategy.[72]

Perhaps the most effective religious commentary in *Left Behind* relates to the general function of religion in the marketplace. The market for Christian products is large, estimated at $6.8 billion in 2003 (excluding Christian books), nearly as much as the $7 billion earned by the videogame industry that year.[73] While most creators of Christian products are deeply devoted to their faith, the very status of the Christian retail industry as an industry pressures its participants toward consumption in addition to belief. Christian games connect faith to products before devotion; they address the consumption of religion as much as, or perhaps before, the principles of religion. A game like *Left Behind: Eternal Forces* does encourage prayer, but it is prayer for nothing in particular. Likewise, games such as *Deus Ex* address morality by simulating its abstract existence. These games take rather limited positions on the proper way to believe, behave, or act in the world.

The absence of procedural rhetorics in religious games recalls the distinction between schooling and education. Just as schooling affirms the values of existing institutions rather than challenging old ideas with new ones, ethical and religious simulations affirm the existence of moral predicament and faith as structures in the world. But they do little to disrupt existing moral and belief systems or to represent the function of desirable (or undesirable) systems of ethics or belief through procedural rhetorics, simulations of *how to live well* rather than affirmations of the mere reality of morality and faith as concepts in the world. This subject remains an open territory for videogames of the future.

Exercise

Dance Dance Revolution (popularly known as *DDR*) is a series of dance simulator games created by the Konami Corporation's Bemani music games division. First released in 1998 as an arcade game in Japan, the game has enjoyed nearly a hundred updated versions, including appearances on Sony Playstation,[1] Sony Playstation 2,[2] Sega Dreamcast,[3] Nintendo 64,[4] Microsoft Xbox,[5] and Nintendo GameCube.[6] *DDR* is a rhythm game; it is played by pressing sensors on a touch-sensitive dance pad in proper time with music. On-screen cues in the form of arrows show the player's proper timing, superimposed on top of visually sensuous animated backdrops representative of the game's characteristic electronic dance music. Whereas the console versions of *DDR* allowed play using the standard controller's directional pad, the physical interface of the arcade game turned it into a platform for public performance—and a physically strenuous one at that.[7]

Dance pad peripherals for home consoles appeared soon after. Home players found the home version especially welcoming, since it reduced some of the cognitive dissonance associated with public arcade performance, and a new community of casual *DDR* players emerged. In the summer of 2004, high-end dance pad peripheral manufacturer Red Octane launched GetUpMove.com, a promotional and information website showcasing the uses of dance pads and the Playstation Dance Dance Revolution as a weight-loss tool.[8] Like weight-loss promotional campaigns of all kinds, GetUpMove highlighted the most astounding successes, including a young woman who lost 95 pounds with no exercise program other than *DDR*. Claims like Red Octane's drew considerable media attention, including highly visible coverage from Fox News,[9] USA Today,[10] CNN,[11] and Good Morning America.[12] In the aftermath of such widespread exposure, anecdotal market reports suggested that consumers were buying PlayStation 2 consoles, dance pad peripherals, and copies of *DDR* titles solely for the purpose of exercise. This newfound trend was quickly labeled "exergaming" by the media: the "combination of exercise and videogames."[13]

Interest in the genre has been tremendous. The 2005 Consumer Electronics Show (CES) in Las Vegas, Nevada featured half a dozen exergaming vendors, and studies have been launched on the effects of such games on physical health and self-esteem.[14] Such research may contribute to helpful justifications for games among an increasingly reviled games industry and an increasingly obese populous. But they tell us little about how these games attempt to motivate players to think about physical activity as a part of their lives: what do they learn about exercise when they play? To understand how games can change attitudes about physical fitness, we must interrogate the procedural rhetorics in exergames, not just the short-term outcomes of individual successes. To understand these recent games, it is useful to explore physical—input games from the last several decades. From the vantage point of procedural rhetoric, I am not concerned with the physiological effects of these games—which games lead to more or "better" health effects. Rather, I seek to understand their core rhetorics—the ways that these games are authored to motivate their players to engage in physical activity.

The Prehistory of Exergaming

The increasing media attention around videogames and obesity (both separately and together) has fueled both public and commercial interest in exergaming. This media blitz might seem to suggest that exergaming is a new phenomenon, but the earliest specimens are at least twenty-five years old. A brief prehistory of videogames that produce or require physical activity will help orient the reader to the past and present examples of exergaming.

Today we've become accustomed to videogames as a sedentary living-room activity, akin to watching television. But in the video arcades of the 1970s and 1980s, playing any game, from *Asteroids*[15] to *Zaxxon*, meant standing up at the cabinet and applying significant body English onto the game cabinet.[16] This physical engagement with the arcade cabinet has its origin in pinball machines popular before and after World War II. Pinball relies on analog mechanical controls, including the familiar plunger, which responded in proportion to the physical effort displaced by the player. Tilting, or nudging the cabinet, was eventually incorporated into the rules of the game, with excessive nudging resulting in the loss of a ball.

Apart from less common cocktail-style arcade cabinets, gamers of the coin-op era played in a fully upright position; playing a particularly successful round of even a standard space shooter like *Galaxian* might require a full half-hour of standing up and jostling the cabinet vigorously.[17] Like pinball machines, many early cabinets were installed in bars and lounges. Later, the video arcade's location in public commercial spaces required travel by foot or bicycle for kids under driving age. For kids and teens of the late 1970s and early '80s, playing videogames implied a brisk walk or ride to the local convenience store, mall, or arcade.

Physical connections to the game did not disappear entirely once players began sitting on living room couches playing Atari, Colecovision, or Intellivision. In the early home consoles, the physical interface between player and screen still had some prominence. The Atari 2600 provided both joystick and paddle controllers, and all game-cartridge labels for that system were imprinted with the proper controller to use ("Use joystick controller"). Despite this foregrounding of the human–computer interface, players lounged in a chair or couch found that the hand-held joystick or joypad constrained movement more than it encouraged it. Over time, playing videogames seemed no more physical than watching television, with the possible and unfortunate addition of repetitive stress injuries. Today, this trend is reversing to some extent. The Nintendo Wii, with its unique physical interface replete with motion sensors, attempts to reincorporate physicality into home videogame play.

Although body English, tilt sensors, and walks to the corner arcade aren't the same as strenuous cardiovascular activity, arcades foregrounded physical interaction with games, even with joystick-based games. Whether or not such activity could be deemed "exercise" is questionable, but it does suggest an intimate relation between physical movement—especially rhythmic, repetitive movement—and videogame play itself.

Running

By the late 1980s the game industry had recovered from the 1983 crash and Nintendo had revitalized the industry with the popular Nintendo Entertainment System (NES). In this second wave of videogame consoles, explicit interest in alternatives to sedentary media consumption became more common. It was this environment that launched game titles created explicitly to promote or produce physical activity.

In 1987, Exus released the Foot Craz pad controller for Atari 2600, the first predecessor of today's more familiar *DDR*-style dance pad.[18] Foot Craz was a small pad with five colored buttons that responded to touch. Exus bundled two games with the pad, their only two games for VCS. These titles came very late in the lifecycle of that console, and Foot Craz and its related games remain among the rarest Atari collectibles, indicating Foot Craz's relative failure in the marketplace. A year later, Nintendo released a new edition of its NES with a similar foot-controlled peripheral, which Nintendo dubbed the Power Pad.[19] Much larger and more complex than the Foot Craz, Power Pad was double sided, one side with a grid of twelve touch-sensitive circles, the other with eight circles in a star configuration (figure 10.1). Nintendo and third-party developers released numerous games for Power Pad in the late 1980s and early 1990s. Many of these games used the pad as a surface for running.

A popular arcade game of the early 1980s was *Track & Field*, which allowed players to compete in six Olympic-style events.[20] The game was the first to feature "hammer the buttons"—style controls. In its most basic events, the player controlled a runner with two buttons on the arcade cabinet. One represented the runner's left foot, one his right. To make the runner run, the player would alternately press the left and right buttons in rapid succession; the faster the player pressed, the faster the runner ran. The challenge of the game was to press the buttons in proper succession; simply banging on them randomly led to mediocre results.[21] *Track & Field* made an appearance on the Atari 2600 (along with a special controller), but neither arcade and console versions of the game required particular physical prowess, save a tolerance for rapidly banging hard plastic buttons.[22]

Among the early exergames for Foot Craz and Power Pad, the vast majority adapted the core game mechanic of *Track & Field*, replacing fingers with feet. Running sports are either contests of speed or endurance, with track

Figure 10.1 Although it was not the first and pad-style controller, the NES Power Pad was the first to enjoy widespread adoption.

events usually privileging the former. Given the affordances of these pads, running games were easy targets for adaptation. A "Power Pack" bundle, which included the NES console, light gun, Power Pad, and a three-game cart with *Super Mario Bros.*, *Duck Hunt*, and *World Class Track Meet* appeared in 1988.[23] *World Class Track Meet* was essentially a replica and simplification of *Track & Field*, designed for use with the Power Pad interface.[24] Players could compete in four different track events—110 meter dash, long jump, 100 meter hurdles, and triple jump. When played with the Power Pad, the game became a running event simulator.

In *World Track Meet*, players performed better the faster they ran. However, since the pad only detected impact on the proper sensors, the player had to sprint in place—a nearly impossible task even without the trouble of a pad. *Track & Field* had used the alternate button mechanic as an abstraction of running track; rapidly pressing buttons was a unit operation for sprinting.

World Class Track Meet thus translated a deliberate limitation in arcade play into the basis for physical play. The rapid movement of the fingers on the buttons was meant to simulate the rapid movement of the professional runner's legs. Games that use the sprinting rhetoric as their primary motivation for exercise simply borrow the model "button-mashing for sprinting" and adapt it to the player's feet. These games attempt to operationalize running, creating an on-screen outcome analogous to the input the player produces.

Real track runners do not exercise by practicing sprints alone. Their regimens usually include plyometric exercises for strength and power, medium-distance for endurance and flexibility, and laddered sprints for event-specific training. In fact, launching into a sprint is generally acknowledged to strain the body, especially for those who don't workout regularly. This model of exergaming is exacerbated by the nature of the pad itself—Foot Craz, Power Pad, and *DDR*-style dance pads are smooth on the bottom, making them very likely to move around underfoot, or even slip out from under the player. Although it is tempting to assume that such design is rudimentary and a function of experimentation with new input devices, even the most recent Olympic sports game, *Athens 2004* for PS2 (played with the dance pad), uses an identical procedural rhetoric.[25]

Agility

Some exergames use modified versions of the sprinting rhetoric. Typically, these games interrupt the sprint mechanic with an orthogonal activity meant to enforce a physical transition, such as one might perform during aerobic exercises.

The most basic version of the interrupted sprint can even be found in games like *World Class Track Meet* and *Athens 2004*, in the form of jumping events like long jump or hurdles. In these events, players must cease to touch the pad sensors (or touch alternate pad sensors) to perform a jump. However, the speed of the runner before the jump determines the power, and therefore the distance and score for such jumps. Thanks to this arrangement, these games still deemphasize jumping compared to sprinting.

Other games offer more balanced running rhetorics. Consider *Video Jogger*, one of the two titles Exus created for the Foot Craz.[26] The game depicts two elliptical tracks on screen, one above the other. Each track features an enemy character (represented as a circle). The player uses the pad to run around the

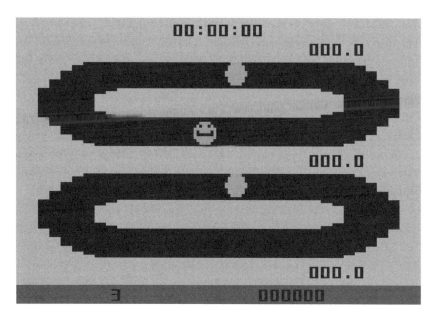

Figure 10.2 One of the two Foot Craz games, *Video Jogger*.

track while avoiding the enemies (figure 10.2). To do so, the player must occasionally switch between the tracks by striking an alternate button on the Foot Craz.

The NES Power Pad game *Athletic World* took this model further in a kind of amateur events simulation.[27] Two of the game's five events exhibit sprinting rhetorics, but the others require the player to run for short distances or even to stand and then shift to different positions on the pad, representing orthogonal physical action. For example, Hop a Log asks the player to run on a central log and then hop on right or left foot to logs on either side. In the Rafting event, the player's character rides a raft down a river, stepping slowly from side to side to avoid obstacles. Occasionally, the player must jump or duck to avoid logs draped across the river (to duck, the player must lean down and press the two forward sensors on the pad while still keeping his feet on the center sensors). Games that rely on multiple, orthogonal physical gestures that disrupt one another attempt to operationalize agility, and thus can be said to exhibit a procedural rhetoric of agility.

Athletic World could be called a camp games simulator; the events resemble casual activities kids might play at summer camp or during an end-of-year "field day" party. As such, the rhetoric of sprinting is abandoned in favor of agility; the rules of the games require players to shift smoothly and carefully—sometimes quickly, sometimes not—between one physical state and another. *Video Jogger* offers a simpler agility rhetoric; the player must run at a slower pace from time to time to avoid the enemies on the track. Likewise, he must stop running entirely to switch tracks. In *Athletic World*, the player transitions much more frequently between jogging, stepping, kneeling, and jumping. In these games, players are rewarded for nimbleness over speed. Moreover, the need to make physical contact with the relatively small and closely spaced sensors on the Power Pad further emphasizes precision.

The most unusual of physical-input games to deploy procedural agility is *Street Cop*, another NES Power Pad game.[28] In *Street Cop*, the player takes the role of a police officer on the beat, looking for crooks and hoodlums (figure 10.3). Play takes place on a horizontal street with three different pedestrian "lanes" the player and other characters can occupy. To control the cop, the player walks, jogs, or runs on the center pads. To shift lanes, the player steps right or left, then resumes walking. To switch directions, the player must press an alternate sensor on the Power Pad; to catch a criminal, he presses another sensor. In an interesting hybrid control method, the player can also use buttons on the regular NES control pad for either of the latter two actions.

Street Cop was a clearly an experiment in using the Power Pad for non-running-sports gameplay. A *Defender*-style inset radar shows the player where to find criminals on the street; the player jogs or walks to reach the criminal, taking care to avoid passing him and avoiding innocent bystanders. Although there is no clear analogue between physical agility and walking a beat, the gameplay encourages deliberate shifts between jog steps, side steps, and diagonal action steps.

A more unusual method of proceduralizing agility is to couple games to an even more specialized physical-input device. Amiga first tried this approach with the Joyboard, a platform on which the player stood and leaned in different directions in lieu of performing normal joystick functions (figure 10.4). To use the Joyboard, the player had to substitute balanced full-body movement for joystick movement. The device came with a skiing game designed specifically for it, *Mogul Maniac*.[29] The side-to-side motion of skiing was ideal for the Joyboard, although in practice the device didn't respond terribly effectively. Amiga prototyped two more games for the Joyboard, neither of which was released: *Off Your Rocker* was a "Simon says"–style game in which the

Figure 10.3 In *Street Cop,* the player uses the Power Pad to control movement rather than rhythm.

player leaned in the proper direction to mimic on-screen color and sound cues.[30] *Surf's Up* was a surfing game in which the player had to carefully direct a surfboard to avoid wiping out.[31]

Despite the paucity of games developed specifically for the Joyboard, the device could also double as standard input device for Atari 2600, so Joyboard owners could attempt to use it with any of the hundreds of games in the VCS library. Success was bound to be limited, especially since the device didn't map precisely to the standard joystick controls, but such an agility test remained possible. Later, LJN released the Roll 'n Rocker for the NES, a peripheral similar to the Joyboard in concept. The player stood on the device

Figure 10.4 One of the earliest physical game controllers for home consoles, the Amiga Joyboard.

(which looked something like a Pogo Ball, a popular toy at the time) and leaned from side to side and front to back to control a character on screen. A standard Nintendo controller plugged into the side of the Roll 'n Rocker, which the player held in a free hand to access button controls.

Unlike the Joyboard, the Roll 'n Rocker was not designed for use with specific games; it was sold as a generic accessory that players could use with most NES games. And unlike *Athletic World* and *Street Cop*, the Roll 'n Rocker leveraged an abstract notion of agility, taking the common need for rapid directional-pad movement necessary to play most NES games and transferring that action from thumb to full body. Like *World Class Track Meet*, Roll 'n Rocker relied on a one-to-one analogue between standard controller input and physical controller input. In so doing, it harnessed the internal mechanics of popular NES games like *Super Mario Bros.*[32] or *Contra*, which required quick fingering on the standard controller.[33] In such games, success is dictated by rapid presses on the proper buttons; Roll 'n Rocker attempts to borrow the carefully crafted agility constraints of standard videogames and couple those to the physical body. The device was a commercial failure, perhaps a testament to the difficulty of leasing existing games for physical input. Still, it offers a lesson in adaptability. Nothing prevents a player from using a *DDR*-style dance pad as standard input for the PlayStation or Xbox. The pad provides four-direction control, and at least two button controls. Playing a game like *Gran Turismo* on the dance pad produces a sensation much like surfing.[34] Still, ill-fated attempts to create generic physical-input devices, such as the Roll 'n Rocker and the Nintendo Power Glove, may have discouraged manufacturers of contemporary dance pads from suggesting their use with other genres of games.

Reflex

I've already argued that arcade games serve as predecessors for exergames in the general sense. But we can find even greater precedent in non-screen-based arcade and carnival games.

Among the commonest types of such games is *Whack-a-Mole*, in which the player hits small animals that pop out of holes in the game cabinet with a large mallet. This game finds its roots in carnival games like shooting galleries and ball tosses, where players have limited time or resources in which to strike a certain number of targets, and even earlier in contests of strength. In the 1990s, as once-popular video arcades shifted to younger audiences, more versions of these games appeared. Today, one popular *Whack-a-Mole* derivative is *Spider Stompin'*. Generally relegated to younger kids' areas of arcades like Chuck E. Cheese's, *Spider Stompin'* has an octagonal platform emblazoned with spiderweb graphics. Scattered among the web are plastic buttons. These buttons are surrounded by graphics of spiders, so that stepping on them gives the impression of squashing spiders. A large score area stands straight up from the front of the platform. During play, the spider buttons light up and dim sequentially, at a speed commensurate with the selected difficulty level. The player must step on the button before the light goes off. Different difficulty levels regulate the number of spiders and the speed at which they disappear.

Games like *Whack-a-Mole* and *Spider Stompin'* don't require constant physical activity like *World Class Track Meet* or *Video Jogger*. Instead, they demand carefully timed physical responses to external stimuli, usually visual stimuli. Games that require physical input based on time-sensitive responses operationalize the rapid response, engendering a procedural rhetoric of *reflex*.

Reflex videogames go back as far as exergames themselves; one of the two games Exus released with the Foot Craz was *Video Reflex*, a highly abstract version of *Spider Stompin'*.[35] In *Video Reflex*, the screen displays five color blocks, each corresponding with one of the color-coded sensors on the Foot Craz. During play, bugs appear on the color blocks, and the player presses the corresponding sensor to squash the bug (a footprint icon appears in the selected square). Nintendo also created a *Whack-a-Mole* knockoff for the Power Pad, *Eggsplode*.[36] In this game, chickens occupy a 3×4 grid that corresponds with the 12-sensor side of the Power Pad. The player presses the appropriate sensor to deactivate bombs set under chickens before they explode.

Contemporary exergames have also deployed the rhetoric of reflex. The Eye Toy camera peripheral for the Sony PlayStation 2 first shipped with a set of minigames called *Eye Toy: Play*, many of which use reflex rhetorics.[37] For example, "Kung Foo" asks the player to disable flying ninjas and monkeys, and "Plate Spinner" requires the player to keep a variety of plates balanced on sticks. Both require sporadic but decisive responses to on-screen stimuli, but not constant, sequential movement as in *World Class Track Meet*, nor constant, disrupted movement as in *Athletic Games*.

Interestingly, *Eye Toy: Play* is often reviled as a single player game but heralded as a perfect party game for a large group of people. Because the Eye Toy detects input not from a small number of fixed sensors on the floor beneath a single player, but rather from a large sensor array in the focus field of the camera itself, many players can take part at the same time, using any part of their bodies to trigger events on screen. Such activity could technically be construed as an exploit, since the game requires configuration for a single player before it starts. But this exploitative play brings to mind similar behavior in the arcade or carnival, by which multiple players might play *Whack-a-Mole* or *Spider Stompin'* at the same time, ensuring much greater success than one player alone. While games with running or agility rhetorics typically score time, as one might in a track meet, games with reflex rhetorics typically score by points; for example, the player might earn one point for the number of bugs squashed. While players can certainly compete for the lowest time in *Athletic World*, points provide a more concrete basis for competition or collaboration. In the arcade, games like *Whack-a-Mole* and *Spider Stompin'* often give out tickets based on final scores, much like skeeball. Players can save these tickets and exchange them for toys as an incentive for continued play and repeat visits. Exergames driven by reflex rhetorics thus appear more social and more competitive than other varieties.

Training

Perhaps the most obvious application of exergaming is the direct remediation of traditional workout methods in videogame form. Bandai made the first such attempt 1988, with *Dance Aerobics* for the NES Power Pad.[38] *Dance Aerobics* used the Power Pad as an input device to monitor traditional aerobic exercise. Bandai reportedly hoped the title would appeal to a female audience, and both the game and its marketing make use of exclusively female characters.

Unlike all the other games previously discussed, *Dance Aerobics* did not attempt to turn the input device into transparent window through which the player interacts with the game. Instead, the game makes it very clear that the Power Pad served as a measurement device for the player's progress. *Dance Aerobics* features an aerobic instructor character on screen, guiding the player just as a trainer might lead a group in a real aerobics class or a home video. As shown in figure 10.5, the game even depicts a Power Pad underneath the on-screen character to help calibrate the player's actions in relation to those of the computer.

During play, the on-screen character first shows the player a number of repetitions of a particular aerobic exercise, such as side-steps or toe-touches. After a countdown, the player must mimic these exercises in time with the on-screen trainer. To enforce the workout, each gesture requires the player to contact a specific set of sensors on the Power Pad. A box of remaining mistake credits display persistently on the side of the screen; failing to complete an aerobic gesture properly docks the player a mistake.

Dance Aerobics assumes that running out of mistake credits indicates that the player has not been completing the designated exercises, and the session is subsequently terminated. But as with many of the running exergames, it's actually quite difficult to strike the proper sensors—or to ensure one doesn't release the wrong sensors by leaning up off of it. The decision to enforce rules on an exercise regimen seems absurdist at first—an imprecise leg stretch should have more value than no action at all. But the game enforces precise sensor presses as an extremely rudimentary unit operation for aerobic training. In a real gym, the trainer leading a session can scan the room and assess

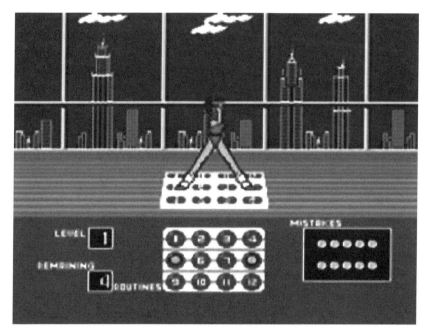

Figure 10.5 *Dance Aerobics* validates the player's workout by requiring timed presses on the Power Pad sensors.

the performance of individuals in a class. A trainer might provide general encouragement ("keep it up!") or single out a particular student in need of reproach ("come on, get your feet up higher"). This kind of "soft" feedback is impossible in *Dance Aerobics*, since the game can get only rudimentary feedback from the player—digital sensor touches on the Power Pad.

Despite this limitation, *Dance Aerobics* is clearly different from other types of exergames. The game could be construed to have a reflex rhetoric; the player is required to touch specific sensors given a particular time horizon. But unlike *Video Jogger* or *Eggsplode*, *Dance Aerobics* relies on an external cultural referent rather than an abstract system to structure its rules: the personal trainer.

A personal trainer is usually a professional hired by an individual or a group to create a specialized exercise regimen. As a tutor and a spotter, the trainer offers both micro- and macroscopic guidance; the trainer both recommends the proper exercises and ensures that the client carries them out properly, for the most efficient result and to avoid injury. While admittedly rudimentary, *Dance Aerobics* enacts precisely this rhetoric. Exergames with a procedural rhetoric of reflex only call for physical action given specific, often random computer-generated events. In a game with a training rhetoric, both the physical gestures and the pauses between those gestures bear equal relevance. Players of *Dance Aerobics* will quickly note the deliberate pacing of the aerobic maneuvers, a rhythm that extends to the character animation, which is constructed to match the familiar beat-counted rhythm of aerobic exercise.

Input devices haven't changed considerably in the twenty or so years since *Dance Aerobics*' release, but computer graphics certainly have. In 2004, ResponDesign tried their hand at a personal training game, *Yourself! Fitness*, built for the much more modern Xbox and PlayStation 2 consoles, as well as the PC.[39] Fitness and athletic shoe executives founded ResponDesign, making it the first independent developer/publisher of fitness games. The company is based in Portland, Oregon, and has a partnership with nearby Nike that allows them to take advantage of the latter's advanced consumer focus groups and athletic experts. ResponDesign's first title, *Yourself! Fitness*, is an attempt to reinvent the home fitness video as videogame.

The game features Maya, an intricately modeled and motion-capture animated "virtual personal trainer" who serves as the game's hostess and primary interface. Maya is a fascinating specimen in herself, a sort of anonymous amalgam of cultural and racial representation who could pass for Caucasian, Persian, or Latina. Maya appears strong yet nonthreatening; she is toned yet soft, approachable.[40] Unlike all of the games previously discussed, *Yourself! Fitness* employs no control inputs whatsoever, save the inconsequential use of the standard controller to make menu selections. Despite the massive innovations in computer technology during the twenty years since *Dance Aerobics*, control inputs have remained largely the same: game consoles are capable of detecting digital button pushes and, on more recent consoles, levels of pressure on analog control sticks. Instead of trying to make strides in the basic technology used for human input, ResponDesign instead decided to let the human player provide most of the input to the program.

The player sets up a profile with height, weight, vital signs, and exercise goals. Maya then crafts a customized training program that typically requires less than thirty minutes per day. The majority of the routines are standard aerobic exercises. Unlike the rudimentary 8-bit *Dance Aerobics*, *Yourself! Fitness* offers a smooth animation of exercise steps. This graphical improvement might risk undermining the regimented nature of the exercise, an unexpected benefit of the former game's 8-bit graphics, but the latter also takes advantage of greater graphical power to vary Maya's behavior. The exercises she performs, her voice instructions, and her rate of activity are generated from physiological inputs provided by the player. Before beginning a session, Maya first asks the player to take a heart rate measurement and asks how the player feels. If the player isn't up to working out, she might offer a pass for the day. The game leaves it up to the player to monitor his performance during the actual exercises; there is no "mistake allocation" as in *Dance Aerobics*. Instead of monitoring an aerobic workout at the microscopic level by simulating the ongoing incantations of a stereotypical aerobic instructor, *Yourself! Fitness* simulates the one-on-one interview style of a personal trainer. Whereas *Dance Aerobics* strives to keep the player on measure with the imaginary class that the on-screen character leads, *Yourself! Fitness* attempts to monitor the player's perception of his or her physical condition and adjust current and future exercise sessions to accommodate both the condition and the player's fitness goals.

In its attempt provide a holistic fitness regimen, the game also offers menus and recipes for healthful eating. Although well intentioned, the menus reveal how desperate the game is to quantify the player's behavior, uncomfortable with the leniency of its procedural trainer. Maya asks the player to input the number of calories he or she plans to consume per day and builds a menu based on that input and other saved settings. Given the computational power of the console, it is surprising that the game forces the player to synthesize such an easily computable concept as calorie intake. This mechanic would seem to complement the exercise management portion more successfully if it were to help the player build a diet profile that determined proper daily calorie range and provided menus accordingly.

As part of the reinvention of the exercise video, *Yourself! Fitness* tries to abet the inevitable repetitiveness of that medium—what creator Phin Barnes called "the same woman saying the same thing on the same beach with the same wave crashing at the same time, day after day."[41] To combat this boredom, the game allows the player to unlock new exercise "arenas" and music much like players of racing games can unlock new tracks. Where a racing game like *Gran Turismo* or *Athens 2004* rewards performance—finish position in the race—*Yourself! Fitness* rewards consistency—the number of workouts completed without missing.[42] In the *Yourself! Fitness* version of a procedural trainer, unlockable content replaces the incremental sensor presses of *Dance Aerobics*. Whereas the latter punishes inconsistency with "game over"—a curious way to encourage exercise indeed—the former rewards regular exercise with a change of scenery. Whether or not unlocking new environments is a sufficient motivation for regular exercise is an open question.

Yourself! Fitness updates the aging exercise video for the videogame console. In fact, ResponDesign's ability to land the funding to create the game in the first case seems predicated on this very market shift—same idea, different medium. ResponDesign clearly hopes that the female consumers who dominate the home fitness market will take advantage of junior's Xbox after bedtime.[43]

But games like *Dance Aerobics* and *Yourself! Fitness* still rely on a traditional rhetoric of personal exercise: the subject of the exercise must muster internal motivation to begin, pursue, and continue the exercise regimen. Both games attempt to improve the player's success in individual aerobic sessions, and the latter strives to encourage players toward regular exercise. Yet both also assume traditional, somewhat tired methods of promoting physical activity. *Yourself! Fitness* re-creates the form of a personal trainer, rather than operationalizing what one *does*.

Earlier I mentioned that games with a procedural rhetoric of reflex like *Whack-a-Mole* and *Eggsplode* often use abstract, numeric scores as a motivator for continued play. In such games, score-based motivation only emerges once the gameplay ends; the player reviews his score after a session and chooses whether to try to surpass it or to quit. Some exergames have moved away from the figure of the trainer and focused instead on more abstract methods of encouraging and sustaining game-based exercise during individual play sessions themselves. Like *Yourself! Fitness*, such games also deploy procedural rhetorics based on personal training, but these games re-create the rules of training rather than the form of the trainer. Each gesture in the game is designed specifically to elicit an additional physical response from the player, just as each gesture in the gym is designed to elicit additional physical response from the participant. Like games with rhetorics of running, these games can engender long stretches of physical activity; but like games with rhetorics of reflex or agility, they also respect breaks in motion and use such breaks to shift and vary players' physical gestures.

A simple example of a generalized procedural trainer is *Short Order*, a game bundled with *Eggsplode* for the Power Pad.[44] *Short Order* is a cross between the playground game hopscotch and the classic arcade game *Burgertime*.[45] The goal of the game is to assemble hamburgers to order from a small number of basic components—bun, burger, lettuce, tomato, cheese. The game displays the target burger, whose difficulty varies as a function of its height (number of components). The player sees the completed burger for a moment, and then must recreate it from memory. To select a burger component, the player must jump and land on two proper contiguous sensors on the grid side of the Power Pad. Unlike a reflex game, no time limit faces the player, but a wrong step will end the sequence and cost the player a life.

Short Order impels the player to consider and execute his next jump carefully to ensure that it selects the desired hamburger part. After that part is placed, the player immediately concentrates on the next one, until the burger is completed. At the end of the sequence, the game moves on to a larger, more difficult burger.

A simple game, *Short Order* affords only one physical action as an input, but it structures each response to the Power Pad device so that each action has a consequence in the game. Even though the game's scoring mechanism bears resemblance to the reflex scoring of *Eggsplode*, *Short Order* contextualizes each physical gesture so that it bears concrete meaning: the player intuitively appreciates the process of constructing a hamburger. It is an everyday activity with a known and measurable outcome and to which the player can relate directly. In comparison, completing a various round of jumping jacks in *Yourself! Fitness* only has meaning in the context of physical fitness.

Dance Dance Revolution, the darling of exergaming with which I began this chapter, offers a sophisticated example of a training rhetoric. To use *Yourself! Fitness* effectively, the player must already be self-motivated to start and continue a fitness regimen. But *DDR* produces exercise as an emergent outcome of play itself.

DDR's core mechanic—step on the pad corresponding to an on-screen arrow at the right beat in the music—is somewhat similar to the aerobic exercises of *Yourself! Fitness*. Aerobics are often done to the beat of music, and the offshoot fitness program Jazzercise explicitly ties aerobic exercise to jazz dance. But despite the appeal of using popular music as a backdrop, these and related programs still create no compulsion for participants to continue physical activity during or between sessions. *DDR*'s principal innovation in the rhetoric of exergaming aims to fill this gap in traditional exercise programs.

DDR's scoring mechanism is twofold. One the one hand, the player must take care to keep a global energy meter at a positive level. For every arrow the player misses, some of this energy is depleted; lose it all and the game is over, just as when making a mistake in *Short Order* or running out of mistake credits in *Dance Aerobics*. The energy meter provides negative motivation to the player, providing him with a disincentive to quit outright.

On the other hand, the game also provides direct feedback for each and every step the player makes. Depending on the accuracy of the player's footing, a textual readout on screen responds to each step: Perfect, Great, Good, Almost, or Miss. Unlike *Dance Aerobics* or the various running games discussed earlier, *DDR* distinguishes degrees of success for individual steps based on the time difference between ideal and actual player steps. More important, the game supports "chains" of success based on individual step scores. Multiple "Perfect" or "Great" scores in a row chain together into a combo, and the numeric total is displayed prominently at center screen. These incremental scores are *DDR*'s procedural rendering of the personal trainer's affirmation after a single repetition; they reinforce not only the player's current gesture, but also the general rhythm that produced that gesture. And because the combo score is numeric, the game encourages the player to maintain that level of activity for as long as possible. To reinforce the numeric feedback, a trainer-like voiceover provides encouragement at key points, using phrases like "You're doing great!" Unlike *Yourself! Fitness*, in which Maya knows nothing about the player's actions, *DDR* generates its verbal feedback procedurally based on the player's global energy level and individual combo patterns. This allows the game to provide encouragement or praise based on the player's current performance, rather than the last set of reps he completed.

Despite the similarity between *DDR*'s voice feedback and the verbal feedback a personal trainer might provide, the game both mechanizes and extends the concept of the trainer into a fluid extension of the player's body. By providing succinct, motivational feedback with each physical gesture, *DDR* grafts the personal trainer directly onto the player's perception. One might compare *DDR* to a lightweight heads-up display for joggers that would project proper footfalls onto the pavement and then provide immediate constructive feedback on the runner's pace and form. And unlike the psychological reinforcement of slot machine and arcade coin-drop incentives, which work against the player, *DDR* couples its procedural rhetoric with the player's own goals: complete a dance performance, finish an exercise routine.

This more sophisticated procedural trainer also appears in games based on other peripherals. Many of the original Eye Toy games offered reflex play, but the most recent title, *Eye Toy Antigrav* evolved the peripheral into a tool for an impelling exergame.[46] Whereas earlier Eye Toy games use the camera to show the player's image on screen, *Antigrav* uses the camera solely as an input device to control an on-screen character, positioned to replicate the player's real-world movement. Harkening back to the Amiga Joyboard, *Antigrav* is a hoverboard game. The player's character rides the board through a complex 3D world, making turns and avoiding obstacles by turning his body, ducking, or jumping. Although similar in principle to the basic agility play in a game like *Athletic World*, *Antigrav* takes advantage of the more granular movement made possible by the Eye Toy bound to a computer vision system that tracks physical movement.

Antigrav shares many features with racing games, and one way of determining score is a measure of elapsed time taken to complete a course, much as in *World Class Track Meet*. But within levels, players can gain powerups and additional points by capturing bonus objects throughout the course. The levels are designed so that acquiring these objects requires careful, constant changes in the orientation of head and arms. For example, while traveling on a slope up a hill a player might need to reach an arm out to the side and slowly extend it up, then down in an arc as he speeds through the turn. Although *Antigrav* doesn't provide the same level of incremental encouragement as *DDR*, each passing moment of its gameplay reorients the player's focus toward a very short-term goal, such as acquiring the next bonus item. This incremental impulsion seeks to persuade the player to continue the full-body physical engagement the game requires, even in the face of fatigue.

Generic physical input devices can also impel continued physical engagement. Earlier I cited the Roll 'n Rocker as an example of a controller that failed to fully translate the reflex requirements of fingers on directional pads to feet on a balance board. More recently, Powergrid Fitness has created a more complex attempt at a general-purpose controller that both demands physical exertion and correlates that exertion to any console game.

The Powergrid Kilowatt is an exercise bike-sized device that facilitates an isometric workout. It has no moving parts, but instead uses force sensors to translate pressure the player exerts on the devices' handlebars into in-game movement. Most of the exergames discussed above offer aerobic exercises, but isometric workouts are anaerobic, building strength in much the same way as weightlifting. The principle behind the Kilowatt workout is no different than that of the Roll 'n Rocker: leverage the internal motivational structures of any videogame to induce players to use their full bodies rather than just their thumbs. But unlike the Roll 'n Rocker, the Kilowatt actually provides a reasonably analogous control mechanism for most games. Moreover, it impels players to continue both gameplay and exercise because of the nature of isometric exercise: it hurts! Unlike aerobics, which can cause a player to break a sweat or raise his heart rate, isometric exercise can be felt immediately in the upper body. This sensation of "knowing it's working" orients both the player's gameplay and workout goals simultaneously.

Even the Nintendo GameCube bongo drum controller leverages a rhetoric of training to motivate physical interaction. The bongo controller contains two touch sensors, one for each drum surface, and a microphone sensor meant to detect two-handed claps directly above it. The bongo was launched with *Donkey Konga*, a music-rhythm game that mimics the gameplay of Namco's home version of a Japanese taiko drum simulator, *Taiko Drum Master* (itself a rhythm game like *DDR*).[47] This game musters some of the same rhetoric as *DDR*, but banging the drum surface proves to be much less exerting than moving one's whole body on the dance pad. But another bongo-compatible game, *Donkey Kong Jungle Beat*, asks the player to use the bongo as a controller for a platform fighting game.[48] Striking the right bongo moves Donkey Kong to the right, left moves him left, and both together make him jump. Clapping grabs bananas in the near vicinity, which are needed to advance to subsequent levels. At the close of each level, the player is also rewarded with special medals based on the number of bananas collected.

Like *DDR*, *Jungle Beat* offers incremental scoring that encourages players to prolong successful maneuvers as much as possible. In *Jungle Beat*, collecting a banana by clapping scores twice the points as walking over it. And collecting multiple bananas while flying through the air increases that multiplier. Furthermore, the player must regularly do battle with small enemies and large bosses at the end of each level, all requiring both positioning maneuvers and *Track & Field*–style alternating strikes on the left and right drum faces. Although bludgeoning a plastic drum may make for sore hands more than toned triceps, the game's rules impel further physical activity, even when that activity borders on agony.

Yourself! Fitness attempts to motivate players through unlockable backgrounds and music, content only vaguely related to the title's aerobic gameplay. Exergames with rhetorics of training like *DDR* and *Antigrav* tend to recontextualize the idea of exercise by creating repeating incentives to continue physical exertion. Nevertheless, *Yourself! Fitness* may offer a much more consistent, formal kind of aerobic exercise; it does use well-established exercise routines, after all. But the physiological value of exergames should not be maximized blindly; rather, more long-term gain may come from consistent physical activity at a lower level of professional fitness. The strength of games like *DDR* lies precisely in their ability to engender physical activity through play without demanding the player to adopt a complex understanding of fitness. These more sophisticated procedural rhetorics of training operationalize the core properties of the trainer—an agent impelling a chain of continuous, high-quality physical movements—rather than the trainer's physical form.

Limits of the Living Room

A wide variety of exergames use gameplay and input devices to motivate physical activity. An analysis would be incomplete without considering the environment in which these games are played in the first place. Today, the majority of games sold commercially are played on videogame consoles (as opposed to personal computers). Consoles need to be connected to televisions, and televisions are generally large, immobile appliances that an entire household shares. The TV is usually positioned in a living room or den surrounded by couches and chairs; many such rooms also house a coffee table or other large furniture between the couches and the television. It is common to eat or drink while watching TV, and coffee tables support the coffee, beer, soda, and other sundries to be consumed while watching primetime comedies, weekend sports events, or the nightly news. Thus the living room is generally an inactive, static space with large, heavy furniture dividing a large, open space into many smaller, closed spaces.

Each and every one of the exergames discussed here requires considerable physical space for successful, safe play. All but the Eye Toy and Nintendo bongo require something to be placed on the floor under the player. And all save the bongo demand considerable freedom of movement around the player, including open space on all sides to avoid injury in the case of a misstep. Although the popular press has not discussed the topic much, the Nintendo Wii also requires considerable freedom of movement for many of its games, including the most novel concepts that map gross motor gestures to in-game actions like swinging a tennis racket or a sword.

Catalogs and home furnishing displays idealize the living room or den as a place of inactivity, with substrates for food and drink flanked by plush seating, eyes oriented toward a television. Given the average American living room or den, it seems that many families would need to move furniture—especially coffee tables—out of the way to facilitate successful exergaming. A device like the Powergrid Kilowatt is heavy, difficult to move, and takes up as much room as a large stationary bike or home weight machine, invoking all the unreasonable spatial demands of ordinary exercise equipment. The infeasibility of such devices cannot be taken for granted in an analysis of exergaming. Even *DDR* dance pads are bulky devices that must be stashed under furniture or stored awkwardly in closets. And bulky plastic peripherals like bongo drums and Joyboards hardly make for aesthetically pleasing decor. Advertisements and media images of these devices typically depict them in an empty space, a white room like a gallery where no activity takes place save exergaming. Such environments go beyond even the idealized spaces of home furnishings catalogs. They apparently exist in a void.

Logistical and technical limitations also stand in the way of exergame play. In general, people place living-room seating at an ideal distance to facilitate comfortable television watching from a seated or reclined position on a chair or couch. Even if no coffee table or other impediment stands in the way of the would-be exergamer, the player usually stands three or more feet closer to the television to play, possibly compromising a clear view of the screen. As high definition TV (HDTV) adoption grows—especially given Microsoft's and Sony's aggressive push for high definition on the Xbox 360 and PlayStation 3 consoles—more potential exergamers will upgrade their conventional sets for plasma, liquid crystal display (LCD), or rear-projection HDTVs. These appliances are expensive and often come with furniture designed specifically for them. Audiovisual experts recommend that HDTV monitors be positioned so that a viewer's eyes are in line with the center of the image when seated in front of it.[49] These new sets—especially the lower-priced rear-projection LCD and digital light processing (DLP) units—often suffer from greatly reduced vertical viewing angles, making the screen dim or even unviewable to a player standing on a *DDR* dance pad or facing an Eye Toy camera.

Playing these exergames on a personal computer is possible, but fraught with equal if not greater challenges. *Yourself! Fitness* was released for PC, Xbox, and PlayStation 2. Since the game targets a nontraditional demographic for videogame consoles, the PC version was probably created to accommodate players who don't have a console or don't want one. Yet, most families do not enjoy neat and tidy offices with space for physical activity, and furthermore most don't have a computer monitor as large as their television to facilitate proper visual feedback from a safe distance.

But the constraints of exergame feasibility do not occur in a vacuum. In U.S. homes of the last sixty years, living-room designs have assumed certain lifestyle considerations. One or more adults are expected to rise early in the morning, shower, shave, eat, and commute to work. Kids leave even earlier for school, so that the house is left unoccupied for much of the day. Upon return from work or school, those households lucky enough to avoid dysfunction might enjoy a meal together before relaxing—not working up a sweat—in front of the television. As telecommuting and home offices become more common, many professionals struggle already to find proper space to devote to work at home, even further reducing the space available for avocational activities like television, pleasure reading, and videogaming, let alone health-conscious activities like aerobics, workout devices, or exergaming. For better or worse, the large majority of suburban U.S. homes with the time and money to afford videogame consoles and exergaming software and hardware are simply not designed to support it; physical exertion is something relegated to the neighborhood sidewalk, the local gym, or, more commonly, nowhere at all.

When combined with easy access to long-term credit, the postwar work ethic we short-handedly call "The American Dream" encourages families to buy homes that they can only afford by spending increasingly longer hours at work. Larger homes require us to move deeper into the suburbs, requiring ever-longer commutes across increasingly crowded urban sprawl. Working and commuting for longer hours reduces the time we have with our families and ourselves, leading to a downward spiral of less and less physical activity of any kind. Thus, no matter the efficacy of any of the rhetorics of exergaming, the most important one may reside in the complex social, political, and material structures that determine the spaces we occupy. Exergames reveal the incongruence of work and exercise or leisure, and the prevalence of the ideological structures that push us to work more and move less.

11

Purposes of Persuasion

When we make claims intended to persuade, how do we know if they were successful? As a goal-oriented activity, persuasion might only seem useful if it actually persuades, that is, if the targets of the persuasion change their minds or change their actions. Aristotle's notion of a final cause explains the reason something is made or done; for example, one might walk in order to get healthy.[1] When applied to rhetoric, final causes involve a persuasion to "right judgment, action, or belief."[2] Each of Aristotle's types of persuasive oratory has a different final cause; forensic oratory strives for justice, deliberative oratory strives for public benefit, and epideictic oratory strives for honor.[3] All of these domains might fall under the purview of procedural rhetoric as well. Computer simulations are used with increasing frequency in courtrooms, where they serve as forensic persuasion. *JFK Reloaded*, discussed in chapter 4, might take on a very different persuasive tone if it had been designed for the kind of conspiracy trial depicted in Oliver Stone's film *JFK*. Many of the public policy games also discussed in the first section persuade on the deliberative register. And the advertising and learning games discussed in the final two sections persuade on the epideictic register.

A statement is persuasive, in Aristotle's words, "because there is someone whom it persuades."[4] But precisely how do we know if and when a procedural "statement" has persuaded someone? In classical rhetoric of the ideal form, persuasion entails deliberation, which yields action through reasoned assent. Interlocutors might indicate success directly: "you have persuaded me." In such cases, the persuasion is immediate, determinate, and directly known to the orator. A court of law is perhaps the best example of this sort of certainty. The defendant offers his defense, awaits the jury's deliberation, and then ceremonially receives notice of the success or failure of the persuasion. Deliberative rhetoric follows suit, albeit less powerfully, by means of the democratic process. We carry over this method of measuring persuasion in modern political elections, but the myriad forms and instances of persuasive propositions—speeches, posters, television advertisements—occlude the individual successes and failures of individual tactics. Epideictic rhetoric usually covers the praise or censure of something, or commonly, someone; this is the domain of the ceremonial harangue. Such cases often mirror the deliberative and the judicial, the orator making an appeal to an audience to trust or distrust another human agent. All of these modes of persuasion enjoy the benefit of direct access to the subjects of persuasion: the law court, the agora, and the private symposium support public interjection and challenge. In religious rhetoric, preaching that leads primarily or exclusively to conversion (missionary sermon) provides equally simple evidence of persuasion: the persuaded agent's acceptance of Christ as savior and subsequent acceptance of the initiation rituals of a particular sect. This type of persuasive outcome is not unlike that of the law court or the public forum, in which some material and measurable gesture affirms the interlocutor's acceptance of the orator's argument.

In these cases, the ability to determine whether someone has been persuaded is clear. The object of the persuasion is held accountable, even held hostage for a response. The jury may not complete its duties without answering for the effectiveness of each candidate's persuasion. The same goes for the electorate, who cannot avoid responding to the relative persuasiveness of each of a set of candidates. The only gestures that avoid such accounting are abstention. But even then, individual abstention is not enough; the entire body of jurors or voters must opt out in order to avoid answering the call of persuasion. In such a case, the group is no longer commenting on the persuasiveness of a candidate or a defendant, but on some inherent problem in the method by which they have been asked to judge him.

Videogames—especially serious games—have been implicated in a similar logic of accountability. The value of a videogame in any particular situation is always related to a method of measurement that already implies players' support of the system that produced the videogame. Consider commercial games, which are judged primarily by two measures. First, a commercial game's success is judged by aggregate reviews in magazines and websites like

Metacritic.com. Metacritic.com compiles reviews from other sources and takes a weighted average to arrive at a "metascore" for the product.[5] These scores are taken seriously by buyers and publishers alike; Electronic Arts Chief Creative Officer Bing Gordon has argued that EA brass use Metacritic as a thermometer for the short- and long-term success of their titles.[6] Second, a commercial game's success is judged by its financial performance. Products that sell well are generally accorded more cultural and artistic relevance than those that do not. Games share these criteria with other commercial entertainment goods such as film and books, for which quality is often, and questionably, elided with marketability. Where niche markets make claims for the quality of such a product, the artifact is usually relegated a special "cult status" outside normal commercial success. Cult movies, comics, books, and videogames are rarely mass-market successes, and thus the commercial industries that produce them literally do not account for their impact. The very use of the word *cult* to describe such works speaks to their isolation from generally accepted practice, just as a religious cult's beliefs are misplaced from the norm. Cult veneration is often characterized as daft or even dangerous, even if those in the mainstream pursue similar activities with equal zeal. Commercial games thus foreclose any judgment save that of the market. And market numbers are literally counted and compared, just like jury votes or ballots.

Serious games impose a distinct but similar strategy to determine their success. In the case of the subject areas I have discussed in the previous chapters—politics, advertising, and learning—each has its own logic that stands in for the marketplace. Politics seeks to establish policy positions that support the political agents and constituencies who advance those positions. Ideology supports these claims by forming a foundation for the goals of political structures. Advertising seeks to produce image-markets that support the agencies that produce advertising. Media buying supports this infrastructure by forming a foundation for the goals of advertisers. Learning seeks to reproduce structures of knowledge. Schooling supports the infrastructure of work and the economy by aligning the goals of education with those of institutionalization and production.

Earlier I argued that the serious games movement in its current form supports and extends the closed goals of such institutions. *Seriousness* helps create an opposition to triviality, positioning the goals of government, business, and educational institutions against those of entertainment. Ironically, as the use of Metacritic example demonstrates, commercial (entertainment) games relate leisure to business, to the exchange of disks and bits for capital. Serious games replace the cycle of capital with the cycle of political regimes, the cycle of industrial production, the cycle of institutionalized social goals. Just as the commercial industry has no means to accept financially unsuccessful products and thus must relegate such titles to the realm of cult, so the serious games industry has no means to accept disruptive products that challenge the very operation of the institutions it hopes to serve.

Where commercial videogames cite financial success as a primary measure of success, serious games cite other, less familiar factors. If big business is measured by the amount of money it brings in, and if the logics of institutions like government and education take the place of capital in serious games, then the latter must measure success by the amount of reinforcement a game generates for a sponsoring institution. Consider David Michael and Sande Chen's explanation of the differences between commercial and serious games development:

Modern education is built around the concept of mastering (and/or memorizing) designated content, progressing through a number of school levels (primary, secondary, college, etc.) until finally graduating with a diploma or degree. Even outside the field of education, corporate and military training works within a similar structure. Material is presented to the students/trainees, and their mastery of that material is tested in various ways before they get credit for learning the material.

For serious games to be considered a useful tool to educators and trainers, they must provide testing and progress tracking. The results of the testing must be recognizable within the context of the education or training.[7]

This analysis clearly argues that serious games must support the goals of educators to prosper. Education, argue Michael and Chen, is built around demonstrable mastery of presented materials, tested within the frame of behaviorist reinforcement, and capped by "credit"—a monetary metaphor that symbolizes the player/learner's "earnings," namely a diploma or other token of value within the sponsoring institution. The refusal to participate in this educational economy simply does not count as learning. Michael and Chen also make it clear that serious games must be "useful" to educators and trainers. The output of such games must be accounted for on the balance sheets of these institutions. This motivation itself is driven by the desire for serious games to grow into a (financially) mature industry like commercial games; the obvious way to accomplish this feat is to support to the goals of institutions that can pay handsome sums for services.

Despite their earlier appeal to behaviorist testing, Michael and Chen further clarify that serious games offer the possibility of moving beyond the written test, instead demonstrating "processes, interactions, systems, causes and consequences," a claim that resonates with the type of persuasion I have called procedural rhetoric.[8] However, the two clarify that such methodologies impose additional requirements. Citing Clark C. Abt's original 1970 notion of serious games, Michael and Chen adopt the former's criteria for judging the "usefulness" of such a game:

active involvement and stimulation of all players;
sufficient realism to convey the essential truths of the simulation;
clarity of consequences and their causes both in rules and gameplay;
repeatability and reliability of the entire process.[9]

The first and last criteria are the most telling. To be useful, a serious game must stimulate and involve *all* players, not merely a subset of players. In the case of a school or business, this means that all students or employees must find commensurate value in such a game; otherwise it loses value in direct proportion to fragmentation of the audience. Just as commercial games strive to appeal to the greatest possible number of buyers, so serious games should strive to appeal to the greatest possible number of learners. In this case, the monetary value of commercial success is transferred to the sponsoring organization, for example, the number of students that will be taught chemistry to state expectations or the lowered opportunity cost of a game-based corporate trainer. Additionally, the outcome of such a game must be repeatable and reliable, not merely in part but throughout the "entire process." In other words, the gameplay session must maintain a tight coupling with the institution's existing processes, so that its support of those processes is ensured. "Realism" and "clarity" help convey the "essential truths" of this coupling.

Michael and Chen offer strategies by which serious games developers can ensure that their projects meet these expectations. Developers are advised to include "extensive, detailed logging of all player choices and actions" to allow postplay correlation of in-game to out-of-game actions. Presumably, any actions that do not produce or forward desirable institutional activity must be excised from gameplay—or, at the very least, developers should amplify those in-game actions that maximize institutional goals. Furthermore, argue Michael and Chen, serious games "are expected to *assist* teachers, not *replace* them. Serious games, therefore, need to be integrated into the education process."[10] That is to say, serious games are tools of the institution, by which it leverages its existing purchase outside the domain of games to drive the gears of progress. The educator or trainer guides the player's advancement to ensure that he doesn't "misplay" the game and thereby consider insights or outcomes outside the purview of desirable, condoned learning. In these cases, serious games may even bind with other measures of institutional success. For example, serious games in educational contexts often help students prepare for written tests. Serious games for corporate training often integrate with learning management systems (LMSs), technology infrastructures that automate written assessment, typically via Web-based interfaces.[11] Inevitably, serious games depend on accountability to authorities.

Assessment

The type of overall accountability of which serious games partake is usually called *assessment*. Used in a variety of learning theories, assessment generically refers to the process by which a teacher or some other authority figure evaluates someone. Educational theorists often disagree about the best methodologies for assessment. Popular approaches include Bloom's taxonomy of six levels of competence;[12] rubrics, or anchors for quantitative and qualitative performance; indirect measures, such as exit surveys; and benchmarks, or quantitative comparisons. In every case, assessment entails the comparison of a student's actual performance with expected, desired, or forecasted performance. Serious games directly adopt this understanding of assessment. For example, in his technical book on developing serious games, Bryan Bergeron offers the following software development–specific definition of assessment: "Assessment involves comparing the goals established during the requirements specification stage of development with measurable behavior changes in players after gameplay."[13]

Assessment always requires an appeal to an existing domain. An assessment equates one form of symbolic action with another form of symbolic action through some mediating measurement. In serious games, gameplay (a form of procedural symbolic action) is compared with desirable behavior within an institution, via material measurements like written tests or job performance.

It is worth noting that *assessment* has another, related meaning: that of valuation in general and taxation in particular. One assesses the value of a house or a diamond just as one assesses the importance of a business problem. The word derives from the Latin *assidere*, which literally means *to sit by*, but which took on the medieval meaning of levying tax. In modern times, we still use the term in relation to taxation; for example, a locality assesses properties at a certain rate. In its Latinate sense, assessment can also imply hostility, besiegement or blockade, and this meaning assuredly informs our notion of assessment as taxation. Taxes are levied in exchange for permission to pass, to carry on.

Assessment is thus fundamentally related to material exchange and economic return. A sovereign or a government provides protection and services in exchange for tax. A corporation provides job and industry training in exchange for the performance of job duties. A public school provides education in exchange for the immediate demonstration of progress toward defined social goals. Often, unspoken demands ride on the heels of such exchanges. Taxpayers have only limited control of their government's use of such moneys. Employees must adopt the goals and values of their employers. And students must ascribe to the implicit social program of institutionalized education. In many cases, the alternatives are dire. Failure to pay taxes leads to monetary penalties or audits; habitual penalty leads to incarceration. Failure to support one's employer leads to dismissal; habitual dismissal leads to starvation. Failure to embrace the educational system leads to social stigma; habitual rejection leads to ignominy.

In most cases, political, corporate, and educational institutions rely on one basic form of assessment, derived directly from the estimation of monetary value for taxation: numerical measurement. This goal motivates Michael and Chen's recommendation that developers store the details of players' every choice and action. If every action is stored, then the game can output any type of numerical report, from average score to average player velocity. Quantitative assessment is pervasive in serious games and educational technology in general. Such data are the foundation of educational assessment; we give students percentile grades, which we calculate based on weighted correct and incorrect responses, which we in turn render correct or incorrect by virtue of a pencil mark in a particular numeric index on a test form. We count academic progress by grade level, in numerical order, with progress incremented in convenient rhythm with the calendar. We judge our sons and daughters and their future college careers by standardized test scores, numbers that have become metaphors for potential. We count college credit by units, and we understand academic effort as a function of the relative number of units assigned to a course. We assign times and durations to intellectual pursuits, each class meeting lasting as much time as the last and the next. We choose our neighborhoods based on the performance ratios of local schools, which in turn win their funding by the same measures of performance. No Child Left Behind amplifies education focus on numerical measurement in the hope of increasing "accountability" by calculating school performance from the net assessments of their students.

In politics, newspapers cover Gallup polls that numerize public opinion. Results are broken down into districts, demographics, interest groups, and every other category imaginable. On election night in the United States, we watch as districts, counties, and states report their results, which are converted into the scrip of electoral votes, then further accrued to establish a winner. Would-be politicos measure success first by how many petition signatures they obtain to get on the ballot, then by dollars raised to run their campaigns, then by public opinion polls, next by exit polls, and finally by raw tallies of votes. Public policy is frequently equated with financial expenditure, and budget figures serve as proxies for moral value. Political consultant Frank Luntz, discussed in chapter 3, pays ordinary people to come to his offices to provide fodder for new message development. Subjects watch recorded interviews and continuously adjust a handheld dial to indicate their relatively positive or negative response to the speaker at a given time. Luntz's "message development" team mines the data and cross-references it with the words and phrases uttered at corresponding time-codes, accepting and rejecting possible terms based on numerical assessment.

In advertising, viewership is measured synecdochically, in "eyeballs." Decades ago, Nielsen Media Research concocted the system of television ratings, which bases the value of a show on sampling and viewer logs. The more viewers, the more valuable the advertising space on the show. Thanks to Nielsen's monopoly of the advertising metrics market, marketing value has become directly correlated to Nielsen's algorithms of viewer share. Value in other marketing media remains principally tied to viewership—the number of cars that pass a billboard, the number of commuters on a subway platform, the number of subscribers to a magazine. Like pollsters, marketers correlate these against demographics, matchmaking for the largest number of matching eyeballs. The Internet has been celebrated in marketing circles for its ability to increase accountability in advertising; now banner ad views could be tracked against click-throughs, showing the number of ad viewers who became website viewers. Coupons, website clicks, and direct mail responses correlate viewership to purchases, producing new measures of response rates and "handraising." Promotions and contests collect consumer information, filling databases with ever-increasing numbers of records, which in turn bear new direct response mailers and email offers.

When applied to videogames, numerical assessment seeks to account for player gestures, immediately and indelibly, in the service of the sponsoring agency's known and predefined goals. Bergeron, Michael, and Chen urge serious game developers to first define fixed goals for a game and then correlate the numerical output of play against these goals. The undeniable empirical result is the efficacy of the game. When compared with other, known methods for achieving the same result, one can determine the game's return on investment (ROI), the relative cost benefit of achieving the desired results. Once again, performance is collapsed into financial expenditure.

Consider the type of advergames discussed earlier. Games with weak procedural rhetorics like *Ms. Match* are created in the image of popular casual games to produce high numbers of plays and high time-per-play. In accordance with Michael and Chen's advice on recorded metrics, the site that houses the game can measure the number of times the page and game have been loaded as well as the duration of play. Furthermore, through their Kewlbox.com portal, the creators are able to leverage multiple plays per user session across several of their advertising clients, thus providing increased numerical metrics. Likewise, in-game ad network Massive has partnered with metrics firm Nielsen to create measurement tools for in-game ad placements.[14] Through a normal Internet connection, Nielsen can record player time in front of a Massive-placed ad, as well as the location of that player and ad in the game or game level, as well as additional geometric details such as the angle of view between the player and the ad image. Such metrics allow the advertising industry to continue to justify advertising value through quantitative measurement. Advertisers continue to extend this model. In early 2006, Montréal-based First Person Plural (FPP) announced their intention to use games as a source for database marketing. The group plans to release a driving game called *HumanLimit* for free, tempting players with the promise of a $1 million prize.[15] FPP would collect registrations for future marketing as well as sell ad space in the game's urban environment through a system much like Massive's. Once again, we have an example of a game striving for results through immediate, numerical evidence.

Other games attempt to account for their success through psychological or physiological metrics. Consider the educational/healthcare game *EyeSpy: The Matrix*, a conditioning game for self-esteem.[16] In the game, players are presented with a 4×4 grid of faces. One face in the grid is smiling; the rest frown or scowl. The player is instructed to click on the "smiling/accepting" face as quickly as possible. The researchers who developed the game conducted interviews and measurements with a control group and with players of the game and published research claiming that self-esteem can be enhanced via the randomized, smiling faces of *The Matrix*.[17] The game, they argue, produces implicit self-esteem merely through exposure to the smiling faces. And Red Octane's pro-*DDR* campaign claims that Tanya Jessen lost ninety-five pounds using the game as her only means of exercise.[18]

In serious games, performance is always assumed to correlate with numerical progress, and numerical progress is often tied directly or indirectly to the accrual of or reduction in capital. Furthermore, such a performance assessment is usually assumed to bear interest very rapidly, perhaps even immediately after a session of the game is completed. The institutions that fund and use serious games—the military, government, educational institutions, healthcare institutions, and corporations—impose such demands. For these institutions, persuasion implies the production of assent as rapidly as possible. But as I have argued, procedural rhetorics can also challenge the situations that contain them, exposing the logic of their operations and opening the possibility for new configurations. Accounting for such results is impossible from within the framework of the system a procedural rhetoric hopes to question; the currency of such a system is no longer valid. If we want to know how persuasive games persuade, we need to find another model.

Deliberation

When we created *The Howard Dean for Iowa Game*, the campaign stood at the peak of its success using grassroots outreach. Convinced that all their work could drive registrations, contributions, and further commitments to volunteer, the campaign asked us to include links to such activities in the game itself. These links registered click-throughs to a metrics server, which the campaign used to track the performance of a variety of campaigns. When I talk to the press about political games like *The Howard Dean for Iowa Game* or *Disaffected!*, they inevitably ask how many people played the game, or how long they played, or if we correlated gameplay with registrations or contributions. They are hoping for information like that stored by the metrics server. But the most interesting results the game produced had nothing to do with the number of plays, clicks from the game to the website, or contributions generated. Rather, those came from conversations about the game's procedural rhetoric itself.

In chapter 4, I argued that digital democracy has failed to represent political issues through computation, favoring encyclopedic artifacts like blogs over procedural ones like videogames. Videogames facilitate player consideration of rule-based systems, but blogs facilitate open discussion. Conveniently, Dean's campaign unfolded the same year weblogs came into their own as a popular medium, and we were fortunate to be able to watch players unpack their experiences with the games in both mass media publications and blogs. Responses were mixed, from "Half-assed mind-control experiment"[19] to "I have yet to decide if it's creative or creepy"[20] to "it is too incredible for words to describe."[21] These qualitative responses were both endearing and amusing, even the harshly negative ones. The more significant responses attempted to understand our procedural representation of grassroots outreach in the context of the broader campaign.

While many bloggers weighed in on their love, hate, or ambivalence for the game, others interrogated its rules and attempted to relate those rules to the meaning of the campaign. Wrote critic Justin Hall, "It's the arcade/action side of a real-time strategy game, resource gathering through fast clicking. But there's no resulting overview, no political resource allocation game."[22] Game journalist David Thomas took Hall's observation further in his own review.

The score in the game is simple—the more people you recruit to the Dean side, the better. . . . You recruit, and while you do it, you get little pro-Dean messages flashing around the corners or your screen. . . .

And in a few cute minutes of play with a simple set of games, politics is revealed for what it is—a raw game of numbers. The Dean game shows that his campaign is no different than Bush's. No different than any other in recent memory. The political process has been hijacked by analysis and planners looking at demographic data and figuring out how to build landslides of word-of-mouth influence. What Dean says doesn't matter in this game, nor in the real world. It's simply the calculus of mobilization. Get enough waves of volunteers recruiting volunteers and you have the perfect Amway pyramid—multi-level marketing your way to the presidency.[23]

Unlike many of the comments we tracked, Thomas's criticism ceases to traverse the game's surface and begins to interrogate the meaning of its rules. Politics, argues *The Howard Dean for Iowa Game*, is a numbers game. Like advertising, like education, like the very notion of assessment addressed above, the game privileges warm bodies over public policy. In such a scenario, political action is postponed. Hall makes an apology for the strategy, noting its credibility as a campaign strategy: *"The Howard Dean for Iowa Game* does remind us that the political process is made up of rote tasks performed by dedicated followers—the earlier in the process the better. So as a political education project, it is rudimentarily successful—recruit early and often." But Thomas worries that the strategy never ends, the candidate never stops campaigning to begin governing. On the one hand, Thomas's critique attacks the Dean campaign in particular; its focus on grassroots outreach and recruitment overwhelmed any semblance of discourse about the candidate's political issues. His progressive supporters overran Dean's record as a moderate in the small, rural state of Vermont. The image of Dean as a rural centrist with a commitment to public and social works was replaced by one of his coastal, urban followers: the latte-swilling, Volvo-driving leftists whose aggregate political persona replaced that of Dean. On the other hand, Thomas's appraisal suggests that it is not just Dean for whom amassing human wealth has replaced policy, but all politicians. Thomas continues, "the Dean for Iowa game tells us everything we need to know about the campaign. It's about votes, not about issues. It's about recruitment, not about people. It's about building momentum, not about being right."[24] Such is the procedural rhetoric of politics: one amasses supporters in support of nothing more than support itself. Political justice becomes, in Alain Badiou's words, "the harmonization of the interplay of interests."[25]

How might we measure David Thomas's interesting reading of the rhetoric of *The Howard Dean for Iowa Game*? Again the imps of numerical proof rear their horned heads. We might consider the influence of Thomas's syndicated newspaper column. We might count the readers on Thomas's buzzcut.com website, where the article was originally published. Perhaps we might count the number of replies in the comment thread attached to the article, or perhaps even the number of unique voices in that thread. Or, Google-like, we might count the inbound links, taking reference as a measure of value. But such measures impose the very criticism Thomas mounts against politics upon his own reading: issues, debate, and consideration are dismissed in favor of symbolic wealth.

The real promise of Thomas's response to the game's argument would come from discursive, not numerical analysis. What do he and his readers do with this new perspective on Dean's campaign, or on campaigns in general? Do they abandon all pretense of faith in the democratic process? Do they move for revolution? Do they challenge the candidate to forgo abstraction in favor of policy? And moreover, is this type of response a success or a failure in persuasion?

The persuasive goal of *The Howard Dean for Iowa Game*, we should remember, was to motivate fencesitter supporters to participate in the campaign. Thomas himself seems to self-identify as one such target: "I, like a lot of other people, have been thinking maybe Howard Dean wouldn't be such a bad guy to be president. The 'fighting centrist' acts like he just wants to do the right thing. And in American politics, that's a rare and possibly mythical beast."[26] If the only type of support valid for persuasion is the contribution of money or volunteer time, then certainly Thomas was not persuaded. But if increasingly sophisticated interrogation of the candidate and the campaign offers sufficient evidence of a progression from curious, possible supporter to inquisitive, prospective supporter, we need not consider the videogame a persuasive failure. Rather than producing assent, which can be measured with a yea or nay, the game produces deliberation, which implies neither immediate assent nor dissent.

There are precedents for styles of rhetoric that muster deliberation as evidence of persuasion. Modes of Judeo-Christian rhetoric outside of missionary sermon are less easily compared to the classical modes of evidence. Old Testament covenant speech follows a fixed pattern: "first, to strengthen the authority of the Lord by reminding the audience of what he has done; second, to add new commandments; and third, to conclude with a warning of what will happen if the commandments are disregarded."[27] Such rhetorical acts are less easily mapped to the classical model—their primary purpose is to reinforce the covenant with God, which in turn guides everyday behavior in relation to prophetic caution. In Christian homiletics, propositions carry calls to duty or repentance, usually making appeals to the truth of scripture as a message "seized by the soul" and then deliberated and accepted through the study of scripture.[28] Here persuasion is held in suspense. In some form, the homily persuades when the parishioner agrees to accept it as a proposition for duty or repentance. In both the Catholic and Protestant church, homily often leads to a direct call to commitment or repentance in the form of prayer or contrition. Such actions could be construed as evidence that the homily has persuaded its audience. But the subsequent (and particularly Protestant) call to hermeneutics, or the interpretation of scripture, complicates matters. George A. Kennedy correlates Christian hermeneutics to Aristotelian dialectic: both involve the discovery of new material to advance as propositions in arguments.[29] But homily is advanced unceremoniously. A clerical authority explicates a scriptural passage for the congregation, including how to make use of it in daily life. The call to hermeneutics helps individual parishioners make personal sense of the homiletic elucidation. *Homily* and *sermon* both mean "conversation" or "being together" in Greek (ὁμιλία) and Latin (*sermō*) respectively, but the intercourse does not take place between the congregation and the cleric; rather the set of possible conversations is framed by the homily. Hermeneutics helps the parishioner specify the general homiletic rule to his particular situation.

Preaching in general and homily in particular take an important stance on the measurement of persuasive success by relinquishing measurement in favor of interrogation. The purpose of the cleric is to open a conceptual space for the parishioner, in relation to which the latter might reconfigure his personal life. Classical persuasion privileges consideration, debate, and response, but it typically closes such debate once the matter is decided. Unlike classical persuasion, homily enforces a set of constraints—one would not be wrong to call them rules—that are intended to structure thought and action for the object of the persuasion. Homily itself is verbal, not procedural, but nevertheless a procedural system founds its verbal rhetoric—in this case the system of belief delineated in scripture. Religious thought in general offers an unusual precedent for the conscious expression of a rule-based system. In this case, persuasion is perhaps never perfected, but rather continuously unfolding over time, challenged and readdressed as new "conversations" with an underlying system.

In religious rhetoric, a procedural system is deliberately codified in artifacts, traditions, and texts. We call ascription to such a system *faith*, a devotion to this system. Alain Badiou uses the term *fidelity* in a different way. For any situation, fidelity is a set of procedures that "separate out . . . those which depend on an event."[30] The event, we should recall, is the disruptive reconfiguration of a situation, one that has the potential to break entirely from its previous structure. Badiou's notion of fidelity is modeled after amorous relations, not religious faith. The relationship of love stands in relation to a disruption in the lives of the lover and the beloved. Love "founds itself upon an intervention."[31] Fidelity to this event comes only in the subsequent protection of its consequences. Marriage, for example, as an emblem of fidelity to love, exists as the ongoing commitment to understand two previous individual lives as one pair of intertwined lives. The gesture that establishes a situation, what Badiou calls the count-as-one and which I have called a unit operation, sets the rules for a fidelity. Or as Badiou puts it, "what allows us to evaluate a fidelity is its result."[32] It is measured by the production of new gestures that can be included in the situation. Fidelity helps us understand the uniqueness of Badiou's concept of the event; the event is not an isolated instance, but rather is something that always subsumes its participants. As Peter Hallward clarifies: "A third person looking in on a loving couple may be charmed or irritated, but is unlikely to share in the experience of love itself."[33] In turn, new events may erupt, reconfiguring the situation and demanding a new fidelity. One might think of the birth of a child as an event that alters the fidelity of a couple in love, requiring fidelity of a new kind.

Badiou reserves the name *subject* for beings transformed by an event into a relationship of fidelity. The event is disruptive, reconfiguring the structure of a situation. Within Badiou's vocabulary, we might then argue that procedural rhetorics make claims about the structure of a situation, in the hopes of inspiring a disruptive event. But events and the subjects they produce are individual, and no one relationship exists between the logic of system (e.g., political campaigning) and a singular agent (e.g., the citizen). Moreover, the event itself is unthinkable within the current structure of a situation. Badiou articulates a trace of this potential event within the configuration of a situation, which he names the *evental site*.[34] The evental site is "an abnormal multiple . . . the *minimal* effect of structure which can be conceived; it is such that it belongs to the situation, whilst what belongs to it in turn does not."[35] This odd multiple is a wormhole into other situations; like a rift in space-time, Badiou locates the evental site "on the edge of the void."[36] The evental site can belong to multiple situations simultaneously without inconsistency, and it gives participants of a situation perspective that can lead to disruption. Peter Hallward attempts to simplify the concept thus: "An evental site is . . . an element of a situation that, as inspected from a perspective within the situation, has no recognizable elements or qualities of its own (no elements in common with the situation)."[37] Hallward offers clear examples as well. The participants of anti-Semitic situations do not conceive of individual Jews but only of an "indistinct gap in the normal social fabric."[38] Likewise, participants of homophobic situations do not see gays as "particular men and women engaged in particular relationships," but only as a singular element in an otherwise heterosexual situation.[39]

The evental site takes on special status in relation to the situation. It is the place where "radical innovation" emerges.[40] Actually changing the situation requires an event, but motivated recognition of the situation's structure can take place at the evental site. Procedural rhetorics couple particularly well with Badiou's set-theoretical ontology. Badiou understands situations as arrangements of elements, founded by the gesture of the count-as-one. The count-as-one explains the situation's state. I have extended this understanding of state in the concept of the unit operation, which refers not only to the organization of elements in a situation, but also to the logic by which the situation operates.

Persuasive games expose the logic of situations in an attempt to draw players' attention to an evental site and encourage them to problematize the situation. Videogames themselves cannot produce events; they are, after all, representations. But they can help members of a situation address the logic that guides it and begin to make movements to improve it. David Thomas's response to *The Howard Dean for Iowa Game* traces this gesture in a surprising way, one that both undermines the campaign's intentions and supports them in a new, more sophisticated way.

Previously, I have argued that videogames represent in the gap between procedural representation and individual subjectivity.[41] The disparity between the simulation and the player's understanding of the source system it models creates a crisis in the player; I named this crisis simulation fever, a madness through which an interrogation of the rules that drive both systems begins.[42] The vertigo of this fever—one gets *simsick* as he might get seasick—motivates criticism.

Procedural rhetoric also produces simulation fever. It motivates a player to address the logic of a situation in general, and the point at which it breaks down and gives way to a new situation in particular. If we adopt Badiou's terminology, a procedural rhetoric persuades when it helps discern the eventual site of a situation—the place where current practice breaks down. Players are persuaded when they enter a crisis in relation to this logic. Persuasion is related to the player's ability to see and understand the simulation author's implicit or explicit claims about the logic of the situation represented.

One can imagine several forms of procedural rhetoric. For one part, a persuasive game might attempt to foreclose the eventual site, reinforcing the existing logic of the situation. *America's Army* is an example of such a game; it hopes to represent and reinforce the value system of the U.S. Army and the commutative nature of U.S. defense and military policy. For another part, a persuasive game might attempt to unseat the existing logic of a situation, highlighting one particular eventual site. *Disaffected!* is an example of such a game; it hopes to convert consumer dissatisfaction into introspection about consumer practices. For yet another part, a persuasive game might sit ambiguously between the support and ouster of an existing logic. *The Howard Dean for Iowa Game* and *Grand Theft Auto: San Andreas* are examples of this type of game; the former intends to support the current state of affairs about campaigning, but in select cases it actually undermines that situation. The latter intends to abstract race and social class more than close readings reveal it to do.

Conversations

David Thomas's critique of *The Howard Dean for Iowa Game* and my own reading of *Grand Theft Auto: San Andreas* show how the production of discourse can help trace the status of persuasion in procedural rhetorics. The notion of reflection as articulated in the rhetorical goals of homily and artistic practice offer a useful extension to acts of gameplay. Procedural rhetorics expose the way things work, but reflection creates and prolongs this process. Criticism is one aspect of the reflective process. But criticism requires formal discourse, often limiting itself to the academic and cultural elite. More generally, persuasive games can produce discourse in the general sense, like the blog conversations that cropped up around the Dean game.

Henry Jenkins and Kurt Squire argue that *Animal Crossing* is architected to create such informal discourse:

At first glance, such simple game interactions as growing flowers may sound mundane, but imagine your spouse's frustration as she discovers that you chopped down her beloved tree for firewood, or the simple pleasures of your best friend leaving you a note to please go to the fresh market on Sunday morning for some produce she needs to complete a quest. Families (of all types) live increasingly disjointed lives, but the whole family can play *Animal Crossing* even if they can rarely all sit down to dinner together. When families do gather, the game offers common points of reference and common projects to discuss. At its best, *Animal Crossing* harkens back to the intense social interactions that surrounded Monopoly, Risk, or Life.[43]

The game's temporal structure—a persistent world directly bound to the console's system clock—creates rifts in the gameplay experience. Children, for example, might miss high-value fish that appear regularly at night and therefore after bedtime. A child might ask his parent to catch one on his behalf and send it via the in-game postal service.[44] This request might take place around the dinner table, as Jenkins and Squire suggest, where it could spur additional, informal discussion about the game's economic system. A parent might ask what the child hopes to do with the spoils of such an expedition, or he might even ask for a commission for the trouble. Such discussions help tease out the procedural rhetoric in the game—an informal, local criticism; they also help players share their ongoing relationship with the game's ambiguous position on consumption and satisfaction.

In advertising, conversations are increasingly valued as well, but only when they can be mustered in support of existing goals. Consider Seth Godin's meditation on the role of community in advertising:

What makes them [groups of people] a community is that they talk to each other. They share ideas and adjust their biases and choices based on what other members of the community do. . . . I've decided to occasionally use the word community instead of market. That's because I think the best marketing goes on when you talk to a group that shares a worldview and also talks about it—a community.[45]

Just as Jenkins and Squire portray their family of *Animal Crossing* players, Godin argues that communities use discourse to establish and refine their beliefs. But the benefit of communities to advertisers comes from their demographic stability, not their discursive potential. Put differently, for advertisers the usefulness and benefit of communities arises from leverage, the ability to address a large group with a single message. Despite Godin's simplistic yet clever linguistic dance, he uses *community* merely as a euphemism for *market*, not as a disruption of it. The ability for a community to consider, refine, revise, and reinvent itself bears fruit for advertisers only if such opinions found a large enough collective to consume media-placed messages. Even a focus on niche markets rallies around the same logic; tools like blog advertising or search keyword networks simply replicate mass-market media advertising on a smaller scale.

Compare this approach to the revisionist demonstrative advertising of a game like *The Toilet Training Game* or *Sea World Adventure Park Tycoon*, which mount procedural rhetorics about the operational claims of products and services. Players contextualize these functional networks in their own social context, where they subject them to uniquely individual consideration. In some cases, these conversations might take place between multiple parties. For example, consider a family reflecting on the applicability of a Jeep Commander while playing *Xtreme Errands*. In other cases, perhaps most cases, the conversation takes place internally; the player asks himself questions about the intersection of a product's features with his own routine and values.

In educational technology, reflection is often measured through the quality or content of conversations that take place outside of a computer-mediated system like a videogame. MIT's Education Arcade created a game called *Revolution*, which simulates life in colonial Williamsburg.[46] Built as a modification of the popular role-playing game *Neverwinter Nights*,[47] *Revolution* gives the player a particular social role, "from an upper class lawyer, to a patriotic blacksmith, to an African American house slave," and allows exploration of the social environment from these varied perspectives.[48] In contrast to most Revolutionary War history curricula, the educational goals of *Revolution* cover the interrelated and often conflicting goals of eighteenth-century life.

Oxford University researcher Russell Francis deployed an unusual technique in an attempt to characterize the learning outcomes of *Revolution*. Because the game's value comes from the interrogation of social history, Francis determined that multiple, intersected conversations about aspects of the game's complex social system would be necessary. Francis started by asking students to synthesize their in-game experiences by composing a diary for a game character. He then extended this approach to machinima, having the students create and narrate short films about their characters' virtual lives as evidence of synthesis.[49] Francis noted that the machinima diaries and their constituent artifacts could become platforms for further learning or discussions in email to friends, creating additional discourse.

Other researchers have attempted to build conversation systems directly into their educational games. Mary Ulicsak et al. describe a game created at the NESTA Futurelab called *Savannah*.[50] In the game, children take on the role of lions in a virtual savannah. Mobile devices map the game world onto the topology of a school playground. Ulicsak et al. explain the game dynamics as follows:

Out in the field children are confronted with the challenges faced by lions (hunger, thirst, human and other hazards, the changing seasons). In the field, children play in a pride of 6 lions and have to develop collective strategies for hunting and survival. A separate space, the "den," is an indoor site in which the children act as "game players" rather than lions, planning strategies for field-play, and in which they have access to advisors, an interactive whiteboard that displays lions' movements in the field, and paper and other resources.[51]

In this case, a space for synthetic performance is architected into the game itself, with teacher interaction and whiteboard/paper scratchings constituting deliverables.

A similar situation takes place in *The Grocery Game*, discussed in chapter 1. The game is actually played in the aisles of the supermarket, but the website serves as a virtual clubhouse for its players. In addition to acquiring the latest bulkfood and coupon lists, players use the site's messageboards for encouragement. Many share their goals, including the things they are saving for or the reasons they are playing. Consider the following reports taken from the game's messageboards:

I . . . paid off 2 credit cards, still working on a few others and have saved up enough for a down on a house. It won't be a huge house for our family of 7, but being able to go from $1,000.00 a month in rent to $400–$500 in a house note and being able to live out in the country is worth it.

I used my savings to hire a housekeeper. So no matter how messy my four kids get, I know the entire house will be spotless at least once a week. For about 60 seconds . . . I saved more than enough to cover the costs by just lowering our out of control grocery/Sam's [Club]/Costco bills.[52]

Goals like these personalize the game's procedural rhetoric—beat the food retail business model and keep the money in your pocket. But more important, they help remind players that *The Grocery Game* itself is orthogonal to the acquisition of capital; the goal is not to save money for additional consumption, but to rethink their personal finances and financial goals after mastering this logic.

Social scientists may note that such conversations could be measured using qualitative analysis. The social construction of meaning is a common subject of qualitative research, especially in fields like sociology. Statistical validity is downplayed or avoided entirely, and *in situ* research like ethnography helps contextualize the meaning-making process in actual rather than ideal social situations. By analyzing the conversations and synthetic artifacts produced—*Revolution* machinima diaries or *Savannah* whiteboard strategies—a social scientist or educational technologist might correlate player performance against desired pedagogical goals. Most frequently, such research relies on field observations, participant interviews, and analysis of materials produced by subjects of study. All of these approaches are potentially applicable to persuasive games, especially games whose procedural rhetoric does not produce simplistic numerical results.

But qualitative research too relies on an economy of return. Such research often establishes commonalities between individual instances through sampling or induction. The common use of qualitative research in general and ethnography in particular among anthropologists helps justify their particular interest in characterizing the general operation of social and cultural systems. Researchers spend time—sometimes considerable time—with their subjects, drawing inferences and establishing subjective accounts of social dynamics. Sometimes these observations are correlated with known or desired behaviors, such as the actual versus desired performance of pupils. But even where predefined goals are set aside, qualitative research still accounts for its observations in theoretical wholes. Based on ethnography, researchers draw conclusions that neatly tie up their observations. A place for every social gesture, and every gesture in its place.

Assessment of all kinds demands accountability, assurance that money, time, and commitment will return value in like kind to the sponsoring institution. Political institutions hope for assent and commitment. Advertisers and businesses hope for commercial return. Educational institutions hope for predictable and desired synthetic response. Like a neurotic or a codependent, assessment always sticks around until it can be certain that a result, positive or negative, has come to pass.

Philosophy has offered numerous meditations on the vicious economic cycle. Jacques Derrida argued that the true gift confounds economics because it neither demands nor expects recompense.[53] Many gifts wear the guise of generosity but still demand some type of benefit in return, even if that benefit comes from an unrelated form of real or simulated currency. The sacrifice, for example, "proposes an offering but only in the form of a destruction against which it exchanges, hopes for, or counts on a benefit, namely a surplus-value or at least an amortization, a protection, and a security."[54] Emmanuel Levinas advances a secular conception of religion as an uncrossable separation between the self and the other, "a link established between the Self and the Other, but one that does not create a totality."[55] This relationship founds ethics as well, which is characterized by a respect for that infinite separation. In Badiou's conception of the situation, the event erupts when the elements in a multiple (a set, in the mathematical sense) no longer suffice. A new situation is constructed out of the void (the empty set, $\emptyset$), which is always a member of every set. Even if a procedural rhetoric produces such intense simulation fever around an eventual site that an event erupts, the event itself can never understand its consequences.

Derrida drew a connection between the gift and what he called *dissemination*, a replacement for communication that admits that the source of a message has no certain knowledge about its successful delivery. Literary expression is disseminated; the reader interprets in the face of the inaccessibility of the author—even if the author is physically present, the separation between his and the reader's subjectivity is impassable. Nevertheless, we continue to read, interpret, and critique literature—or art, or film, or even videogames. Assessment strives to close down expressive systems by accounting for their output as a function of their design. Assessment helps affirm the institutions that structure our world, giving them evidence that their tactics support existing strategies. In the eyes of these institutions, we are always on trial, and "evidence" serves to prove our guilt or innocence. Assessment demands wholesale accountability, in advance, for how something serves an authority.

But if procedural rhetorics challenge the logics of structures that contain them, then the only way to address their success is through transformation. In Badiou's ontology, the individuals who reconfigure situations—for example by falling in love—never cease to pay tribute to this event. The new logic that rules their situation can never be assessed in the present, at a single moment in time, because it must always play out over time through a process of fidelity. Once a procedural rhetoric advances a new logic that a subject interrogates, it no longer remains possible to feign ignorance about that logic. Like love and revolution, procedural rhetorics persuade through intervention, by setting the stage for a new understanding unthinkable in the present.

Like literature, poetry, and art, videogames cannot necessarily know their effects on individual players. As an expressive practice, procedural rhetoric is intimately related to humanism. The *humanities* were originally coextensive with the liberal arts, which formed the basis of the classical trivium and quadrivium, discussed earlier in relation to Dorothy Sayers' medieval classicism. Today, we use the term more generally, usually referring to subjects concerned with human culture, such as literature, history, art, philosophy, music. These domains of human production create discourse—they express our joys, anger, fears, confusion, affection, and hope. The humanities attempt to get to the bottom of human experience in specific situations, to expose their structures. Procedural media like videogames get to the heart of things by mounting arguments about the processes inherent in them. When we create videogames, we are making claims about these processes, which ones we celebrate, which ones we ignore, which ones we want to question. When we play these games, we interrogate those claims, we consider them, incorporate them into our lives, and carry them forward into our future experiences. When we read books, watch cinema, view art, attend theater, listen to music, pore over comics—and indeed when we play videogames—these media influence and change us. They contribute to the type of person each of us becomes, each text, each film, each song, each game making a mark, a unique inspiration or aversion. Humanistic approaches to cultural artifacts could be seen to trace the procedural construction of human subjectivity—the interlocking logics, histories, and cultural influences recent and past that drive our perspectives on new challenges. As the name suggests, the humanities help us understand what it means to be human, no matter the contingencies of profession, economics, or current affairs. The humanities offer insights into human experience that we need when industries, militaries, governments, game engines, middleware, and all else fails. This is the knowledge that helps us to recover from heartbreak, to make sense of tragedy, to understand betrayal.

Most importantly, these observations take place over time. In part, they take place over the time of an individual's life. Just as we return to books, films, and art that have challenged the ways we understand the world, so we return to videogames for the same reason—to renew our fidelity to their procedural rhetorics, or to revise our relationship to their claims based on new experiences. And the cultural value of videogames goes beyond even the longitudinal experience of an individual life. It takes place over the course of many lives, generations—entire eras of human experience. The videogames we make and play today may have meaning for us now, but they also defer that meaning for future players, who will experience these artifacts in different contexts. Meaning takes place on the historical scale.

We must recognize the persuasive and expressive power of procedurality. Processes influence us. They seed changes in our attitudes, which in turn, and over time, change our culture. As players of videogames and other computational artifacts, we should recognize procedural rhetoric as a new way to interrogate our world, to comment on it, to disrupt and challenge it. As creators and players of videogames, we must be conscious of the procedural claims we make, why we make them, and what kind of social fabric we hope to cultivate through the processes we unleash on the world. Despite the computers that host them, despite the futuristic and mechanical fictional worlds they often render, videogames are not expressions of the machine. They are expressions of being human. And the logics that drive our games make claims about who we are, how our world functions, and what we want it to become.

Notes

Preface

1. To wit, some $7.3 billion in 2004. See the Entertainment Software Association, "Essential Facts about the Computer and Video Game Industry" (Washington, D.C.: The Entertainment Software Association, 2005).

2. James Newman, *Videogames* (London: Routledge, 2004), 5.

3. The first videogame, *Spacewar!*, was created by Steve Russell in 1962 at the Massachusetts Institute of Technology (Steve Russell, *Spacewar!*, Cambridge, Mass.: Massachusetts Institute of Technology, 1962). Nolan Bushnell's 1971 coin-op adaptation of *Spacewar!*, called *Computer Space* (Nolan Bushnell, *Computer Space*, Mountain View, Calif.: Nutting Associates, 1971) and the Atari follow-up *Pong* (Atari, *Pong*, Sunnyvale, Calif.: Atari, 1972) were largely deployed in venues like bars and pool halls. Arcade culture of the 1970s primarily took place in such adult spaces. While the video arcades and home consoles of the late 1970s and early 1980s catered to children more than adults, the prehistory of such videogames (the 1950s to the 1970s) make simplistic games about videogames as children's media untenable.

4. See http://muse.jhu.edu/journals/childrens_literature/.

5. See http://www.hollins.edu/grad/childlit/childlit.htm/.

6. See Les Daniels, *Comix: A History of Comic Books in America* (New York: Outerbridge and Deinstfrey, 1971).

7. See http://www.english.ufl.edu/comics/; http://www.english.ufl.edu/imagetext/.

8. Newman, *Videogames*, 5.

9. Atticus XI (pseudonym), *A Conversation with Dr. Henry Jenkins* (2004 [cited February 4, 2005]); available from http://www.penny-arcade.com/lodjenkins.php/.

10. Ian Bogost, *Unit Operations: An Approach to Videogame Criticism* (Cambridge, Mass.: MIT Press, 2006).

11. Ian Bogost, "Videogames and Ideological Frames," *Popular Communication* 4, no. 2 (2006).

12. Ian Bogost, "Frame and Metaphor in Political Games," in *Worlds in Play*, ed. Suzanne de Castell and Jen Jenson (Berlin and New York: Peter Lang, forthcoming).

13. Ian Bogost, "Videogames and the Future of Education," *On the Horizon* 13, no. 2 (2005).

14. 12. Ian Bogost, "Playing Politics: Videogames for Politics, Activism, and Advocacy," *First Monday* 11, no. 9 (2006).

15. See http://www.watercoolergames.org/.

Chapter 1

1. Owen Gaede, *Tenure* (Minneapolis: Control Data Corporation, 1975). PLATO was a computer instruction system first developed at the University of Illinois in 1960. The name is an acronym for Programmed Logic for Automatic Teaching Operations. The system was commercially produced by Control Data Corporation (CDC) until the 1990s, and despite its eventual failure PLATO is acknowledged to have pioneered now-familiar tools like online forums, instant messaging, and multiplayer games. I am indebted to Noah Falstein for introducing me to this particular PLATO title.

2. Owen Gaede has also written a Windows version of *Tenure*, available at http://home.earthlink.net/~tenure/abouttenure.html/.

3. This is similar to Marshall McLuhan's suggestion that we see a medium only when we are moving beyond it.

4. Seymour M. Hersh, "Torture at Abu Ghraib," *New Yorker*, May 10, 2004.

5. Janet Murray, *Hamlet on the Holodeck* (New York: Free Press, 1997), 71.

6. Ibid.

7. Ibid., 72.

8. Bogost, *Unit Operations*.

9. Stevan Harnad, "Computation Is Just Interpretable Symbol Manipulation; Cognition Isn't," *Minds and Machines* 4, no. 4 (2004): 379.

10. Ibid.

11. Max Weber, *The Protestant Ethic and the Spirit of Capitalism*, trans. Talcott Parsons (London: Unwin Hyman, 1930), 181.

12. Bogost, *Unit Operations*, 3.

13. Jared Diamond, *Guns, Germs, and Steel* (New York: W. W. Norton, 1999).

14. Steven J. Levitt and Stephen J. Dubner, *Freakonomics: A Rogue Economist Explores the Hidden Side of Everything* (New York: William Morrow, 2005), 7.

15. Ibid., 137–141.

16. Ibid., 139. My emphasis.

17. Joseph Weizenbaum, "ELIZA—A Computer Program for the Study of Natural Language Communication between Man and Machine," *Communications of the ACM* 9, no. 1 (1966).

18. Ibid., 36–37.

19. For example, see Michael Mateas and Andrew Stern, "A Behavior Language for Story-Based Believable Agents," *IEEE Intelligent Systems* 7, no. 4 (2002).

20. The assembly instructions given here apply to the 6502 processor. The 6502 is an 8-bit processor widely used in microcomputers of the 1980s, including the Apple

II, the Commodore 64, the Atari 400 and 800, and, with modifications, as the 6507 in the Atari VCS (2600) and the Nintendo Entertainment System (NES). Assembly instructions may vary from processor to processor.

21. Noah Wardrip-Fruin, "Expressive Processing: On Process-Intensive Literature and Digital Media," Doctoral dissertation (Brown University, 2006).

22. For more on game engines and unit operations, see Bogost, *Unit Operations*, 56–66.

23. Infocom, *Zork* (Cambridge, Mass.: Infocom, 1980).

24. For more on the use of n-grams to construct computational, textual artifacts, see Noah Wardrip-Fruin, "Playable Media and Textual Instruments," *Dichtung Digital, Journal für Digitale Ästhetik* 5, no. 34 (2005).

25. Lawrence Lessig, *Code and Other Laws of Cyberspace* (New York: Basic Books, 1999), 6.

26. *Plato: Complete Works* (New York: Hackett, 1997), 453a.

27. Ibid., 266d.

28. Ibid., 266d–267d.

29. George A. Kennedy, *Classical Rhetoric and Its Christian and Secular Tradition* (Chapel Hill: University of North Carolina Press, 1999), 33.

30. Ibid., 34.

31. *Plato: Complete Works*, 464c.

32. Aristotle, *Physics*, trans. Robin Waterfield (Oxford and New York: Oxford University Press, 1999), 39 (II.33, 194b132).

33. Aristotle, *The Rhetoric and Poetics of Aristotle* (New York: McGraw Hill, 1984), 32 (I.33, 1358b–1355).

34. Ibid., 24 (I.22, 1355b–1326).

35. Ibid., 30–31 (I.32, 1358a–1358b).

36. Ibid., 199 (III.112, 1414a–1414b).

37. Kennedy, *Classical Rhetoric and Its Christian and Secular Tradition*, 3.

38. Sonja K. Foss, Karen A. Foss, and Robert Trapp, *Contemporary Perspectives on Rhetoric* (Prospect Heights, Ill.: Waveland Press, 1985), 11.

39. Kevin Michael DeLuca, *Image Politics: The New Rhetoric of Environmental Activism* (New York: Guilford Press, 1999), 14.

40. Foss, Foss, and Trapp, *Contemporary Perspectives on Rhetoric*, 12.

41. Kenneth Burke, *A Rhetoric of Motives* (Berkeley and Los Angeles: University of California Press, 1969), 19.

42. Ibid., 41.

43. Ibid., 20.

44. Foss, Foss, and Trapp, *Contemporary Perspectives on Rhetoric*, 193.

45. Burke, *A Rhetoric of Motives*, 172.

46. See Foss, Foss, and Trapp, *Contemporary Perspectives on Rhetoric*, 214.

47. Marguerite Helmers and Charles A. Hill, "Introduction," in *Defining Visual Rhetorics*, ed. Charles A. Hill and Marguerite Helmers (Mahwah, N.J.: Lawrence Erlbaum Associates, 2004), 2.

48. Charles A. Hill, "The Psychology of Rhetorical Images," in *Defining Visual Rhetorics*, 25.

49. Ibid., 33.

50. Ibid., 37.

51. Ibid.

52. Ibid., 38.

53. J. Anthony Blair, "The Rhetoric of Visual Arguments," in *Defining Visual Rhetorics*, 44.

54. Ibid.

55. Ibid., 47.

56. Ibid., 49.

57. Ibid., 51.

58. Jacques Derrida, *Of Grammatology*, trans. Gayatri Chakravorty Spivak (Baltimore: The Johns Hopkins Press, 1974), 3, 11–23.

59. David S. Birdsell and Leo Groarke, "Toward a Theory of Visual Argument," *Argumentation and Advocacy* 33 (1996): 2.

60. Randall A. Lake and Barbara A. Pickering, "Argumentation, the Visual, and the Possibility of Refutation: An exploration," *Argumentation and Advocacy* 12 (1988): 82.

61. Keith Kenney, "Building Visual Communication Theory by Borrowing from Rhetoric," in *Visual Rhetoric in a Digital World*, ed. Carolyn Handa (New York: Bedford St. Martins, 2004).

62. DeLuca, *Image Politics*, 1.

63. James P. Zappen, "Digital Rhetoric: Toward an Integrated Theory," *Technical Communication Quarterly* 14, no. 3 (2005): 319.

64. Ibid., 321.

65. Laura J. Gurak, *Cyberliteracy: Navigating the Internet with Awareness* (New Haven: Yale University Press, 2001), 29.

66. Ibid., 44.

67. Barbara Warnick, *Critical Literacy in a Digital Era: Technology, Rhetoric, and the Public Interest* (Mahwah, N.J.: Lawrence Erlbaum Associates, 2002), 82.

68. Richard A. Lanham, *The Electronic Word: Democracy, Technology, and the Arts* (Chicago: University of Chicago Press, 1995), 17, 39, 76, 152.

69. Lev Manovich, *The Language of New Media* (Cambridge, Mass.: MIT Press, 2001), 77–78.

70. For concise coverage of these two important works, see their respective chapters in Nick Montfort and Noah Wardrip-Fruin, eds., *The New Media Reader* (Cambridge, Mass.: MIT Press, 2003), 35–48, 301–338.

71. Chris Crawford, "Process Intensity," *Journal of Computer Game Development* 1, no. 5 (1987).

72. Manovich, *The Language of New Media*, 77.

73. Elizabeth Losh, *Virtualpolitik: Digital Rhetoric and the Subversive Potential of Information Culture*, manuscript in progress.

74. See chapter 7 for more on anti-advergames.

75. Patrick Dugan, "Hot off the Grill: la Molleindustria's Paolo Pedercini on The McDonald's Video Game," *Gamasutra*, February 27, 2006.

76. Richard Linklater, *Fast Food Nation* (Participant Productions, 2006); Eric Schlosser, *Fast Food Nation: The Dark Side of the All-American Meal* (New York: Harper, 2001).

77. See http://demo.fb.se/e/girlpower/retouch/.

78. See http://www.pbskids.com/. PBS is the American Public Broadcasting System, a public television network.

79. See http://pbskids.org/dontbuyit/.

80. See http://pbskids.org/dontbuyit/advertisingtricks/foodadtricks_burger2.html/.

81. Hill, "The Psychology of Rhetorical Images," 31.

82. Blair, "The Rhetoric of Visual Arguments," 51–52.

83. One might wonder if this omission suggests rhetoricians' general blindness toward computational media.

84. One could make additional claims about the relative vividness of different types of procedural interaction, for example screen-based applications as compared with augmented reality (AR), virtual reality (VR), or other forms. This is a valid question which I do not intend to address in the present context. That said, I do discuss physical interfaces in chapter 10, and the reader is referred there for more on this topic.

85. Hill, "The Psychology of Rhetorical Images," 33.

86. The spot is available online at http://www.pbs.org/30secondcandidate/timeline/years/1964b.html/.

87. See http://en.wikipedia.org/wiki/Daisy_(television_commercial)/.

88. Blair, "The Rhetoric of Visual Arguments," 52.

89. Ibid.

90. This does not imply that all procedural arguments are logically consistent, but merely that computationally implemented procedural arguments are assured to execute according to the particular logic a human author has imposed upon them.

91. Sherry Turkle, "Seeing through Computers," *American Prospect* 8, no. 31 (March 1997).

92. Maxis, *Sim City* (Alameda, Calif.: Brøderbund, 1989).

93. Bogost, *Unit Operations*, 106–109.

94. Http://www.thegrocerygame.com/.

95. This sample was collected in October 2003 from the game's old messageboard system at http://pub28.ezboard.com/bterisshoppinglist/. The site has since created a new board and purged these previous messages.

96. The mathematician Laplace devised a solution to Buffon's needle problem that provided an efficient means of estimating the value of π.

97. Chris Crawford, *Balance of the Planet* (Self-published, 1990).

98. Murray, *Hamlet on the Holodeck*, 128.

99. Ibid.

100. Ibid., 74.

101. Katie Salen and Eric Zimmerman, *Rules of Play: Game Design Fundamentals* (Cambridge, Mass.: MIT Press, 2004), 28.

102. Rockstar Games, *Grand Theft Auto III* (New York: Take Two Interactive, 2001).

103. Eric Qualls, "*Grand Theft Auto: San Andreas* (Review)" (GamesFirst, 2004 [cited March 2, 2006]); available from http://www.gamesfirst.com/index.php?id=188/.

104. Adam Woolcott, "*Grand Theft Auto* Retrospective" (Gaming Target, 2005 [cited March 1, 2006]); available from http://www.gamingtarget.com/article.php?artid=4739/.

105. Bogost, *Unit Operations*, 107.

106. Chris Crawford, *The Art of Interactive Design: A Euphonious and Illuminating Guide to Building Successful Software* (San Francisco: No Starch Press, 2002).

107. When I say "videogames," I mean to include non- or low-graphical procedural works like interactive fiction and text adventures.

108. Friedrich Kittler, "There Is No Software," in *Literature, Media, Information Systems*, ed. John Johnston (Amsterdam: Overseas Publishers Association, 1997).

109. Andrew Rollings and Ernest Adams, *Andrew Rollings and Ernest Adams on Game Design* (New York: New Riders, 2003), 200.

110. Bushnell, *Computer Space*.

111. Rollings and Adams, *Andrew Rollings and Ernest Adams on Game Design*, 46.

112. Geoffrey R. Loftus and Elizabeth F. Loftus, *Mind at Play: The Psychology of Video Games* (New York: Basic Books, 1983).

113. Shuen-shing Lee, "I Lose, Therefore I Think: A Search for Contemplation amid Wars of Push-Button Glare," *Game Studies* 3, no. 2 (2003).

114. We discuss this matter further in Ian Bogost and Gonzalo Frasca, "Videogames Go to Washington: the Story Behind Howard Dean's Videogame Propaganda," in *Second Person: Roleplaying and Story in Games and Playable Media*, ed. Pat Harrigan and Noah Wardrip-Fruin (Cambridge, Mass.: MIT Press, 2007), 233–246.

115. Alelo Inc. and USC Information Sciences Institute, *Tactical Iraqi* (Los Angeles: Tactical Language Training LLC, 2005).

116. Elizabeth Losh, "In Country with Tactical Iraqi: Trust, Identity, and Language Learning in a Military Video Game" (paper presented at the Digital Arts and Cultures Conference, IT University, Copenhagen, Denmark, December 1–4, 2005).

117. See http://www.watercoolergames.org/archives/000526.shtml#c7429/.

118. Republican National Committee, *Tax Invaders* (Washington, D.C.: RNC/gop.com, 2004); Taito, *Space Invaders* (Tokyo: Taito, 1978).

119. Ben Woodhouse and Martyn Williams, *Congo Jones and the Raiders of the Lost Bark* (London: The Rainforest Foundation, 2004).

120. Nintendo, *Super Mario Bros.* (Kyoto, Japan: Nintendo, 1985).

121. Banff Centre and Global Arcade, *P.o.N.G* (San Francisco: Global Arcade, 1999).

122. See http://www.globalarcade.org/pong/index.html/.

123. Dunhill Electronics, *Tax Avoiders* (American Videogame, 1982).

124. So reads the game's packaging and the cartridge label.

125. Some have observed that the mechanics of *Tax Avoiders* bear very close resemblance to those of the Atari 2600 title *Porky's*, based on the 1982 film of the same name. Dunhill Electronics created both games, although *Porky's* enjoyed much greater success, and perhaps understandably so. *Tax Avoiders* was the sole title released by American Videogame, which went bankrupt soon after its release, a victim of the so-called videogame crash of 1983. Bob Clark, *Porky's* (20th Century Fox, 1982); Dunhill Electronics, *Porky's* (Santa Clara, Calif.: Fox Video Games, 1983).

126. Brian Sutton-Smith, *The Ambiguity of Play* (Cambridge, Mass.: Harvard University Press, 1997), 8.

127. Katie Salen and Eric Zimmerman, *Rules of Play: Game Design Fundamentals* (Cambridge, Mass.: MIT Press, 2004).

128. Sutton-Smith, *The Ambiguity of Play*, 9–12.

129. Ibid.

130. Salen and Zimmerman, *Rules of Play*, 520.

131. I discuss ideology in more detail in the next section.

132. Salen and Zimmerman, *Rules of Play*.

133. Johan Huizinga, *Homo ludens* (New York: Beacon, 1955), 5.

134. Ibid.

135. Ibid., 8.

136. Ibid., 45.

137. Clark C. Abt, *Serious Games* (New York: Viking, 1970), 9.

138. Michael Schrage, *Serious Play: How the World's Best Companies Simulate to Innovate* (Cambridge, Mass.: Harvard Business School Press, 1999), 12–15.

139. The report in question is Ben Sawyer, "Serious Games: Improving Public Policy through Game-Based Learning and Simulation" (Washington, D.C.: Woodrow Wilson International Center for Scholars, 2002). The origin of the title was related to me in a personal communication with Ben Sawyer, March 31, 2006.

140. See http://www.seriousgames.org/.

141. See http://www.seriousgames.org/about2.html/.

142. See http://www.seriousgamessummit.com/home.html/. This messaging may change in the future, but it has been used for the last three Serious Games Summits,

one each per year held in Washington, D.C., in the fall and at the Game Developers Conference in the spring.

143. I have jokingly suggested that this particular use of *serious* must always be preceded by the informal vocative *dude*, as if to signal that the alternative, slang use of the term *serious* will follow. Cf. Stuart Moulthrop, "Taking Cyberculture Seriously" (paper presented at the Digital Arts and Culture Conference, ITU, Copenhagen, Denmark, December 1–4, 2005).

144. Alain Badiou, *Being and Event*, trans. Oliver Feltham (London and New York: Continuum, 2005), 25.

145. Ibid., 26.

146. Bogost, *Unit Operations*, 11–14.

147. Badiou, *Being and Event*, 95.

148. Ibid., 179.

149. See http://captology.stanford.edu/index.html#captologyOverview/.

150. B. J. Fogg, *Persuasive Technology: Using Computers to Change What We Think and Do* (San Francisco: Morgan Kauffman, 2003).

151. Ibid., 17.

152. Ibid., 33.

153. Ibid., 34.

154. Ibid., 37.

155. Ibid., 41.

156. Ibid., 44.

157. Ibid., 46.

158. Ibid., 49.

159. Ibid., 24.

160. Ibid.

161. Ibid., 51.

162. Bogost, *Unit Operations*, 55–64.

163. Jacques Derrida uses the term dissemination in his critique of Plato's preference of spoken to written discourse, arguing that centrality and authority elude meaning in all forms, whether textual, verbal, or otherwise. See "Plato's Pharmacy," in Jacques Derrida, *Dissemination*, trans. Barbara Johnson (Chicago: University of Chicago Press, 1981), 61–84.

164. Gonzalo Frasca, "Videogames of the Oppressed" (master's thesis, The Georgia Institute of Technology, 2001).

165. One form of this type of critical activity has been called "Software Studies," although much of this work still does not interrogate the cultural implications of computational systems through close readings of the software or hardware architectures that underlie them. For two good examples of the latter, see Brett Camper, "Reveling in Restrictions: Technical Mastery and Game Boy Advance Homebrew Software" (paper presented at the Digital Arts and Cultures 2005, IT University, Copenhagen, Denmark, December 1–3, 2005); Michael Mateas and Nick Montfort, "A Box, Darkly: Obfuscation, Weird Languages, and Code Aesthetics" (paper presented at the Digital Arts and Cultures 2005, IT University, Copenhagen, Denmark, December 1–3, 2005).

Chapter 2

1. 3D Pipeline Corporation, *BioChemFX* (La Jolla, Calif.: 3D Pipeline Corporation, 2003).

2. For another discussion of *BioChemFX*, see Bogost, *Unit Operations*, 98–99.

3. Mary Foster, "The Search for the Dead Is Renewed," *Louisiana Weekly*, March 6, 2006.

4. Select Bipartisan Committee to Investigate the Preparation for and Response to Hurricane Katrina, "A Failure of Initiative: The Final Report of the Select Bipartisan

Committee to Investigate the Preparation for and Response to Hurricane Katrina" (Washington, D.C.: U.S. House of Representatives, 2006), 1.

5. Ibid., 2, 87–97.

6. Ibid., 2–3, 131–146, 151–158.

7. Ibid., 3–4, 183–195, 241–260.

8. Ibid., 1.

9. Ibid.

10. The Committee was not tasked with recommendations: "We hope our findings will prompt the changes needed to make all levels of government better prepared and better able to respond the next time." Ibid., 359.

11. The Department of Homeland Security, "The Federal Response to Hurricane Katrina: Lessons Learned" (Washington, D.C.: The White House and the Department of Homeland Security, 2006), 36.

12. Select Bipartisan Committee to Investigate the Preparation for and Response to Hurricane Katrina, "A Failure of Initiative."

13. The Department of Homeland Security, "The Federal Response to Hurricane Katrina: Lessons Learned," 5.

14. For an interesting interpretation of the cause of the Chicago fire, see Richard F. Bales, *The Great Chicago Fire and the Myth of Mrs. O'Leary's Cow* (New York: McFarland, 2002).

15. Select Bipartisan Committee to Investigate the Preparation for and Response to Hurricane Katrina, "A Failure of Initiative," 359.

16. Ibid., 1.

17. Joan Walsh, "Flushing Out the Ugly Truth" (Salon.com, 2005 [cited November 12, 2005]); available from http://www.salon.com/opinion/feature/2005/09/01/katrina_race/index_np.html/.

18. Associated Press, "Video Shows Bush Warned before Katrina Hit," *CBS News*, March 2, 2006.

19. The fungus traveled westerly from Britain's southern port cities, from ships that had unknowingly carried it from the New World.

20. James T. Richardson, *Contending Liberalisms in World Politics* (Boulder, Colo.: Lynne Rienner Publishers, 2001), 34.

21. Ibid.

22. Ibid., 35.

23. *Plato: Complete Works*, 515a–516a.

24. Raymond Boudon, *The Analysis of Ideology* (Chicago: University of Chicago Press, 1989), 25.

25. Ibid.

26. Karl Marx, *Capital*, volume 1: *A Critique of Political Economy* trans. Ben Fowkes (New York: Penguin, 1992), 166–167. Translation modified.

27. Dialectic in the Hegelian and Marxist sense is different from the Platonic sense discussed in chapter 1. For Plato, dialectic is philosophical investigation, pursuit of truth through discourse and, especially for Socrates, dispute. For Hegel and Marx, dialectic is the process by which opposing ideas (a thesis and antithesis) combine and reconcile in a new unified whole (synthesis), which in turn becomes the thesis of a new dialectic. For Hegel, this process grounds historical progress.

28. Antonio Gramsci, *Selections from the Prison Notebooks*, trans. Quintin Hoare and Geoffrey Nowell-Smith (New York: International, 1971), 164–165, 183–185.

29. Louis Althusser, *Lenin and Philosophy and Other Essays*, trans. Ben Brewster (New York: Monthly Review, 1971), 145.

30. Ibid., 166.

31. Ibid., 175.

32. Michel Foucault, *The Archaeology of Knowledge*, trans. A. M. Sheridan Smith (New York: Pantheon, 1972), 117.

33. Slavoj Žižek, *The Sublime Object of Ideology* (New York: Verso, 1989), 21.

34. Badiou, *Being and Event*, 95.

35. Peter Hallward, *Badiou: A Subject to Truth* (Minneapolis: University of Minnesota Press, 2003), 96.

36. Modeling, Simulation, and Virtual Environments Institute (MOVES), *America's Army: Operations* (Washington, D.C.: U.S. Army, 2002).

37. Michael Zyda et al., "Entertainment R&D for Defense," *IEEE Computer Graphics and Applications* 23, no. 1 (2003): 28.

38. Ibid., 34.

39. Ibid., 28.

40. Valve, *Half-Life: Counter-Strike* (Bellevue, Wash.: Sierra Online, 2000).

41. Shenja van der Graaf and David B. Nieborg, "Together We Brand: America's Army" (paper presented at the Digital Games Research Conference, Utrecht, Netherlands, November 2003), 6.

42. Zyda et al., "Entertainment R&D for Defense," 29.

43. Ibid., 30.

44. Ibid.

45. Ibid.

46. Ibid., 29.

47. Van der Graaf and Nieborg, "Together We Brand," 8.

48. BreakAway Games, *A Force More Powerful* (Washington, D.C.: The International Center for Nonviolent Conflict, 2006).

49. Peter Ackerman and Jack DuVall, *A Force More Powerful* (New York: Palgrave Macmillan, 2001); Steve York, *A Force More Powerful* (PBS, 1999).

50. Gene Sharp, *Power and Struggle* (Boston: Porter Sargent, 1973).

51. Serbian Ministry of Information, "Microsoft Invests in Serbian Government's Electronic Initiatives" (Serbia Info, 2001 [cited 2005 May 3, 2005]); available from http://www.serbia-info.com/news/2001-06/08/23825.html/.

52. See http://www.aforcemorepowerful.org/game/index.php/.

53. See Gene Sharp, *Dynamics of Nonviolent Action* (Boston: Porter Sargent, 1973); Gene Sharp, *Methods of Nonviolent Action* (Boston: Porter Sargent, 1973); Sharp, *Power and Struggle*.

54. Roger Cohen, "Who Really Brought Down Milosevic?," *New York Times*, November 26, 2000.

55. Josh On, *Antiwargame* (San Francisco: Futurefarmers, 2001).

56. Lee, "I Lose, Therefore I Think."

57. Stef & Phil, *New York Defender* (Paris: Uzinagaz, 2002).

58. Gonzalo Frasca, *Kabul Kaboom* (Montevideo, Uruguay: Ludology.org, 2001).

59. Powerful Robot Games, *September 12* (Montevideo, Uruguay: Newsgaming.com, 2003).

60. Lee, "I Lose, Therefore I Think."

61. For example, cf. Greg Costikyan, "I Have No Words but I Must Design: Toward a Critical Vocabulary for Games" (paper presented at the Computer Games and Digital Cultures, Tampere, Finland, June 6–8, 2002).

62. Powerful Robot Games, *Madrid* (Montevideo, Uruguay: Newsgaming.com, 2004).

63. Such an interpretation was offered in the discussion of the game on the website for Grand Text Auto: http://grandtextauto.gatech.edu/2004/03/14/newsgamings-imadridi/.

64. Steve Beck, *Save the Whales* (Self-published, 2002).

65. See http://www.atariage.com/software_page.html?SoftwareLabelID=2059/.

66. Kaneko, *Socks the Cat Rocks the Hill* (1993), unpublished videogame.

67. See, for example, http://en.wikipedia.org/wiki/Socks_(cat)/.

68. Strategic Simulations Inc., *President Elect* (Sunnyvale, Calif.: Strategic Simulations Inc., 1988).

69. Randy Chase, *Power Politics* (Portland, Ore.: Cineplay Interactive, 1992).

70. Randy Chase, *The Doonesbury Election Game: Campaign '96*, (Novato, Calif.: Mindscape, 1996).

71. Stardock, *The Political Machine* (San Francisco: Ubisoft Entertainment, 2004).

72. Kellogg Creek Software, *Power Politics III* (Portland, Ore.: Kellogg Creek Software, 2004).

73. Eighty Dimensional Software, *President Forever* (Vancouver: Eighty Dimensional Software, 2004); Eighty Dimensional Software, *Prime Minister Forever* (Vancouver: Eighty Dimensional Software, 2005); Eighty Dimensional Software and Deutsches Institut für Public Affairs, *Chancellor Forever* (Vancouver: Eighty Dimensional Software, 2005).

74. Magic Lantern, *Frontrunner* (Monmouth, Ill.: Lantern Games, 2004).

75. Scott Hilyard, "New Video Game Mimics Race for the Oval Office," *USA Today*, April 23, 2004.

76. Brad Wardell, "Postmortem: Stardock's *The Political Machine*," *Game Developer*, October 11, 2004.

77. Alain Badiou, *Infinite Thought*, trans. Oliver Feltham and Justin Clemens (London and New York: Continuum, 2003), 73.

78. Persuasive Games, *The Howard Dean for Iowa Game* (Burlington, Vermont: Dean for America, 2003).

79. For more on the design of *The Howard Dean for Iowa Game* as well as depictions of the alternative designs, see Bogost and Frasca, "Videogames Go to Washington."

80. iTraffic, *Staffers Challenge* (New York: Discovery Channel, 2004); Steve Rosenbaum, *Staffers* (Discovery Channel, 2004).

81. Sorrent Games, *Bush vs. Kerry Boxing* (London: Sorrent Games, 2004); Sorrent Games, *Fox Sports Boxing* (London: Sorrent Games, 2004).

82. Michael D. Santos, Craig Leve, and Anthony R. Pratkanis, "Hey Buddy Can You Spare Seventeen Cents? Mindful Persuasion and Pique Technique," *Journal of Applied Social Psychology* 24 (1994). I discuss piques in more detail in chapter 7.

83. Blockdot, *White House Joust* (Dallas, Texas: Kewlbox.com, 2004).

84. "UN's Darfur Death Estimate Soars," *BBC News*, March 14, 2005.

85. See http://www.darfurisdying.com.

86. Susana Ruiz et al., *Darfur Is Dying* (New York: mtvU, 2006).

87. See http://www.darfurthesis.net.

88. Personal email from mtvU, May 23, 2006.

89. Ibid.

90. Julian Dibbell, "Game from Hell: Latest Plan to Save Sudan: Make a Video Game Dramatizing Darfur," *Village Voice*, February 13, 2005.

91. Gerard Prunier, *Darfur: The Ambiguous Genocide* (Ithaca: Cornell University Press, 2005).

92. Ibid., 124–128.

93. Diana Richards, *Political Complexity: Nonlinear Models of Politics* (Ann Arbor: University of Michigan Press, 2000), 8.

94. Ibid.

Chapter 3

1. Robert J. Vanderbei, "Election 2004 Results" (2004), http://www.princeton.edu/~rvdb/JAVA/election2004/.

2. Steve Schifferes, "Election Reveals Divided Nation," *BBC News*, November 3, 2004.

3. Peter Wallsten and Nick Anderson, "Democrats Map Out a Different Strategy," *Los Angeles Times*, November 6, 2004.

4. Steve Schifferes, "What next for the Democrats," *BBC News*, November 3, 2004.

5. Carla Marinucci, "In Postmortem on Kerry Bid, Dems Seek Clues to New Life," *San Francisco Chronicle*, November 7, 2004.

6. George Lakoff, *Women, Fire, and Dangerous Things* (Chicago: University of Chicago Press, 1990); George Lakoff and Mark Johnson, *Metaphors We Live By* (Chicago: University of Chicago Press, 1980).

7. George Lakoff, *Moral Politics: How Liberals and Conservatives Think* (Chicago: University of Chicago Press, 1996), 63.

8. George Lakoff, *Don't Think of an Elephant: Know Your Values and Frame the Debate—The Essential Guide for Progressives* (New York: Chelsea Green, 2004).

9. Frank I. Luntz, "The Environment: A Cleaner, Safer, Healthier America" (Luntz Research Companies, 2003), 131–135.

10. Frank I. Luntz, "Energy, Preparing for the Future" (Luntz Research Companies, 2002); Frank I. Luntz, "The Best and Worst Language of 2004: Key Debate Phrases" (Luntz Research Companies, 2004).

11. William Booth, "For Norton, a Party Mission," *Washington Post*, January 8, 2001.

12. Julie Cart, "Bush Opens Way for Counties and States to Claim Wilderness Roads," *Los Angeles Times*, January 21, 2003.

13. Chris Crawford, *Balance of Power* (Novato, Calif.: Mindscape, 1985).

14. Larry Barbu, *Crisis in the Kremlin* (Alameda, Calif.: Spectrum Holobyte, 1991).

15. Maxis, *Sim Earth* (Alameda, Calif.: Microprose, 1990).

16. Crawford, *Balance of the Planet*.

17. On, *Antiwargame*.

18. Josh Oda, *Bushgame: The Anti-Bush Online Adventure* (Allston, Mass.: Starvingeyes, 2004).

19. Persuasive Games, *The Howard Dean for Iowa Game*); Republican National Committee, *Tax Invaders*.

20. Persuasive Games, *Activism: The Public Policy Game* (Atlanta, Georgia: Persuasive Games, 2004).

21. Persuasive Games, *Take Back Illinois* (Atlanta, Georgia: Persuasive Games/Illinois House Republicans, 2004).

22. Powerful Robot Games, *Cambiemos* (Montevideo, Uruguay: Frente Amplio Nueva Mayoria/Powerful Robot Games, 2004).

23. Republican National Committee, *Tax Invaders*; Taito, *Space Invaders*.

24. Reuters, "Minister: Bush Must Be 'Shot Down,'" *CNN.com*, October 10, 2005, http://www.cnn.com/2005/WORLD/europe/09/08/germany.bush.reut/.

25. Lakoff, *Moral Politics: How Liberals and Conservatives Think*, 181.

26. Ibid., 189.

27. Chris Carter, *The X Files* (Fox, 1993).

28. H. G. Wells, *The War of the Worlds* (New York: Aerie, 1898; reprint, 2005).

29. Roland Emmerich (dir.), *Independence Day* (Fox, 1996).

30. See J. L. Austin, *How to Do Things with Words* (Cambridge, Mass.: Harvard University Press, 1962); John Searle, *Speech Acts: An Essay in the Philosophy of Language* (Cambridge: Cambridge University Press, 1969).

31. Martin Le Chevallier, *Vigilance 1.0* (Helsinki: Kiasma Museum, 2000).

32. Lakoff, *Moral Politics*, 44–45.

33. Ibid., 46.

34. Ibid., 61.

35. Ibid.

36. The panopticon is a prison building first conceived by Jeremy Bentham in which a guard could see the prisoners, but the prisoners could not detect if they were being observed or not. See Jeremy Bentham, *The Panopticon and Other Prison Writings* (London: Verso, 1995). Michel Foucault used the panopticon as an example of modern discipline as unseen observation, a theme explored in *Vigilance 1.0*; see Michel Foucault, *Discipline and Punish: The Birth of the Prison* (New York: Vintage, 1995), 209–216.

37. Rockstar Games, *Grand Theft Auto: San Andreas* (New York: Take Two Interactive, 2004).

38. Rockstar Games, *Grand Theft Auto III*; Rockstar Games, *Grand Theft Auto: Vice City* (New York: Take Two Interactive, 2003).

39. Howard Markel, "Fast Food, Obesity, and Hospitals," *Medscape Pediatrics* 5, no. 2 (2003). The reader is encouraged to test this claim in his or her own community. After a visit to the doctor, I walked through the nearby hospital lobby and indulged in a Chick-Fil-A meal, the only food being sold in the building I passed through.

40. Marion Nestle, *Food Politics: How the Food Industry Influences Nutrition and Health* (Berkeley, Calif.: University of California Press, 2002), 175.

41. Ibid., 231.

42. Morgan Spurlock (dir.), *Super Size Me* (Hard Sharp, 2004).

43. Lakoff, *Moral Politics*, 74.

44. Ibid.

45. Ibid., 116.

46. Ibid., 83.

47. Ibid., 75.

48. When eaten with the dressing it comes with, the salad totals nearly as many calories as a Big Mac. Some configurations of salad plus dressing even offer more grams of total fat than a Big Mac. See http://www.mcdonalds.com/app_controller.nutrition.index1.html.

49. For a discussion of the representation of urban space in *Grand Theft Auto*, see Ian Bogost and Daniel Klainbaum, "Presence and the Mediated Cities of *Grand Theft Auto*," in *The Meaning and Culture of Grand Theft Auto*, ed. Nathan Garrelts (Jefferson, N.C.: McFarland, 2006), 162–176.

50. Will Wright has demonstrated such a get-up on his *San Andreas* character. See Will Wright, "The Future of Content" (paper presented at The Game Developers Conference, San Francisco, 2005).

51. See Mateas and Stern, "A Behavior Language for Story-Based Believable Agents."

52. Lakoff, *Moral Politics*, 385.

53. Ibid., 387–388.

54. Lakoff, *Don't Think of an Elephant*, 33–34.

55. Michael Moore (dir.), *Fahrenheit 9/11* (Sony Pictures, 2004).

56. Madeline Smithberg and Lizz Winstead, *The Daily Show* (Comedy Central, 1996).

Chapter 4

1. See http://www.grassroots.com/, a paradigmatic case for marriages between Silicon Valley and Beltway interests.

2. Institute for Politics Democracy and the Internet (IPDI), "Post-Election 2000 Survey on Internet Use for Civics and Politics" (Washington, D.C.: IPDI, 2000).

3. Bruce A. Brimber and Richard Davis, *Campaigning Online: The Internet in U.S. Elections* (New York and Oxford: Oxford University Press, 2003).

4. Michael Cornfield, "Commentary on the Impact of the Internet on the 2004 Election" (Pew Internet and American Life Project, March 6, 2005 [cited March 23, 2005]); available from http://www.pewinternet.org/PPF/r/151/report_display.asp/.

5. Ibid.

6. Far from being relegated to the world of politics, MeetUp.com supports communities of almost every kind, from pug owners to anime fans.

7. See http://www.friendster.com and http://www.myspace.com/.

8. See http://www.linkedin.com. LinkedIn was founded by former PayPal EVP Reid Hoffman. PayPal was an early innovator in person-to-person networks for ad hoc financial transactions. The company was acquired by eBay in 2002. LinkedIn and PayPal serve different functions, but both attempt to facilitate ad hoc person-to-person transactions.

9. See http://www.spritofamerica.net/.

10. Despite the popularity of this term among political cyberpundits, *emergence* is an imprecise way to characterize ad hoc person-to-person networking. The term is adapted from its use in complex systems theory, where it refers to coherent structures and patterns that come from small-scale interactions over time. An often-cited example of emergent systems is the ant colony, in which each ant acts in accordance with its own surroundings rather than receiving commands from some centralized source.

11. John Berry and Ed Keller, *The Influentials: One American in Ten Tells the Other Nine How to Vote, Where to Eat, and What to Buy* (New York: Free Press, 2003); Institute for

Politics Democracy and the Internet (IPDI), "Political Influentials Online in the 2004 Presidential Campaign" (Washington, D.C.: IPDI, 2004).

12. Firaxis Games, *Civilization* (Paris: Infogrames, 1991).

13. Stainless Steel Studios, *Empire Earth* (Burbank, Calif.: Sierra Studios, 2001).

14. Impressions Games, *Zeus: Master of Olympus* (Burbank, Calif.: Sierra Studios, 2000).

15. Creative Assembly, *Medieval: Total War* (Los Angeles: Activision, 2002).

16. Kurt Squire, "Replaying History: Learning World History trough Playing Civilization" (dissertation, Indiana University, 2004), 247–261.

17. Ibid., 116–117.

18. Anne-Marie Schleiner, *Velvet-Strike*, 2002.

19. Chris Crawford, *Chris Crawford on Game Design* (New York: New Riders, 2003), 383.

20. DreamWorks Interactive, *Medal of Honor* (Redwood Shores, Calif.: Electronic Arts, 1999).

21. Electronic Arts, *Medal of Honor: Rising Sun* (Redwood City, Calif.: Electronic Arts, 2003).

22. C-level (Mark Allen, Peter Brinson, Brody Condon, Jessica Hutchins, Eddo Stern, and Michael Wilson), *Waco Resurrection* (Los Angeles: C-Level, 2003).

23. Kinematic, *9–11 Survivor* (Kinematic.com, 2003).

24. Kuma Reality Games, *Kuma\War* (New York: Kuma Reality Games, 2003).

25. Traffic Games, *JFK Reloaded* (Edinburgh, Scotland: Traffic Games, 2004).

26. Tracy Fullerton, "'Documentary' Games: Putting the Player in the Path of History" (paper presented at the Playing the Past: Nostalgia in Video Games and Electronic Literature, The University of Florida, Gainesville, Florida, 2005).

27. Ubisoft Montreal Studios, *Tom Clancy's Splinter Cell: Chaos Theory* (San Francisco: Ubisoft Entertainment, 2005).

28. One conspiracy theory even suggests that Greer himself might have fired the fatal shot. See http://community-2.webtv.net/Larry762/fontcolor3300FF/page4.html for a typical explanation.

29. The Teamsters Union leader didn't disappear until 1975, more than ten years after Kennedy's assassination. However, the Kennedy administration in particular saw Republican-tied Hoffa as both a racketeer and a political threat, and it attempted to disrupt the Teamsters both through direct action and through support of the rival AFL-CIO.

30. Persuasive Games, *The Howard Dean for Iowa Game.*

31. See Ian Bogost, "Asynchronous Multiplay: Futures for Casual Multiplayer Experience" (paper presented at the Other Players Conference on Multiplayer Phenomena, Copenhagen, Denmark, December 1–3, 2004).

32. Bogost and Frasca, "Videogames Go to Washington."

33. See http://www.popmatters.com/multimedia/reviews/d/dean-for-iowa-game.shtml.

34. Persuasive Games, *Take Back Illinois.*

35. James Paul Gee, *What Video Games Have to Teach Us about Learning and Literacy* (New York: Palgrave Macmillan, 2003), 24.

Chapter 5

1. Frank Presbrey, *The History and Development of Advertising* (New York: Doubleday, 1929), 1–2.

2. J. R. Hulbert, "Some Medieval Advertisements of Rome," *Modern Philology* 20, no. 4 (1923): 403.

3. Raymond Williams, *Problems in Materialism and Culture: Selected Essays* (London: Verso, 1980), 170.

4. James B. Twitchell, "Bur First, a Word from Our Sponsor," *Wilson Quarterly* 20, no. 3 (1996): 68.

5. Ibid., 68–69.

6. Ibid., 70

7. See http://www.yaya.com/why/index_why.html/.

8. Jane Chen and Matthew Ringel, "Can Advergaming Be the Future of Interactive Advertising?" in *<kpe> Fast Forward* (Los Angeles: <kpe>, 2001). <kpe> was bought by Agency.com in 2002 and their website summarily vanished. Various archive copies can be found online; as of early 2006, a version was available at http://www.locz.com.br/loczgames/advergames.pdf./

9. See http://www.blockdot.com/.

10. See http://www.skyworks.com/.

11. Fredric Jameson, *Postmodernism, or the Cultural Logic of Late Capitalism* (Durham: Duke University Press, 1991).

12. Jean Baudrillard, *Selected Writings*, ed. Mark Poster (Palo Alto, Calif.: Stanford University Press, 1988).

13. Deborah Solomon, "Continental Drift: An Interview with Jean Baudrillard," *New York Times*, November 20, 2005.

14. Sulake, *Virtual Magic Kingdom* (Burbank, Calif.: Disney, 2005).

15. T. L. Stanley, "Disney Hopes Virtual Park Delivers Real-World Results," *AdAge*, January 3, 2005. Also see Michael McCarthy, "Disney Plans to Mix Ads, Video Games to Target Kids, Teens," *USA Today*, January 17, 2005.

16. Claude S. Fischer, "Succumbing to Consumerism? Underlying Models in the Historical Claim" (paper presented at the American Sociological Association Conference, Atlanta, Georgia, 2003).

17. Baudrillard, *Selected Writings*, 48.

18. Donald N. McCloskey, "The Economics of Choice," in *Economics for Historians*, ed. Thomas G. Rawski and Susan B. Carter (Berkeley, Calif.: University of California Press, 1996), 150.

19. Seth Godin, *All Marketers Are Liars: The Power of Telling Authentic Stories in a Low-Trust World* (New York: Penguin, 2005), 19.

20. Ibid., 47.

21. Seth Godin, *Permission Marketing: Turning Strangers into Friends and Friends into Customers* (New York: Simon and Schuster, 1999), 23–24.

22. Godin, *All Marketers Are Liars*, 140.

23. Or more precisely, the viewer can then speed through the ads using rapid digital fast-forward.

24. Frank Rose, "The Lost Boys," *Wired* 12:08 (2004).

25. Richard W. Lewis, *Absolut Book: The Absolut Vodka Advertising Story* (North Clarendon, Vermont: Tuttle Publishing, 1996); Judith Rosen, "Is Tuttle Ready for Fall? Absolutely," *Publishers Weekly*, August 1, 2005. The sales figure appears in the Rosen article, which also announces Tuttle's plans for a 100,000 copy first run of the sequel, Richard W. Lewis, *Absolut Sequel: The Absolut Advertising Campaign Continues* (North Clarendon, Vermont: Tuttle Publishing, 2005).

26. Marguerite Reardon, "NFL to Re-air Super Bowl Commercials" (CNet, 2006 [cited February 10 2006]); available from http://news.com.com/2100-1024_3-6033515.html/.

27. See, for example, http://www.photoshoplab.com/tutorial_Make-Your-Own-iPod-style-Photo.html/.

28. Rose, "The Lost Boys."

29. Godin, *All Marketers Are Liars*, 34, 36.

30. EA Canada, *SSX 3* (Redwood Shores, Calif.: Electronic Arts, 2003).

31. Paul Milgrom and John Roberts, "Relying on the Information of Interested Parties," *Rand Journal of Economics* 17 (1986).

32. Luca Lambertini and Marco Trombetta, "Delegation and Firms' Ability to Collude" (Copenhagen, Denmark: University of Copenhagen/Department of Accounting and Finance, LSE, 1997).

33. Gerard R. Butters, "Equilibrium Distributions of Sales and Advertising Prices," *Review of Economic Studies* 44, no. 3 (1977).

34. Gary S. Becker and Kevin M. Murphy, "A Simple Theory of Advertising as a Good or Bad," *Quarterly Journal of Economics* November (1993); Avinash Dixit and Victor Norman, "Advertising and Welfare," *Bell Journal of Economics* 9 (1978).

35. Bryan Peterson, *Understanding Exposure*, revised edition (New York: Amphoto, 2004), 80–81.

36. Richard E. Kihlstrom and Michael H. Riordan, "Advertising as a Signal," *Journal of Political Economy* 92, no. 3 (1984); Paul Milgrom and John Roberts, "Price and Advertising Signals of Product Quality," *Journal of Political Economy* 94, no. 796–821 (1986).

37. See, for example, Ronald D. Michman, *Lifestyle Marketing: Reaching the New American Consumer* (New York: Praeger, 2003).

38. Ibid., 1–2.

39. Chen and Ringel, "Can Advergaming Be the Future of Interactive Advertising?," 3.

40. Ibid.

41. Ibid., 4.

42. Ibid.

43. Ibid.

44. Ibid.

45. See http://www.postopia.com/.

46. See http://www.candystand.com/. Since the site opened, Kraft sold its Life Savers and Altoids business units to Wrigley in 2004, and now the site is owned and maintained by the Wm. Wrigley Jr. Co.

47. See http://www.skyworks.com/.

48. Groove Alliance, *Mountain Dew Skateboarding* (Somers, N.Y.: PepsiCo, 2003).

49. Zach Whalen, "Product Placement and Virtual Branding in Video Games" (Gameology.com, 2003 [cited April 30 2006]); available from http://www.gameology.org/node/121/.

50. Namco, *Pac-Man* (Chicago: Midway Games, 1980).

51. Kaneko, *Chester Cheetah: Too Cool to Fool* (Dallas, Texas: Recot, 1992).

52. Whalen, *Product Placement and Virtual Branding in Video Games.*

53. Bally/Midway, *Tron* (Chicago: Bally/Midway, 1982).

54. Atari, *E.T.* (Sunnyvale, Calif.: Atari, 1982).

55. M Network, *Kool-Aid Man* (El Segundo, Calif.: Mattel, 1982).

56. Rose, "The Lost Boys."

57. Tim Gnatek, "Just for Fun, Casual Games Thrive Online," *New York Times,* February 23, 2006; David Kushner, "The Wrinkled Future of Online Gaming," *Wired* 12:06 (2004).

58. Astraware Limited, *Bejeweled* (Seattle, Wash.: PopCap Games, 2000). A different version of the original *Bejeweled* went by the name *Diamond Mine.*

59. Blockdot, *Ms. Match* (Dallas, Texas: Kewlbox.com, 2005).

60. Fuji Electronics, *Sporstron S3300 Coca-Cola* (Tokyo: Fuji Electronics, 1978).

61. The Pepsi Nintendo DS was available only in the Japanese market. Both the DS and the Coca-Cola GameGear are highly sought-after collectibles.

62. SEGA, *Coca Cola Kid* (Tokyo: SEGA Entertainment, 1994).

63. Virgin Games, *M.C. Kids* (London: Virgin Games, 1992). According to one of the developers, McDonald's apparently didn't like the final product and refused to promote it in-store. See http://greggman.com/games/mckids.htm/.

64. I originally culled and reformatted these claims based on the "Why Games?" page of advergame consultant YaYa Media's website, circa 2002 (http://www.yaya.com/why/index_why.html/). They were presented in this form in Ian Bogost, "Persuasive Games: Play in Advocacy and Pedagogy" (paper presented at the Cyberspace @ UCLA Symposium on Playing, Gaming, and Learning, Los Angeles, October 23, 2003). Since then, I have found the list adopted by another advergame consultant, Wright Games, in a similar "why games" webpage on their corporate website, http://www.wrightstrategies.com/wrightgames/why_brand.asp/.

65. See http://www.kewlbox.com/.

66. See http://www.massiveincorporated.com/.

67. See http://www.doublefusion.com/.

68. See http://www.ingameadvertising.com/.

69. Kevin Newcomb, "Massive Scores $10 Million," *ClickZ News*, January 19, 2005. Also see http://www.prnewswire.co.uk/cgi/release?id=157815/; http://www.prnewswire.co.uk/cgi/release?id=157815/.

70. Kris Graft, "Microsoft Acquisition a Sign of Ad Revenue," *Business Week*, April 28, 2006.

71. See http://www.doublefusion.com. This statement was current as of February 2006.

72. Ibid.

73. Funcom, *Anarchy Online* (Durham, N.C.: Funcom, 2001).

74. Irrational Games, *SWAT 4* (Bellevue, Wash.: Sierra Entertainment, 2005).

75. Ubisoft Montreal Studios, *Tom Clancy's Splinter Cell: Chaos Theory*.

76. See http://www.doublefusion.com/. These examples were accurate as of February 2006.

77. James Brightman, "In-Game Ads Evolving, Becoming More Effective," *GameDaily*, October 17, 2005.

78. See http://games.slashdot.org/comments.pl?sid=176151&cid=14636210/.

79. Valve, *Half-Life: Counter-Strike*.

80. Dyslexia (pseudonym), *Ad-Nauseam?* (February 3, 2006 [cited February 6, 2006]); available from http://www.mlgpro.com/news/Ad-Nauseam%253F/1.html/.

81. Brendan Sinclair, "Study Suggests In-game Ads a Win-Win Proposition," *Gamespot*, December 5, 2005.

82. Isabella M. Chaney, Ku-Ho Lin, and James Chaney, "The Effect of Billboards with the Gaming Environment," *Journal of Interactive Advertising* 5, no. 1 (2004).

83. Namco, *Pole Position* (Sunnyvale, Calif.: Atari, 1983).

84. Namco, *Dig Dug* (Sunnyvale, Calif.: Atari, 1982).

85. Rockstar Games, *Grand Theft Auto: San Andreas*.

86. Ubisoft Paris Studios, *XIII* (San Francisco: Ubisoft Entertainment, 2003). Admittedly, *XIII* uses cel-shaded (cartoon-style) graphics, and so photorealism is not part of the game's expressive goals. I am indebted to Zach Whalen for this example.

87. Rockstar Games, *Grand Theft Auto: Vice City*.

88. David McNally (dir.), *Coyote Ugly* (Touchstone, 2000).

89. Reena Jana, "Is That a Video Game—Or an Ad?," *Business Week*, January 26, 2006.

90. See http://www.more-public-toilets-ny.org/.

91. For images from this campaign, see http://leighhouse.typepad.com/advergirl/2006/02/why_we_love_pro.html/.

92. For images from this campaign which also won an Epica award, see http://www.epica-awards.com/epica/2004/winners/cat31.htm/.

93. For images from this campaign, see http://garicruze.typepad.com/ad_blather/2006/02/fedex.html/.

94. Chris Isidore, "Signs of the Times," *CNN Money*, May 7, 2004.

Chapter 6

1. Robert Levine, "Video Games Struggle to Find the Next Level," *New York Times*, May 8, 2006.

2. Chris Morris, "EA's Big Deal: Touchdown or Fumble?," *CNN Money*, December 14, 2004.

3. Namco, *Pac-Man*.

4. Williams Entertainment, *Joust* (Chicago: Midway Games, 1982).

5. Data East, *BurgerTime* (Chicago: Midway Games, 1982).

6. Namco, *Pole Position*.

7. Namco, *Dig Dug*.

8. Atari, *E.T.*

9. Richard Ow, "Harnessing Hollywood," *License!*, June 1, 2004.

10. Ibid.

11. Admittedly, the *Harry Potter* games have improved in players' and critics' eyes since the first title.

12. Electronic Arts, *Harry Potter and the Chamber of Secrets* (Redwood City, Calif.: Electronic Arts, 2002); Electronic Arts, *Harry Potter and the Goblet of Fire* (Redwood City, Calif.: Electronic Arts, 2005); Electronic Arts, *Harry Potter and the Prisoner of Azkaban* (Redwood City, Calif.: Electronic Arts, 2005); Electronic Arts, *Harry Potter and the Sorcerer's Stone* (Redwood City, Calif.: Electronic Arts, 2001); Electronic Arts, *Harry Potter: Quidditch World Cup* (Redwood City, Calif.: Electronic Arts, 2003); Electronic Arts, *LEGO Creator: Harry Potter and the Chamber of Secrets* (Redwood City, Calif.: Electronic Arts, 2002).

13. In the fourth game, *Harry Potter and the Goblet of Fire*, this isn't the case. Collectible beans replenish magic and stamina, and collector's cards can be equipped on characters to give them special abilities. Although the new features probably enhance the experience, they make a less powerful statement about the nature of licensed products.

14. Anna Gunder, "As If by Magic: On Harry Potter as a Novel and Computer Game" (paper presented at the Digital Games Research Association [DiGRA] Conference, Utrecht, the Netherlands, November 2003).

15. Electronic Arts, *Harry Potter: Quidditch World Cup*.

16. Steven Waldman, "No Wizard Left Behind," *Slate*, March 18, 2004.

17. J. K. Rowling, *Harry Potter and the Philosopher's Stone* (London: Bloomsbury Press, 1997); J. K. Rowling, *Harry Potter and the Sorcerer's Stone* (New York: Scholastic, 1999).

18. Maxis, *Sim City*.

19. Holistic Design, *Mall Tycoon* (New York: Take-Two Interactive, 2002).

20. Jaleco Entertainment, *Trailer Park Tycoon* (Buffalo, N.Y.: Jaleco Entertainment, 2002).

21. Software 2000, *Fast Food Tycoon* (Santa Monica, Calif.: Activision Value Publishing, 2000).

22. Chris Sawyer Productions, *Transport Tycoon* (Hunt Valley, Maryland: Microprose, 1994).

23. Microprose, *Sid Meier's Railroad Tycoon* (Hunt Valley, Maryland: Microprose, 1991).

24. The two most notable mainstream successes have been *Roller Coaster Tycoon* and *Zoo Tycoon*. Blue Fang Games, *Zoo Tycoon* (Redmond, Wash.: Microsoft Game Studios, 2001); Chris Sawyer Productions, *RollerCoaster Tycoon* (Hunt Valley, Maryland: Microprose, 1999).

25. Artex Software, *Carnival Cruise Lines Tycoon* (Santa Monica, Calif.: Activision Value Publishing, 2005); Cat Daddy Games, *Cruise Ship Tycoon* (Santa Monica, Calif.: Activision Value Publishing, 2003).

26. Bullfrog Productions, *Theme Park* (Redwood City, Calif.: Electronic Arts, 1994); Deep Red Games, *SeaWorld Adventure Parks Tycoon* (Santa Monica, Calif.: Activision Value Publishing, 2003).

27. Bold Games, *John Deere American Farmer* (Mississauga, Ontario, Canada: Global Star Software, 2004).

28. Activision, *Caterpillar Construction Tycoon* (Santa Monica, Calif.: Activision Value Publishing, 2005).

29. PlayerThree and DeepEnd, *WFP Food Force* (Rome: World Food Programme, 2005).

30. Cyberlore, *Playboy: The Mansion* (Toronto, Ontario, Canada: Groove Games, 2005).

31. Success, *Yoshinoya* (Tokyo: Success, 2004).

32. Dorasu, *Curry House CoCo Ichibanya: Kyo mo Genki da! Curry ga Umai!* (Tokyo: Dorasu, 2004). The game's full title translates to English as: *Curry House CoCo Ichibanya: Today I am energetic again! The curry is fantastic!*

33. Frank Capra (dir.), *It Happened One Night* (Columbia, 1934).

34. See http://www.imdb.com/title/tt0025316/trivia/.

35. Vera Caspary, *Laura* (New York: The Feminist Press at CUNY, 1943; reprint, 2005); Otto Preminger (dir.), *Laura* (Fox, 1944).

36. Michael Curtiz (dir.), *Mildred Pierce* (Warner Brothers, 1945).

37. Hal Needham (dir.), *Smokey and the Bandit* (Universal Pictures, 1977).

38. Steven Spielberg (dir.), *E.T.: The Extra Terrestrial* (Universal Studios, 1982).

39. See http://www.imdb.com/title/tt0083866/trivia/.

40. Martin Campbell (dir.), *GoldenEye* (MGM, 1995).

41. Robert Cochran and Joel Surnow, *24* (ABC, 2001–).

42. Lawrence Trilling and J. J. Abrams, *Blowback* (season 3, episode 14) (ABC, 2004).

43. Quentin Tarantino (dir.), *Four Rooms* (Miramax, 1995); Quentin Tarantino (dir.), *From Dusk Til Dawn* (Dimension, 1996); Quentin Tarantino (dir.), *Kill Bill, Vol. 1* (Miramax, 2003); Quentin Tarantino (dir.), *Pulp Fiction* (Miramax, 1994); Quentin Tarantino (dir.), *Reservoir Dogs* (Live/Artisan, 1992).

44. David Foster Wallace, *Infinite Jest* (New York: Back Bay, 1997), 15, 35, 53.

45. Steven Spielberg (dir.), *Minority Report* (DreamWorks, 2002).

46. Anonymous, "Lexus Concepts Star in Spielberg's Minority Report" (2002 [cited January 2 2006]); available from http://www.cardesignnews.com/news/2002/020724minority-report/.

47. Mark Burnett et al., *The Restaurant* (NBC, 2003).

48. EA Canada, *SSX 3* (Redwood City, Calif.: Electronic Arts, 2003).

49. Neversoft, *Tony Hawk Pro Skater 3* (Santa Monica, Calif.: Activision, 2003).

50. Amusement Vision, *Super Monkey Ball 2* (Tokyo: SEGA Entertainment, 2002).

51. Ryan Vance, *Ads in Games: Who's Buying?* (G4TV, 2002 [cited November 10, 2003]); available from http://www.g4tv.com/techtvvault/features/36254/Ads_in_Games_Whos_Buying.html/.

52. EA Canada, *Fight Night Round 3* (Redwood City, Calif.: Electronic Arts, 2006).

53. See http://forum.xbox365.com/ubb-data/ultimatebb.php?/ubb/get_topic/f/66/t/003409/p/2/.

54. See http://www.subservientchicken.com. The subservient chicken is an Internet-based application that allows the player to "control" a video image of a man in a chicken suit by typing simple commands like "eat," "die," "strip," or "read." It is an example of so-called viral marketing, an attempt to create brand discourse through furtive, advertiser-seeded subculture discourse.

55. Namco, *Pole Position*; SEGA, *Turbo* (Tokyo: SEGA Entertainment, 1981).

56. Polyphony Digital, *Gran Turismo* (Tokyo: SCIE, 1997).

57. Maxis, *The Sims Online* (Redwood Shores, Calif.: Electronic Arts, 2002).

58. Maxis, *The Sims* (Redwood Shores, Calif.: Electronic Arts, 2000).

59. Jana, "Is That a Video Game—Or an Ad?" The *Sims Online* objects were later released as downloads for the single-player game.

60. Ubisoft Annecy Studios and Ubisoft Shanghai Studios, *Tom Clancy's Splinter Cell: Pandora Tomorrow* (San Francisco: Ubisoft Entertainment, 2004).

61. Andy Wachowski and Larry Wachowski (dir.), *The Matrix* (Warner Bros., 1999). The sliding-face Nokia phone Neo receives in the second scene was the subject of considerable gadget lust among the film's fans.

62. Mark Burnett, *The Apprentice* (ABC, 2004–).

Chapter 7

1. Jana, "Is That a Video Game—Or an Ad?"

2. For more on the history of fan fiction, including considerable discussion of *Star Trek*, see Henry Jenkins, *Textual Poachers; Television Fans and Participatory Culture* (London and New York: Routledge, 1992).

3. Paul Bartel (dir.), *Death Race 2000* (New World Pictures, 1975); Exidy, *Death Race* (Sunnyvale, Calif.: Exidy Systems, 1976). The videogame has the distinction of becoming the first title to be pulled from the market after complaints about violence. It's a humbling story from our contemporary perspective; the game challenged two players to run over as many pixilated people as possible.

4. Atari, *Night Driver* (Sunnyvale, Calif.: Atari, 1976), Midway, *Datsun 280 Zzzap* (Chicago: Midway Games, 1976). *Night Driver* was released for the Atari VCS 2600 in 1979, and the Commodore64 in 1982.

5. DSD/Camelot, *Tooth Protectors* (New Brunswick, N.J.: Johnson and Johnson, 1983).

6. As a result, *Tooth Protectors* is a very rare title, highly sought after by collectors.

7. See, for example, http://www.atariage.com/software_page.html?SoftwareLabelID=76/.

8. D. B. Weiss, *Lucky Wander Boy* (New York: Plume, 2003).

9. Singularity Design, *Fiskars Prune to Win* (Madison, Wisc.: Fiskars Brands, 2005).

10. Sensodyne, *Sensodyne Food Fear Challenge* (Philadelphia: GlaxoSmithKline, 2005).

11. Spurlock, *Super Size Me*.

12. Namco, *Pac-Man*; SuperSizeMe.com, *Burger Man* (New York: The Con, 2004).

13. See http://www.supersizeme.com/home.aspx?page=aboutmovie/.

14. Agency.com, *Agency.com Snowball Fight* (New York: Agency.com, 2005).

15. The game can be found at http://www.mtbireland.com/dodge.html/; Mountain Bike Ireland's website is at http://www.mtbireland.com/. As of early 2006, the game page looks quite different than it did when Berger (and I) first viewed it; it now sports a banner ad and some commentary about the game; the direct link to Mountain Bike Ireland has been removed, which rather changes the experience.

16. Murray, *Hamlet on the Holodeck*, 143–144.

17. Moroch Partners, *Shark Bait* (Oak Brook, Ill.: McDonald's, 2006).

18. From commentary by AdLand, http://ad-rag.com/127922.php/.

19. Microsoft, *Volvo Drive for Life* (Göthenberg, Sweden: Volvo, 2005).

20. Stuart Elliott, "Grand Theft Auto? No, Make Mine Volvo," *New York Times*, November 11, 2005.

21. For example, Volvo maintains a "Volvo Saved My Life Club" photo gallery on its website, at http://www.volvocars.us/_Tier2/WhyVolvo/Safety/Volvo_Saved_My_Life_Club_Photo_Album.htm.

22. Judith Williamson, *Decoding Advertisements: Ideology and Meaning in Advertising* (London: Marion Boyers, 1978; reprint, 2002), 75.

23. Ibid., 77.

24. WildTangent, *Dodge Stow 'n Go Challenge* (Detroit, Mich.: DaimlerChrysler Corporation, 2005).

25. See http://chrysler.homefieldgames.com/chryslersng/htdocs/stowngo.aspx/.

26. Persuasive Games, *Xtreme Errands* (Detroit, Mich.: DaimlerChrysler, 2005).

27. Intelligent Systems Co., *Advance Wars* (Redmond, Wash.: Nintendo of America, 2001).

28. Bogost, *Unit Operations*, 134–135.

29. See http://www.ameribev.org/about/industrybasics.asp/. Coke's internal use of the "TLI" acronym may be apocryphal, but the term seems to have gained general use in the trade.

30. M Network, *Kool-Aid Man* (Hawthorne, Calif.: Mattel Electronics, 1983).

31. The flyer was used in both in-store promotions and as a print advertisement. The copy I have is a full-page ad from a copy of the comic book *The Fantastic Four*.

32. Despite ongoing speculation about the poison taken by members of the People's Temple cult, historians disagree on whether the grape-flavored drink its members used to deliver the potassium cyanide was in fact Kool-Aid, Flavorade, or yet some other powder-and-sugar drink mix.

33. The creation of two totally different games for the two consoles was very unusual. Mattel's engineers argued for different designs to take advantage of each platform's strengths, while its marketers wanted consistency across the platforms. In the end, the marketers won, and later Mattel games—as well as contemporary games—strive for identical gameplay across myriad platforms.

34. Perfect Fools, *Coca-Cola Nordic Christmas* (Atlanta, Georgia.: Coca-Cola Company, 2004).

35. And perhaps unfortunately so, as this book hopes to demonstrate.

36. Jennifer Privateer, "A Personal Account from Bioneers 2002," *Natural Products and Organic Food*, January 2003.

37. Framfab, bone, and FHV/bbdo, *Pickwick Afternoon* (Utrecht, the Netherlands: Pickwick Tea/Sara Lee International, 2005).

38. Bally/Midway, *Tapper* (Chicago: Bally/Midway, 1983).

39. Atari, *Pong*.

40. See http://www.britvic.com/retail/Brands/J2O/default.htm/.

41. Graphico, *J$_2$O Toilet Training Game* (Chelmsford: Britvic, 2003).

42. The game only depicts a male point of view. Although the player selects a gender at the start of the game via toilet-door style iconography, women are forced to take the role of men to play the game.

43. Williamson, *Decoding Advertisements*, 65.

44. Robert B. Cialdini and David A. Schroeder, "Increasing Compliance by Legitimizing Paltry Contributions: When Even a Penny Helps," *Journal of Personality and Social Psychology* 34, no. 4 (1976); Anthony Pratkanis and Elliot Aronson, *Age of Propaganda: The Everyday Use and Abuse of Persuasion* (New York: W. H. Freeman, 2001); Santos, Leve, and Pratkanis, "Hey Buddy Can You Spare Seventeen Cents?"

45. Pratkanis and Aronson, *Age of Propaganda*, 12.

46. Ibid., 355.

47. Naomi Klein, *No Logo: Taking Aim at the Brand Bullies* (New York: Picador, 2000); Pratkanis and Aronson, *Age of Propaganda*.

48. Juliet B. Schor, *Born to Buy* (New York: Scribner, 2004), 19.

49. Alyssa Quart, *Branded: The Buying and Selling of Teenagers* (New York: Basic Books, 2004).

50. Ibid., 103.

51. I first used this term to describe the game *Disaffected!*, which my studio released in January 2006, and which is discussed below.

52. Tony Walsh, *Big Mac Attacked* (2002 [cited December 12, 2004]); available from http://www.alternet.org/story/14530/.

53. See http://nationalcheeseemporium.org/.

54. Forterra Systems, *There.com* (San Mateo, Calif.: Makena Technologies, 2003–).

55. Tobi Elkin, "Nike, Levi Strauss Test Virtual World Marketing," *Advertising Age*, October 27, 2003.

56. Betsy Book, *Virtual World Business Brands: Entrepreneurship and Identity in Massively Multiplayer Online Gaming Environments* (2005 [cited June 15, 2005]); available from http://ssrn.com/abstract=736823/.

57. Adam Cadre et al., *Coke Is It!*, 1999.

58. Nick Montfort, *Book and Volume*, (Philadelphia: Auto Mata, 2005).

59. Shawn McGough, *Melting Mitsubishi* (self-published, 2003).

60. Atari, *Missile Command* (Sunnyvale, Calif.: Atari, 1980).

61. Andre Allen and Bill Berner, *Chappelle's Show* (Comedy Central, 2003).

62. Powerful Robot Games, *September 12*.

Chapter 8

1. Edward Thorndike, *Educational Psychology: The Psychology of Learning* (New York: Teachers College Press, 1913).

2. B. F. Skinner, *The Technology of Teaching* (New York: Appleton Century Crofts, 1968).

3. G. E. Zuriff, *Behaviorism: A Conceptual Reconstruction* (New York: Columbia University Press, 1985), 1.

4. Charles J. Brainerd, *Piaget's Theory of Intelligence* (New York: Prentice Hall, 1978).

5. See, for example, Jerome Bruner, *Going Beyond the Information Given* (New York: W. W. Norton, 1973).

6. John Dewey, *How We Think* (New York: Dover, 1997).

7. Lev Semenovich Vygotsky, *Mind in Society* (Cambridge, Mass.: Harvard University Press, 1978), 55–58.

8. Jean Lave and Etienne Wenger, *Situated Learning: Legitimate Peripheral Participation* (Cambridge: Cambridge University Press, 1991), 29–31.

9. James K. Doyle, "The Cognitive Psychology of Systems Thinking," *System Dynamics Review* 13, no. 3 (1997): 253.

10. Ibid., 254.

11. Edith Ackermann, *Piaget's Constructivism, Papert's Constructionism: What's the Difference?* (2001 [cited February 10, 2006]); available from http://learning.media.mit.edu/content/publications/EA Piaget%20_%20Papert.pdf/.

12. This oversimplification excludes, for example, nativism, the epistemological position that people are born with knowledge, but that such knowledge must be coaxed out of latency before it can be used. The Socratic method—directed questions whose responses come from deduction rather than experience—is the commonest example of this epistemology. Despite our familiarity with this form of nativism thanks to Plato, it is a relatively rare strategy in contemporary postsecondary educational settings, let alone in primary and secondary classrooms.

Some will object to the use of the term "constructivism" to refer to subtly different and sometimes contrasting viewpoints, for example those of Piaget and Papert. However, a fundamental similarity—learners as constructors of their own cognitive realities—justifies the common term.

13. Friedrich Fröbel, *Die Menschenerziehung* (Leipzig: Weinbrach, 1826), 2.

14. See Maria Montessori, *The Montessori Method* (New York: Schocken, 1964).

15. Maria Montessori, *The Absorbent Mind* (New York: Dell, 1967), 205.

16. Bill Buxton, "Simulation and Learning" (paper presented at the Age of Simulation, Linz, Austria, January 12, 2006).

17. Maxis, *Sim City* (Alameda, Calif.: Brøderbund, 1989).

18. Tecmo, *Ninja Gaiden* (NES), (Tokyo, Japan: Tecmo, Ltd., 1989).

19. Tecmo, *Ninja Gaiden* (Xbox), (Tokyo, Japan: Tecmo, Ltd., 2004).

20. David Grossman, *Teaching Kids to Kill* (2000 [cited January 23, 2005, no longer online]); available from http://www.killology.org/article_teachkid.htm/.

21. CNN.com, "Microsoft to Alter 'Flight Simulator' Game" (CNN.com, September 14, 2001 [cited January 23, 2006]); available from http://archives.cnn.com/2001/TECH/ptech/09/14/microsoft.flight.sim/.

22. Ibid.

23. Andrew Orlowski, "Flight Sim Enquiry Raises Terror Alert," *Register*, January 8, 2004, http://www.theregister.co.uk/2004/01/08/flight_sim_enquiry_raises_terror/.

24. Bogost, *Unit Operations*, 103–104.

25. Turkle, "Seeing through Computers."

26. Paul Starr, "Policy as a Simulaton Game," *American Prospect* 5, no. 17 (March 17, 1994), http://www.prospect.org/print/V5/17/starr-p.html/.

27. Bogost, *Unit Operations*, 129–135.

28. Maria Montessori, "The Child," *Theosophist* 30, no. 6 (1942).

29. Seymour Papert, *Mindstorms: Children, Computers, and Powerful Ideas* (New York: Basic Books, 1980).

30. Courtney Cazden, "Performance before Competence: Assistance to Child Discourse in the Zone of Proximal Development," *Quarterly Newsletter of the Laboratory of Comparative Human Cognition* 3 (1981).

31. Jay Forrester, *Urban Dynamics* (Cambridge, Mass.: Wright Allen, 1969).

32. Bogost, *Unit Operations*, 96–97.

33. Gee, *What Video Games Have to Teach Us about Learning and Literacy*, 42–43.

34. James Paul Gee, "Demonstrating the Important Learning Found in COTS Games" (paper presented at the Serious Games Summit 2005, San Francisco, 2005). Also see a summary in Brandon Sheffield, "Playing Games with Jim: Demonstrating the Important Learning Found in COTS Games," *Gamasutra*, March 8, 2005.

35. James Paul Gee, *The Classroom of Popular Culture* (Harvard University, 2005 [cited February 2, 2006]); available from http://www.edletter.org/past/issues/2005-nd/gee.shtml/.

36. James Paul Gee, *Situated Language and Learning: A Critique of Traditional Schooling* (London: Routledge, 2004), 66. Also in James Paul Gee, *Learning about Learning from a Video Game* (Academic Advanced Distributed Learning Co-Lab, February 10, 2005 [cited February 10, 2006]); available from http://web.reed.edu/cis/tac/meetings/Rise%20of%20Nations.pdf/.

37. John C. Beck and Mitchell Wade, *Got Game: How the Gamer Generation Is Reshaping Business Forever* (Cambridge, Mass.: Harvard Business School Press, 2004), 167.

38. Gee, "Demonstrating the Important Learning Found in COTS Games."

39. Gee, *What Video Games Have to Teach Us about Learning and Literacy*, 48.

40. Ibid., 86.

41. Jesper Juul, *Half-Real: Video Games between Real Rules and Fictional Worlds* (Cambridge, Mass.: MIT Press, 2005), 13.

42. Ibid., 15.

43. Raph Koster, *A Theory of Fun for Game Design* (Scottsdale, Ariz. Paraglyph Press, 2004), 168.

44. Ibid.

45. Ibid.

46. Gee, *What Videogames Have to Teach Us about Learning and Literacy*, 18.

47. Ibid., 19.

48. Ibid., 26–27.

49. Ibid., 9.

50. Alan Kay and Adele Goldberg, "Dynamic Personal Media," in *The New Media Reader*, ed. Noah Wardrip-Fruin and Nick Montfort (Cambridge, Mass.: The MIT Press, 1977). Xerox PARC was a hub of computer innovation in the 1970s. Among many other innovations, Kay and his colleagues developed the graphical user interface, incorporated into the Xerox Star, which was the basis for the Apple Macintosh.

51. Papert, *Mindstorms: Children, Computers, and Powerful Ideas*.

52. B. A. Sheil, "Teaching Procedural Literacy," in *Proceedings of the ACM 1980 Annual Conference* (New York: ACM Press, 1980).

53. Ken Perlin, Mary Flanagan, and Andrea Hollingshead, "RAPUNSEL Manifesto," *RAPUNSEL Research Web* (2005), available from http://www.maryflanagan.com/rapunsel/manifesto.htm/.

54. Engineering Committee on Science, and Public Policy, "Rising above The Gathering Storm: Energizing and Employing America for a Brighter Economic Future" (Washington, D.C.: The National Academy of Sciences, 2005), 79–80.

55. Crawford, "Process Intensity."

56. Michael Mateas, "Procedural Literacy: Educating the New Media Practitioner," *On the Horizon* 13, no. 2 (2005): 101–102.

57. Dorothy Sayers, "The Lost Tools of Learning" (Oxford University, Reprinted in *National Review*, 1947).

58. Ibid. The original publication is out of print, but the reader may confer the many online reprints of "The Lost Tools of Learning," e.g., http://www.gbt.org/text/sayers.html/.

59. Ibid.

60. Ibid.

61. The traditional quadrivium consisted of four subjects, arithmetic, geometry, music, and astronomy. These form the basis for the original liberal arts taught in medieval universities.

62. Jessie Wise and Susan Wise Bauer, *The Well-Trained Mind: A Guide to Classical Education at Home* (New York: W.W. Norton, 1999).

63. Ibid., 210.

64. Sayers, "The Lost Tools of Learning."

65. Wise and Bauer, *The Well: Trained Mind*, 200.

66. A word or phrase that reads the same forward and backward. Among the most notable are Georges Perec's "Le grand palindrome" (roughly 1,500 words), in *La clôture et autre poèmes* (Paris: Hachette/Collection P.O.L., 1980); and Nick Montfort and William Gillespie's *2002* (2,002 words) (Edwardsville, Ill.: Spineless Books, 2002).

67. A text in which use of a particular letter is forbidden. The most famous lipogrammatic text is Georges Perec's *La disparition*, a lipogram in E (that is, the letter "e" appears nowhere in the work). Georges Perec, *La disparition* (Paris: Gallimard, 1990). English translation, Georges Perec, *A Void*, trans. Gilbert Adair (Boston: Verba Mundi, 2005).

68. A text in which use of letters with ascenders or descenders, i.e., b, d, f, g, h, j, k, l, p, q, t, and y, is forbidden.

69. Mateas, "Procedural Literacy," 103.

70. Martin Greenberger, *Computers and the World of the Future* (Cambridge, Mass.: MIT Press, 1962), 206. Cited in Mateas, "Procedural Literacy," 105.

71. Gee, *What Video Games Have to Teach Us about Learning and Literacy*, 8.

72. Ibid.

73. Stephen Johnson, *Everything Bad Is Good for You: How Today's Popular Culture Is Actually Making Us Smarter* (New York: Riverhead, 2005), 59.

74. Ibid., 176–177.

75. Ibid., 148–151.

76. See http://education.mit.edu/starlogo/.

77. See Mitchel Resnick, *Turtles, Termites, and Traffic Jams: Explorations in Massively Parallel Microworlds* (Cambridge, Mass.: MIT Press, 1997); Vanessa Stevens Colella, Eric Klopfer, and Mitchel Resnick, *Adventures in Modeling: Exploring Complex Dynamic Systems with StarLogo* (New York: Teachers College Press, 2001).

78. Diamond, *Guns, Germs, and Steel*.

79. Sid Meier and Firaxis Games, *Civilization* (Paris, France: Infogrames, 1991).

80. Stainless Steel Studios, *Empire Earth*.

81. Paradox Entertainment, *Europa Universalis*, Montreal: Strategy First, 2000.

82. Heather Chaplin and Aaron Ruby, *Smartbomb: The Quest for Art, Entertainment, and Big Bucks in the Videogame Revolution* (Chapel Hill, N.C.: Algonquin Books, 2005), 2.

83. Ibid.

84. David Williamson Shaffer, "Epistemic Games," *Innovate* 1, no. 6 (2005), David Williamson Shaffer, "Pedagogical Praxis: The Professions as Models for Post-industrial Education," *Teachers College Record* 10 (2004).

85. David Williamson Shaffer, "Epistemic Frames and Islands of Expertise: Learning from Infusion Experiences" (paper presented at the International Conference of the Learning Sciences [ICLS], Santa Monica, Calif., 2004).

86. Shaffer, "Epistemic Games."

87. Persuasive Games, *Take Back Illinois*.

88. Maxis, *The Sims*.

89. Chaplin and Ruby, *Smartbomb*, 138.

90. Gonzalo Frasca, "*The Sims*: Grandmothers Are Cooler Than Trolls," *Game Studies* 1, no. 1 (2001).

Chapter 9

1. See http://www.buildfreedom.com/tl/wua3.shtml/.

2. For example, see the NBC News/Wall Street Journal poll at http://www .pollingreport.com/prioriti.htm/. The other three are usually foreign policy, security, and healthcare.

3. See http://www.policyalmanac.org/education/index.shtml/.

4. General information on the No Child Left Behind legislation can be found at http://www.whitehouse.gov/news/reports/no-child-left-behind.html#1/.

5. See http://www.brookings.edu/views/op-ed/loveless/20040108.htm/.

6. John Stuart Mill, *On Liberty* (New York: Penguin, 1975), 177.

7. What follows are not Laurel's exact words, but a kind of narrative summary of the notes I took during her talk. While I believe I have captured the spirit of Laurel's message quite well, I make no claims of direct citation.

8. See http://www.watercoolergames.org/archives/000142.shtml#laurel/.

9. Louis Althusser, "Ideology and Ideological State Apparatuses," *Lenin and Philosophy and Other Essays*, trans. Ben Brewster (New York: Monthly Review Press, 2003).

10. See http://www.johntaylorgatto.com/.

11. For a good introduction to Jackson and his book, see http://www.sociology.org .uk/tece1el2.htm/.

12. See, for example, http://www.eagleforum.org/educate/2002/apr02/pre-school .shtml/.

13. 3Form, *Mansion Impossible* (Jersey, U.K.: Jersey Insight, 2003).

14. Dolf de Roos and Robert T. Kiyosaki, *Real Estate Riches: How to Become Rich Using Your Banker's Money* (New York: Warner, 2001), 5.

15. Ibid., 53, 81.

16. Ibid., 42, 126.

17. Nintendo, *Animal Crossing* (Kyoto, Japan: Nintendo, 2002).

18. See Bogost, "Asynchronous Multiplay."

19. Henry Jenkins and Kurt Squire, "Playing Together, Staying Together," *Computer Games Magazine*, December 2003.

20. Just to give the reader a sense of the magnitude of work that faces players of *Animal Crossing*, the final renovation mortgage is over 700,000 "bells" (the currency unit in the game). The most lucrative fish and insects one can catch in the game sell for 10,000 bells, but they are quite rare. More typical items sell for 300–1,000 bells.

21. John de Graaff, David Wann, and Thomas H. Naylor, *Affluenza: The All-Consuming Epidemic* (San Francisco: Berrett Koehler, 2005), xvi.

22. Ibid., 11–22.

23. Will Wright, "Design Learning: How Other Fields Can Inform Interactive Design" (paper presented at the Living Game Worlds 2006: Designers on Design, The Georgia Institute of Technology, Atlanta, Georgia, 2006).

24. De Graaff, Wann, and Naylor, *Affluenza*, 15.

25. In particular, see http://www.animalcrossingcommunity.com/.

26. See http://www.animalcrossingcommunity.com/hra_guide.asp/.

27. De Graaff, Wann, and Naylor, *Affluenza*, 39.

28. Michael Ashkenazi and Jeanne Jacob, *The Essence of Japanese Cuisine* (Philadelphia: University of Pennsylvania Press, 2002), 142.

29. For more on the seasonal appearance of fish and insects, see http://www .animalcrossingcommunity.com/items_list.asp/.

30. De Graaff, Wann, and Naylor, *Affluenza*, 44.

31. Bogost, *Unit Operations*, 134–135.

32. In 2005 Nintendo released a version of *Animal Crossing* for the Nintendo DS handheld console: Nintendo, *Animal Crossing: Wild World* (Kyoto, Japan: Nintendo, 2005). By this time, the GameCube version had been available for three years, and the majority of tie-ins had been built around the console version.

33. Bandai, *Catch a Coke* (Atlanta, Georgia: The Coca-Cola Company, 1983); Bandai, *Monkey Coconut* (Tokyo: Bandai, 1981).

34. Atari, *Pepsi Invaders* (Atlanta, Georgia: The Coca-Cola Company, 1983).

35. ROM (read only memory) chips are programmed at manufacture and cannot be altered once created. EPROM (erasable programmable read only memory) chips can be erased and reused, making them appropriate for both debugging and small production runs. EPROMs are typically erased by exposing the chip to an ultraviolet light source or an electrical field (in the case of an EEPROM, electrically erasable programmable read only memory).

36. Price guides value the title at $400–500, but in 2005 a copy sold on eBay for over $1,800. David Ellis, *Price Guide to Classic Video Games* (New York: House of Collectibles, 2004), 99.

37. David Michael and Sande Chen, *Serious Games: Games That Educate, Train, and Inform* (Boston: Thompson Course Technology, 2006), 145.

38. Ibid., 149.

39. Ibid.

40. Ibid., 147.

41. James E. Driskell and Daniel J. Dwyer, "Microcomputer Videogame Based Training," *Educational Technology* (February 1984): 11.

42. Ibid., 13.

43. Ibid., 11.

44. Michael and Chen, *Serious Games*, 164.

45. Persuasive Games, *Cold Stone Creamery: Stone City* (Scottsdale, Ariz.: Cold Stone Creamery, 2005).

46. Tor Thorsen, "San Andreas Rated AO, Take-Two Suspends Production," *GameSpot*, July 20, 2005.

47. Mystique, *Custer's Revenge* (Northridge, Calif.: Mystique, 1982). The game's manual claims that Custer "scores" (scare quotes included) rather than rapes the "maiden." The description is clearly intended as a pun on the convention of numerical scoring in videogames. See http://www.atariage.com/manual_html_page.html?SoftwareLabelID=119/.

48. Ren Reynolds, "Playing a 'Good' Game: A Philosophical Approach to Understanding the Morality of Games," *International Game Developers Association* (2002), http://www.igda.org/articles/rreynolds_ethics.php/.

49. Henry Jenkins, "Reality Bytes: Eight Myths about Video Games Debunked," *PBS: The Videogame Revolution* 1 (2005), available from http://www.pbs.org/kcts/videogamerevolution/impact/myths.html/.

50. Ibid.

51. Reynolds, "Playing a 'Good' Game."

52. Miguel Sicart, "The Ethics of Computer Game Design" (paper presented at the Digital Games Research Conference 2005, Vancouver, June 2005), 3.

53. BioWare, *Star Wars: Knights of the Old Republic* (San Francisco: LucasArts, 2003).

54. Lionhead Studios, *Black & White* (Redwood City, Calif.: Electronic Arts, 2001).

55. SEGA, *Sonic the Hedgehog* (Tokyo: SEGA Entertainment, 1991).

56. SEGA, *Shadow the Hedgehog* (Tokyo: SEGA Entertainment, 2005).

57. Gee, *What Video Games Have to Teach Us about Learning and Literacy*, 139–143.

58. Ion Storm, *Deus Ex* (San Francisco: Eidos, 2000).

59. Looking Glass Studios, *Thief* (San Francisco: Eidos, 1998).

60. Warren Spector, "Are Games Educational?" (paper presented at the Education Arcade Conference, Los Angeles, May 10, 2004).

61. Wisdom Tree, *Bible Buffet* (Tucson, Ariz.: Wisdom Tree, 1992).

62. Wisdom Tree, *Menace Beach* (Tucson, Ariz.: Wisdom Tree, 1990); Wisdom Tree, *Sunday Funday* (Tucson, Ariz.: Wisdom Tree, 1995).

63. Wisdom Tree, *Exodus* (Tucson, Ariz.: Wisdom Tree, 1991).

64. Wisdom Tree, *Bible Aventures* (Tucson, Ariz.: Wisdom Tree, 1991).

65. Nintendo, *The Legend of Zelda* (Kyoto, Japan: Nintendo, 1986); Wisdom Tree, *Spiritual Warfare* (Tucson, Ariz.: Wisdom Tree, 1992).

66. N'Lightning Software, *Catechumen* (Medford, Ore.: N'Lightning Software Development, 2000).

67. Mass Media and Crave Entertainment, *The Bible Game* (Newport Beach, Calif.: Crave Entertainment, 2005).

68. Left Behind Games, *Left Behind: Eternal Forces* (Murietta, Calif.: Left Behind Games, 2006). The comments here are based on a pre-release version of the game, as demonstrated to the author by the developers at the Electronic Entertainment Expo (E3) in May 2006.

69. The first book in the series is Tim F. LaHaye and Jerry B. Jenkins, *Left Behind: A Novel of the Earth's Last Days* (Carol Stream, Ill.: Tyndale, 1996). As of spring 2006, fourteen books have been published, along with two movies and numerous children's books.

70. Ian Bogost, interview with Troy Lyndon and Greg Bauman, May 9, 2006.

71. Ibid.

72. Ibid.

73. Packaged Facts, "The U.S. Market for Religious Publishing and Products" (New York: Packaged Facts, 2004); The Entertainment Software Association, "Essential Facts about the Computer and Video Game Industry."

Chapter 10

1. Konami, *Dance Dance Revolution* (Tokyo: Konami, 1999).

2. Konami, *DDRMAX: Dance Dance Revolution 6thMIX* (Tokyo: Konami, 2002).

3. Konami, *Dance Dance Revolution 2ndMIX Dreamcast Edition* (Tokyo: Konami, 2000).

4. Konami, *Dance Dance Revolution Disney Dancing Museum* (Tokyo: Konami, 2000).

5. Konami, *Dance Dance Revolution Ultramix* (Tokyo: Konami, 2003).

6. Konami, *Dance Dance Revolution Mario Mix* (Kyoto: Nintendo, 2005).

7. DDR Freak, "Tournament Performance and Strategy" (2004); available from http://www.ddrfreak.com/library/contributor-article.php?postID=7890162/.

8. Red Octane, *GetUpMove.com* (Red Octane, 2004 [cited March 3 2005]); available from http://www.getupmove.com/.

9. Catherine Donaldson-Evans, "Players Break a Sweat with Video Games," *Fox News*, July 9, 2004.

10. Associated Press, "Video Game Fans Dance Off Extra Pounds," *USA Today*, May 23, 2004.

11. Anita Chiang, "Video Game Helps Players Lose Weight," *CNN.com*, May 24, 2004.

12. ABC News, "Toys to Get Kids Off the Couch," *ABC News Good Morning America*, December 15, 2005.

13. Star Lawrence, "Exercise, Lose Weight with 'Exergaming,'" *WebMD*, January 18, 2005.

14. Red Octane, "Dance Video Game Supports Academic Success," *GetUpMove.com research report*, June 29, 2005.

15. Atari, *Asteroids* (Sunnyvale, Calif.: Atari, 1980).

16. SEGA, *Zaxxon* (Tokyo: Sega Entertainment, 1982).

17. Namco, *Galaxian* (Chicago: Midway Games, 1979).

18. Exus, *Foot Craz* (Exus, 1987).

19. The Power Pad had originally been developed by frequent Nintendo third-party developer Bandai, and released a year earlier under the name *Family Trainer*. Nintendo bought the rights to the device from Bandai and released it as their own. Power Pad took the name *Family Fun Fitness* in Europe.

20. Konami, *Track & Field* (arcade) (Tokyo: Konami, 1982).

21. Some clever *Track & Field* players found an exploit: holding a plastic ruler over the cabinet buttons and then pressing a pencil or pen on top of the ruler between the buttons allowed the player to achieve significantly better results just by moving a hand or fist back and forth across the ruler. Later versions of the arcade console sported bevels overtop of the buttons to prevent this kind of play, which was perceived as socially disruptive and abusive toward the hosting arcade.

22. Konami, *Track & Field* (Atari 2600) (Tokyo: Konami, 1983).

23. Bandai had released *Stadium Events* in 1987; *World Class Track Meet* was Nintendo's rebranded 1988 reissue of the same title, converted for use with Power Pad.

24. Bandai, *World Class Track Meet* (Tokyo: Nintendo, 1988).

25. Eurocom, *Athens 2004* (Foster City, Calif.: SCEA, 2004).

26. Exus, *Video Jogger* (Exus, 1987).

27. Bandai, *Athletic World* (Tokyo: Bandai, 1987).

28. Bandai, *Street Cop* (Tokyo: Bandai, 1987).

29. Amiga, *Mogul Maniac* (Santa Clara, Calif.: Amiga Corp., 1983).

30. Amiga, *Off Your Rocker* (Santa Clara, Calif.: Amiga Corp., unreleased).

31. Amiga, *Surf's Up* (Santa Clara, Calif.: Amiga Corp., unreleased).

32. Nintendo, *Super Mario Bros.*

33. Konami, *Contra* (Tokyo: Konami, 1988).

34. Polyphony Digital, *Gran Turismo* (Tokyo: SCIE, 1997).

35. Exus, *Video Reflex* (Exus, 1987).

36. Nintendo, *Eggsplode* (Kyoto, Japan: Nintendo, 1990).

37. SCEE, *Eye Toy: Play* (Sony Computer Entertainment Europe, 2003).

38. Bandai, *Dance Aerobics* (Tokyo: Nintendo, 1988).

39. ResponDesign, *Yourself! Fitness* (Portland, Ore.: ResponDesign, 2004).

40. I am indebted to Vish Unnithan for this observation.

41. Phineas Barnes, "A Fitness Game for Xbox and PC" (paper presented at the Games for Health Conference, Madison, Wisc., September 20, 2004).

42. Nintendo's increasingly popular *Brain Age* series of cognitive training games also rewards consistency with new exercises.

43. As of late 2006, ResponDesign remains mired in a two-year long infringement lawsuit (see http://xbox.ign.com/articles/567/567385pl.html), which has hampered the company's ability to release new products.

44. Nintendo, *Short Order* (Kyoto, Japan: Nintendo, 1990).

45. Data East, *BurgerTime.*

46. Harmonix Music Systems, *Eye Toy: Antigrav* (Foster City, Calif.: SCEA, 2004).

47. Namco, *Taiko Drum Master* (Tokyo: Namco, 2004); Nintendo, *Donkey Konga* (Kyoto, Japan: Nintendo, 2004).

48. Nintendo, *Donkey Kong Jungle Beat* (Kyoto, Japan: Nintendo, 2005).

49. See http://www.myhometheater.homestead.com/viewingdistancecalculator.html/.

Chapter 11

1. Aristotle, *Physics*, 39 (II.33, 194b132).

2. Kennedy, *Classical Rhetoric and Its Christian and Secular Tradition*, 77.

3. Aristotle, *The Rhetoric and Poetics of Aristotle*, 32–33 (1358b).

4. Ibid., 27 (1356b).

5. See http://www.metacritic.com/about/scoring.html/ for a complete description of the process.

6. Bing Gordon, "Developing and Educating Creative Leaders at EA" (paper presented at the Living Game Worlds 2005, The Georgia Institute of Technology, March 16, 2005).

7. Michael and Chen, *Serious Games*, 37.

8. Ibid., 38.

9. Ibid.

10. Ibid.

11. Mark Prensky, *Digital Game-Based Learning* (New York: McGraw-Hill, 2001), 340.

12. See Benjamin Bloom, *Taxonomy of Educational Objectives: The Classification of Educational Goals* (White Plains, N.Y.: Longman, 1956).

13. Bryan Bergeron, *Developing Serious Games* (Hingham, Mass.: Charles River Media, 2006), 216.

14. Chris Marlowe, "Nielsen to Measure Massive Ads," *Inside Branded Entertainment*, December 16, 2004.

15. Paul Hyman, "Technology Seeks to Measure Game Ad ROI," *Hollywood Reporter*, February 24, 2006.

16. Mark Baldwin, *EyeSpy: The Matrix* (Montréal, Quebec: McGill University, 2004).

17. Mark Baldwin, Jodene Baccus, and Dominic J. Packer, "Increasing Implicit Self-Esteem through Classical Conditioning," *Psychological Science* 7 (2004).

18. Michael and Chen, *Serious Games*, 185.

19. See http://www.thegamersforum.com/showthread.php?t=7506/.

20. See http://www.radiosilent.org/mt/http:/www.radiosilent.org/mt/000152.html/ (no longer online).

21. See http://www.gendeanblog.com/ (no longer online).

22. Justin Hall, *Clicking for Dean* (Game Girl Advance, 2003 [cited December 23, 2003]); available from http://www.gamegirladvance.com/archives/2003/12/23/ clicking_for_dean.html/.

23. David Thomas, *The Dean of Political Games* (Buzzcut: Critical Videogame Theory, December 24, 2003); available from http://www.buzzcut.com/article.php? story=20031224234034103/.

24. Ibid.

25. Badiou, *Infinite Thought*, 73.

26. Thomas, *The Dean of Political Games*.

27. Kennedy, *Classical Rhetoric and Its Christian and Secular Tradition*, 141.

28. Ibid., 159.

29. Ibid., 157.

30. Badiou, *Being and Event*, 232.

31. Ibid.

32. Ibid., 233.

33. Hallward, *Badiou*, 128.

34. Badiou, *Being and Event*, 175.

35. Ibid.

36. Ibid.

37. Hallward, *Badiou*, 118.

38. Ibid.

39. Ibid.

40. Ibid., 120.

41. Bogost, *Unit Operations*, 107.

42. Ibid., 108.

43. Jenkins and Squire, "Playing Together, Staying Together." Also available at http://educationarcade.org/node/102/.

44. For more on this topic, see Bogost, "Asynchronous Multiplay."

45. Godin, *All Marketers Are Liars*, 55.

46. MIT Education Arcade, *Revolution* (Cambridge, Mass.: MIT, 2004).

47. BioWare, *Neverwinter Nights* (New York: Infogrames, 2003).

48. See http://educationarcade.org/revolution/.

49. Russell Francis, "Revolution: Learning about History through Interactive Role Play in a Virtual Environment" (paper presented at The Education Arcade Conference, Los Angeles, May 19, 2005).

50. Mary Ulicsak et al., "Time Out? Exploring the Role of Reflection in the Design of Games for Learning."

51. Ibid.

52. Grocery Game message boards are found at http://www.terismessageboard.com/. The site's administrators appear to archive and remove old posts regularly, and these particular posts are no longer visible.

53. Jacques Derrida, *Given Time 1. Counterfeit Money*, trans. Peggy Kamuf (Chicago: University of Chicago Press, 1992), 137–138.

54. Ibid., 137.

55. Emmanuel Levinas, *Totalité et Infini* (Paris: Kluwer, 1971), 30.

Bibliography

ABC News. "Toys to Get Kids off the Couch." *ABC News Good Morning America*, December 15, 2005.

Abt, Clark C. *Serious Games*. New York: Viking, 1970.

Ackerman, Peter, and Jack DuVall. *A Force More Powerful*. New York: Palgrave Macmillan, 2001.

Ackermann, Edith. 2001. "Piaget's Constructivism, Papert's Constructionism: What's the Difference?" *MIT Media Lab Publications*, http://learning.media.mit.edu/content/publications/EA.Piaget%20_%20Papert.pdf/ (accessed February 10, 2006).

Activision. *Caterpillar Construction Tycoon* (videogame). Santa Monica, Calif.: Activision Value Publishing, 2005.

Agency.com. *Agency.com Snowball Fight* (videogame). New York: Agency.com, 2005.

Alelo, Inc., and USC Information Sciences Institute. *Tactical Iraqi* (videogame). Los Angeles, Calif.: Tactical Language Training LLC, 2005.

Allen, Andre, and Bill Berner. *Chappelle's Show*. Edited by Dave Chappelle. Comedy Central, 2003.

Alliance, Groove. *Mountain Dew Skateboarding* (videogame). Somers, N.Y.: PepsiCo, 2003.

Althusser, Louis. *Lenin and Philosophy and Other Essays*. Translated by Ben Brewster. New York: Monthly Review, 1971.

Amiga. *Mogul Maniac* (videogame). Santa Clara, Calif.: Amiga Corp., 1983.

———. *Off Your Rocker* (videogame). Santa Clara, Calif.: Amiga Corp., unreleased.

———. *Surf's Up* (videogame). Santa Clara, Calif.: Amiga Corp., unreleased.

Anonymous. 2002. "Lexus concepts star in Spielberg's *Minority Report*." In *Car Design News*, http://www.cardesignnews.com/news/2002/020724minority-report/ (accessed January 2, 2006).

Aristotle. *Physics*. Translated by Robin Waterfield. Oxford and New York: Oxford University Press, 1999.

———. *The Rhetoric and Poetics of Aristotle*. New York: McGraw Hill, 1984.

Artex Software. *Carnival Cruise Lines Tycoon* (videogame). Santa Monica, Calif.: Activision Value Publishing, 2005.

Ashkenazi, Michael, and Jeanne Jacob. *The Essence of Japanese Cuisine*. Philadelphia: University of Pennsylvania Press, 2002.

Associated Press. "Video Game Fans Dance Off Extra Pounds." *USA Today*, May 23, 2004.

———. "Video Shows Bush Warned before Katrina Hit." *CBS News*, March 2, 2006.

Astraware Limited. *Bejeweled* (videogame). Seattle, Wash.: PopCap Games, 2000.

Atari. *Asteroids* (videogame). Sunnyvale, Calif.: Atari, 1980.

———. *E.T.* (videogame). Sunnyvale, Calif.: Atari, 1982.

———. *Missile Command* (videogame). Sunnyvale, Calif.: Atari, 1980.

———. *Night Driver* (videogame). Sunnyvale, Calif.: Atari, 1976.

——. *Pepsi Invaders* (videogame). Atlanta, Georgia: The Coca Cola Company, 1983.

——. *Pong* (videogame). Sunnyvale, Calif.: Atari, 1972.

Atticus XI (pseudonym). 2004. "A Conversation with Dr. Henry Jenkins." In *Penny Arcade*, http://www.penny-arcade.com/lodjenkins.php/ (accessed February 4, 2005).

Austin, J. L. *How to Do Things with Words*. Cambridge, Mass.: Harvard University Press, 1962.

Badiou, Alain. *Being and Event*. Translated by Oliver Feltham. London and New York: Continuum, 2005.

——. *Infinite Thought*. Translated by Oliver Feltham and Justin Clemens. London and New York: Continuum, 2003.

Baldwin, Mark. *EyeSpy: The Matrix*. Montréal, Quebec: McGill University, 2004.

Baldwin, Mark, Jodene Baccus, and Dominic J. Packer. "Increasing Implicit Self-Esteem Through Classical Conditioning." *Psychological Science* 7 (2004): 498–502.

Bales, Richard F. *The Great Chicago Fire and the Myth of Mrs. O'Leary's Cow*. New York: McFarland, 2002.

Bally/Midway. *Tapper* (videogame). Chicago: Bally/Midway, 1983.

——. *Tron* (videogame). Chicago: Bally/Midway, 1982.

Bandai. *Athletic World* (videogame). Tokyo: Bandai, 1987.

——. *Catch a Coke* (videogame). Atlanta, Georgia: The Coca Cola Company, 1983.

——. *Dance Aerobics* (videogame). Kyoto: Nintendo, 1988.

——. *Monkey Coconut* (videogame). Tokyo: Bandai, 1981.

——. *Street Cop* (videogame). Tokyo: Bandai, 1987.

——. *World Class Track Meet* (videogame). Kyoto: Nintendo, 1988.

Banff Centre, and Global Arcade. *P.o.N.G.* (videogame). San Francisco, Calif.: Global Arcade, 1999.

Barbu, Larry. *Crisis in the Kremlin*. Alameda, Calif.: Spectrum Holobyte, 1991.

Barnes, Phineas. "A Fitness Game for Xbox and PC." Paper presented at the Games for Health Conference, Madison, Wisconsin, September 20, 2004.

Bartel, Paul (dir.). *Death Race 2000*. New World Pictures, 1975.

Baudrillard, Jean. *Selected Writings*. Edited by Mark Poster. Palo Alto, Calif.: Stanford University Press, 1988.

BBC News. "UN's Darfur Death Estimate Soars." *BBC News*. March 14, 2005.

Beck, John C., and Mitchell Wade. *Got Game: How the Gamer Generation Is Reshaping Business Forever*. Cambridge, Mass.: Harvard Business School Press, 2004.

Beck, Steve. *Save the Whales*. Self-published, 2002.

Becker, Gary S., and Kevin M. Murphy. "A Simple Theory of Advertising as a Good or Bad." *Quarterly Journal of Economics* (November 1993): 941–964.

Bentham, Jeremy. *The Panopticon and Other Prison Writings*. London: Verso, 1995.

Bergeron, Bryan. *Developing Serious Games*. Hingham, Mass.: Charles River Media, 2006.

Berry, John, and Ed Keller. *The Influentials: One American in Ten Tells the Other Nine How to Vote, Where to Eat, and What to Buy*. New York: Free Press, 2003.

BioWare. *Neverwinter Nights* (videogame). New York: Infogrames, 2003.

———. *Star Wars: Knights of the Old Republic* (videogame). San Francisco, Calif.: LucasArts, 2003.

Birdsell, David S., and Leo Groarke. "Toward a Theory of Visual Argument." *Argumentation and Advocacy* 33 (1996): 1–10.

Blair, J. Anthony. "The Rhetoric of Visual Arguments." In *Defining Visual Rhetorics*, edited by Marguerite Helmers and Charles A. Hill, 41–61. Mahwah, N.J.: Lawrence Erlbaum Associates, 2004.

Blockdot. *Ms. Match* (videogame). Dallas, Texas: Kewlbox.com, 2005.

———. *White House Joust* (videogame). Dallas, Texas: Kewlbox.com, 2004.

Bloom, Benjamin. *Taxonomy of Educational Objectives: The Classification of Educational Goals*. White Plains, N.Y.: Longman, 1956.

Blue Fang Games. *Zoo Tycoon* (videogame). Redmond, Wash.: Microsoft Game Studios, 2001.

Bogost, Ian. "Asynchronous Multiplay: Futures for Casual Multiplayer Experience." Paper presented at the Other Players Conference on Multiplayer Phenomena, Copenhagen, Denmark, December 1–3, 2004.

———. "Frame and Metaphor in Political Games." In *Worlds in Play*, edited by Suzanne de Castell and Jen Jenson. Berlin and New York: Peter Lang, forthcoming.

———. "Persuasive Games: Play in Advocacy and Pedagogy." Paper presented at the Cyberspace @ UCLA Symposium on Playing, Gaming, and Learning, Los Angeles, Calif., October 23, 2003.

———. "Playing Politics: Videogames for Politics, Activism, and Advocacy." *First Monday* 11, no 9. Edited by Thomas Malaby and Sandrd Bremen.

———. *Unit Operations: An Approach to Videogame Criticism*. Cambridge, Mass.: MIT Press, 2006.

———. "Videogames and Ideological Frames." *Popular Communication* 4, no. 2 (2006).

———. "Videogames and the Future of Education." *On the Horizon* 13, no. 2 (2005): 119–125.

Bogost, Ian, and Gonzalo Frasca. "Videogames Go to Washington: The Story Behind Howard Dean's Videogame Propaganda." In *Second Person: Roleplaying and Story in*

Games and Playable Media, 233–246, edited by Pat Harrigan and Noah Wardrip-Fruin. Cambridge, Mass.: MIT Press, 2006.

Bogost, Ian, and Daniel Klainbaum. "Presence and the Mediated Cities of Grand Theft Auto." In *The Meaning and Culture of "Grand Theft Auto,"* edited by Nathan Garrelts, 162–176. Jefferson, N.C.: McFarland, 2006.

Bogost, Ian, Troy Lyndon, and Greg Bauman. Interview. May 9, 2006.

Bold Games. *John Deere American Farmer* (videogame). Mississauga, Ontario, Canada: Global Star Software, 2004.

Book, Betsy. 2005. "Virtual World Business Brands: Entrepreneurship and Identity in Massively Multiplayer Online Gaming Environments." In *SSRN*, http://ssrn.com/abstract=736823/ (accessed June 15, 2005).

Booth, William. "For Norton, a Party Mission." *Washington Post*, January 8, 2001, A01.

Boudon, Raymond. *The Analysis of Ideology*. Chicago: University of Chicago Press, 1989.

Brainerd, Charles J. *Piaget's Theory of Intelligence*. New York: Prentice Hall, 1978.

BreakAway Games. *A Force More Powerful* (videogame). Washington, D.C.: The International Center for Nonviolent Conflict 2006.

Brightman, James. "In-Game Ads Evolving, Becoming More Effective." *GameDaily* (October 17, 2005).

Brimber, Bruce A., and Richard Davis. *Campaigning Online: The Internet in U.S. Elections*. New York and Oxford: Oxford University Press, 2003.

Bruner, Jerome. *Going Beyond the Information Given*. New York: W. W. Norton, 1973.

Bullfrog Productions. *Theme Park* (videogame). Redwood City, Calif.: Electronic Arts, 1994.

Burke, Kenneth. *A Rhetoric of Motives*. Berkeley and Los Angeles: University of California Press, 1969.

Burnett, Mark. *The Apprentice*. ABC, 2004–.

Burnett, Mark, Mark Koops, H. T. Owens, and Ben Silverman. *The Restaurant*. NBC, 2003.

Bushnell, Nolan. *Computer Space* (videogame). Mountain View, Calif.: Nutting Associates, 1971.

Butters, Gerard R. "Equilibrium Distributions of Sales and Advertising Prices." *Review of Economic Studies* 44, no. 3 (1977): 465–491.

Buxton, Bill. "Simulation and Learning." Paper presented at The Age of Simulation, Linz, Austria, January 12, 2006.

Cadre, Adam, David Dyte, Michael Fessler, Dan Shiovitz, Lucian P. Smith, Adam Thornton, and J. Robinson Wheeler. *Coke Is It!* (videogame). 1999.

Campbell, Martin (dir.). *GoldenEye*. MGM, 1995.

Camper, Brett. "Reveling in Restrictions: Technical Mastery and Game Boy Advance Homebrew Software." Paper presented at the Digital Arts and Cultures 2005, IT University, Copenhagen, Denmark, December 1–3, 2005.

Capra, Frank (dir.). *It Happened One Night*. Columbia, 1934.

Cart, Julie. "Bush Opens Way for Counties and States to Claim Wilderness Roads." *Los Angeles Times*, January 21, 2003, 1.

Carter, Chris. *The X Files*. Edited by Chris Carter. Fox, 1993.

Caspary, Vera. *Laura*. New York: The Feminist Press at CUNY, 1943. Reprint, 2005.

Cat Daddy Games. *Cruise Ship Tycoon* (videogame). Santa Monica, Calif.: Activision Value Publishing, 2003.

Cazden, Courtney. "Performance before Competence: Assistance to Child Discourse in the Zone of Proximal Development." *Quarterly Newsletter of the Laboratory of Comparative Human Cognition* 3 (1981): 5–8.

Chaney, Isabella M., Ku-Ho Lin, and James Chaney. "The Effect of Billboards with the Gaming Environment." *Journal of Interactive Advertising* 5, no. 1 (2004).

Chaplin, Heather, and Aaron Ruby. *Smartbomb: The Quest for Art, Entertainment, and Big Bucks in the Videogame Revolution.* Chapel Hill, N.C.: Algonquin Books, 2005.

Chase, Randy. *Power Politics* (videogame). Portland, Ore.: Cineplay Interactive, 1992.

———. *The Doonesbury Election Game: Campaign '96* (videogame). Novato, Calif.: Mindscape, 1996.

Chen, Jane, and Matthew Ringel. "Can Advergaming Be the Future of Interactive Advertising?" In *<kpe> Fast Forward.* Los Angeles: <kpe>, 2001.

Chiang, Anita. "Video Game Helps Players Lose Weight." *CNN.com*, May 24, 2004.

Chris Sawyer Productions. *RollerCoaster Tycoon* (videogame). Hunt Valley, Maryland: Microprose, 1999.

———. *Transport Tycoon* (videogame). Hunt Valley, Maryland: Microprose, 1994.

Cialdini, Robert B., and David A. Schroeder. "Increasing Compliance by Legitimizing Paltry Contributions: When Even a Penny Helps." *Journal of Personality and Social Psychology* 34, no. 4 (1976): 599–604.

Clark, Bob (dir.). *Porky's.* 20th Century Fox, 1982.

C-level (Mark Allen, Peter Brinson, Brody Condon, Jessica Hutchins, Eddo Stern, and Michael Wilson). *Waco Resurrection* (videogame). Los Angeles, Calif.: C-Level, 2003.

Cnn.com. 2001. "Microsoft to Alter 'Flight Simulator' Game." *CNN.com Sci-Tech*, CNN.com, http://archives.cnn.com/2001/TECH/ptech/09/14/microsoft.flight.sim/ (accessed January 23, 2006).

Cochran, Robert, and Joel Surnow. *24.* ABC, 2001–.

Cohen, Roger. "Who Really Brought Down Milosevic?" *New York Times*, November 26, 2000.

Committee on Science, Engineering, and Public Policy. "Rising above The Gathering Storm: Energizing and Employing America for a Brighter Economic Future." Washington, D.C.: The National Academy of Sciences, 2005.

Cornfield, Michael. 2005. "Commentary on the Impact of the Internet on the 2004 Election." In Pew Internet and American Life Project, http://www.pewinternet.org/PPF/r/151/report_display.asp/ (accessed March 23, 2005).

Costikyan, Greg. "I Have No Words but I Must Design: Toward a Critical Vocabulary for Games." Paper presented at the Computer Games and Digital Cultures, Tampere, Finland, June 6–8, 2002.

Crawford, Chris. *Balance of Power* (videogame). Novato, Calif.: Mindscape, 1985.

——. *Balance of the Planet* (videogame). Self-published, 1990.

——. *Chris Crawford on Game Design*. New York: New Riders, 2003.

——. "Process Intensity." *Journal of Computer Game Development* 1, no. 5 (1987).

——. *The Art of Interactive Design: A Euphonious and Illuminating Guide to Building Successful Software*. San Francisco, Calif.: No Starch Press, 2002.

Creative Assembly. *Medieval: Total War* (videogame). Los Angeles, Calif.: Activision, 2002.

Criterion Games. *Burnout 3: Takedown* (videogame). Redwood City, Calif.: Electronic Arts, 2004.

Curtiz, Michael (dir.). *Mildred Pierce*. Warner Brothers, 1945.

Cyberlore. *Playboy: The Mansion* (videogame). Toronto, Ontario: Groove Games, 2005.

Daniels, Les. *Comix: A History of Comic Books in America*. New York: Outerbridge and Deinstfrey, 1971.

Data East. *BurgerTime* (videogame). Chicago: Midway Games, 1982.

DDR Freak. 2004. "Tournament Performance and Strategy." At http://www
.ddrfreak.com/library/contributor-article.php?posted=7890162/ (accessed May 4,
2004).

Deep Red Games. *SeaWorld Adventure Parks Tycoon* (videogame). Santa Monica, Calif.:
Activision Value Publishing, 2003.

de Graaff, John, David Wann, and Thomas H. Naylor. *Affluenza: The All-Consuming
Epidemic*. San Francisco, Calif.: Berrett Koehler, 2005.

DeLuca, Kevin Michael. *Image Politics: The New Rhetoric of Environmental Activism*. New
York: Guilford Press, 1999.

de Roos, Dolf, and Robert T. Kiyosaki. *Real Estate Riches: How to Become Rich Using
Your Banker's Money*. New York: Warner, 2001.

Derrida, Jacques. *Dissemination*. Translated by Barbara Johnson. Chicago: University
of Chicago Press, 1981.

———. *Given Time 1. Counterfeit Money*. Translated by Peggy Kamuf. Chicago: University of Chicago Press, 1992.

———. *Of Grammatology*. Translated by Gayatri Chakravorty Spivak. Baltimore: The
Johns Hopkins Press, 1974.

Dewey, John. *How We Think*. New York: Dover, 1997.

Diamond, Jared. *Guns, Germs, and Steel*. New York: W. W. Norton, 1999.

Dibbell, Julian. "Game from Hell: Latest Plan to Save Sudan: Make a Video Game
Dramatizing Darfur." *Village Voice*, February 13, 2005.

Dixit, Avinash, and Victor Norman. "Advertising and Welfare." *Bell Journal of Economics* 9 (1978): 1–17.

Donaldson-Evans, Catherine. "Players Break a Sweat with Video Games." *Fox News*,
July 9, 2004.

Dorasu. *Curry House CoCo Ichibanya: Kyo mo Genki da! Curry ga Umai!* (videogame).
Tokyo: Dorasu, 2004.

Doyle, James K. "The Cognitive Psychology of Systems Thinking." *System Dynamics Review* 13, no. 3 (1997): 253–265.

DreamWorks Interactive. *Medal of Honor* (videogame). Redwood Shores, Calif.: Electronic Arts, 1999.

Driskell, James E., and Daniel J. Dwyer. "Microcomputer Videogame Based Training." *Educational Technology* (February 1984): 11–16.

DSD/Camelot. *Tooth Protectors* (videogame). New Brunswick, N.J.: Johnson and Johnson, 1983.

Dugan, Patrick. "Hot Off the Grill: la Molleindustria's Paolo Pedercini on The McDonald's Video Game." *Gamasutra*, February 27, 2006.

Dunhill Electronics. *Porky's* (videogame). Santa Clara, Calif.: Fox Video Games, 1983.

———. *Tax Avoiders* (videogame). American Videogame, 1982.

Dyslexia (pseudonym). February 3, 2006. "Ad-Nauseam?" In *Major League Gaming*, http://www.mlgpro.com/news/Ad-Nauseam%253F/1.html/ (accessed February 6, 2006).

EA Canada. *Fight Night Round 3* (videogame). Redwood City, Calif.: Electronic Arts, 2006.

———. *SSX 3* (videogame). Redwood City, Calif.: Electronic Arts, 2003.

Eighty Dimensional Software. *President Forever* (videogame). Vancouver, British Columbia: Eighty Dimensional Software, 2004.

———. *Prime Minister Forever* (videogame). Vancouver, British Columbia: Eighty Dimensional Software, 2005.

Eighty Dimensional Software, and Deutsches Institut für Public Affairs. *Chancellor Forever* (videogame). Vancouver, British Columbia: Eighty Dimensional Software, 2005.

Electronic Arts. *Harry Potter and the Chamber of Secrets* (videogame). Redwood City, Calif.: Electronic Arts, 2002.

——. *Harry Potter and the Goblet of Fire* (videogame). Redwood City, Calif.: Electronic Arts, 2005.

——. *Harry Potter and the Prisoner of Azkaban* (videogame). Redwood City, Calif.: Electronic Arts, 2005.

——. *Harry Potter and the Sorcerer's Stone* (videogame). Redwood City, Calif.: Electronic Arts, 2001.

——. *Harry Potter: Quidditch World Cup* (videogame). Redwood City, Calif.: Electronic Arts, 2003.

——. *LEGO Creator: Harry Potter and the Chamber of Secrets* (videogame). Redwood City, Calif.: Electronic Arts, 2002.

——. *Medal of Honor: Rising Sun* (videogame). Redwood City, Calif.: Electronic Arts, 2003.

Elkin, Tobi. "Nike, Levi Strauss Test Virtual World Marketing." *Advertising Age*, October 27, 2003.

Elliott, Stuart. "Grand Theft Auto? No, Make Mine Volvo." *New York Times*, November 11 2005, C15.

Ellis, David. *Price Guide to Classic Video Games*. New York: House of Collectibles, 2004.

Emmerich, Roland (dir.). *Independence Day*. Fox, 1996.

Eurocom. *Athens 2004* (videogame). Foster City, Calif.: SCEA, 2004.

Exidy. *Death Race* (videogame). Sunnyvale, Calif.: Exidy Systems, 1976.

Exus. *Foot Craz* (videogame). Exus, 1987.

——. *Video Jogger* (videogame). Exus, 1987.

——. *Video Reflex* (videogame). Exus, 1987.

Firaxis Games. *Civilization* (videogame). Paris, France: Infogrames, 1991.

Fischer, Claude S. "Succumbing to Consumerism? Underlying Models in the Historical Claim." Paper presented at the American Sociological Association Conference, Atlanta, Georgia, 2003.

Flanagan, Mary, Ken Perlin, and Andrea Hollingshead. "RAPUNSEL Manifesto." *RAPUNSEL Research Web*, http://www.maryflanagan.com/rapunsel/manifesto.htm/.

Fogg, B. J. *Persuasive Technology: Using Computers to Change What We Think and Do.* San Francisco, Calif.: Morgan Kauffman, 2003.

Forrester, Jay. *Urban Dynamics.* Cambridge, Mass.: Wright Allen, 1969.

Forterra Systems. *There.com* (website). San Mateo, Calif.: Makena Technologies, 2003–.

Foss, Sonja K., Karen A. Foss, and Robert Trapp. *Contemporary Perspectives on Rhetoric.* Prospect Heights, Ill.: Waveland Press, 1985.

Foster, Mary. "The Search for the Dead Is Renewed." *Louisiana Weekly*, March 6, 2006.

Foster Wallace, David. *Infinite Jest.* New York: Back Bay, 1997.

Foucault, Michel. *Discipline and Punish: The Birth of the Prison.* New York: Vintage, 1995.

———. *The Archaeology of Knowledge.* Translated by A. M. Sheridan Smith. New York: Pantheon, 1972.

Framfab, bone, and FHV/bbdo. *Pickwick Afternoon* (videogame). Utrecht, the Netherlands: Pickwick Tea/Sara Lee International, 2005.

Francis, Russell. "Revolution: Learning about History through Interactive Role Play in a Virtual Environment." Paper presented at The Education Arcade Conference, Los Angeles, May 19, 2005.

Frasca, Gonzalo. *Kabul Kaboom* (videogame). Montevideo, Uruguay: Ludology.org, 2001.

———. "The Sims: Grandmothers Are Cooler Than Trolls." *Game Studies* 1, no. 1 (2001).

——. "Videogames of the Oppressed." Master's thesis, The Georgia Institute of Technology, 2001.

Fröbel, Friedrich. *Die Menschenerziehung*. Leipzig: Weinbrach, 1826.

Fullerton, Tracy. "'Documentary' Games: Putting the Player in the Path of History." Paper presented at the Playing the Past: Nostalgia in Video Games and Electronic Literature, The University of Florida, Gainesville, 2005.

Fuji Electronics. *Sportstron S3300 Coca-Cola* (videogame). Tokyo: Fuji Electronics, 1978.

Funcom. *Anarchy Online* (videogame). Durham, N.C.: Funcom, 2001.

Gaede, Owen. *Tenure* (videogame). Minneapolis: Control Data Corporation, 1975.

Gee, James Paul. "Demonstrating the Important Learning Found in COTS Games." Paper presented at the Serious Games Summit 2005, San Francisco, 2005.

——. Learning about Learning from a Video Game. In *Games and Professional Practice Simulations*, Academic Advanced Distributed Learning Co-Lab, 2005. At http://web.reed.edu/cis/tac/meetings/Rise%20of%20Nations.pdf/ (accessed February 10, 2006).

——. *Situated Language and Learning: A Critique of Traditional Schooling*. London: Routledge, 2004.

——. The Classroom of Popular Culture. In *Harvard Education Letter*, Harvard University, 2005. At http://www.edletter.org/past/issues/2005-nd/gee.shtml/ (accessed February 2, 2006).

——. *What Video Games Have to Teach Us about Learning and Literacy*. New York: Palgrave MacMillan, 2003.

Gnatek, Tim. "Just for Fun, Casual Games Thrive Online." *New York Times*, February 23, 2006.

Godin, Seth. *All Marketers Are Liars: The Power of Telling Authentic Stories in a Low-Trust World*. New York: Penguin, 2005.

———. *Permission Marketing: Turning Strangers into Friends and Friends into Customers*. New York: Simon and Schuster, 1999.

Gordon, Bing. "Developing and Educating Creative Leaders at EA." Paper presented at the Living Game Worlds 2005, The Georgia Institute of Technology, March 16, 2005,

Graft, Kris. "Microsoft Acquisition a Sign of Ad Revenue." *Business Week*, April 28, 2006.

Gramsci, Antonio. *Selections from the Prison Notebooks*. Translated by Quintin Hoare and Geoffrey Nowell-Smith. New York: International, 1971.

Graphico. *J₂O Toilet Training Game* (videogame). Chelmsford, U.K.: Britvic, 2003.

Greenberger, Martin. *Computers and the World of the Future*. Cambridge, Mass.: MIT Press, 1962.

Grossman, David. 2000. Teaching Kids to Kill. In *Phi Kappa Phi National Forum*, http://www.killology.org/article_teachkid.htm/ (accessed January 23, 2005; no longer online).

Gunder, Anna. "As if by Magic: On Harry Potter as a Novel and Computer Game." Paper presented at the Digital Games Research Association (DiGRA) Conference, Utrecht, the Netherlands, November 2003.

Gurak, Laura J. *Cyberliteracy: Navigating the Internet with Awareness*. New Haven: Yale University Press, 2001.

Hall, Justin. 2003. Clicking for Dean. In *Weblog*, Game Girl Advance, http://www.gamegirladvance.com/archives/2003/12/23/clicking_for_dean.html/ (accessed December 23, 2003).

Hallward, Peter. *Badiou: A Subject to Truth*. Minneapolis: University of Minnesota Press, 2003.

Harmonix Music Systems. *Eye Toy: Antigrav* (videogame). Foster City, Calif.: SCEA, 2004.

Harnad, Stevan. "Computation Is Just Interpretable Symbol Manipulation; Cognition Isn't." *Minds and Machines* 4, no. 4 (2004): 379–390.

Helmers, Marguerite, and Charles A. Hill. "Introduction." In *Defining Visual Rhetorics*, edited by Charles A. Hill and Marguerite Helmers, 1–23. Mahwah, N.J.: Lawrence Erlbaum Associates, 2004.

Hersh, Seymour M. "Torture at Abu Ghraib." *New Yorker*, May 10, 2004.

Hill, Charles A. "The Psychology of Rhetorical Images." In *Defining Visual Rhetorics*, edited by Marguerite Helmers and Charles A. Hill, 25–40. Mahwah, N.J.: Lawrence Erlbaum Associates, 2004.

Hilyard, Scott. "New Video Game Mimics Race for the Oval Office." *USA Today*, April 23, 2004.

Holistic Design. *Mall Tycoon* (videogame). New York: Take-Two Interactive, 2002.

Huizinga, Johan. *Homo ludens*. New York: Beacon, 1955.

Hulbert, J. R. "Some Medieval Advertisements of Rome." *Modern Philology* 20, no. 4 (1923): 403–424.

Hyman, Paul. "Technology Seeks to Measure Game Ad ROI." *Hollywood Reporter*, February 24, 2006.

Impressions Games. *Zeus: Master of Olympus* (videogame). Burbank, Calif.: Sierra Studios, 2000.

Infocom. *Zork* (videogame). Cambridge, Mass.: Infocom, 1980.

Institute for Politics Democracy and the Internet (IPDI). "Political Influentials Online in the 2004 Presidential Campaign." Washington, D.C.: IPDI, 2004.

———. "Post-Election 2000 Survey on Internet Use for Civics and Politics." Washington, D.C.: IPDI, 2000.

Intelligent Systems Co. *Advance Wars* (videogame). Redmond, Wash.: Nintendo of America, 2001.

Ion Storm. *Deus Ex* (videogame). San Francisco: Eidos, 2000.

Irrational Games. *SWAT 4* (videogame). Bellevue, Wash.: Sierra Entertainment, 2005.

Isidore, Chris. "Signs of the Times." *CNN Money*, May 7, 2004.

iTraffic. *Staffers Challenge* (videogame). New York: Discovery Channel, 2004.

Jaleco Entertainment. *Trailer Park Tycoon* (videogame). Buffalo, N.Y.: Jaleco Entertainment, 2002.

Jameson, Fredric. *Postmodernism, or the Cultural Logic of Late Capitalism*. Durham: Duke University Press, 1991.

Jana, Reena. "Is That a Video Game—Or an Ad?" *Business Week*, January 26, 2006.

Jenkins, Henry. "Reality Bytes: Eight Myths about Video Games Debunked." *PBS: The Videogame Revolution*, http://www.pbs.org/kcts/videogamerevolution/impact/myths.html.

——. *Textual Poachers: Television Fans and Participatory Culture*. London and New York: Routledge, 1992.

Jenkins, Henry, and Kurt Squire. "Playing Together, Staying Together." *Computer Games Magazine*, December 2003.

Johnson, Stephen. *Everything Bad Is Good for You: How Today's Popular Culture Is Actually Making Us Smarter*. New York: Riverhead, 2005.

Juul, Jesper. *Half-Real: Video Games between Real Rules and Fictional Worlds*. Cambridge, Mass.: MIT Press, 2005.

Kaneko. *Chester Cheetah: Too Cool to Fool* (videogame). Dallas, Texas: Recot, 1992.

——. *Socks the Cat Rocks the Hill* (unpublished video game). 1993.

Kay, Alan, and Adele Goldberg. "Dynamic Personal Media" (1977). In *The New Media Reader*, edited by Noah Wardrip-Fruin and Nick Montfort, 391–404. Cambridge, Mass.: MIT Press, 2003.

Kellogg Creek Software. *Power Politics III* (videogame). Portland, Ore.: Kellogg Creek Software, 2004.

Kennedy, George A. *Classical Rhetoric and Its Christian and Secular Tradition*. Chapel Hill: University of North Carolina Press, 1999.

Kenney, Keith. "Building Visual Communication Theory by Borrowing from Rhetoric." In *Visual Rhetoric in a Digital World*, edited by Carolyn Handa, 321–343. New York: Bedford St. Martins, 2004.

Kihlstrom, Richard E., and Michael H. Riordan. "Advertising as a Signal." *Journal of Political Economy* 92, no. 3 (1984): 427–450.

Kinematic. *9–11 Survivor* (videogame). Kinematic.com, 2003.

Kittler, Friedrich. "There Is No Software." In *Literature, Media, Information Systems*, edited by John Johnston, 147–155. Amsterdam: Overseas Publishers Association, 1997.

Klein, Naomi. *No Logo: Taking Aim at the Brand Bullies*. New York: Picador, 2000.

Konami. *Contra* (videogame). Tokyo: Konami, 1988.

——. *Dance Dance Revolution* (videogame). Tokyo: Konami, 1999.

——. *Dance Dance Revolution 2ndMIX Dreamcast Edition* (videogame). Tokyo: Konami, 2000.

——. *Dance Dance Revolution Disney Dancing Museum* (videogame). Tokyo: Konami, 2000.

——. *Dance Dance Revolution Mario Mix* (videogame). Kyoto: Nintendo, 2005.

——. *Dance Dance Revolution Ultramix* (videogame). Tokyo: Konami, 2003.

——. *DDRMAX: Dance Dance Revolution 6thMIX* (videogame). Tokyo: Konami, 2002.

——. *Track & Field* (arcade videogame). Tokyo: Konami, 1982.

——. *Track & Field* (Atari 2600 videogame). Tokyo: Konami, 1983.

Koster, Raph. A Theory of Fun for Game Design. Scottsdale, Ariz.: Paraglyph Press, 2004.

Kuma Reality Games. *Kuma\War* (videogame). New York: Kuma Reality Games, 2003.

Kushner, David. "The Wrinkled Future of Online Gaming." *Wired* 2004.

LaHaye, Tim F., and Jerry B. Jenkins. *Left Behind: A Novel of the Earth's Last Days*. Carol Stream, Ill.: Tyndale, 1996.

Lake, Randall A., and Barbara A. Pickering. "Argumentation, the Visual, and the Possibility of Refutation: An Exploration." *Argumentation and Advocacy* 12 (1988): 79–93.

Lakoff, George. *Don't Think of an Elephant: Know Your Values and Frame the Debate—The Essential Guide for Progressives*. New York: Chelsea Green, 2004.

——. *Moral Politics: How Liberals and Conservatives Think*. Chicago: University of Chicago Press, 1996.

——. *Women, Fire, and Dangerous Things*. Chicago: University of Chicago Press, 1990.

Lakoff, George, and Mark Johnson. *Metaphors We Live By*. Chicago: University of Chicago Press, 1980.

Lambertini, Luca, and Marco Trombetta. "Delegation and Firms' Ability to Collude." Copenhagen, Denmark: University of Copenhagen/Department of Accounting and Finance, LSE, 1997.

Lanham, Richard A. *The Electronic Word: Democracy, Technology, and the Arts*. Chicago: University of Chicago Press, 1995.

Lave, Jean, and Etienne Wenger. *Situated Learning: Legitimate Peripheral Participation*. Cambridge: Cambridge University Press, 1991.

Lawrence, Star. "Exercise, Lose Weight with 'Exergaming.'" *WebMD*, January 18, 2005.

Le Chevallier, Martin. *Vigilance 1.0* (videogame). Helsinki: Kiasma Museum, 2000.

Lee, Shuen-shing. "I Lose, Therefore I Think: A Search for Contemplation amid Wars of Push-Button Glare." *Game Studies* 3, no. 2 (2003).

Left Behind Games. *Left Behind: Eternal Forces* (videogame). Murietta, Calif.: Left Behind Games, 2006.

Lessig, Lawrence. *Code and Other Laws of Cyberspace*. New York: Basic Books, 1999.

Levinas, Emmanuel. *Totalité et infini*. Paris: Kluwer, 1971.

Levine, Robert. "Video Games Struggle to Find the Next Level." *New York Times*, May 8, 2006.

Levitt, Steven J., and Stephen J. Dubner. *Freakonomics: A Rogue Economist Explores the Hidden Side of Everything*. New York: William Morrow, 2005.

Lewis, Richard W. *Absolut Book: The Absolut Vodka Advertising Story*. North Clarendon, Vermont: Tuttle Publishing, 1996.

———. *Absolut Sequel: The Absolut Advertising Campaign Continues*. North Clarendon, Vermont: Tuttle Publishing, 2005.

Linklater, Richard. "Fast Food Nation." Participant Productions, 2006.

Lionhead Studios. *Black & White* (videogame). Redwood City, Calif.: Electronic Arts, 2001.

Loftus, Geoffrey R., and Elizabeth F. Loftus. *Mind at Play: The Psychology of Video Games*. New York: Basic Books, 1983.

Looking Glass Studios. *Thief* (videogame). San Francisco: Eidos, 1998.

Losh, Elizabeth. "In Country with Tactical Iraqi: Trust, Identity, and Language Learning in a Military Video Game." Paper presented at the Digital Arts and Cultures Conference, IT University, Copenhagen, Denmark, December 1–4, 2005.

Luntz, Frank I. "Energy, Preparing for the Future." Luntz Research Companies, 2002.

———. "The Best and Worst Language of 2004: Key Debate Phrases." Luntz Research Companies, 2004.

———. "The Environment: A Cleaner, Safer, Healthier America." Luntz Research Companies, 2003.

Magic Lantern. *Frontrunner* (videogame). Monmouth, Illinois: Lantern Games, 2004.

Manovich, Lev. *The Language of New Media*. Cambridge, Mass.: MIT Press, 2001.

Marinucci, Carla. "In Postmortem on Kerry Bid, Dems Seek Clues to New Life." *San Francisco Chronicle*, November 7, 2004, A1.

Markel, Howard. "Fast Food, Obesity, and Hospitals." *Medscape Pediatrics* 5, no. 2 (2003).

Marlowe, Chris. "Nielsen to Measure Massive Ads." *Inside Branded Entertainment*, December 16, 2004.

Marx, Karl. *Capital*, volume 1: *A Critique of Political Economy*. Translated by Ben Fowkes. New York: Penguin, 1992.

Mass Media, and Crave Entertainment. *The Bible Game* (videogame). Newport Beach, Calif.: Crave Entertainment, 2005.

Mateas, Michael. "Procedural Literacy: Educating the New Media Practitioner." *On the Horizon* 13, no. 2 (2005): 101–111.

Mateas, Michael, and Nick Montfort. "A Box, Darkly: Obfuscation, Weird Languages, and Code Aesthetics." Paper presented at the Digital Arts and Cultures 2005, IT University, Copenhagen, Denmark, December 1–3, 2005.

Mateas, Michael, and Andrew Stern. "A Behavior Language for Story-Based Believable Agents." *IEEE Intelligent Systems* 7, no. 4 (2002): 39–47.

Maxis. *Sim City* (videogame). Alameda, Calif.: Brøderbund, 1989.

———. *Sim Earth* (videogame). Alameda, Calif.: Microprose, 1990.

———. *The Sims* (videogame). Redwood Shores, Calif.: Electronic Arts, 2000.

———. *The Sims Online* (videogame). Redwood Shores, Calif.: Electronic Arts, 2002.

McCarthy, Michael. "Disney Plans to Mix Ads, Video Games to Target Kids, Teens." *USA Today*, January 17, 2005.

McCloskey, Donald N. "The Economics of Choice." In *Economics for Historians*, edited by Thomas G. Rawski and Susan B. Carter, 122–158. Berkeley, Calif.: University of California Press, 1996.

McGough, Shawn. *Melting Mitsubishi*, 2003. At http://www.shawnmcgough.com/index.cgi?article=24.

McNally, David (dir.). *Coyote Ugly*. Touchstone, 2000.

Meier, Sid, and Firaxis Games. *Civilization* (videogame). Paris, France: Infogrames, 1991.

Michael, David, and Sande Chen. *Serious Games: Games That Educate, Train, and Inform*. Boston, Mass.: Thompson Course Technology, 2006.

Michman, Ronald D. *Lifestyle Marketing: Reaching the New American Consumer*. New York: Praeger, 2003.

Microprose. *Sid Meier's Railroad Tycoon* (videogame). Hunt Valley, Maryland: Microprose, 1991.

Microsoft. *Volvo Drive for Life* (videogame). Göthenberg, Sweden: Volvo, 2005.

Midway. *Datsun 280 Zzzap* (videogame). Chicago: Midway Games, 1976.

Milgrom, Paul, and John Roberts. "Price and Advertising Signals of Product Quality." *Journal of Political Economy* 94, no. 796–821 (1986).

——. "Relying on the Information of Interested Parties." *Rand Journal of Economics* 17 (1986): 18–31.

Mill, John Stuart. *On Liberty*. New York: Penguin, 1975.

MIT Education Arcade. *Revolution* (videogame). Cambridge, Mass.: MIT, 2004.

M Network. *Kool-Aid Man* (videogame). El Segundo, Calif.: Mattel, 1982.

M Network. *Kool-Aid Man* (videogame). Hawthorne, Calif.: Mattel Electronics, 1983.

Modeling, Simulation, and Virtual Environments Institute (MOVES). *America's Army: Operations* (videogame). Washington, D.C.: U.S. Army, 2002.

Montessori, Maria. *The Absorbent Mind*. New York: Dell, 1967.

———. "The Child." *Theosophist* 30, no. 6 (1942): 144.

———. *The Montessori Method*. New York: Schocken, 1964.

Montfort, Nick. *Book and Volume* (videogame). Philadelphia, Penn.: Auto Mata, 2005.

Montfort, Nick, and William Gillespie. *2002*. Edwardsville, Ill.: Spineless Books, 2002.

Montfort, Nick, and Noah Wardrip-Fruin, eds. *The New Media Reader*. Cambridge, Mass.: MIT Press, 2003.

Moore, Michael (dir.). *Fahrenheit 9/11*. Sony Pictures, 2004.

Moroch Partners. *Shark Bait* (videogame). Oak Brook, Ill.: McDonald's, 2006.

Morris, Chris. "EA's Big Deal: Touchdown or Fumble?" *CNN Money*, December 14, 2004.

Moulthrop, Stuart. "Taking Cyberculture Seriously (Dude)." Paper presented at the Digital Arts and Culture Conference, ITU, Copenhagen, Denmark, December 1–4, 2005.

Murray, Janet. *Hamlet on the Holodeck*. New York: Free Press, 1997.

Mystique. *Custer's Revenge* (videogame). Northridge, Calif.: Mystique, 1982.

Namco. *Dig Dug* (videogame). Sunnyvale, Calif.: Atari, 1982.

———. *Galaxian* (videogame). Chicago: Midway Games, 1979.

———. *Pac-Man* (videogame). Chicago: Midway Games, 1980.

——. *Pole Position* (videogame). Sunnyvale, Calif.: Atari, 1983.

——. *Taiko Drum Master* (videogame). Tokyo: Namco, 2004.

National Environmental Trust. Luntzspeak.com (website), http://www.luntzspeak .com/ (accessed October 10, 2005).

Needham, Hal (dir.). *Smokey and the Bandit*. Universal Pictures, 1977.

Nestle, Marion. *Food Politics: How the Food Industry Influences Nutrition and Health*. Berkeley, Calif.: University of California Press, 2002.

Neversoft. *Tony Hawk Pro Skater 3* (videogame). Santa Monica, Calif.: Activision, 2003.

Newcomb, Kevin. "Massive Scores $10 Million." *ClickZ News*, January 19, 2005.

Newman, James. *Videogames*. London: Routledge, 2004.

Nintendo. *Animal Crossing* (videogame). Kyoto, Japan: Nintendo, 2002.

——. *Animal Crossing: Wild World* (videogame). Kyoto, Japan: Nintendo, 2005.

——. *Donkey Konga* (videogame). Kyoto, Japan: Nintendo, 2004.

——. *Donkey Kong Jungle Beat* (videogame). Kyoto, Japan: Nintendo, 2005.

——. *Eggsplode* (videogame). Kyoto, Japan: Nintendo, 1990.

——. *Short Order* (videogame). Kyoto, Japan: Nintendo, 1990.

——. *Super Mario Bros.* (videogame). Kyoto, Japan: Nintendo, 1985.

——. *The Legend of Zelda* (videogame). Kyoto, Japan: Nintendo, 1986.

N'Lightning Software. *Catechumen* (videogame). Medford, Ore.: N'Lightning Software Development, 2000.

Oda, Josh. *Bushgame: The Anti-Bush Online Adventure* (videogame). Allston, Mass.: Starvingeyes, 2004.

On, Josh. *Antiwargame* (videogame). San Francisco: Futurefarmers, 2001.

Orlowski, Andrew. "Flight Sim Enquiry Raises Terror Alert." *Register* (January 8, 2004), http://www.theregister.co.uk/2004/01/08/flight_sim_enquiry_raises_terror/.

Ow, Richard. "Harnessing Hollywood." *License!*, June 1, 2004.

Packaged Facts. "The U.S. Market for Religious Publishing and Products." New York: Packaged Facts, 2004.

Papert, Seymour. *Mindstorms: Children, Computers, and Powerful Ideas*. New York: Basic Books, 1980.

Perec, Georges. *A Void*. Translated by Gilbert Adair. Boston: Verba Mundi, 2005.

———. *La disparition*. Paris: Gallimard, 1990.

———. "Le grand palindrome." In *La clôture et autre poèmes*. Paris: Hachette/Collection P.O.L., 1980.

Perfect Fools. *Coca-Cola Nordic Christmas* (videogame). Atlanta, Georgia: Coca-Cola Company, 2004.

Persuasive Games. *Activism: The Public Policy Game* (videogame). Atlanta, Georgia: Persuasive Games, 2004.

———. *Cold Stone Creamery: Stone City* (videogame). Scottsdale, Ariz.: Cold Stone Creamery, 2005.

———. *Disaffected!* (videogame). Atlanta, Georgia: Persuasive Games, 2006.

———. *Take Back Illinois* (videogame). Atlanta, Georgia: Persuasive Games/Illinois House Republicans, 2004.

———. *The Howard Dean for Iowa Game* (videogame). Burlington, Vermont: Dean for America, 2003.

———. *Xtreme Errands* (videogame). Detroit, Mich.: DaimlerChrysler, 2005.

Peterson, Bryan. *Understanding Exposure*, revised edition. New York: Amphoto, 2004.

Plato. *Plato: Complete Works*. New York: Hackett, 1997.

PlayerThree, and DeepEnd. *WFP Food Force* (videogame). Rome: World Food Programme, 2005.

Polyphony Digital. *Gran Turismo* (videogame). Tokyo: SCIE, 1997.

Powerful Robot Games. *Cambiemos* (videogame). Montevideo, Uruguay: Frente Amplio Nueva Mayoria/Powerful Robot Games, 2004.

——. *Madrid* (videogame). Montevideo, Uruguay: Newsgaming.com, 2004.

——. *September 12* (videogame). Montevideo, Uruguay: Newsgaming.com, 2003.

Pratkanis, Anthony, and Elliot Aronson. *Age of Propaganda: The Everyday Use and Abuse of Persuasion*. New York: W. H. Freeman, 2001.

Preminger, Otto (dir.). *Laura*. 20th Century Fox, 1944.

Prensky, Mark. *Digital Game-Based Learning*. New York: McGraw-Hill, 2001.

Presbrey, Frank. *The History and Development of Advertising*. New York: Doubleday, 1929.

Privateer, Jennifer. "A Personal Account from Bioneers 2002." *Natural Products and Organic Food*, January 2003.

Prunier, Gerard. *Darfur: The Ambiguous Genocide*. Ithaca, N.Y.: Cornell University Press, 2005.

Qualls, Eric. 2004. "Grand Theft Auto: San Andreas (Review)." GamesFirst, http://www.gamesfirst.com/index.php?id=188/ (accessed March 2, 2006).

Quart, Alyssa. *Branded: The Buying and Selling of Teenagers*. New York: Basic Books, 2004.

Reardon, Marguerite. 2006. "NFL to Re-air Super Bowl Commercials." CNet *News.com*, http://news.com.com/2100–1024_3–6033515.html/ (accessed February 10, 2006).

Red Octane. "Dance Video Game Supports Academic Success." *GetUpMove.com Research Report*, June 29, 2005.

———. GetUpMove.com (2004). Promotional website, Red Octane, http://www.getupmove.com/ (accessed March 3, 2005).

Republican National Committee. *Tax Invaders* (videogame). Washington, D.C.: RNC/gop.com, 2004.

Resnick, Mitchel. *Turtles, Termites, and Traffic Jams: Explorations in Massively Parallel Microworlds*. Cambridge, Mass.: MIT Press, 1997.

ResponDesign. *Yourself! Fitness* (videogame). Portland, Ore.: ResponDesign, 2004.

Reuters. "Minister: Bush Must Be 'Shot Down.'" *CNN.com*. October 10, 2005, http://www.cnn.com/2005/WORLD/europe/09/08/germany.bush.reut/.

Reynolds, Ren. "Playing a 'Good' Game: A Philosophical Approach to Understanding the Morality of Games." *International Game Developers Association* (2002), http://www.igda.org/articles/rreynolds_ethics.php/.

Richards, Diana. *Political Complexity: Nonlinear Models of Politics*. Ann Arbor, Mich.: University of Michigan Press, 2000.

Richardson, James L. *Contending Liberalisms in World Politics*. Boulder, Colo.: Lynne Rienner Publishers, 2001.

Rockstar Games. *Grand Theft Auto III* (videogame). New York: Take Two Interactive, 2001.

———. *Grand Theft Auto: San Andreas* (videogame). New York: Take Two Interactive, 2004.

———. *Grand Theft Auto: Vice City* (videogame). New York: Take Two Interactive, 2003.

Rollings, Andrew, and Ernest Adams. *Andrew Rollings and Ernest Adams on Game Design*. New York: New Riders, 2003.

Rose, Frank. "The Lost Boys." *Wired* (2004).

Rosen, Judith. "Is Tuttle Ready for Fall? Absolutely." *Publishers Weekly*, August 1, 2005.

Rosenbaum, Steve. *Staffers*. Edited by Steve Rosenbaum. Discovery Channel, 2004.

Rowling, J. K. *Harry Potter and the Philosopher's Stone*. London: Bloomsbury Press, 1997.

——. *Harry Potter and the Sorcerer's Stone*. New York: Scholastic, 1999.

Ruiz, Susana, Ashley York, Huy Truong, Alexander Tarr, Mike Stein, Corey Jackson, Ramiro Cazaux, Noah Keating, Ellee Santiago, and Scott Gillies. *Darfur Is Dying* (videogame). New York: mtvU, 2006.

Russell, Steve. *Spacewar!* (videogame). Cambridge, Mass.: Massachusetts Institute of Technology, 1962.

Salen, Katie, and Eric Zimmerman. *Rules of Play: Game Design Fundamentals*. Cambridge, Mass.: MIT Press, 2004.

Santos, Michael D., Craig Leve, and Anthony R. Pratkanis. "Hey Buddy Can You Spare Seventeen Cents? Mindful Persuasion and Pique Technique." *Journal of Applied Social Psychology* 24 (1994): 755–764.

Sawyer, Ben. "Serious Games: Improving Public Policy through Game-Based Learning and Simulation." Washington, D.C.: Woodrow Wilson International Center for Scholars, 2002.

Sayers, Dorothy. "The Lost Tools of Learning." Oxford University. Reprinted in *National Review* 1947.

SCEE. *Eye Toy: Play* (videogame). Sony Computer Entertainment Europe, 2003.

Schifferes, Steve. "Election Reveals Divided Nation." *BBC News*, November 3, 2004.

——. "What Next for the Democrats." *BBC News*, November 3, 2004.

Schleiner, Anne-Marie. *Velvet-Strike*. New York, 2002.

Schlosser, Eric. *Fast Food Nation: The Dark Side of the All-American Meal.* New York: Harper, 2001.

Schor, Juliet B. *Born to Buy.* New York: Scribner, 2004.

Schrage, Michael. *Serious Play: How the World's Best Companies Simulate to Innovate.* Cambridge, Mass.: Harvard Business School Press, 1999.

Searle, John. *Speech Acts: An Essay in the Philosophy of Language.* Cambridge: Cambridge University Press, 1969.

SEGA. *Coca Cola Kid* (videogame). Tokyo: SEGA Entertainment, 1994.

———. *Shadow the Hedgehog* (videogame). Tokyo: SEGA Entertainment, 2005.

———. *Sonic the Hedgehog* (videogame). Tokyo: SEGA Entertainment, 1991.

———. *Turbo* (videogame). Tokyo: SEGA Entertainment, 1981.

———. *Zaxxon* (videogame). Tokyo: Sega Entertainment, 1982.

Select Bipartisan Committee to Investigate the Preparation for and Response to Hurricane Katrina. "A Failure of Initiative: The Final Report of the Select Bipartisan Committee to Investigate the Preparation for and Response to Hurricane Katrina." Washington, D.C.: U.S. House of Representatives, 2006.

Sensodyne. *Sensodyne Food Fear Challenge* (videogame). Philadelphia, Penn.: GlaxoSmithKline, 2005.

Serbian Ministry of Information. 2001. "Microsoft Invests in Serbian Government's Electronic Initiatives." In *Government Activities*, Serbia Info, http://www.serbia-info.com/news/2001–06/08/23825.html/ (accessed May 3, 2005).

Shaffer, David Williamson. "Epistemic Frames and Islands of Expertise: Learning from Infusion Experiences." Paper presented at the International Conference of the Learning Sciences (ICLS), Santa Monica, Calif., 2004.

———. "Epistemic Games." *Innovate* 1, no. 6 (2005).

——. "Pedagogical Praxis: The Professions as Models for Post-industrial Education." *Teachers College Record* 10 (2004): 1401–1421.

Sharp, Gene. *Dynamics of Nonviolent Action*. Boston, Mass.: Porter Sargent, 1973.

——. *Methods of Nonviolent Action*. Boston, Mass.: Porter Sargent, 1973.

——. *Power and Struggle*. Boston, Mass.: Porter Sargent, 1973.

Sheffield, Brandon. "Playing Games with Jim: Demonstrating the Important Learning Found in COTS Games." *Gamasutra*, March 8, 2005.

Sheil, B. A. "Teaching Procedural Literacy." In *Proceedings of the ACM 1980 Annual Conference*, 125–126. New York: ACM Press, 1980.

Sicart, Miguel. "The Ethics of Computer Game Design." Paper presented at the Digital Games Research Conference 2005, Vancouver, British Columbia, June 2005.

Sinclair, Brendan. "Study Suggests In-Game Ads a Win-Win Proposition." *Gamespot*, December 5, 2005.

Singularity Design. *Fiskars Prune to Win* (videogame). Madison, Wisc.: Fiskars Brands, 2005.

Skinner, B. F. *The Technology of Teaching*. New York: Appleton Century Crofts, 1968.

Smithberg, Madeline, and Lizz Winstead. *The Daily Show*. Comedy Central, 1996.

Software 2000. *Fast Food Tycoon* (videogame). Santa Monica, Calif.: Activision Value Publishing, 2000.

Solomon, Deborah. "Continental Drift: An Interview with Jean Baudrillard." *New York Times*, November 20, 2005.

Sorrent Games. *Bush vs. Kerry Boxing* (videogame). London: Sorrent Games, 2004.

——. *Fox Sports Boxing* (videogame). London: Sorrent Games, 2004.

Spector, Warren. "Are Games Educational?" Paper presented at the Education Arcade Conference, Los Angeles, Calif., May 10, 2004.

Spielberg, Steven (dir.). *E.T.: The Extra Terrestrial*. Universal Studios, 1982.

—— (dir.). *Minority Report*. DreamWorks, 2002.

Spurlock, Morgan (dir.). *Super Size Me*. Hart Sharp, 2004.

Squire, Kurt. "Replaying History: Learning World History through Playing Civilization." Doctoral dissertation, Indiana University, 2004.

Stainless Steel Studios. *Empire Earth* (videogame). Burbank, Calif.: Sierra Studios, 2001.

Stanley, T. L. "Disney Hopes Virtual Park Delivers Real-World Results." *AdAge* (January 3, 2005), 4.

Stardock. *The Political Machine* (videogame). San Francisco, Calif.: Ubisoft Entertainment, 2004.

Starr, Paul. "Policy as a Simulaton Game." Review of Reviewed Item. *American Prospect* no. 5 (17) (March 17, 1994), http://www.prospect.org/print/V5/17/starr-p.html/.

Stef & Phil. *New York Defender* (videogame). Paris: Uzinagaz, 2002.

Stevens Colella, Vanessa, Eric Klopfer, and Mitchel Resnick. *Adventures in Modeling: Exploring Complex Dynamic Systems with StarLogo*. New York: Teachers College Press, 2001.

Strategic Simulations Inc. *President Elect* (videogame). Sunnyvale, Calif.: Strategic Simulations Inc., 1988.

Success. *Yoshinoya* (videogame). Tokyo: Success, 2004.

Sulake. *Virtual Magic Kingdom* (videogame). Burbank, Calif.: Disney, 2005.

SuperSizeMe.com. *Burger Man* (videogame). New York: The Con, 2004.

Sutton-Smith, Brian. *The Ambiguity of Play*. Cambridge, Mass.: Harvard University Press, 1997.

Taito. *Space Invaders* (videogame). Tokyo: Taito, 1978.

Tarantino, Quentin (dir.). *Four Rooms*. Miramax, 1995.

—— (dir.). *From Dusk Til Dawn*. Dimension, 1996.

—— (dir.). *Kill Bill, Vol. 1*. Miramax, 2003.

—— (dir.). *Pulp Fiction*. Miramax, 1994.

—— (dir.). *Reservoir Dogs*. Live/Artisan, 1992.

Tecmo. *Ninja Gaiden* (NES videogame). Tokyo, Japan: Tecmo, Ltd., 1989.

——. *Ninja Gaiden* (Xbox videogame). Tokyo, Japan: Tecmo, Ltd., 2004.

The Department of Homeland Security. "The Federal Response to Hurricane Katrina: Lessons Learned." Washington, D.C.: The White House and the Department of Homeland Security, 2006.

The Entertainment Software Association. "Essential Facts about the Computer and Video Game Industry." Washington, D.C.: The Entertainment Software Association, 2005.

Thomas, David. December 24, 2003. "The Dean of Political Games." Buzzcut: Critical Videogame Theory. Available from http://www.buzzcut.com/article.php ?story= 20031224234034103/ (accessed December 24, 2003).

Thorndike, Edward. *Educational Psychology: The Psychology of Learning*. New York: Teachers College Press, 1913.

Thorsen, Tor. "San Andreas Rated AO, Take-Two Suspends Production." *GameSpot*, July 20, 2005.

3D Pipeline Corporation. *BioChemFX* (videogame). La Jolla, Calif.: 3D Pipeline Corporation, 2003.

3Form. *Mansion Impossible* (videogame). Jersey, UK: Jersey Insight, 2003.

Traffic Games. *JFK Reloaded* (videogame). Edinburgh, Scotland: Traffic Games, 2004.

Trilling, Lawrence, and J. J. Abrams. "Blowback." Season 3, episode 14 of *Alias*. ABC, 2004.

Turkle, Sherry. "Seeing through Computers." *American Prospect* 8, no. 31 (March 1997).

Twitchell, James B. "But First, a Word from Our Sponsor." *Wilson Quarterly* 20, no. 3 (1996): 68–77.

Ubisoft Annecy Studios, and Ubisoft Shanghai Studios. *Tom Clancy's Splinter Cell: Pandora Tomorrow* (videogame). San Francisco, Calif.: Ubisoft Entertainment, 2004.

Ubisoft Montreal Studios. *Tom Clancy's Splinter Cell: Chaos Theory* (videogame). San Francisco, Calif.: Ubisoft Entertainment, 2005.

Ubisoft Paris Studios. *XIII* (videogame). San Francisco, Calif.: Ubisoft Entertainment, 2003.

Ulicsak, Mary, Steve Sayers, Keri Facer, and Ben Williamson. "Time Out? Exploring the Role of Reflection in the Design of Games for Learning." 2005.

Valve. *Half-Life: Counter-Strike* (videogame). Bellevue, WA: Sierra Online, 2000.

Vance, Ryan. 2002. "Ads in Games: Who's Buying?" G4TV, http://www.g4tv.com/techtvvault/features/36254/Ads_in_Games_Whos_Buying.html/ (accessed November 10, 2003).

Vanderbei, Robert J. "Election 2004 Results." *Princeton Research Report*, http://www.princeton.edu/~rvdb/JAVA/election2004/.

van der Graaf, Shenja, and David B. Nieborg. "Together We Brand: America's Army." Paper presented at the Digital Games Research Conference, Utrecht, Netherlands, November 2003.

Virgin Games. *M.C. Kids* (videogame). London: Virgin Games, 1992.

Vision, Amusement. *Super Monkey Ball 2* (videogame). Tokyo: SEGA Entertainment, 2002.

Vygotsky, Lev Semenovich. *Mind in Society*. Cambridge, Mass.: Harvard University Press, 1978.

Wachowski, Andy, and Larry Wachowski (dir.). *The Matrix*. Warner Bros., 1999.

Waldman, Steven. "No Wizard Left Behind." *Slate*, March 18, 2004.

Wallsten, Peter, and Nick Anderson. "Democrats Map Out a Different Strategy." *Los Angeles Times*, November 6, 2004.

Walsh, Joan. 2005. "Flushing Out the Ugly Truth." *Opinion*, Salon.com, http://www.salon.com/opinion/feature/2005/09/01/katrina_race/index_np.html/ (accessed November 12, 2005).

Walsh, Tony. 2002. "Big Mac Attacked." *AlterNet*, http://www.alternet.org/story/ 14530/ (accessed December 12, 2004).

Wardell, Brad. "Postmortem: Stardock's *The Political Machine*." *Game Developer*, October 11, 2004.

Wardrip-Fruin, Noah. "Expressive Processing: On Process-Intensive Literature and Digital Media." Doctoral dissertation, Brown University, 2006.

———. "Playable Media and Textual Instruments." *Dichtung Digital, Journal für Digitale Ästhetik* 5, no. 34 (2005).

Warnick, Barbara. *Critical Literacy in a Digital Era: Technology, Rhetoric, and the Public Interest*. Mahwah, N.J.: Lawrence Erlbaum Associates, 2002.

Weber, Max. *The Protestant Ethic and the Spirit of Capitalism*. Translated by Talcott Parsons. London: Unwin Hyman, 1930.

Weiss, D. B. *Lucky Wander Boy*. New York: Plume, 2003.

Weizenbaum, Joseph. "ELIZA—A Computer Program for the Study of Natural Language Communication between Man and Machine." *Communications of the ACM* 9, no. 1 (1966): 36–45.

Wells, H. G. *The War of the Worlds*. New York: Aerie, 1898. Reprint, 2005.

Whalen, Zach. 2003. "Product Placement and Virtual Branding in Video Games." *Essays*, Gameology.com, http://www.gameology.org/node/121/ (accessed April 30, 2006).

WildTangent. *Dodge Stow 'n Go Challenge* (videogame). Detroit, Mich.: DaimlerChrysler Corporation, 2005.

Williams Entertainment. *Joust* (videogame). Chicago: Midway Games, 1982.

Williams, Raymond. *Problems in Materialism and Culture: Selected Essays.* London: Verso, 1980.

Williamson, Judith. *Decoding Advertisements: Ideology and Meaning in Advertising.* London: Marion Boyers, 1978. Reprint, 2002.

Wisdom Tree. *Bible Adventures* (videogame). Tucson, Ariz.: Wisdom Tree, 1991.

——. *Bible Buffet* (videogame). Tucson, Ariz.: Wisdom Tree, 1992.

——. *Exodus* (videogame). Tucson, Ariz.: Wisdom Tree, 1991.

——. *Menace Beach* (videogame). Tucson, Ariz.: Wisdom Tree, 1990.

——. *Spiritual Warfare* (videogame). Tucson, Ariz.: Wisdom Tree, 1992.

——. *Sunday Funday* (videogame). Tucson, Ariz.: Wisdom Tree, 1995.

Wise, Jessie, and Susan Wise Bauer. *The Well-Trained Mind: A Guide to Classical Education at Home.* New York: W. W. Norton, 1999.

Woodhouse, Ben, and Martyn Williams. *Congo Jones and the Raiders of the Lost Bark* (videogame). London: The Rainforest Foundation, 2004.

Woolcott, Adam. 2005. "Grand Theft Auto Retrospective." Gaming Target, http://www.gamingtarget.com/article.php?artid=4739/ (accessed March 1, 2006).

Wright, Will. "Design Learning: How Other Fields Can Inform Interactive Design." Paper presented at the Living Game Worlds 2006: Designers on Design, The Georgia Institute of Technology, Atlanta, Georgia, 2006.

——. "The Future of Content." Paper presented at The Game Developers Conference, San Francisco, 2005.

York, Steve. *A Force More Powerful.* PBS, 1999.

Zappen, James P. "Digital Rhetoric: Toward an Integrated Theory." *Technical Communication Quarterly* 14, no. 3 (2005): 319–325.

Žižek, Slavoj. *The Sublime Object of Ideology*. New York: Verso, 1989.

Zuriff, G. E. *Behaviorism: A Conceptual Reconstruction*. New York: Columbia University Press, 1985.

Zyda, Michael, John Hiles, Alex Mayberry, Casey Wardynski, Michael V. Capps, Brian Osborn, Russell Shilling, Martin Robaszewski, and Margaret J. Davis. "Entertainment R&D for Defense." *IEEE Computer Graphics and Applications* 23, no. 1 (2003): 28–36.

Index